MISBEHAVIOR IN ORGANIZATIONS

This revised edition of *Misbehavior in Organizations* updates and expands upon the integrative OMB (organizational misbehavior) framework pioneered by the authors. Streamlined for improved readability, it covers key topics that have emerged in the scholarly literature in the past decade such as insidious workplace behavior, bullying and harassment in the workplace, information hiding, cyberbullying, and organizational spirituality. A thorough and up-to-date resource on this crucial and evolving topic in organizational studies, this book provides insights on misbehavior at the individual, position, group, and organizational levels.

Yoav Vardi (PhD, ILR School, Cornell University) is retired from the Department of Labor Studies at Tel Aviv University. He is affiliated with the Israel Academic College and the Faculty of Economics at the University of Ljubljana, Slovenia. His main research interests are managing organizational misbehavior and careers.

Ely Weitz, Department of Labor Studies, Tel Aviv University, heads the department's Executive Master Program in Labor Studies. His research interests include organization theory, management history, management and organization development, and misbehavior in organizations. Dr. Weitz is the past chair of the Israeli Industrial Relations Research Association.

Series in Applied Psychology

Series Editors

Jeanette N. Cleveland, Colorado State University
Kevin R. Murphy, Landy Litigation and Colorado State University

Edwin A. Fleishman, Founding series editor (1987–2010)

Winfred Arthur, Jr., Eric Day, Winston Bennett, Jr., and Antoinette Portrey
Individual and Team Skill Decay: The Science and Implications for Practice

Gregory Bedny and David Meister
The Russian Theory of Activity: Current Applications to Design and Learning

Winston Bennett, David Woehr, and Charles Lance
Performance Measurement: Current Perspectives and Future Challenges

Michael T. Brannick, Eduardo Salas, and Carolyn Prince
Team Performance Assessment and Measurement: Theory, Research, and Applications

Zinta S. Byrne
Understanding What Employee Engagement Is and Is Not: Implications for Theory, Research, and Practice

Neil D. Christiansen and Robert P. Tett
Handbook of Personality at Work

Jeanette N. Cleveland, Margaret Stockdale, and Kevin R. Murphy
Women and Men in Organizations: Sex and Gender Issues at Work

Aaron Cohen
Multiple Commitments in the Workplace: An Integrative Approach

Russell Cropanzano
Justice in the Workplace: Approaching Fairness in Human Resource Management, Volume 1

Russell Cropanzano
Justice in the Workplace: From Theory to Practice, Volume 2

David V. Day, Stephen Zaccaro, Stanley M. Halpin
Leader Development for Transforming Organizations: Growing Leaders for Tomorrow's Teams and Organizations

Stewart I. Donaldson, Mihaly Csikszentmihalyi and Jeanne Nakamura
Applied Positive Psychology: Improving Everyday Life, Health, Schools, Work, and Safety

James E. Driskell and
Eduardo Salas
Stress and Human Performance

Sidney A. Fine and
Steven F. Cronshaw
*Functional Job Analysis: A Foundation for
Human Resources Management*

Sidney A. Fine and
Maury Getkate
*Benchmark Tasks for Job Analysis:
A Guide for Functional Job Analysis
(FJA) Scales*

J. Kevin Ford, Steve W. J.
Kozlowski, Kurt Kraiger,
Eduardo Salas, and
Mark S. Teachout
*Improving Training Effectiveness in
Work Organizations*

Jerald Greenberg
*Organizational Behavior: The State of
the Science, Second Edition*

Jerald Greenberg
Insidious Workplace Behavior

Itzhak Harpaz and Raphael Snir
*Heavy Work Investment: Its Nature,
Sources, Outcomes and Future Directions*

Edwin Hollander
*Inclusive Leadership: The Essential
Leader-Follower Relationship*

Ann Hergatt Huffman and
Stephanie R. Klein
*Green Organizations: Driving Change
with I-O Psychology*

Jack Kitaeff
Handbook of Police Psychology

Uwe E. Kleinbeck, Hans-Henning
Quast, Henk Thierry, and
Hartmut Häcker
Work Motivation

Laura L. Koppes
*Historical Perspectives in Industrial and
Organizational Psychology*

Ellen Kossek and Susan Lambert
*Work and Life Integration: Organizational,
Cultural, and Individual Perspectives*

Martin I. Kurke and
Ellen M. Scrivner
Police Psychology into the 21st Century

Joel Lefkowitz
*Ethics and Values in Industrial and
Organizational Psychology*

John Lipinski and
Laura M. Crothers
*Bullying in the Workplace: Causes,
Symptoms, and Remedies*

Manuel London
*Job Feedback: Giving, Seeking, and Using
Feedback for Performance Improvement,
Second Edition*

Manuel London
*How People Evaluate Others in
Organizations*

Manuel London
*Leadership Development: Paths to
Self-Insight and Professional Growth*

Manuel London
The Power of Feedback: Giving, Seeking, and Using Feedback for Performance Improvement

Robert F. Morrison and Jerome Adams
Contemporary Career Development Issues

Michael D. Mumford
Pathways to Outstanding Leadership: A Comparative Analysis of Charismatic, Ideological, and Pragmatic Leaders

Michael D. Mumford, Garnett Stokes, and William A. Owens
Patterns of Life History: The Ecology of Human Individuality

Kevin R. Murphy
A Critique of Emotional Intelligence: What Are the Problems and How Can They Be Fixed?

Kevin R. Murphy
Validity Generalization: A Critical Review

Kevin R. Murphy and Frank E. Saal
Psychology in Organizations: Integrating Science and Practice

Susan E. Murphy and Ronald E. Riggio
The Future of Leadership Development

Susan E. Murphy and Rebecca J. Reichard
Early Development and Leadership: Building the Next Generation of Leaders

Margaret A. Neal and Leslie Brett Hammer
Working Couples Caring for Children and Aging Parents: Effects on Work and Well-Being

Robert E. Ployhart, Benjamin Schneider, and Neal Schmitt
Staffing Organizations: Contemporary Practice and Theory, Third Edition

Steven A.Y. Poelmans
Work and Family: An International Research Perspective

Erich P. Prien, Jeffery S. Schippmann, and Kristin O. Prien
Individual Assessment: As Practiced in Industry and Consulting

Robert D. Pritchard, Sallie J. Weaver, and Elissa L. Ashwood
Evidence-Based Productivity Improvement: A Practical Guide to the Productivity Measurement and Enhancement System

Ned Rosen
Teamwork and the Bottom Line: Groups Make a Difference

Eduardo Salas, Stephen M. Fiore, and Michael P. Letsky
Theories of Team Cognition: Cross-Disciplinary Perspectives

Heinz Schuler, James L. Farr, and Mike Smith
Personnel Selection and Assessment: Individual and Organizational Perspectives

MISBEHAVIOR IN ORGANIZATIONS

A Dynamic Approach

Second edition

Yoav Vardi and Ely Weitz

Routledge
Taylor & Francis Group

NEW YORK AND LONDON

Second edition published 2016
by Routledge
711 Third Avenue, New York, NY 10017

and by Routledge
2 Park Square, Milton Park, Oxfordshire OX14 4RN

Routledge is an imprint of the Taylor & Francis Group, an informa business

Library of Congress Cataloging in Publication Data
A catalog record for this book has been requested

ISBN: 978-1-138-84097-3 (hbk)
ISBN: 978-1-138-84098-0 (pbk)
ISBN: 978-1-315-73256-5 (ebk)

Typeset in Bembo
by Out of House Publishing

Printed and bound in the United States of America by Publishers Graphics, LLC on sustainably sourced paper.

This book is dedicated to our dear families.

CONTENTS

PART III
Implications for Research and Management 221

FIGURES AND TABLES

Figures

Tables

SERIES FOREWORD

The goal of the Applied Psychology series is to create books that exemplify the use of scientific research, theory, and findings to help solve real problems in organizations and society. Vardi and Weitz's *Misbehavior in Organizations: A Dynamic Approach* (2nd edn) exemplifies this approach. This volume updates and significantly expands their 2004 edition, preserving the strengths of this previous work and incorporating a significant amount of new material.

The topic of misbehavior in organizations is a timely and important one. Major corporations, from Enron to Barings Bank, have been ruined because of fraud and misrepresentation. Misbehaviors ranging from bullying and abusive supervision to sexual harassment in the workplace provide frequent headlines. Vardi and Weitz bring together wide-ranging scholarship to help us understand the roots, the effects, and the implications of misbehavior in organizations. One particularly important addition to their previous text is the attention this volume pays to the consequences of organizational misbehavior for the careers of those who misbehave and those who their behaviors affect. One sobering message of this book is that there are a range of misbehaviors that can, at least in the short run, *enhance* one's career prospects, and that one explanation for organizational misbehavior is that it is often rewarded by organizations.

Vardi and Weitz develop and apply a multilevel framework for studying and understanding misbehavior in organization. This volume examines individual, group, and organizational antecedents of misbehavior and it considers the effects of misbehavior over time. The authors combine a high level of scholarship with a clear and vivid writing style to present a timely and thought-provoking analysis of the nature, antecedents, and effects of misbehavior in organizations. We are thrilled to add *Misbehavior in Organizations: A Dynamic Approach* (2nd edn) to the Applied Psychology series.

Kevin R. Murphy
Jeanette N. Cleveland

PREFACE TO SECOND EDITION

Ideas for new constructs come from different sources. The idea for Organizational Misbehavior (OMB) came from a surprise at being caught off guard. The incident was recorded in Vardi's personal file and is quoted from there. It happened during the fall term of 1990 when he taught a course in an Executive MBA program at Cleveland State University. The course title was: Behavioral Sciences for Organizations. All of the 24 students attending the class on those Saturday mornings were either managers or had previous experience as managers in a wide variety of industries. Their real-life experiences, as well as their natural preference for the practical over the academic, were often shared in class vocally and enthusiastically. Dr. Vardi wrote the following in his notes for an essay on teaching Organizational Behavior to managers:

> During the class on work motivation, I posed a general question to the group: How can we design the work to be done so that people will want to expend more effort? Eventually we got to discuss different theories of work motivation. They particularly liked Adams' inequity theory. We also explored the classical job design model by Hackman and Oldham. The students seemed to appreciate it, as many OB students do. It is one of these Organizational Behavior models that makes good theoretical sense and also seems to have practical value because it clearly demonstrates how employees react to their own jobs; as a consequence, it has implications for supervisors and managers. As we explored the model with its different facets and emphasized the role of the intervening "critical psychological states" in eliciting good performance, satisfaction, and motivation, John M. (who at the time ran a large manufacturing department) said, quite cynically: "You know, professor, I like this model, but there is one problem with it." Expecting the

usual comments about subjectivity versus objectivity or about the role of individual differences, I was taken by surprise when he said: "The way I see it, the problem is that this model has nothing to do with reality. Excuse me, but only academics who don't really manage people can view the world like this. My job as a manager is not to make work more interesting or more satisfying. My job is to make sure people don't waste time, don't steal, don't cheat their supervisors, don't take drugs, and don't fight with one another. Believe me, I am more of a cop than a cheerleader. I don't want to give them more autonomy, I just want them to be honest and do their jobs."

This quite uncharacteristic outburst started a heated class debate about misconduct at work—issues that had never come up in class before. They all recalled incidents at their organizations. They felt that there is a lot of improper behavior going around. Not only employees do this, they observed; executives engage in it. They even admitted that they, too, stray from time to time (small stuff you know, like making long-distance phone calls, doing their term papers on company time, etc.). I was completely caught off guard and taken aback. The model indeed says nothing about predicting misbehavior on the job. I promised to do a quick search of the OB literature for next class to see whether anybody writes about misconduct at work and why it happens. I was intrigued and spent the week skimming management and OB textbooks and found very little. I read several scholarly reviews of the field in the prominent *Annual Review of Psychology*—not a word.

It was then when I began to suspect that Organizational Behavior as a discipline has for some reason neglected to explore what I decided to call Organizational Misbehavior. Quite apologetically, I told my students that indeed there are no OB models that systematically explain why members of organizations are motivated to engage in misconduct and concluded that they were right to feel quite cynical toward them. If these models indeed fail to account for the negative aspects of work behavior, they offer only partial explanations for the wide range of organizational behaviors in the "real world." I added that because we have a formal concept to describe exceptionally good behavior (OCB—Organizational Citizenship Behavior), we might as well have a new concept to tap "bad" behavior: (OMB—Organizational Mis-Behavior). It caught on.

A decade has passed since our book was published by Lawrence Erlbaum Associates. Much has come to pass—even LEA has undergone major transformation, demonstrating the volatility and shift in the publishing sector in particular, and business in general. Now we are under the auspices of Taylor & Francis, which has so generously offered us the opportunity to update and revise our 2004 book. We seized this opportunity with much excitement and enthusiasm because the interest in organizational misbehavior (OMB), which we helped instill, in organizational behavior and management scholarship seems to have flourished since then. Our purpose in the new book is to revisit our previous framework and its sources, bring it up-to-date, and to expand it to areas and topics that are relatively unexplored.

While we strived to maintain the original line of thinking about OMB following the path laid down by Vardi and Wiener (1992, 1996) and Vardi and Weitz (2004), we offer a look at the dark sides of organizations that bear special interest for both researchers of OMB and practitioners who must inevitably face and manage misbehavior in work organizations. There is no doubt that managers nowadays are more aware of the plethora of manifestations of misconduct in all kinds of organizations and are more amenable to addressing and managing them. Thus, we offer this book as another useful and practical guideline for both types of endeavors.

During the past few years, while contemplating on our OMB framework, we began to realize that our initial view of the phenomenon of misbehavior in organizations had been quite static. We focused our attention on misbehavior and searched for its possible causes. Our empirical approach could be characterized as cross-sectional: Measure patterns of misconduct in different organizations and search for their correlates. This is all nice, and academically publishable, but is it a realistic depiction of organizations? We began to suspect that a more temporal and dynamic approach is called for. Our insight was that what was missing from our thinking was the linkage between OMB and careers. We started to ask ourselves such questions as: What happens to individuals who exhibit certain misbehaviors over time? Do acts of misbehavior impact their career choices and moves? What are the career consequences, as viewed by the organizations, to such behaviors? Do careers have dark sides as well? Thus, in this book we offer the reader a new perspective about misbehavior in organizations that explores both causes and consequences of OMB from a temporal perspective. Namely, over time, members of organizations behave both properly and improperly and these behaviors are inseparable from their unfolding organizational careers. We believe that these insights will trigger both research and practice innovation in managing individual careers as well as career systems.

We launched our current project by reviewing the vast literature pertaining to organizational misbehavior that has emerged during the past decade. We then combed through the vast OMB topics and chose to include themes that have been relatively unexplored. Such topics, in addition to misbehavior and careers, are the flourishing of corruption, academic fraud, abusive supervision, workplace bullying, sexual harassment, misbehavior as a contagious phenomenon, the role of individual and organizational spirituality, knowledge and information hiding as misbehavior, workarounds, and the spread of incivility and deception in organizations. Thus, our extensive bibliography has also been significantly updated.

We extend our thanks to the Department of Labor Studies for its generous financial and administrative support. We are thankful for our colleagues, Yinon Cohen, David DeVries, Yitzhak Haberfeld, Gideon Kunda, Lilach Luria, Hadas Mandel, Sami Miaari, Guy Mundlak, Tammie Ronen Rosenbaum, Moshe Semyonov, Yehouda Shenhav, Haya Stier, Shay Tzafrir and Isaac Waisberg for their helpful and insightful advice. Daphna Kanner Cohen, our departmental secretary, deserves our heartfelt thanks.

Yehuda Baruch and Ora Setter were our research partners in investigating the dark side of organizational careers and the role of spirituality vis-à-vis misbehavior at work. Our Slovenian colleagues Miha Skerlavaj and Matej Cerne shared with us their expertise about knowledge-hiding. Yasmin Alkalai has, as always, been very helpful in data analysis. Their contributions are acknowledged and greatly appreciated.

Last, but most important to us. Our talented and intelligent research assistant, Ms. Alin Weingarten, has been extremely diligent and insightful from day one. Alin added her ideas to our writing, has managed the technical work, and has been a real colleague with her maturity and wisdom. We are especially indebted to Alin for her work on the topic of bullying and abusive supervision. Thank you Alin and best of luck in pursuing your academic goals!

PART I

Organizational Misbehavior (OMB)

1

ORGANIZATIONAL BEHAVIOR AND MISBEHAVIOR

Problematic behavioral manifestations in the organized workplace are not new. F. W. Taylor (1895, 1903) brought the practice of *soldiering* or *goldbricking*—deliberately slowing down production—to light. The early proponents of the Human Relations School reported extensively on production restriction and rate-busting (and their consequences) as early as the 1920s (Roethlisberger & Dickson, 1964). Greenberg and Scott (1996) dated employee theft (a major form of organizational misbehavior) to ancient times. These phenomena are unquestionably universal. Therefore, it is safe to assume that most, if not all, members of work organizations, throughout their employment, engage in some form of misbehavior related to their jobs, albeit in varying degrees of frequency and intensity. Hence, to achieve a better understanding of organizational behavior (OB), we must study organizational misbehavior as well. *Organizational misbehavior* (OMB) is defined as acts in the workplace that are committed intentionally and constitute a violation of rules pertaining to such behaviors. We strongly believe that, to truly comprehend the behavior of people at work and the functioning of organizations, social scientists need to explore and research both the positive and negative aspects of work-life. After all, how can we understand the functional if we fail to recognize the dysfunctional and unconventional?

During the past three decades, organization scholars have become more willing to acknowledge that various forms of work-related misbehavior by employees and managers are prevalent, and that their consequences for employers are indeed quite significant and costly (e.g., Neuman & Baron, 2005; Griffin & Lopez, 2005; Berry et al., 2007; Greenberg, 2010; Hershcovis & Barling, 2010; Tepper & Henle, 2011). Such behaviors range a full spectrum from minor to serious—a mere perception of violation of the psychological contract (e.g., Bordia et al., 2008); minor workplace incivility (e.g., Lim et al., 2008; Reich & Hershcovis, 2015); insulting behaviors (e.g., Francis et al., 2015); workplace social undermining (e.g., Duffy et al., 2006); knowledge-hiding (e.g., Connelly et al., 2012); theft of company assets (e.g., Tomlinson & Greenberg, 2007); cyberloafing (e.g., Weatherbee, 2010; Kidwell, 2010); acts of destructiveness, vandalism, and sabotage (e.g., Skarlicki et al., 2008); substance abuse while at work (Frone, 2008, 2013); aggression perpetrated against fellow employees or toward the organization (e.g., Neuman & Baron, 2005; Barling et al., 2009; Hershcovis & Barling, 2010; Hershcovis & Reich, 2013); bullying (e.g., Einarsen et al., 2011); and abusive supervision (Tepper, 2007; Mackey et al., 2015).

Although such forms of misconduct appear to be rampant and universal, systematic OB research of these phenomena is lacking (Vardi & Wiener, 1992, 1996). There is also conceptual confusion in describing them (O'Leary-Kelly et al., 2000a; Bowling & Gruys, 2010; Tepper & Henle, 2011). Until recently, OB, as a distinct academic discipline devoted to exploring and expanding our understanding of work behavior, has lagged behind other social science disciplines in exploring this vast domain. This is quite surprising given that OMB, referred to by other scholars as antisocial (Giacalone & Greenberg, 1997; Thau et al., 2007), dysfunctional (O'Leary-Kelly & Collins, 1998; Griffin & Lopez, 2005), deviant (Hollinger & Clark, 1982; Robinson & Bennett, 1995), or counterproductive behavior (Sackett & DeVore, 2001; Fox & Spector, 2005), is not restricted to certain marginal members. It has been recorded for workers of all types of organizations—for employees at all levels of the organizational hierarchy, salaried professionals and non-professionals, and both non-supervisory and managerial employees (cf. Giacalone & Greenberg, 1997; Griffin et al., 1998a; Robinson & Greenberg, 1998; Vardi & Weitz, 2002a).

This chapter is devoted to the ubiquity of OMB. First, we discuss the prevalence of misbehavior and then employ a historical perspective to search the literature for previously proposed typologies and definitions for employee misbehavior. Second, we address the question why the field of OB has overlooked OMB and has, in fact, evolved into a (positively) "skewed" discipline focusing on more normative aspects of work behavior. Last, we describe the emergence of the current interest in OMB from the early sociological research of white-collar crime, focusing on employee deviance, workplace aggression, and political organizational behavior as selected examples.

Prevalence of Misbehavior at Work

Undoubtedly, OMB comes with a hefty price tag. With its cost comes a growing awareness of it. Estimates of the costs of the most prevalent misbehavior—employee theft—run as high as $51 billion annually in the United States alone (Global Retail Theft Barometer, 2011). Estimates of the costs resulting from problem drinking in the workplace run as high as $162 billion in 2006 (Frone, 2013). The economics of OMB are indeed staggering once the costs of fraud, sabotage, vandalism, substance abuse, litigation, and so on are factored in, although some costs may be offset by benefits that often follow organizational improvements launched due to misbehavior such as blocking the promotion of a fraudulent candidate, or installing new quality and monitoring practices in the wake of exposure of misconduct by whistleblowers. Moreover, information concerning intellectual property theft by employees has become publicly available on the internet by governmental agencies and private security firms (e.g., www.symantec.com). One site (www.whistleblowing.co.za) offers employees an opportunity to anonymously blow the whistle on fraud, pilfering, and embezzlement in their companies. Case-based and practitioner-oriented literature flourished in the 1990s under such telling titles as *Dirty business* (Punch, 1996) and *Are your employees stealing you blind?* (Bliss & Aoki, 1993). Some semi-academic (e.g., Denenberg & Braverman, 1999) and academic (e.g., Kelloway et al., 2006) books offer solid practical advice on how to prevent violent behavior in the workplace or handle employee problem drinking (Frone, 2013). Shulman (2007) has, quite convincingly, made the case for the prevalence of employee deception in the workplace.

Research in work organizations has provided ample evidence for the large variety of OMB. Mars (1974) studied deviant work practices among dockworkers, Hollinger and Clark (1982) found it in all sectors of the economy, and Analoui and Kakabadse (1992) conducted a longitudinal study of an entertainment and hospitality organization and found unconventional practices among both managers and employees. Greenberg (1990a, 1997) extensively examined the causes of employee theft in organizations, Treviño (1986) investigated unethical managerial decisions, Raelin (1984) studied deviant behavior among professionals, and Giacalone and Rosenfeld (1987) researched sabotage behavior. "As the organizational misbehavior literature has grown and terminology has been added to the academic lexicon" (Tepper & Henle, 2011, p. 487) researchers have begun to incorporate a variety of definitions, typologies and models into organizational studies (see Greenberg, 2010; Van Wijhe et al., 2014; Neall & Tuckey, 2014; Ashforth et al., 2008). In fact, there is a growing research interest in specific OMB phenomena such as incivility (Cortina & Magley, 2009; Lim et al., 2008; Reich & Hershcovis, 2015), lying and deceiving (Grover, 2010; Shulman, 2007), whistleblowing (Miceli et al., 2008), substance abuse (Frone, 2013), sexual harassment (McDonald, 2012; Popovich & Warren, 2010; Willness et al., 2007), and bullying (Glambek et al., 2014). Remember, this is just a sample. As Moberg (1997) once observed, both employee virtue and employee vice seem endless.

Misbehavior in Organizational Behavior Discourse

OB is an interdisciplinary field of research that explores the behavior of individuals and groups within organizational contexts, as well as the structure and behavior of organizations (see Greenberg, 1994; Miner, 2002 on the state of the science). At the macro-level, OB is rooted in sociology, political science, and economics; it deals with questions of organizational form, design, and action in the socioeconomic context. At the micro-level, OB stems from psychology, especially industrial and organizational (I-O) psychology, focusing on the individual and dealing with his or her attitudes and behavior and how these affect and are affected by the organizational system (Staw, 1984). During its years of development, OB was primarily influenced by its psychological origins, as may be evidenced by the objects of its research and subjects of its practice (Cappelli & Sherer, 1991; Mowday & Sutton, 1993). Similarly, the social psychology roots of OB have contributed to the extensive interest in workgroups and teams in organizations (the meso-level).

Most OB research focuses on the individual (micro) level, rather than on the effects of culture and environment on behavior (Porter & Schneider, 2014). Some scholars argue that this tendency to emphasize interpersonal differences over situational variables is somewhat of a universal approach in OB (Erez & Early, 1993), which may indeed be its main drawback (Cappelli & Sherer, 1991). This line of thought led researchers such as Mowday and Sutton (1993) to conclude that the field is exhausted—that scholars should redirect their attention to the macro-level and search for new relationships between the organizational context and its individual members' behaviors. We found, however, that although the research concerning the positive-normative behavior of the individual in the organization seems somewhat saturated, the systematic study of the darker side of human behavior at work (Vaughan, 1999) has only just begun.

An examination and tabulation of organizational behavior reviews (e.g., Shafir & LeBoeuf, 2002; Sackett & Lievens, 2008; Avolio et al., 2009; Bakker et al., 2014) highlights the tendency of theory and research to focus on a positive depiction of organizational life. Approximately 88 percent of the reviews are positively skewed, with attitudes toward work, motivation, and performance being the main areas of interest (see Appendix 2). For instance, reviews dealing with motivation refer to positive motivational frameworks such as self-efficacy theory, intrinsic motivation theories, goal theories, and self-regulation. Although workplaces may encompass a variety of negative as well as positive behaviors or attitudes, most of the reviews employ a traditional human resource management viewpoint of organizational productivity and address topics such as training, group performance and team effectiveness, appraisal and feedback, job design, job autonomy and job enrichment. Only a few authors addressed negative or dysfunctional forms of behavior in the workplace and reviewed topics such as organizational injustice, employee retaliation, withdrawal behaviors, workplace aggression, violence, and victimization, discrimination, deviance and dissent. Interestingly, when searching for the term "organizational citizenship behavior" (OCB), Google registers 357,000 results as compared with only 21,000 for the term "organizational misbehavior."

The state of affairs is not much better in OB textbooks. A cursory study of some of the widely used OB textbooks (e.g., Daft, 2000; Daft & Noe, 2001; Greenberg & Baron, 1997; Hellriegel et al., 2001; Steers, 1991) reveals that most of the terms defined in the glossaries are positively skewed. None of these textbooks seriously relates to negative types of organizational behaviors. A notable exception is the widely used management textbook by Ivancevich, Konopaske, and Matteson (2014), which devotes a whole chapter to organizational misbehavior. Terms such as those used in our book to describe various forms of employee misconduct (*misbehavior, dysfunctional, counterproductive,* or *antisocial behaviors*) are hardly mentioned and certainly not discussed as prevalent work-related phenomena that need to be understood, explained, and controlled. Clearly, the depiction of organizations in most textbooks is incomplete.

Finally, we examined titles of articles pertaining to OB in the leading journals (presented in alphabetic order): *Academy of Management Journal* (1958–2015), *Academy of Management Review* (1976–2015), *Administrative Science Quarterly* (1956–2015), *American Journal of Sociology* (1895–2015), *American Sociological Review* (1936–2015), *Journal of Applied Psychology* (1967–2015), *Organizational Behavior and Human Performance* (1966–1984), and *Organizational Behavior and Human Decision Process* (1985–2015). Not surprisingly, these titles reflect the discipline's inherent positive orientation. The number of titles referring to OMB phenomena (misconduct, deviance, unethical behavior, political behavior, theft, violence, harassment, etc.), compared with the enormous amount of research concerning issues such as productivity, motivation, leadership, job satisfaction, career development, team effectiveness, and creativity, is notably lower. Thus, the inevitable question is: How did this happen and where has misbehavior gone?

We suggest that the paucity of empirical research into the darker side of organizational life, and the lack of well-developed mainstream models of organizational misbehavior, may be explained by four interrelated reasons: (1) the field's inherent tendency toward specialization and the predominance of functionalism, (2) the predominance of a congruence paradigm, (3) the tendency to address managerial needs, and (4) the lack of methodologies to adequately capture misbehavior in organizations.

Specialization and Functionalism

OB emerged as an interdisciplinary academic field and has prospered primarily in schools of management and business administration (Kreitner & Kinicki, 1995). It is grounded, however, in traditional I-O psychology, which has had a profound impact on its formation and may have inadvertently limited its fields of inquiry (Cappelli & Sherer, 1991; Mowday & Sutton, 1993). Because of its importance in this analysis, we now turn to a brief review of the history of I-O psychology.

During the first part of the twentieth century, I-O psychologists concentrated their efforts on recruitment and selection, work methods, and job design (Katzell & Austin, 1992). These new practices became part of the academic discourse during World War I, at which time the US government turned to psychologists for help in developing recruitment and selection procedures for the military (see Cappelli & Sherer, 1991). Their apparent success in this endeavor accorded the emerging field of I-O psychology legitimization and contributed to its official and widespread recognition, which in turn helped practitioners market professional tools to the prospering postwar private sector for seeking and hiring new employees. During the 1930s, the core practices of the field were employee selection, appraisal, and training. On the whole, academic research in those years was characterized by retesting and re-examining what was already achieved, rather than by breaking new ground and defining new directions (Katzell & Austin, 1992).

The number of universities offering programs in I-O psychology was growing. By 1930, Pennsylvania State College, Ohio State University, the University of Minnesota, and Stanford University were offering PhD degrees in I-O psychology. As the decade progressed, several more academic institutions began offering programs to train students for careers in I-O psychology. Of course, this offered additional respectability to the new discipline and facilitated its institutionalization as a professional and academic pursuit. Yet even with this growing recognition, there was no marked change in I-O psychology's objects of inquiry. Researchers continued to further their knowledge in the familiar areas, reassess previous studies, and re-examine well-established theories and models. The core objects of I-O psychology remained employee selection, performance appraisal, and training techniques.

World War II had a significant influence on the evolution and development of I-O and OB. As in World War I, hundreds of I-O psychologists representing a variety of specialties were employed by the US military, developing even more sophisticated selection tests. The war gave rise to additional sub-specializations within the areas of appraisal, group processes, and attitude change (Katzell & Austin, 1992). The exposure I-O psychologists received in the military during WWII had once again helped them legitimize and expand their professional endeavors in the rapidly growing postwar economy. The 1950s, 1960s, and early 1970s were characterized by rapid economic growth. I-O psychology scholars and practitioners were again in demand by growing companies, giving them opportunities to expand and test their knowledge of employee selection, appraisal, and training. Human resource management was elevated to an academic discipline in its own right.

Work motivation (Locke, 1968; Vroom, 1964), job satisfaction (Herzberg, 1968), job redesign (Hackman & Oldham, 1980), and career development (Hall,

1976) were also widely addressed both scientifically and in practice. This tendency toward the non-economic and personal rewards was explained in light of Maslow's (1954) general theory of human motivation. The I-O psychology literature of the postwar era was characterized by writings highly critical of the stultifying nature of most jobs and called for expanding opportunities for self-expression and personal growth (Argyris, 1957; McGregor, 1960). Although the starting point for the need deficiency approach may have been the sense of worthlessness and alienation experienced by employees (e.g., Blauner, 1964), the workplace was fast reframed as the arena in which the employee should fulfill his or her various needs—from security and a decent wage to self-esteem and self-actualization. Less pleasant aspects of the human experience at work were, by and large, neglected.

Years later, in the first *Annual Review of Psychology* state-of-the-art analysis of OB, Mitchell (1979) rightly noted the saturation of research in some areas as opposed to the non-existence of study in others. Others (e.g., O'Reilly, 1991) argued that most studies in OB contribute to the progress of already existing areas or methodologies, but tend not to seek new concepts or objects of inquiry. Following this, House, Rousseau, and Themas-Hurt (1995) suggested that the field needs new theories and a wider range of objects, and Daft and Lewin (1993) openly called for a new research agenda, including the development of issues such as leadership in flexible and non-hierarchical organizations, employee empowerment, organizational learning, computer communication, and inter-organizational cooperation. Still, this agenda did not include a call for systematic research, which may shed some light on the shady aspects of organizational life, misbehavior among them.

The exclusion of misbehavior from OB discourse is apparently the result of a long process of institutionalization of several practices leading to a positive-normative bias in the field. This process was further reinforced by the dominant approach in the social sciences, especially at the formative stage of OB development as a distinct discipline—functionalism. As a paradigm, functionalism was neither reflexive nor critical. Therefore, it was not sensitive to the problems and conflicts of the society at large (Smelser, 1999) and the work organization in particular (Bensman & Gerver, 1963).

Although this trend was typical of I-O psychology, sociology was no different. Early on, the academic field of sociology also ventured into the workplace. The famous Hawthorne studies, which seem to mark the shift from scientific management to human relations, have become the cornerstone of every course dealing with industrial sociology. In 1914, when Henry Ford faced grave organizational problems, he created a sociology department that employed 250 people. Aiming to reduce a daily absentee rate exceeding 10 percent, compounded by a huge yearly turnover rate that required nearly $2 million a year just to train new workers, and facing fierce negotiations with one of the most militant unions in the country, Ford designed a new program for commitment, loyalty, and conformity. Every qualified employee was paid $5 per day (Marcus & Segal, 1989).

The sociology department was charged with determining who was qualified to receive this remuneration. These agents of social control visited homes and interviewed friends, neighbors, and priests to determine who conformed to the code of conduct, family values, community values, thrift, and personal character. They used strict criteria for unsuitability and norms of exclusion: Single young men, men who were engaged in divorce, those who did not spend their evenings wisely, those who drank alcohol, or those who did not speak English. They also gave lessons in home management to workers and their families and taught them how to shop and preserve moral values (Marcus & Segal, 1989).

Sociology, as a form of social praxis, sought to establish rational control over human nature and society (Shenhav, 2002). Although these social agents focused on improving good and proper behavior and expunging what they considered to be evil or deviant, they, like I-O psychologists, failed to further investigate these darker sides of work-life and the reasons for their prevalence. Even when crime and deviance were discussed, they were considered as pathologies or problems to be solved through the mechanisms of equilibrium (hence, need not be worried about) or as functional to the system in the long run and thus no longer categorized as a problem (Bensman & Gerver, 1963). Crozier (1964), in his classic study of the French bureaucracy, described an organization in which a lack of integration between the staff and the firm's goals caused negative employee attitudes toward the workplace. However, he concluded, "this lack of integration does not seem to have much influence over other aspects of the staff's behavior and attitudes... The staff's dissatisfaction and pessimism do not prevent a satisfactory basic pattern of adjustment. Indeed, they can be viewed as a specific way, a grumbling way, of achieving it" (p. 50). Moreover, "they adjust to it [to the bureaucratic hierarchy] in a grumbling way, but, one way or another, they adjust" (p. 55). Although aware of the possibility of irregularities, backdoor deals, and subtle blackmail, Crozier argued that no organization could survive if it were run solely by such individual and backdoor deals. This was due to "the rational side of the organization and the series of social controls that prevent people from taking too much advantage over their own strategic situation" (p. 166). Management control in the workplace has indeed been a dominant notion for the better part of the twentieth century (see Edwards, 1979).

A Congruence Paradigm

Functionalism, however, does not stand alone. Later mainstream approaches to the study of organization behavior, emerging from Katz and Kahn's (1966) adaptation of the open system model, also focus on the positive-normative aspects of work and organizational life (e.g., Nadler & Tushman, 1980; Porter et al., 1975). These approaches contend that, for the enterprise to be efficient, there needs to be a fit (a congruence, a match) among its components. The implication that its absence may lead to problems, dysfunctional behavior, and underperformance has somehow remained unaddressed, which is our second concern regarding OMB research. The influence of the congruence argument has permeated several key areas of interest in OB. The following are some well-known examples from both macro- and micro-OB.

At the *strategic* level, the best-known theory promoting the tenet of congruency is Miles and Snow's (1978) work on the fit between organization types and their environments. In another realm, one of the most influential models of *occupational careers* is based on the assumption that personal career fulfillment is a function of the fit between a person's occupational orientation and a commensurate occupational environment (Holland, 1985). In the study of *organizational careers*, Hall (1976) and Schein (1978) promoted the view that successful careers are a result of a good match between the needs of the employee and opportunities provided by the organization through its career management system. This was in line with the predominant person–environment fit approach to personal adjustment promoted by work psychologists (see Pazy & Zin, 1987). Finally, at the *person–organization interaction* level, the popular notion of the psychological contract promoted the proposition that congruency of expectations and obligations between employer and employee should lead to desirable outcomes (e.g., Kotter, 1973).

Perhaps a good example of the congruence paradigm's influence on OB is Nadler and Tushman's (1980) framework for organizational diagnosis. They (following Katz & Kahn, 1966; Leavitt, 1972) proposed a general model in which organizational effectiveness is a function of fit among key organization components: Mission or task, formal structure, informal structure, and the individual. Despite their logical appeal, the weakness of such theories is that they strongly imply that congruence is desirable and incongruence is not. Thus, they portray a normative bias and shy away from dealing with potential or actual misfit. Certainly, misbehavior at work may result from such mismatches (e.g., when individual values are incongruent with the organization's policy). Yet they may also emerge when fit between person and work exists (e.g., when loyalty leads to acting illegally or unethically on behalf of the organization).

In summary, traditional research on attitudes toward work—job satisfaction in particular—tended to focus on improving the fit between the individual and his or her occupation. The consequences of lack of fit or mismatch between the individual and his or her work were not adequately explored or researched (Pazy & Zin, 1987). Similarly, the positive consequences of lack of fit, such as certain friction and tension that may enhance creativity and change, were ignored. Such conditions could indeed be important precursors of misbehavior on the job.

Organizational Behavior and Management

The third reason for the lack of OMB research again goes back to the early days of management—namely, the rise of scientific management and, later, the emergence of the Human Relations School. Both focused their attention on issues of productivity and motivation (Farrell & Petersen, 1982; Katzell & Austin, 1992) mostly because, in the wake of the two world wars and the Depression, times of vast opportunities and economic growth unfolded. The main focus was on enhancing organizational productivity and developing work organizations and their managers. Perhaps in the search for yet higher levels of effectiveness, especially in the footsteps of the Human Relations School, many of the founding fathers of OB (e.g., Argyris, 1957; Herzberg, 1968; McGregor, 1960; Porter & Lawler, 1968; Schein, 1969) emphasized behavior and de-emphasized misbehavior. The models depicting employee behavior at work, which were attractive to practitioners and management, were and perhaps had to be positively skewed. Management fads such as efficiency improvement, job enrichment and sociotechnical programs, career development, quality circles, total quality management, sensitivity training (Abrahamson, 1996, 1997), positive psychology (Ben-Shahar, 2007) and the like caught the public's fancy because they seemed to be appealing and sold well. Understandably, programs with more realistic names, such as insensitivity treatment, defect correction, or inefficiency prevention, would not have had the same appeal, although these might have better reflected their contents. Most telling of this trend in OB is the way Adams' (1963) theory of *inequity* came to be commonly known as *equity* theory. Perceived equity is not a motivator. Rather, the theory subsumes that individuals are driven to cope with cognitive dissonance that results from perceived incomparable worth—not equal worth—and are thus motivated to act to restore an internal sense of balance. Later, in fact, Greenberg (1990a) demonstrated how perceived inequity at work might lead to theft.

Practitioners, consultants, and academics, offering solutions to managers' ever more demanding perceived or real problems, tend to wrap their goods in attractive packages and promote positive aspects of behavior while mostly ignoring the negative ones. The venerable *Harvard Business Review* (HBR), which during its long years of influential existence offered managers up-to-date practical programs and prescriptions designed to increase the firm's efficiency and profitability, and the employees' well-being, clearly demonstrates this bias. A thorough review of HBR publications (Sibbet, 1997) reveals that models, research, or practical advice for the daily and cumbersome confrontation with misbehavior in the workplace occupy negligible space, if at all.

Many questions come to mind. Does mainstream OB literature portray behavior in organizations accurately? Is it reasonable to assume that management and organizational scholars do not encounter misbehavior in the workplace? Does management avoid dealing with dysfunctional behaviors? Does it not experience manifestations of theft of company property by employees, aggression, sexual harassment, and the like? Are HR managers not aware of the effects of employee misconduct on employee careers? Are researchers not aware of these phenomena? Why do managers and practitioners prefer to deal only with techniques such as cooperative management, interpersonal communication, total quality management, and the like while ignoring the more murky aspects of the workplace? Have researchers attempting to study negative aspects of organizational life encountered a total lack of cooperation from management?

It appears that top management generally has had no interest in studying unconventional practices in their firms and even less interest in publishing—going public with—such findings. It may be that they are wary of tarnishing the reputation of themselves or the company (Analoui & Kakabadse, 1992), preferring to sweep the bad news under the proverbial corporate rug. Unquestionably, this lack of cooperation creates difficulties for would-be OMB researchers in the quest for valid data, which leads us to our fourth concern regarding the paucity of OMB research: The methodological problems in the study of OMB (see Chapter 10).

Methodological Limitations

The methodology in use by the majority of organizational researchers has no doubt influenced the development of OB. It may also explain OB's tendency to focus on a relatively small number of phenomena. Historically, OB researchers have specialized in cross-sectional correlational designs, whereas laboratory and field experiments were left to psychologists and ethnographic research was left to anthropologists. For example, most of the studies published in the *Administrative Science Quarterly* between 1959 and 1979 tended to be empirical (Daft, 1980). These methods, using quantitative, precise, and rigorous language to describe organizational phenomena, narrow the scope of organizational issues that can be investigated. That is, they limit research projects to relatively accessible, tangible, prior-defined characteristics of individuals and organizations, and therefore do not tap the amorphous and often hidden dimensions of everyday organizational life. Generally speaking, OB research sheds light on only a narrow range of organizational reality. It misses, as Daft (1980) argued, "the complex, intangible, emotional dimensions of organizations [that] probably cannot be processed through the fine filter of linear statistics" (p. 632).

In addition to the lack of agreement among scholars as to the nature of OB, the tools they use to encompass the dimensions of OB are limited. Most instruments used in OB research tap a fairly limited amount of behavioral variance because of the manner in which behavior is operationalized. In many ways, it is a myopic view of both the fidelity and bandwidth of human behavior in organizations. For example, take one of OB's most studied variables: Job satisfaction. Traditionally, research captures this affect or attitude on a preset numerical (i.e., arbitrary) scale. Yet those individuals who are either euphoric or utterly miserable at work, by definition, cannot convey their true feelings toward their job on such a scale. Similarly, organization climate scales (e.g., Litwin & Stringer, 1968) are not designed to assess the extent to which manipulative managerial behavior is predominant in an organization. Leadership questionnaires (e.g., Fleishman & Harris, 1962) typically ignore the possible abuse of supervisory power, and most commitment measures tap neither betrayal intentions nor addiction to work or workaholism. We believe our tools, with their limited measures, provide some explanation for the institutionalization of the positively leaning descriptions of organizational life that OB has generated.

Qualitative, long-term ethnographic research has definite advantages over quantitative methodology in revealing new fields of knowledge, but it tends to be highly time-consuming and evokes many ethical dilemmas. To conduct such research, generous funding, a commitment by management, and academic support are required. For example, it took Ferhad Analoui six years of undercover work to record and analyze some 450 incidents of OMB in one particular British organization (see Analoui & Kakabadse, 1992). This may not be suitable for academics struggling with the pressure to publish within given time constraints and incommensurate with the lack of funding, as well as management's unwillingness to participate in research examining company-sensitive issues (Analoui & Kakabadse, 1992). In addition to the increasing difficulty to publish in leading academic periodicals, these constraints may explain the scarcity of rigorous OMB research.

Finally, the lack of agreement among scholars about common descriptions, explanations, and definitions of observed phenomena of misbehavior also makes it difficult for this new theoretical and empirical body of knowledge to be developed. Furthermore, the fact that OB scholars come from varied academic disciplines makes it more difficult to agree on what is instrumental and what is evil (Near & Miceli, 1984), what is prosocial and what is antisocial (Giacalone & Greenberg, 1997), and what is functional and what is dysfunctional (Bamberger & Sonnenstuhl, 1998). We believe there is a need to resolve such conceptual and methodological dilemmas.

A Historical Perspective

After almost five decades of OB research, three distinct phases in the evolution of the newly emergent area of OMB can be identified: The mid-1950s to the late 1970s—*the early phase*, a period of sporadic and non-systematic research; the early 1980s to the mid-1990s—*the formative phase*, a period of wide scholarly calls for systematic research and the evolvement of the major areas of interest in the new field; and the mid-1990s to date—*the current phase*, toward the full integration of the emerging subfield of OMB into mainstream OB.

The Early Phase

Although OB scholars and practitioners tend to ignore the dark side of organizational life, other disciplines such as industrial sociology, occupational psychology, criminology, and organizational anthropology did in fact deal with it (Hollinger & Clark, 1982). For instance, Quinney (1963) investigated the impact of an occupational structure on employees' criminal behavior at work. Larceny, in the form of embezzlement (Altheide et al., 1978; Cressey, 1953), fiddling · (Mars, 1973), pilferage (Altheide et al., 1978; Ditton, 1977; Mars, 1973), and employee theft (Horning, 1970; Kemper, 1966; Mars, 1974; Merriam, 1977), was explored extensively. Sabotage, whether referred to as industrial sabotage (Taylor & Walton, 1971), vandalism (Cohen, 1973; Fisher & Baron, 1982), or destruction (Allen & Greenberger, 1980), also received widespread attention mainly because it was harmful, costly, and easy to track. Restriction of output (Collins et al., 1946; Harper & Emmert, 1963), goldbricking (Roy, 1952), informal coworker interaction (Roy, 1959), and unauthorized use of time-saving tools (Bensman & Gerver, 1963) were other types of deviant behaviors addressed by scholars, perhaps following management's growing attention to efficiency and productivity in the 1950s and 1960s.

The only extensive attempt to explore improper work behavior was made by sociologists and criminologists using the concept of white-collar crime proposed by Sutherland (1940) in his presidential address to the American Sociological Society in 1939. Later Sutherland (1949) defined it as "crime committed by a person of respectability and high social status in the course of his occupation" (p. 9). Although the notion was never developed into a full and coherent theory, and despite its inherent deficiencies (for review of the critiques, see Coleman, 1987; Shapiro, 1990), it offered a significant contribution to criminology, sociology, and, later, OB research as well (Braithwaite, 1985).

From an analytical viewpoint, the term *white-collar crime* has three foci: Illegality of the act, social status of the actor, and identity of the beneficiary. Most definitions comply with the first—that is, writers (e.g., Coleman, 1994; Horning, 1970) emphasize the formal definition of acts of misbehavior as criminal.

Originally, a class distinction was made between white- and blue-collar crime or more accurately between white-collar crime and blue-collar theft (Horning, 1970). Later, more widely accepted conceptualizations were suggested by Clinard and Quinney (1973) and Coleman (1994, 1987) based on the identity of the beneficiary of the illegal act. Clinard and Quinney decomposed the concept of white-collar crime into *occupational crime*, defined as "offenses committed by individuals for themselves in the course of their occupation and the offenses of employees against their employers," and *corporate crime*, which, in contrast, is defined as "the offenses committed by corporate officials for the corporation and the offenses of the corporation itself" (cited in Braithwaite, 1985, p. 18). The definition of *occupational crime* encompasses many blue-collar crimes. Coleman (1987), in a somewhat different classification, called for the distinction between *occupational crime*, which he defined as "[crimes] committed for the benefit of individual criminals without organizational support," and *organizational crime*, which refers to "[crimes] committed with support from an organization, that is, at least in part, furthering its own ends" (p. 406). A more clear-cut distinction, supplementing Clinard and Quinney's (1973) work, emphasizes the difference between crimes committed against coworkers and those committed against the organization (Greenberg & Scott, 1996). In fact, Greenberg and Scott (1996) took the definition a step further by adopting the distinction made by Hollinger and Clark (1982) between production deviance and property deviance, thus adding a third dimension to the conceptualization of organizational crime.

The evolving definitions of *white-collar crime* demonstrate the long way Sutherland's term traveled during its 75 years of existence. However, the history of the white-collar crime concept has its share of controversy. Sutherland's overarching definition "has been criticized, refined and debated" more than supported (Shapiro, 1990, p. 347). Although Sutherland's conceptualization was incorporated into popular culture, it has proved to be somewhat confusing and obfuscating. Currently, the term has come to be used generically, dealing with a wide variety of work-related illegal acts by persons at all organizational levels (Greenberg & Scott, 1996; Jensen & Hodson, 1999). "Taken as a whole," Coleman (1987) observed, "the literature on the etiology and development of white-collar crime is a hodgepodge of studies looking at different crimes from different levels of analysis" (p. 408). These studies "confuse acts with actors, norms with norm breakers, the modus operandi with the operator" (Shapiro, 1990, p. 347), resulting in "an unfortunate mixing of definition and explanation" (Braithwaite, 1985, p. 3). Although the white-collar crime construct offers important insights into the darker side of organizations, it fails to develop a systematic theory of OMB.

The Formative Phase

Besides Blauner's (1964) groundbreaking work on alienation in the American workplace, systematic thinking about employee reactions to work dissatisfaction has its most profound roots in Hirschman's (1970) *Exit, voice, and loyalty: Responses to decline in firms, organizations and states*. Identifying *voice* as employees' political response to job dissatisfaction, and defining it as "any attempt at all to change rather than to escape from an objectionable state of affairs" (p. 30), was a major contribution to the OB field (Farrell, 1983). Not only did Hirschman bring the darker aspects of organizations into the forefront, but he also set the basis for one of the most important conceptual frameworks in OB. The Exit, Voice, Loyalty, and Neglect (EVLN) model, for example, derived from Hirschman's work by

Rusbult, Zembrodt, and Gunn (1982), is a useful conceptual framework for analyzing the relationships among responses to job dissatisfaction (Farrell, 1983). Although Hirschman's conceptualization was developed to explain the responses of organizations to decline, it could also prove useful in understanding how individuals act when things are not going well (Withey & Cooper, 1989). Thus, the EVLN model may serve as a general framework for understanding a variety of workplace behaviors.

We posit that loyalty may be viewed as organizational citizenship behavior (Organ, 1988), prosocial organizational behavior (Brief & Motowidlo, 1986), extra-role behavior, and the like (see Van Dyne et al., 1994). That is, *loyalty* may be defined as individual acts that are first and foremost supportive of the organization (for a discussion in the variety of meanings attached to loyalty, see Withey & Cooper, 1989). Similarly, antisocial behaviors (Giacalone & Greenberg, 1997) may be viewed as related to *voice* and *exit* and, to a lesser degree, *neglect*. However, unlike Rusbult et al. (1982) and Farrell (1983), we do not view voice as merely a contributive behavior, but more as a variety of behaviors ranging from acts aimed at restoring past situations (e.g., filing a grievance) to destructive behaviors aimed at causing damage to the organization (e.g., sabotage) or its members (e.g., aggression and violence). Moreover, although the EVLN responses were found to be both conceptually and empirically distinguishable (Farrell, 1983; Withey & Cooper, 1989), their boundaries are somewhat blurred. For instance, exit and voice could be independent, sequential, or co-occurring (Withey & Cooper, 1989). In any case, during the 1980s in particular, with the exception of the EVLN model and some work on workplace deviance (Hollinger & Clark, 1982, 1983; Raelin, 1984), interest in organizational misbehavior was marginal in OB, but the seeds for the rapid development in the 1990s were sown.

The Mature Phase

Interdisciplinary and eclectic by nature, the emerging approach to OMB is in a unique position because it can appropriate and enjoy the fruits of the research conducted in other disciplines. For the sake of parsimony and focus, in this section, we only discuss the evolution of selected OMB sub-interests: *Employee deviance, workplace aggression*, and *political behavior*. Each domain has a somewhat different focus: The employee deviance literature is concerned with the social conditions under which certain behaviors are considered counternormative or deviant. Workplace aggression research is limited to exploring mainly harmful and damaging behaviors. Political behavior research attempts to shed light on the use and misuse of power and influence as means to achieve particular individual and group interests. Evidently, these three scientific branches are not totally distinct. In fact, to a large extent, they are interrelated and overlap at times (we explore these topics further throughout the book).

Employee Deviance

Several early attempts have been made to classify employee deviance, also referred to as *workplace deviance* or *organizational deviance*. For instance, Wheeler (1976) classified forms of organizational rule-breaking into serious and non-serious offenses. Mangione and Quinn (1975) proposed two categories of deviance: *Counterproductive behavior*, defined as "purposely damaging employer's property," and *doing little on the job*, defined as "producing output of poor quality or low quantity" (p. 114)—somewhat similar to Taylor's (1895, 1903) definition of *soldiering* more than a century ago.

A significant breakthrough in understanding workplace deviance was made by Hollinger and Clark (1982). They noted, "for the student of occupational behavior a relatively unexplored area of inquiry is the deviance [which] occurs in the workplace, particularly those unauthorized acts by employees which are intended to be detrimental to the formal organization" (p. 97). Following Mangione and Quinn (1975), they classified the findings of Cressey (1953), Mars (1973), Ditton (1977), Horning (1970), and others into two distinct categories of employee deviance: *Property deviance* and *production deviance*. Property deviance focuses on those instances when employees acquire or damage the tangible property or assets of the organization without authorization, whereas production deviance concerns behaviors that violate the formally proscribed norms delineating the quality and quantity of work to be accomplished. Unlike white-collar crime, their definitions of production deviance and property deviance classify the act as anormative, not as a crime. That is, occupational white-collar crime against the company is now replaced by employee deviance (mostly toward property); however, the former focuses on the illegality of the act (yet possibly normative), whereas the latter underlines it as being counter-normative (yet possibly legal).

More than a decade later, Robinson and Bennett (1995) called for expanding this framework, arguing that an accurate typology of employee deviance should consider not only behavior directed at organizations, but also behavior that targets other individuals. Their typology—derived from a statistical analysis of survey-based data—offers two solid dimensions: Type of target chosen by the perpetrator (other persons or the organization) and extent of damage inflicted (minor or serious). Bennett and Robinson (2000) further developed a measure called the Workplace Deviance Scale that distinguishes between organization and interpersonal deviant behavior.

Workplace Aggression

The phenomenon of workplace aggression was rarely studied within OB until the early 1990s. Perhaps this reflects a more benign work atmosphere in organizations in the post-WWII era characterized by rapid growth and full employment. Since the early 1980s, the workplace in the United States and Europe has become markedly more vulnerable and unsettled, accompanied by new-age forms of employee alienation and the breakdown of the traditional psychological contract. The term *aggression* is employed to describe many different behaviors, not all of which are necessarily antisocial in either their intents or effects. As Neuman and Baron (1997) noted, for example, there is a distinction between aggressive (with mostly negative connotation) and assertive (with mostly positive connotation) forms of behavior, and the difference is not always clear-cut. Yet the recent literature seems to tilt toward the hostile dimension of the behavior (e.g., O'Leary-Kelly et al., 1996). Again, this may not be surprising in view of the rapid growth of reported cases of aggression, homicide included, within the workplace (see Chapter 11).

The proposition that aggression is a plausible outcome of frustration in the workplace is not new (Spector, 1978). Blauner (1964) observed that "machine-breaking was a common response in the early stages of industrialization when new factory conditions appeared oppressive" (p. 106), suggesting that aggression is a result of employees' frustration brought on by their lack of control, perhaps "ways of getting even with a dominating technology" (p. 107). However, despite Blauner's depiction of powerlessness and alienation in industry, and although early work motivation theories (Adams, 1965; Herzberg, 1968; Vroom, 1964) alluded to the possibility of hostile behavior at work, aggression as an intentionally harmful behavior was not fully conceptualized until the mid-1970s (Spector, 1975, 1978). This is quite surprising considering that a significant amount of research outside the organizational context was devoted to factors that cause, facilitate, or exacerbate human aggression or that tend to prevent or reduce it. Unfortunately, Neuman and Baron (1997) observed that there is little evidence to suggest that this large body of knowledge has been systematically applied to the social context in which most adults spend most of their waking time—their work environment.

Workplace violence and aggression are often discussed in the popular literature (for a review, see Barling et al., 2009), suggesting that a number of workplace factors are associated with these forms of misbehavior such as organizational injustice, pressures of widespread job losses and fewer job opportunities, lower levels of organizational loyalty, souring peer relationships, authoritarian styles of management, and substance abuse. Although this literature offers anecdotal evidence regarding elements that have been or are postulated to be associated with workplace aggression and violence, there has been little systematic research explaining their effects. In social psychology, for example, human aggression is considered an adaptive reaction to frustration—an instinct resulting from internal excitation or a learned social behavior that is part drive-based and part learned behavior. The social learning perspective posits that organizational aggression is prompted by external factors (social-situational cues and reinforcers), rather than internal factors (instincts and drives; O'Leary-Kelly et al., 1996).

An early adaptation of the social psychology models to the organizational setting was proposed by Korman (1971, 1976), who presented a framework relating environmental antecedents to motivational processes and suggested that a high level of aggression toward self and others stems from the workplace's environmental characteristics. This model, although novel, is undeveloped and lacks a definition of aggression. Similarly, Spector (1975, 1978) explored the relationship between frustration caused by factors in the work setting and aggression. He defined *aggression* as "behaviors designed to hurt the employer or the organization" (Spector, 1975, p. 635) and noted that aggression was traditionally conceptualized as a reaction to an organization's control and punishment systems. He concluded that frustrating events, which interfere with employees' goal attainment and/or maintenance in organizational settings, might indeed cause aggressive behavior.

Two further distinctions regarding aggression can be made. The first distinguishes organizational aggression and interpersonal aggression. Whereas the former is intended to harm the organization, the latter is intended to hurt other employees and "is primarily verbal" (Spector, 1975, p. 637). The second distinction accounts for the visibility of the act. It differentiates between *overt* (work slowdowns, grievances) and *covert* (sabotage, withholding of output) forms of aggression. Neuman and Baron (1997) noted that research concerning aggression tends to focus almost exclusively on the covert forms of aggression. In any case, as suggested earlier, except for Spector and a few others (for reviews, see O'Leary-Kelly et al., 1996; Neuman & Baron, 1997; Robinson & Bennett, 1997), workplace aggression and violence per se remained almost unexplored until the 1990s.

Political Organizational Behavior

Crozier (1964) studied power relations and the problem of control in organizations, concepts that gained respect in the Marxist sociological tradition (e.g., Baritz, 1960; Bendix, 1956; Braverman, 1974; Edwards, 1979). During the 1970s and early 1980s, there was a surge of theoretical and empirical work on the acquisition and exercise of power within complex organizations (e.g., Bacharach & Lawler, 1980; Pfeffer, 1981). This body of research focused primarily on structural and environmental factors affecting the distribution and dynamics of power in organizations. It made clear that power reflects the degree to which organizational members cope with critical demands facing the organization, and the degree to which members control critical resources or information on which others must depend. However, little research attention was paid to the more psychological determinants of individual acquisition of power, let alone its manipulative use in organizations.

Although widely recognized by organizational members, instrumental political behavior of individuals within organizations was not integrated into organizational theory until the mid-1980s. Empirical studies of the processes by which individuals select the target of political behavior in which they engage have rarely been conducted (Farrell & Petersen, 1982; Kacmar & Carlson, 1998). The main reason for this apparent paradox is, as already noted, that the Scientific Management and Human Relations schools, with their managerial perspective and prescriptive biases, focused on issues of motivation and productivity at the expense of understanding resource allocation and the related intra-organizational conflict, which is an integral part of it.

Scholarly interest in the political behavior of individuals stems from waves of growing attention to the way power is used in organizations in the 1970s (Farrell & Petersen, 1982; Kacmar & Carlson, 1998). Other social science disciplines also investigated the roots of such behaviors at various levels. Political scientists addressed unrest as antecedent to political protests, psychologists considered personality variables such as Machiavellianism as potential antecedents of political behaviors, and anthropologists studied leveling behaviors—behaviors that reduce others to one's own level or status within a social context (Robinson & Bennett, 1997). In addition, sociologists began to explore mechanisms of neutralization, which allow individuals in social situations to justify and rationalize improper conduct (Sykes & Matza, 1957b).

Political behavior in organizations is defined as "those activities that are not required as part of one's organizational role but that influence, or attempt to influence, the distribution of advantages and disadvantages within the organization" (Farrell & Petersen, 1982, p. 405). This definition emphasizes the instrumental nature of political behavior by conceptualizing it as residing in informal structures and relating to the promotion of self and group interests, especially the expansion of the available resources for mobilization. Farrell and Petersen (1982) presented a preliminary multidimensional typology of political behavior in organizations consisting of three dimensions: Internal–external, vertical–lateral, and legitimate–illegitimate.

The first dimension relates to the focus of resources sought by those engaging in political behavior. The second recognizes the difference between influence processes relating superiors to subordinates and those relating to equals. The third, and perhaps the most relevant to our discussion, acknowledges that in organizations there is a distinction between normal, everyday, and even positive and beneficial politics, and extreme political behavior that violates the rules. As to the question of who engages in this kind of behavior, Farrell and Petersen (1982) argue that illegitimate political behavior is likely to be action taken by alienated members and those who feel they have little to lose.

More than three decades after Farrell and Petersen's (1982) work was published, it is now clear that the real contribution of their work was not in its adaptation of political behavior to organizational context, or their definition of the new concept, or the typology they presented. Their main contribution to OB, with which we concur, was in identifying an inherent positive-normative bias in its perspective, thus in effect calling for the expansion of the field's boundaries to encompass the more sinister sides of human behavior in organizations.

Toward a Framework for Misbehavior

In this chapter, we showed that, since its formation as a distinct discipline in the mid-1950s, OB research tended to (1) focus on the micro-level and (2) emphasize the positive-normative side of human behavioral patterns in work organizations. Undoubtedly, the field failed to pay proper attention to the unconventional aspects of organizational behavior, despite its aspirations to become a scholarly field of inquiry. We, among other scholars, have been attempting to rectify this omission.

Today more than ever we are witnessing a surge in OMB research and literature. Certainly we do not yet have the time perspective necessary to judge its impact on and contribution to management and the OB field. The emergence of this relatively new and distinct body of knowledge is the reason the field has moved from the early, formative stage to its current mature phase—even if this stage is yet to reach full bloom. Beginning in the late 1970s, and especially during the 1990s, we can clearly identify a *corrective tendency* of the OB field—an increasing awareness of as well as research into OMB. Thus, together with OMB and OCB, the OB discipline forms a new, distinguishable, and expanding body of knowledge rooted in academic discourse as well as practice.

We suggest that the classical models of behavior in work organizations, relating principally to enhancing positive outcomes of work-life, be reconsidered and expanded to cover the whole range of human behavior in organizational settings. This is necessary because misbehavior is both a *pervasive* and *universal* phenomenon. It cuts across individuals, jobs, hierarchical levels, occupations, organizations, and geographic borders. Only by further broadening our focus, intensively combining new knowledge to what we already understand, and tirelessly reconsidering our existing theories and our models, can OB become the scholarly, multileveled, overarching, and encompassing field it aspires to be. For instance, to date little is known about the effects of group-level variables on individual misbehavior at work (Robinson & O'Leary-Kelly, 1998). Thus, in our discussions about manifestations and antecedents of OMB we attach relatively more importance to the organizational, positional, and individual determinants of OMB. Most importantly, we view OMB in a dynamic, temporal manner: We emphasize the effects over time of misbehavior manifestations on both individuals and organizations. Since all organization members experience misbehavior during their careers, these eventually affect each other over time.

The next chapter adopts Vardi and Wiener's (1992, 1996) original motivational model and extends it to an overall *Antecedents–Intentions–Manifestations* framework for OMB analysis. The new framework serves as our guide and roadmap for this book, distinguishing various levels of antecedents of intentional OMB and its large variety of manifestations in the workplace. As is seen, both expositions deal with the challenges and demands presented earlier: They are anchored in classical models of OB, and they allow us to extend the discussion of OMB to the effects of micro-level (person and job), group, and macro-level (organization) factors.

2

A GENERAL FRAMEWORK FOR OMB ANALYSIS

The growing awareness of the prevalence of workplace misbehavior, briefly demonstrated in Chapter 1, can be coupled with a wide array of scholarly definitions and conceptualizations. Based on a review of the literature, Robinson and Greenberg (1998) identified eight terms and definitions that relate to the phenomenon of *employees behaving badly* at work (presented here in a chronological order):

- Non-compliant behavior (Puffer, 1987).
- Organizational misbehavior (Vardi & Wiener, 1992, 1996).
- Workplace deviance (Robinson & Bennett, 1995).
- Workplace aggression (Baron & Neuman, 1996).
- Organization-motivated aggression (O'Leary-Kelly et al., 1996).
- Antisocial behavior (Giacalone & Greenberg, 1997).
- Employee vice (Moberg, 1997).
- Organizational retaliation behaviors (Skarlicki & Folger, 1997).

Of these constructs, three appear to be especially relevant to our framework: *Antisocial behavior*—any behavior that brings or is intended to bring harm to the organization, its employees, or its stakeholders (Giacalone & Greenberg, 1997); *workplace deviance*—voluntary behavior of organization members, which violates significant organizational norms and, in so doing, threatens the well-being of the organization or its members (Robinson & Bennett, 1995); and *OMB*—any intentional act by organization members that violates core organizational or societal norms (Vardi & Wiener, 1992). The other definitions pertain to specific behaviors, such as acts of aggression and retaliation, which are considered special cases of organizational misbehavior.

Building upon prior work, researchers constantly suggest new constructs in an attempt to explain what misbehaviors are and what their antecedents and consequences may be. Below is a sample of several new constructs that were recently introduced to the growing OMB literature:

- Employee deviance (Warren, 2003).
- Generalized workplace harassment (GWH; Rospenda & Richman, 2004).
- Dysfunctional behavior (Griffin & Lopez, 2005).
- Pathological workplace behavior (Babiak & Hare, 2006).
- Insidious workplace behavior (IWB; Greenberg, 2010).
- Organizational wrongdoing (Palmer, 2012).
- Workplace idleness (Paulsen, 2014).
- Detrimental citizenship behavior (Pierce & Aguinis, 2015).

Evidently, behavioral science scholars view this complex and multifaceted phenomenon of misbehavior at work from different vantage points, which is neither new nor discouraging. Most behaviors in organizations (e.g., employee attachment and leadership) have attracted varied perspectives and interpretations, resulting in a wide array of definitions and concepts. Some definitions achieve more acceptance than others, especially as they gain sound empirical support. Thus, at this early stage of conceptual development, we should not expect consensus among scholars. We should be able to recognize the differences in emphases and implications and continue to build on them.

The flux of constructs, typologies, and models emerging since the 1990s, typical of the interdisciplinary and somewhat amorphous nature of OB, makes the mapping of research trends in the emerging OMB field extremely difficult (O'Leary-Kelly et al., 2000a). However, we define the main issues around which this field is evolving and furnish the necessary historical–epistemological dimension to the plethora of definitions and dimensions of workplace misbehavior (e.g., Robinson & Greenberg, 1998; Sackett & DeVore, 2001). In this book we strive to contribute to solidify a body of knowledge from which various OMB frameworks can be structured, researched, and applied.

This chapter is devoted to the development of one analytic OMB framework that integrates our understanding and exploration of the antecedents and manifestations of intentional misconduct so prevalently exhibited by organization members. First, we discuss the current need for such a framework. Then we describe the initial Vardi and Wiener (1992, 1996) motivational OMB model, and finally we conclude by offering a general framework for OMB. As the book progresses, we break down the model into its component parts and then, in the last chapter, reassemble the parts into a comprehensive, generic, model of OMB analysis and OMB management.

Need for Conceptual Clarification

The most prominent characteristic of research on unconventional practices within organizational settings is the attempt to define the essence of these phenomena and capture their vitality and the many human behaviors that fall within them (O'Leary-Kelly et al., 2000a; Robinson & Greenberg, 1998). Indeed, the field is still searching for its unique identity. As early as the 1980s, we began to see attempts to define and refine the field. We saw a flood of related constructs (e.g., organizational aggression, unconventional practices at the workplace, and employee deviance) that describe the phenomenon, typologies (e.g., Farrell & Petersen, 1982; Gardner & Martinko, 1998; Neuman & Baron, 1997; Robinson & Bennett, 1995) designed to encompass its scope and variance, and models (e.g., Martinko & Zellars, 1998; O'Leary-Kelly et al., 1996) that attempt to explain why these behaviors occur (either as a generic phenomenon or specific type of behavior) as well as how to manage and contain them. The contribution of this emerging and growing body of knowledge to our understanding of the OMB phenomena is yet to be truly understood and fully evaluated.

Of course, in their attempt to explore the other, darker side of organizational life, OB researchers are not alone. Scholars study related fields including management ethics (e.g., Brown et al., 2005; Treviño & Nelson, 2011) and industrial relations (e.g., Ackroyd & Thompson, 1999; Paulsen, 2014). In the field of business ethics, for example, scholars offer different models of ethical and unethical decision-making (see Treviño et al., 2014; Kish-Gephart et al., 2010). Overall, these models suggest a number of individual (e.g., moral identity, moral disengagement, locus of control, and Machiavellianism), interpersonal (e.g., peer influence, management influence) and organizational (e.g., culture, climate, codes of conduct) antecedents that may interact to effect unethical behaviors in organizations.

Some Related Concepts

Several attempts to systematize the treatment of phenomena related to OMB have been reported in the academic literature, especially in the areas of sociology and management. We offer the reader a few frameworks to exemplify how different academic perspectives produce different classifications and definitions.

Hollinger (1986) observed that sociological research on employee misbehavior (which he defined as *workplace deviance*) centers around two foci: Production deviance and property deviance. Although both constitute rule-breaking behavior, the first includes various types that are counterproductive (e.g., substandard work slowdowns and insubordination), and the second pertains to acts against property and assets of the organization (e.g., theft, pilferage, fiddling, embezzlement, and vandalism). Based on empirical analyses, he concluded that such individual acts are more likely to occur when personal attachment to the organization (e.g., commitment) is low.

Other antecedents found to affect productivity deviance are mostly related to group, peer, and competitive pressures (e.g., Hegarty & Sims, 1978; Zey-Ferrell & Ferrell, 1982); conflict and maladjustment (Raelin, 1986); employee recalcitrance (Ackroyd & Thompson, 1999); or implicit disagreements with organizational goals and expectations. Similarly, antecedents contributing to property deviance, such as theft, may be feelings of injustice or exploitation (Hollinger & Clark, 1983; Mars, 1974), attempts to ease personal financial pressure (Merton, 1938), moral laxity (Merriam, 1977), available opportunities (Astor, 1972), dissatisfaction with work (Mangione & Quinn, 1975), perceptions of pay inequity (Greenberg, 1990a), and feelings of frustration (Analoui & Kakabadse, 1992; Spector, 1997b) or revenge (Bies et al., 1997). Vandalism, as property deviance, was also found to be associated with perceptions of inequity and mistreatment (DeMore et al., 1988).

Treviño (1986) developed a novel approach to conceptualize OMB among managers by developing a model that explains the role personality, job, and situational factors play in determining ethical and unethical decisions. She identified individual-level variables such as the stage of moral development, ego strength, field dependence, and locus of control, as well as situational contingencies, such as the immediate job context and organization culture, as antecedents. Treviño then developed an extensive set of interactional propositions articulating specific predictions. Although the dependent variable *ethical–unethical behavior* was not formally defined, one may assume that intentionally making an unethical decision constitutes an important precursor of OMB. Because we attach special importance to managers' actions, we dedicate a separate chapter (Chapter 6) to corruption and unethical managerial behavior in organizations, its antecedents, and implications.

An empirically based typology of deviant workplace behavior was developed by Robinson and Bennett (1995), who conceived of employee deviance as voluntary behavior that violates significant organizational norms and, in so doing, threatens the well-being of an organization, its members, or both. This definition is problematic for several reasons: (1) by emphasizing organizational norms, Robinson and Bennett distinguished workplace deviance from unethical behavior as the latter form of behavior relates to societal and moral, rather than local, conventions; (2) they included in their definition the harmful consequences of employee misconduct, thus precluding potential benefits of engaging in acts that defy local norms; and (3) they emphasized the role of significant norms espoused by the dominant coalitions in the organization. This could preclude less crystallized, yet important norms of conduct defined by other stakeholders such as customers or legislators.

Robinson and Bennett's (1995) typology of employee deviance consists of two dimensions: One ranging from personal to organizational targets, and the other from minor to serious infractions. Four types of voluntary and harmful misconduct emerged from a multidimensional scaling analysis: Production deviance (e.g., wasting resources), property deviance (e.g., stealing from the company), political deviance (e.g., showing undue favoritism), and personal deviance (e.g., sexual harassment). Robinson and Bennett also developed a workplace deviance scale specifically devised to measure organizational and interpersonal targeted misbehavior (Bennett & Robinson, 2000). This fairly concise and useful measure taps into forms of both personal and organizational misbehavior (Chapter 10 further discusses OMB measurement issues).

Robinson and Greenberg (1998) proposed an integrative model of workplace deviance consisting of five sequential components: (1) perpetrator (insider–outsider), (2) intention (intentional–unintentional), (3) target (internal–external and individual–organizational), (4) action (direct–indirect, active–passive, and verbal–physical), and (5) consequences (harmful–beneficial). This scheme allows for the identification of a variety of workplace activities that violate organizational norms of proper conduct. However, the Robinson and Greenberg model fails to deal with a major component in the process—the motivation to intentionally violate organizational norms. This issue, the motivation to engage in misbehavior, is the primary issue of this book.

The models discussed above reflect an ongoing debate as to whether the decision to misbehave is more a function of bad apples or bad barrels (Treviño & Youngblood, 1990). That is, are misbehaviors a function of the personal characteristics of individuals (the bad apples perspective) or organizational and societal variables (the bad barrels perspective)? However, Granovetter (1992) argued that neither the under-socialized perspective of individuals acting in isolation nor the over-socialized perspective of individuals obedient to norms and culture is adequate to explain behavior. Following this argument, researchers contend that neither the individual nor the organizational and societal perspectives alone fully explain OMB.

Frameworks in the OMB literature

Greenberg (2010) introduced the term *insidious workplace behavior* (IWB), defined as "a form of intentionally harmful workplace behavior that is legal, subtle, and low level (rather than severe), repeated over time and directed at individuals or organizations" (p. 4). IWB refers to a subset of misbehaviors, such as lying, incivility, sexist humor, revenge, sabotage, and passive or verbal forms of aggression. These behaviors share an underlying motive—the desire to inflict harm to individuals or organizations—yet their outcomes may not be harmful in the short term. Nonetheless, their cumulative effect may be detrimental since they are inclined to occur all the time, and will often remain undetected or unreported (we further discuss insidious forms of behavior in Chapters 4, 5, and 6). Palmer

(2012) introduced the conceptual framework of *organizational wrongdoing*, and suggested three underlying criteria to qualify behaviors as wrongful: Illegality, non-conformity to ethical codes of conduct, and social irresponsibility. His primary argument is that much organizational wrongdoing cannot be considered to be motivated behavior. Palmer delineates two contrasting perspectives of wrongdoing. First, the "dominant" approach that views organizational wrongdoing as an abnormal phenomenon, and assumes that wrongdoers are rational decision-makers, who deliberately and discretionally decide to engage in wrongdoing, and are positively inclined to do so. The second "alternative" approach views organizational wrongdoing as a normal phenomenon, and assumes that wrongdoers act under constraints of bounded rationality within their immediate social context. Their behaviors may escalate with time, yet wrongdoers are not positively inclined to engage in wrongdoing.

Warren (2003) emphasizes organizational consequences of *employee deviance*, defined as "behavioral departures from the norms of reference group" (p. 622). Her typology entails two dimensions: Conformity versus deviancy and global norms (hypernorms) versus behavioral norms (reference group norms). Hence, four categories emerge: (1) destructive deviance—behavior that falls outside both sets of norms (e.g., embezzlement); (2) destructive conformity—behavior that falls within reference group norms but deviates from hypernorms (e.g., selling an unsafe product); (3) constructive conformity—behavior that falls within both sets of norms (e.g., performing job assignments); and (4) constructive deviance—behavior that deviates from the reference group norms but conforms to hypernorms, and thereby can benefit the organization, its members, or both (e.g., whistleblowing).

Griffin and Lopez (2005) suggested the term *dysfunctional behavior* to describe "motivated behavior by an employee or group of employees that is intended to have negative consequences for another individual and/or group and/or the organization" (p. 1001). They reviewed a spectrum of misbehaviors and reassessed them using five dimensions: (1) definitional precision, (2) temporal consistency, (3) construct dimensionality, (4) behavioral motives, and (5) behavioral consequences. Subsequently, Griffin and Lopez created a typology of four dysfunctional behaviors: (1) workplace deviance (destructive and constructive), (2) workplace aggression (destructive and constructive), (3) workplace violence (towards persons or objects), and (4) antisocial behavior (described as an alternative term for dysfunctional behavior).

A different substantive construct, named *generalized workplace harassment* (GWH; Rospenda et al., 2005) refers to "Negative workplace interactions that affect the terms, conditions, or employment decisions related to an individual's job, or create a hostile, intimidating or offensive working environment, but which are not based on legally-protected social status characteristics" (p. 96). The GWH construct addresses four conceptual dimensions: Verbal hostility, covert hostility, manipulation, and physical hostility. Furthermore,

Rospenda and colleagues (Rospenda et al., 2005, 2006) as well as others (e.g., Raver & Nishii, 2010) have suggested the broad term *workplace harassment* (WH) in referring to both *sexual harassment* (SH) and GWH. Drawing on this, Neall and Tuckey (2014) recently suggested a more comprehensive conceptualization of GWH that encompasses various content domains within harassment research, such as bullying, aggression, incivility, abusive supervision, violence, abuse, mobbing, victimization, and hostile behavior.

Using a narrower approach, scholars have utilized the term *workplace mistreatment* (Yang et al., 2014; Cortina & Magley, 2003; Lim & Cortina, 2005), to describe a "specific, antisocial variety of organizational deviance, involving a situation in which at least one organizational member takes counternormative negative actions—or terminates normative positive actions—against another member… interpersonal mistreatment can thus range from subtle social slights to general incivility to blatant harassment and violence" (Cortina & Magley, 2003, p. 247). Workplace mistreatment incorporates three commonly occurring interpersonal OMBs: Incivility, bullying, and workplace aggression.

An emerging conceptual framework refers to pathological and psychopathological workplace behavior (see Babiak & Hare, 2006). Although related literature has its roots in industrial psychology, different scholars have recently sought to bridge the gap between clinical psychology and organizational (mis) behavior (e.g., Baysinger et al., 2014; Smith & Lilienfeld, 2013). Of particular salience are notions of *dark triad personalities* at work or *toxic employees* (e.g., Jonason et al., 2012) who display "behavior tendencies toward self-promotion, emotional coldness, duplicity and aggressiveness" (Paulhus & Williams, 2002, p. 557), and terms such as *aberrant* (Wille et al., 2013) or *dysfunctional* personalities at work characterized by 'dark side traits' (Furnham et al., 2014).

The concept of *corporate psychopaths*, popularized by Boddy (e.g., 2006, 2011, 2014), denotes "a psychopath who works and operates in the organizational area" (Boddy, 2011, p. 369) and implies a toxic link between corporate organizations and psychopathy. Gabriel (2012) used a psychoanalytic approach to describe a state of corporate organizational pathology, called *miasma*: "a highly toxic state of affairs capable of afflicting everybody and of corrupting the institutional and moral fabric of a social unit" (p. 1145). Drawing on Stein (2001), Gabriel (2012) maintains that corporate organizations have turned "into a place of darkness where emotional brutality is commonplace and different forms of psychological violence… have become the norm" (p. 1142). His theory enlists a variety of psychological consequences (i.e., depression, anxiety) to organizational members as a result of miasma.

Taken together, it is evident that current OMB literature is still characterized by construct proliferation. Many scholars call for synergy; while others state the importance of capturing theoretical differences between concepts (see Tepper & Henle, 2011). We now turn to theoretically crystallize our conceptualization of OMB following the foundations laid down by Vardi and Wiener (1992, 1996).

OMB

Our review of the literature suggests that misbehavior in organizations should not only be viewed as *pervasive*, but also as *intentional* work-related behavior, mostly resulting in *negative consequences* for both individuals (perpetrators and targets) and the organization. Thus, we view OMB as an integral and common aspect of organizational reality and an important facet of individual, group, and organization conduct. It is not, we argue, a marginal, deviant organizational occurrence, . but as real as proper and conventional workplace behavior.

Definitions of workplace misbehavior may take on a variety of approaches and properties depending on theoretical positions concerning (1) the criterion against which OMB is determined, (2) the agent(s) who decide what constitutes OMB, and (3) the personal and organizational consequences of OMB. The position we take in this book concerning these requirements is guided by one overriding principle: The resulting definition should be broad enough to integrate various types of misbehavior, yet capable of providing a foundation for a constructive and explanatory model of OMB. We selected the concepts of values and norms as the criteria determining OMB and viewed both society at large and the organization as the defining agents. Because consequences of OMB can vary in different situations (e.g., functional or dysfunctional, negative or positive, and short-term or long-term), we do not include them in the definition, but rather as dependent variables in the overall model.

The term OMB has its roots in the industrial relations field. Our conceptualization and definition of *misbehavior*, however, is quite different from the Marxist conceptualization (Edwards, 1979). Ackroyd and Thompson (1999) referred to it as "anything you do at work you are not supposed to do" (p. 2). They claimed misbehavior occurs when there is a mismatch between what is expected from the employees by their employers and what they are actually willing to do. This conceptualization of OMB deals with non-compliance, counterproductivity, and sabotage as part of employees' attempts to increase their own control over their work-lives in today's capitalistic labor market. The authors presented four dimensions of appropriation in the organization on which owners and workers may agree or disagree: (1) appropriation of work, (2) appropriation of resources, (3) appropriation of time, and (4) appropriation of identity. Inherent conflicts between employees and employers about these dimensions is what may lead employees to misbehave; the various forms of misbehavior reflect different levels and intensity of disagreement.

This Marxist explanation of OMB posits that it is an expression of employees' resistance to managerial control. Hence, misbehavior is an endemic condition produced by the organization resulting from the inevitable class conflict and is by no means new. Although it is reasonable to believe that OMB is widespread, there is no reason to treat it as an inevitable product of class conflict. For example, in some cases, employee theft may reflect an employee's attempt to take revenge for maltreatment and be a means of protest against employers. Undeniably, it may also be motivated by personal needs and intended to benefit the perpetrators (Greenberg, 1993).

Our view is that OMB is voluntary and committed by choice. Thus, we adopt Vardi and Wiener's (1996) definition for OMB as "any intentional action by member/s of organization/s which defies and violates (a) shared organizational norms and expectations, and/or (b) core societal values, mores and standards of proper conduct" (p. 151). Clearly, this definition requires some qualification. Before we do that, it is crucial to emphasize that we explicitly rule out unintentional acts of misbehavior such as accidental damage to a machine or inadvertent injury to a coworker. Such mishaps occur as a result of human error. However, accidents resulting from intentional violation of rules and procedures are considered as OMB. That is, we include in the OMB construct only those acts that are intentional and purposeful, regardless of their eventual consequences.

First, the violation of organizational norms and values is a fundamental component in the OMB construct. Work organizations are complex social entities often comprised of multiple subunits and constituencies, thus the term *organization* does not necessarily convey a determinate entity. Rather, it represents the relevant unit of analysis of an investigator, manager, or consultant interested in the OMB phenomenon. Depending on their perspectives and special interests, researchers and practitioners may refer to a work organization as a whole or any significant sector within it, such as a workgroup or one of the divisions or strategic business units. The choice regarding the identity of the unit of interest must be made explicit in order to identify the relevant core values against which a violation (and therefore OMB) may occur. Thus, whenever the term *organization* is used herein, it is meant to convey exactly this meaning.

Second, both the overt action and its underlying intention(s) are necessary to identify misbehavior; to define OMB without its antecedent intention(s) may result in erroneously including behaviors that may be unintentional or accidental. Hence, work-related actions that involve errors, mistakes, or even unconscious and unintended negligence (e.g., a harmful mistake in a surgical procedure that is committed unintentionally) do not constitute OMB despite their similar consequences to the organization as well as to the actors involved.

Third, in studying OMB, we focus on the individual level of analysis rather than the group or organization levels. Although it may be possible to apply the concept of OMB to misbehavior by groups (e.g., Trice & Beyer, 1993, on deviant organizational subcultures) or organizations (e.g., Baucus & Near, 1991, on illegal corporate behavior), we direct our attention to individual members who are intentionally and directly involved in some form of OMB because the role of individual motivation and choice as the source and driver of OMB.

Fourth, for OMB to occur, it needs to run counter to existing core values and norms. These pertain to both formal (laws, rules, regulations, standard operating procedures, etc.) and informal organizational or social expectations. Our definition acknowledges the importance of both internal (intra-organizational) and external (societal) value systems in determining OMB.

The Role of Values

Personal and organizational values play a central role in the understanding of OMB. Therefore, a quick review of the concept is necessary. In the social psychology literature, there are some inconsistencies in the definition of the concept and the distinctions between values and related constructs such as attitudes, beliefs, and norms. Nevertheless, certain formulations, which allow for operational definitions and empirical measurement, have gained a fair degree of acceptance (see Brown, 1976; Fallding, 1965; Meglino et al., 1989; Wiener, 1988). One such definition, proposed by Rokeach (1973), is that "a value is an enduring belief that a specific mode of conduct or end-state of existence is personally or socially preferable to an opposite or converse mode of conduct or end-state of existence" (p. 5). To Rokeach, values are forms of beliefs that may stem from social expectations, particularly when shared. Thus, social values may be viewed as normative beliefs complementing instrumental beliefs as antecedents of behavior (Fishbein & Ajzen, 1975). Further, values may be construed as internalized normative beliefs. Once established, they may act as a built-in normative compass, a guide for behavior independent from the effect of rewards and punishments that result from actions (Wiener, 1982).

The concepts of values and norms apply to various types of social units, including the three most congruous with the definition of OMB: Workgroups, work organizations, and society at large. Rokeach's (1973) definition suggests that values shared by group members, particularly values concerning modes of conduct, become similar to norms guiding members toward uniformity in behavior. Others (e.g., Kilman, 1985), however, distinguish between norms and values, arguing that the former offer more specific and explicit behavioral expectations, whereas the latter are broader in scope than norms (for a more extensive review of organizational value systems, see Wiener, 1988; for a discussion on societal-level values, see Rokeach, 1973). Personal and organizational value systems play important roles in forming people's intention to behave and misbehave.

Definitional Implications

The definition of OMB implies three important and distinct features that are useful for constructing an integrative model of misbehavior: Measuring the variables, deriving relevant predictions, and implications for management in dealing with OMB. These are the foci of this book.

The Construct

Our definition of OMB does not necessitate that the act violate both societal and organizational values to be categorized as such. Although such behaviors are not uncommon (e.g., unauthorized use of company property), it would be theoretically too narrow and not constructive to limit OMB to just those acts. According to the proposed definition, a behavior that may be consistent with organizational expectations but violates societal values (e.g., misleading customers) would be considered OMB. Such organizationally condoned misbehaviors may be detrimental to the employee involved, and to the organization in the long run. Similarly, member behavior that is consistent with societal values but violates organizational expectations would also be classified as OMB (e.g., whistleblowing in an organization that does not sanction such behavior). Unacceptable as these behaviors may be at the time and particular location, they may be beneficial to organizations in the long run. We deem this definitional broadness as essential in any attempt to construct an integrative and inclusive OMB model. Our definition also provides a solid basis for a meaningful typology of misbehaviors that would be useful for the overall understanding and prediction of organizational outcomes.

OMB—Pernicious or Beneficial?

Another feature of the OMB construct is that it does not necessarily equate the violation of norms or values with negative and undesirable behavior. First, our definition does not make reference to the consequences of misbehavior, as these may be positive or negative. Second, the desirability of any value-breaking behavior is inherently a matter of judgment. In general, value-violating behavior would be deemed undesirable by a collective of individuals sharing that value, but it may be perceived as desirable by another collective that views this behavior as desirable and beneficial. If we examine the all-too-prevalent phenomenon of cheating customers, it may be valued as undesirable by members of society at large, while it may be deemed acceptable, and even necessary, in an organization strapped for cash. By the same token, whistleblowing may be viewed as commendable action by members of society at large, but unacceptable to the top management of a particular organization.

Consequences of OMB

Unlike some definitions (e.g., Robinson & Bennett, 1995), our definition does not deal with eventual or real consequences of misbehavior. We argue that the consequences of OMB may only be evaluated by their degree of constructiveness or destructiveness for any given organization. The basic premise is that an organization may not be successful in the long run if it expects or even permits members to violate values and norms of the larger society within which it operates. Thus, using the same example, cheating customers would in the long run tend to be detrimental to organizations that allow it, but whistleblowing may prove constructive (Miceli & Near, 1992). OMB that violates both societal and organizational values, such as undermining and harassing members, engaging in corporate fraud, sabotaging work, or vandalizing equipment, is clearly harmful.

OMB as a Complex Variable

Because OMB is defined in relation to a set of core values of a particular social unit, and because such core values can be measured, OMB can be considered a variable. Moreover, because of the complex phenomenon it may tap, OMB should be treated as a multidimensional construct. Such an approach is useful in order to generate significant predictions about the phenomenon. In general, OMB may range from a low (benign) degree of misbehavior, such as minor workplace incivility, to a high (severe) degree of misbehavior, such as the murder of coworkers, and the measurement may take two forms: Behavioral and attitudinal.

The behavioral aspect of OMB can be measured using frequency counts of acts of misbehavior with respect to a given organizational unit or individual members. This frequency measure can also be weighted by an index of severity of the misbehavior. Such an index may be comprised of two facets: (1) the centrality of the violated norm or value (for proposals related to the measurement of the centrality of a core value, see Wiener, 1988), and (2) the degree of planning involved in the misbehavior.

The attitudinal aspect of OMB may tap the individual's strength or intensity of the intention, predisposition, or propensity to engage in work and organization-related misconduct. Although people tend to be quite reluctant to openly express their intentions to misbehave, instruments that tap into these intentions could be designed and developed (e.g., in a questionnaire form. For a discussion on OMB measurement issues, see Chapter 10). Multifaceted indices (behavioral and attitudinal) are routinely used by OB researchers to measure specific work behaviors that individuals hesitate to report—withdrawal behavior (e.g., actual incidents of turnover and intentions to leave the organization) or organizational citizenship behavior (e.g., actual altruistic deeds and prosocial attitudes). Using both behavioral and attitudinal observations may facilitate a more meaningful classification of the misbehavior phenomenon.

Basic Types of OMB

An examination of a broad range of norm-violating behaviors suggests that all such actions may be classified into three basic categories based on the underlying intention of the misbehaving individual:

- Misbehaviors intended to benefit the self (*OMB Type S*): These are mostly internal to the organization and usually victimize the employing firm or its members. Such behaviors may have three categories of internal targets: (a) the work (e.g., distorting data); (b) the organization's property, resources, symbols, or regulations (e.g., stealing and selling manufacturing secrets); and (c) other members (e.g., harassing peers). An exception is a member's behavior that appears to benefit the organization (e.g., overcharging customers), but is in fact intended to eventually benefit the individual (e.g., gaining a promotion).
- Misbehaviors that primarily intend to benefit the member's employing organization (*OMB Type O*): These (e.g., falsifying records to improve chances of obtaining a contract for the organization) are usually directed toward external victims such as other organizations, social institutions, public agencies, suppliers or customers. If the intention underlying this form of behavior is self-serving (e.g., for career considerations, such as making one's visibility more pronounced) and not primarily benefiting the organization, it should not be classified as OMB Type O; more likely, this would be OMB Type S.
- Misbehaviors that primarily intend to inflict damage and cause harm (*OMB Type D*): Targets of these behaviors could be both internal and external. Whereas the intentions underlying Type S and Type O misbehaviors are to benefit either the individual or organization, the intention underlying OMB Type D is to hurt others or harm the organization. Such intentional misbehaviors (e.g., sabotaging company-owned equipment) may be perpetrated by members either on their own volition (e.g., as revenge or a response to perceived or actual mistreatment) or on behalf of significant others (e.g., interfering with organizational operations to comply with a union's dictates). However, the intention must be to cause some type of damage, whether be it minor or considerable, subtle or visible.

The OMB Type S, O, D typology is based on the intentions of the actor. As a rule, when more than one intention seem to underlie an act of OMB, and when observations yield equivocal data, the predominant intention would determine the classification. For example, when a part-time fireman sets a national forest on fire to generate work for himself, this would be OMB Type S because benefiting the self, rather than causing damage, was the primary intention (*New York Times*, July 2002). To emphasize the intention principle, which is at the core of the OMB classification, it is necessary to analyze OMB within a behavioral-motivational framework. We elaborate on this in the following section.

Conceptual Anchors

Any willful (motivated) violation of shared expectations (norms or values) constitutes misbehavior, regardless of its consequences. Therefore, mainstream OB paradigms that make distinctions between normative, value-based processes, and instrumental-calculative ones in determining individual behavior in organizations, might be useful as a basis for an individual misbehavior model. One such paradigm, which has been often used to explain determinants of individual behavior in organizations, is Fishbein and Ajzen's (1975) reasoned action theory.

Their conceptualization focuses primarily on understanding and predicting behavioral intentions. It hypothesizes that an individual's behavior is a result of the intention to perform that behavior. A person's behavioral intention, in turn, is determined by two basic components: (1) the person's attitude toward performing the act and (2) the subjective norm or, specifically, perception of the totality of the normative pressures concerning the behavior.

The first component—the person's attitude toward performing the act—is a function of beliefs concerning the consequences of the act and the value of the outcomes, as the specific individual perceives them. These may be referred to as instrumental-cognitive beliefs. The second component—the subjective norm—is a function of the person's beliefs about what referent others think he or she should do, weighted by the motivation to comply with their expectations. Such significant others may include specific individuals, a particular reference group, the work organization, or society at large (see Vardi & Weitz, 2002c).

The manner by which members of a social unit acquire norms and values is not a simple one. How do members know when they act in defiance of existing norms? How do they identify situations in which they engage in certain forms of OMB? Salancik and Pfeffer's (1978) social information theory may be particularly helpful. To them, the social context affects a person's behavior by shaping his or her perceptions and beliefs about organizational situations. Yet one can argue that sense-making cues, transmitted through both formal and informal social interactions, pertain not only to desirable behavior but also, and perhaps more dramatically, to misbehavior. Such cues may carry important symbolic and affective meanings, as well as instrumental ones. Thus, individual attitudes and beliefs, which are formed through such socially constructed realities (Berger & Luckmann, 1966), may determine the intentions that lead to the various types of OMB.

In addition, several researchers (e.g., Jaccard & Davidson, 1975; Pomazal & Jaccard, 1976; Schwartz & Tessler, 1972) have suggested that the subjective norm is determined not only by social normative beliefs (i.e., a person's beliefs of how others expect him or her to act), but also by personal normative beliefs—personal moral standards (Jones, 1991) concerning a particular mode of conduct are established when a person internalizes expectations of others concerning a particular behavior. These determinants of the subjective norm may be termed *internalized subjective beliefs*. When behavioral acts are guided by internalized forces, they are no longer dependent on their linkage with the reinforcements and sanctions on which they were initially based (e.g., Jones & Gerard, 1967). To Fishbein and Ajzen, attitudes and subjective norms may be viewed as predictors and the behavioral intention as the criterion. The model incorporates both cognitive and affective components because attitudes, by definition, include affective or evaluative considerations concerning ensuing acts (in our case, intentional acts of misbehavior).

In our proposed framework, one major determinant of OMB is the rational calculations of utility of the behavior to the employee. Therefore, it is important to determine the considerations that go into this decision-making process. March and Simon's (1958) seminal book on organizations offers important insights (e.g., inducement-contribution trade-offs) about causes of work-related behavior. According to their paradigm, individuals in organizations decide not only to join or leave, but also how to perform and how much effort to exert in any given circumstance. Granted, these decisions are constrained by imperfect (bounded) rationality, yet individuals are, by and large, aware of both constraints and opportunities in their organizational environment. For instance, they use such information in their decisions to come to work or call in sick. This rationale can be readily adapted to explain forms of misbehavior because individuals are aware (albeit imperfectly) of the opportunities as well as the consequences of engaging in misconduct. Such knowledge, in turn, provides the sources of most instrumental or calculative considerations that, like any sort of work behavior, may be limited. Thus, March and Simon's and Fishbein and Ajzen's paradigms provide us with an essential attribute of the major cognitions contributing to the formation of individual interests that determine certain types of OMB.

OMB as Intentional Behavior

A motivational OMB framework is shown in Figure 2.1. The core relationships are based on the Fishbein and Ajzen model as adapted by Wiener (1982) to form a normative–instrumental framework of individual commitment, and by Wiener and Vardi (1990) to conceptually integrate organizational culture and individual motivation. In the basic OMB system, misbehavior is not always a function of the two predictor categories: Instrumental and normative. Instead, depending on its type, OMB may be determined by either one of the two predictors or simultaneously by both.

OMB Type S

OMB Type S reflects the intention to benefit the individual rather than the employing organization. It is determined primarily by attitude, which in turn is a function of the sum of the beliefs concerning the consequences of the individual's misbehavior. Because such misbehavior is self-serving, it stands to reason that it would be influenced by a person's beliefs concerning the extent to which the misbehavior is likely to result in favorable or unfavorable outcomes. For instance, the probability of misusing company resources is reduced if the person believes that punishment may readily result from such act than when no sanctions are

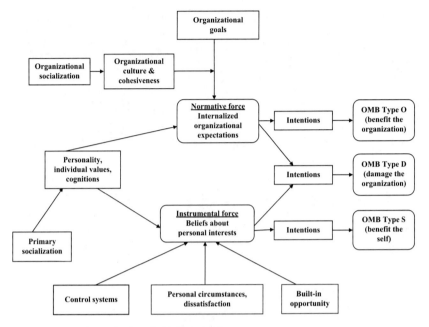

FIGURE 2.1 A motivational OMB model

anticipated. Thus, the motivational process underlying OMB Type S is primarily calculative-instrumental. Nevertheless, although this type of misconduct is a function of instrumental processes, these behaviors may be constrained by factors such as the degree of cohesiveness among members, the organization culture, and organization control mechanisms.

OMB Type O

Although less common, OMB Type O reflects the intentions to benefit the employing organization rather than the individual directly. It is primarily determined by subjective norms that are a function of the totality of internalized normative beliefs concerning expectations from organizational members. As a rule, Type O misbehaviors are anchored in ideology and values and are carried out by individuals who strongly identify with their organization, its mission, and its leadership, and who are often willing to sacrifice self-interest for greater causes. Intentionally breaking the law to protect company interests, while knowingly risking personal well-being, is a case in point. Although normative pressures determine this type of OMB, one could also argue that certain instrumental factors serve as constraints (e.g., situations in which the potential actors refrain from misbehavior because they perceive the likelihood of being punished by external agencies as being too high for them). Of course, it is possible that an individual may break the law on behalf of the company for personal interests. This form of misbehavior should be classified as OMB Type S because the predominant motive is self-serving.

OMB Type D

Unlike OMB Types S and O, Vardi and Wiener (1992, 1996) classified acts as OMB Type D as reflected by the intention to damage or harm a particular individual, organization asset, or social unit. Underlying such intentions may be normative forces, as in the case of speaking publicly against the employing organization or damaging company property as a show of solidarity with striking union members. This kind of behavior may also be determined by instrumental forces—deriving personal satisfaction from an act of revenge or vandalism. This is why we contend that, in principle, both normative and instrumental forces may converge simultaneously to determine Type D misbehavior.

Antecedents of Misbehavior

Our definition of OMB and proposed conceptual framework, which emphasizes the distinction between normative and instrumental determinants of misbehavior, suggests the existence of identifiable antecedents that may affect the formation of the motivational components in the model. We believe that antecedents (determinants) contributing to the instrumental component would primarily influence Type S misbehavior, and antecedents contributing to the normative component would affect Type O misbehavior. Both forces may influence OMB Type D. We now offer general categories and a selected sample of antecedents that may contribute most to the variance of the normative and instrumental components of the model and, consequently, to OMB. The antecedents are categorized according to levels of analysis: Organization, group, position/career, and individual.

Organization-Level Antecedents

Organizations differ in terms of the contextual conditions, at different levels, that may affect the propensity of an individual member to engage in work-related misbehavior. Clusters of such factors are listed as follows.

Organizational Goals

Organizational goals—those implicit and declared targets that serve to translate organization strategy to actual plans, closely reflecting top management values and expectations—are likely to strongly influence members' job performance and productivity levels. However, the pursuit of organizational goals may also encourage employee misbehavior, particularly when they are conflicting, highly demanding, vague, or unrealistic (e.g., Bowling & Eschleman, 2010; Frone, 2008; Mazzetti et al., 2014; Yang & Diefendorff, 2009) and supported by a strong culture or by corporate psychopath executives (Boddy, 2014). For example, Ackroyd and Thompson (1999) posited that employee misconduct is mostly a form of protest against arbitrary managerial control.

Control Systems

Control systems are not uniform across organizations and may not be similar across departments within the same workplace. Control systems are physical or procedural entities within the workplace designed specifically to reduce the occurrence of events judged to be detrimental to the organization. Typically, control systems such as disciplinary systems and special monitoring arrangements serve to increase the risk of detection and thus the likelihood of the perpetrators of such acts to be sanctioned (Sackett & DeVore, 2001). However, oppressive systems, as well as lax controls, may contribute to the emergence of OMB. Although methods of control permeate the workplace (Sewell, 1998), there is still little sound empirical evidence of their effectiveness (for exceptions, see Henle & Blanchard, 2008; Ugrin & Pearson, 2013). Certain jobs in work organizations involve operations for which external control of employee behavior is inherently difficult. Home delivery, operating cash registers, professional or food services, operations in which cash transactions cannot be directly monitored or recorded, and inventory counts are only a few examples of work processes that may be difficult to monitor at times. Thus, control systems may have a direct impact on members' instrumental considerations of whether to engage in or refrain from acts of misconduct (Vardi & Wiener, 1996). On the one hand, when confronted with blatant control systems (e.g., surveillance), employees might attempt to resist and protest by engaging in damaging behavior (OMB Type D). On the other hand, lax control systems may be perceived as a sign of trust and lead to exemplary behavior—or may be viewed as a form of organizational weakness and present a built-in opportunity to misbehave.

Organizational Culture and Climate

Organizational culture is widely regarded as a construct denoting the extent to which members share core organizational values (Trice & Beyer 1993; Wiener, 1988). Several writers (e.g., Kunda, 1992, 2006) demonstrated the power of culture as a tool used by certain dominant groups (e.g., top management) to shape members' values and reduce counterproductive behavior (Boye & Jones, 1997). An organization's *climate of honesty*—defined by Cherrington and Cherrington (1985) as employees' perception of the presence of an accepted code of ethics, the perceived level of top management honesty, the internal controls, the disciplinary system, and the perception that those engaging in counterproductive behavior will in fact be punished—acts to reduce misbehavior. Vardi (2001) indicated a significant negative relationship between organizational climate and OMB. Specifically, the more the organizational climate was perceived as supportive and the more the organization reward system was perceived as equitable, employees reported lower levels of OMB. Furthermore, *ethical climate*, conceptualized as "the prevailing perceptions of typical organizational practices and procedures that have ethical content" (Victor & Cullen, 1988, p. 101), was negatively related to employees and managers' OMB, especially when the company emphasized adherence to rules and regulations.

The ways employees perceive the fairness of their treatment and the perceived equity of the distribution of resources are important antecedents of misbehavior. Skarlicki and Folger (1997) posited that procedural justice might be further broken down into the fairness of the decisions, the manner in which they are presented, and the treatment accorded the affected employees once the decision has been made. This is termed *interactional justice.* Organizational policies and practices influence the ways in which employees work and misbehave. For example, an employee may choose to sabotage the assembly line in reaction to a perceived injustice. Inequity theory (Adams, 1963) posits that workers compare the sum of the intrinsic and extrinsic rewards they receive for the effort they put in to the remuneration others get for their work. If the effort–reward ratio is not proportional, some will feel that they are overpaid, whereas others will feel they are underpaid. The former may experience feelings of guilt, whereas the latter group's sense of inequity may lead to feelings of resentment and anger. This felt inequity—the sense of organizational injustice—might serve as an antecedent to misbehavior. Greenberg (1990a) showed that inequity alone might not be enough to trigger misbehavior. He argued that the interaction between perceived inequity and the manner in which the manager chooses to explain and deal with it determines the likelihood of the worker to misbehave. For example, empathetically explaining to employees why pay cuts need to be put in place will reduce the likelihood of them engaging in theft.

Organizational Cohesiveness

Cohesiveness refers to the degree of social bonding and normative closeness. In cohesive work environments, the pressure to adhere to norms of work conduct is especially high. Therefore, cohesiveness may affect misbehavior in a manner similar to the way organizational culture affects OMB. Indeed it may be more powerful. We regard this organization characteristic as a significant antecedent that may strongly contribute to wrongdoing in the name of ideology and organizational causes. Also, drawing on the concept of *groupthink* (Janis, 1982), one may propose that extreme organizational cohesiveness could also produce a kind of *organiza-tionthink*, potentially leading to misguided strategic behavior.

Group-Level Antecedents

As Goffman (1959) vividly demonstrated, the self only exists in relation to others. In the workplace, the workgroup is indeed a significant other. The importance of groups and work teams and their relationship to individual behavior and organizational performance has been widely documented, beginning with the early human relationists (Mayo, 1933; Roethlisberger & Dickson, 1964). Griffin et al. (1998b) emphasized the importance of groups in terms of both the causes and consequences of what they termed *dysfunctional behavior* in organizations. They argued that group misbehavior is both intentional and damaging and has internal as well as external antecedents.

Internal Pressures

Since group affiliation was demonstrated to be a major determinant of work behavior, it has received significant research attention (Homans, 1950). Studies of groups and their effects within the organizational setting indicate both positive (productivity) and negative (restriction) effects. Most theorists (for a thorough review, see Feldman, 1981) and researchers (e.g., Gladstein, 1984; Tziner & Vardi, 1982), however, have posited that workgroups bear a positive influence on individual work behavior by reinforcing normative performance and attitudes. Such influential social-psychological approaches as Bandura's (1973) social learning theory and Salancik and Pfeffer's (1978) social information-processing theory attempt to explain why and how groups exercise (positive) power over their members. Social information-processing theory posits that individuals adapt their behavior based on consequences that are observed and not experienced directly. That is, if one is a member of a workgroup in which misbehavior, such as pilfering or false reporting, goes unsanctioned, he or she is more likely to engage in such misbehavior as well. If a worker is aware of misbehavior by a fellow employee and knows that he or she was punished for it, that worker may change his intention toward that misbehavior.

Furthermore, employees who are inclined to misbehave may be attracted to and selected by workgroups that support and reinforce this behavior. Robinson and O'Leary-Kelly (1998), Ferguson (2007), and Vardi, Weitz, and Gottfrid-Oz (2014) found that the group aggregate measure of misbehavior has a significant effect, a contagion effect, on individual misbehavior. Another body of work demonstrated that groups might create internal dynamics that may be considered negative. Janis (1982) showed the effects of groupthink on decision-making, and others have demonstrated such consequences as performance restriction and social loafing (see meta-analysis by Karau & Williams, 1993). Hollinger (1986) demonstrated that the more attached an employee is to non-deviant workers, the less likely he or she will engage in misbehavior. Following Hirschi's (1969) social bonding theory, Lasley (1988) argued that the existence of a common and shared value system in the workgroup might act to frame misbehavior in a permissible and legal manner. Similarly, the more cohesive the workgroup, the more likely it is to condone or prohibit misbehavior by its members.

External Pressures

Interest in group behavior has received a significant boost from situational (Fiedler, 1967), contingency (Hersey & Blanchard, 1982; Reddin, 1967), leader–member exchange (Liden & Green, 1980), charismatic leaders (Shamir et al., 1993), and team leadership theories (Avolio, 1999). These approaches, however, tend to emphasize the role of managers/leaders in influencing subordinate (individual and group) normative behavior. Overlooked is the fact that leaders may also encourage negative attitudes and behaviors. Bandura (1969) applied social learning theory to explain how aggressive behavior may be learned from significant others. In much the same vein, Greenberg (1997) explicated the role of groups in increasing not only prosocial, but also antisocial work behavior (e.g., stealing).

Position/Career-Level Antecedents

Job Design

Some built-in opportunities to take advantage of or misuse various organizational resources (e.g., time, office equipment, telephone and mail, work tools, internet, etc.) exist in most jobs. In many cases, the degree to which such built-in opportunities exist may enter into instrumental calculations concerning the benefits, consequences, and risks of capitalizing on such opportunities (Bliss & Aoki, 1993). Some work organizations apply stringent mechanisms to determine what their employees are doing at any given moment, whereas others employ lax systems or none at all. Clearly, these may affect employee behavior and misbehavior in the workplace. For example, Vardi and Weitz (2001) demonstrated that job autonomy may be a potential source of misbehavior—they found a positive correlation for measures of OMB and job autonomy.

Job Demands

A prominent element of job characteristics that serves as an antecedent to OMB is the *job demands-resources model* (JD-R; Demerouti et al., 2001). The JD-R model maintains that employees' work environments may be categorized by two conditions: Job demands and job resources. *Job demands* refer to "those physical, psychological, social, or organizational aspects of the job that require sustained physical and/or psychological (cognitive and emotional) effort and are therefore associated with certain physiological and/or psychological costs" (Bakker et al., 2003, p. 344). *Job resources* refer to those job aspects that may reduce job demands and its associated consequences, may help to achieve work goals, and to provide opportunities for growth, development, and learning (Schaufeli et al., 2009). In a longitudinal study, Schaufeli et al. (2009) found that when job demands increase and job resources decrease, burnout—defined as "a syndrome of exhaustion, cynicism, and lack of professional efficacy" (p. 895)—increases. They also found that burnout positively predicts the duration of absences due to sick leave.

Careers

Hall (1976) defined "career" to include all meaningful work-related experiences over a person's life. Certainly promotions are important and meaningful career moves in most organizations, and are aspired to by management-anchored employees (Schein, 1978). Career aspirations and choices affect the intentions to behave and misbehave, and the consequences of such choices and behaviors, in turn, affect careers in work organizations. Chapter 3 elaborates on this by exploring the conceptual connections between acts of misbehavior and careers.

Individual-Level Antecedents

Personality

Although there is no doubt that personality affects behavior, Robinson and Greenberg (1998), argued that there is little empirical evidence for the relationship between personality variables and misbehavior. We disagree. Our reading of the voluminous body of literature regarding personality and organization behavior suggests otherwise.

Two personality variables, in particular, affect motivational components and, in turn, the intention to engage in OMB. These are the normative process of value internalization and the calculations involved in forming instrumental beliefs about personal interests. First is the level of moral development of an organizational member (Kohlberg, 1969). Kish-Gephart et al. (2010) demonstrated the usefulness of this factor in the context of unethical behavior. Second is the degree of sociopathic predisposition—the state characterized by disregard for social norms and obligations without the inhibiting experience of guilt. Of course, extreme degrees of sociopathic tendencies characterize only a marginal portion of any organization's workforce.

Significant relationships between certain personality traits and workplace delinquency were reported by Ashton (1998). Treviño et al. (2014) proposed the usefulness of such traits as locus of control in predicting unethical decision-making. Griffin et al. (1998b) also included individual ethics, values, and morality as antecedents of dysfunctional work behavior. Fox and Spector (1999) found that personality variables affect misbehavior. They reported significant relationships among irascibility, anxiety, impulsiveness, and OMB.

Similarly, Raelin (1986, 1994) reported on the relationship between personality variables and OMB. He found that professionals with low self-esteem tend to express their frustration by engaging in counterproductive behaviors. Moreover, he found that achievement motivation is negatively related to employee deviance—the higher the employees' achievement motivation, the lower their tendency to misbehave. Also, professionals who feel depressed at work are more likely to misbehave (Raelin, 1994). Galperin and Aquino (1999) found a significant relationship between personality variables and misbehavior. A tendency to behave aggressively moderates the relationship between the perception of injustice and organizational deviance. Thus, employees with a strong tendency to behave aggressively are more likely to respond negatively (e.g., to fake sickness, be late for work, etc.) as a result of their perception of injustice than those with low aggressive tendencies.

Personality researchers (e.g., Barrick & Mount, 1991; Digman, 1990) agree that it is possible to organize the non-cognitive dimensions of personality. The five major components are *extroversion, agreeableness, conscientiousness, emotional stability*, and *openness to experience*. This categorization is useful for OMB research: It lends itself well to the formulation of research questions. A person low on emotional stability is expected to exhibit misbehavior toward the organization and fellow workers, while an employee low on agreeableness is expected to engage in interpersonal misbehavior (Krigel, 2001). Indeed, researchers have found agreeableness, conscientiousness, and emotional stability traits to be the strongest negative predictors of organizational misconduct (Berry et al., 2007; Jensen & Patel, 2011; Le et al., 2014). Indubitably, personality plays a role in determining whether a worker will misbehave. This is further explored in Chapter 7.

Value Congruence

This antecedent refers to the degree to which personal values held by the individual are consistent with core organizational and group norms (Vardi & Wiener, 1996). The higher such congruence, the more likely a member is to identify with a referent social unit and be guided by its values and norms (Chatman, 1989; Hall & Schneider, 1972). Individual values, if incongruent with those of top management, may lead to adaptive behavior characterized by frustration and aggression (Ackroyd & Thompson, 1999; Argyris, 1964). Extreme commitment and high identification with the organization may lead to blind loyalty, which might bear negative behavioral consequences as well (Wiener, 1982). Hence, this variable represents a strong contribution to the normative component of the model and, in turn, to OMB.

The generalized value of loyalty and duty is a personal value acquired in the process of primary socialization. It represents a generalized sense of duty and obligation—namely, the belief by individuals that they have a moral obligation to exhibit loyalty in all significant social situations in which they are involved (Wiener, 1982). Regardless of their other values, individuals who rank high on generalized loyalty and duty would tend to identify with their organization and (mis) behave accordingly.

Attitudes

When individuals perceive that they are mistreated by their peers, managers or the organization, the likelihood of misbehavior may increase (Burton et al., 2014). This may indirectly influence the way organizational expectations are learned and internalized. On the one hand, it is less likely for a member to be successfully socialized by, and identify with, an organization when mistreatment of self and others is perceived. On the other hand, high levels of employees' trust in senior management, supervisors and the organization increase their feelings of attachment to the firm and/or its members, which in turn leads them to refrain from antisocial work behaviors (Thau et al., 2007). The lack of fulfillment of members' needs by an organization primarily affects the instrumental component of motivation to misbehave, but it can indirectly contribute to the normative forces as well. Attitudes, especially job dissatisfaction, have long been associated with counterproductive behaviors and absenteeism (e.g., Bowling, 2010; Lau et al., 2003).

Personal Circumstances

When an individual faces a compelling need or deprivation—material or otherwise—he or she might be more inclined to engage in misbehavior that may help resolve such a need (e.g., Merton, 1938). Conversely, when anticipating being at risk of losing membership and employment, both workers and managers may be less inclined to misbehave. Thus, specific personal circumstances partially determine one's tendencies to engage in OMB—primarily by shaping instrumental beliefs about the value of the ensuing consequences of any given misbehavior. When individuals perceive being mistreated by their employing organizations, the valence of self-benefiting misbehavior may increase (e.g., Ackroyd & Thompson, 1999; Analoui & Kakabadse, 1992; Greenberg, 1990b; Hollinger, 1986; Mangione & Quinn, 1975).

A General Framework

Our discussion of OMB has thus far focused on the wide range of antecedents that may lead individuals to choose some form of misconduct. Following Vardi and Wiener's (1992, 1996) typology, we classified such behaviors into three categories based on their predominant motive for choosing the mode of behavior. We now expand this initial conceptualization into a more general framework articulating both antecedents of the intention to misbehave and the actual forms of misbehavior, as manifested in organizations. Our extended model (Figure 2.2), a general framework for OMB, formally depicts the multilevel effects on the intentions to misbehave at work. It also provides a new categorization of manifested behaviors regarded as OMB. It subsumes that each manifestation may result from any one or more of the antecedents, ediated by the intention to misbehave. A determination as to the actual causes of organizational misbehaviors is an empirical question.

OMB Manifestations

Trying to list all possible expressions of OMB seems an endless and perhaps futile task because, as discussed earlier, the perception of a certain act to be counternormative is highly contingent on situational factors. Moreover, researchers often use different designations for the same or similar classes of actions. For instance, workplace aggression (Hershcovis & Barling, 2010; Hershcovis & Reich, 2013), workplace victimization (Aquino & Thau, 2009), workplace bullying (Einarsen et al., 2011), abusive supervision (Tepper, 2007) and destructive leadership (Schyns & Schilling, 2013) all refer to interpersonal mistreatment at work, albeit with some definitional differences between them. For example, abusive supervision is defined as downward hostility, whereas the definition of bullying refers to downward, as well as coworker hostility. Much the same, cyberdeviancy (Weatherbee, 2010), cyberloafing (Henle & Blanchard, 2008), and cyberslacking (Ugrin & Pearson, 2013) typically refer to "the use of internet and mobile technology during work hours for personal purposes" (Vitak et al., 2011).

We organized the expressions of OMB into five distinct categories: Intrapersonal misbehavior (e.g., self-deception, substance abuse, and workaholic behavior), interpersonal misbehavior (e.g., incivility, aggressive behavior, bullying, and sexual harassment), production misbehavior (e.g., rule breaking, loafing, withdrawal behavior), property misbehavior (e.g., corruption, theft, vandalism, espionage, and computer hacking), and political misbehavior (e.g., misuse of power, impression management, politicking, favoritism, and nepotism). It should be emphasized that the manifestations we discuss in this book are definitely representative of the phenomenon but are by no means exhaustive.

OMB Antecedents

Our model (Figure 2.2) categorizes OMB antecedents into classes representing four levels of analysis: Individual, position/career, group, and organization. The choice of variables is based on studies and models that have previously established evidence for the role these factors have in explaining misbehavior.

ANTECEDENTS   MANIFESTATIONS

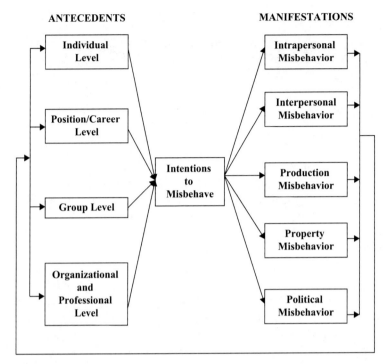

FIGURE 2.2 A general framework for OMB

Individual Level

This category includes personality variables such as the *Big Five* (e.g., Berry et al., 2007) and locus of control (e.g., Kish-Gephart et al., 2010); attitudes such as job satisfaction (e.g., Bowling, 2010), frustration (e.g., Spector & Fox, 2002), and organizational commitment (Dalal, 2005); affect and emotion (e.g., Barling et al., 2009); and stress (Grant, 2013).

Position and Career Level

This category consists of variables considered to be relevant properties of the job, such as job type and design and built-in opportunity to misbehave (e.g., Baruch & Vardi, 2015; Vardi & Weitz, 2001).

Group Level

This category includes such variables as norms (e.g., Robinson & O'Leary-Kelly, 1998), leadership styles (e.g., Schyns & Schilling, 2013; Van Gils et al., 2015), and contagion effects (e.g., Robinson et al., 2014).

Organizational Level

This group of determinants consists of variables such as climate and culture (e.g., Treviño et al., 2014; Vardi, 2001), socialization (Liu et al., 2015; Ofer, 2003), and control systems (e.g., Bacharach et al., 2002; Bergeron et al., 2013).

Mediators

All current models dealing with OMB posit intentionality (O'Leary-Kelly et al., 2000a; Vardi & Wiener, 1992, 1996). That is, they automatically exclude acts—even those that may be harmful—that are accidental. Robinson and Greenberg (1998) identified five defining characteristics of any behavior that would be considered antisocial in the workplace: Perpetrator, intention, target, action, and consequence. The intention to engage in the act would be the mediating variable. Thus, in O'Leary-Kelly et al.'s (2000a) terms, antisocial work behavior is defined as any attempted behavior that is intentional and potentially harmful.

Following Vardi and Wiener (1992, 1996), the intention to misbehave is assumed to mediate the relationships between the antecedents and expressions or manifestations of misbehavior. This intention, in turn, is assumed to be the result of two major independent—yet possibly correlated—forces: The instrumental force, reflecting the actor's beliefs about his or her own personal interests; and the normative force, reflecting the actor's internalized organizational expectations. These two forces may influence the intention to misbehave as well as the specific type of misbehavior. That is, the intention to misbehave may be translated into action in more than one form, reflecting two different sets of considerations. For example, an aggravated employee may seek to harm his supervisor to satisfy his own need for revenge (instrumental force), restrict his output in protest, like his fellow employees do (normative force), or both.

General Propositions

The process of engagement in OMB by organizational stakeholders can be summarized as follows:

- OMB is a motivational process in which the intention to misbehave is assumed to mediate the relationship between the antecedents of the intention and the expressions of the ensuing act.
- The intention to misbehave reflects two different, yet possibly interrelated sets of considerations—normative and instrumental—which in turn are a function of one or more antecedents, at one or more levels.

- The intention to misbehave may translate into action in one or more manifestations of misbehavior.
- OMB is a temporal and dynamic phenomenon in which antecedents lead to intentions, which lead to manifestations, which in turn affect antecedents.

A Roadmap

The framework described in this chapter serves as our conceptual roadmap for the entire book. Our starting point is the argument underlying our dynamic approach to the phenomenon we regard as OMB, that life in organizations entails both positive and negative work-related experiences. These experiences, as they accumulate over time, make up one's organizational career. Thus, inevitably, members of organizations—rank and file as well as management—both behave properly and misbehave on their jobs. Chapter 3 is devoted to the connection between the two constructs: Careers and misbehavior. We then embark on our journey with a description of the expressions of OMB and work our way back to the various antecedents that may account for them. We begin with three chapters devoted to the numerous OMB manifestations found in work organizations. Chapter 4 deals with intra- and interpersonal manifestations, Chapter 5 with production and political manifestations, and Chapter 6 with corruption, unethical managerial behavior, and property manifestations—both tangible and intellectual. Three chapters dealing with OMB antecedents follow. Chapter 7 deals with individual-level antecedents, Chapter 8 deals with job- and group-level antecedents, and Chapter 9 is devoted to organization-level antecedents. This leads us to the research dilemmas facing anyone who studies these phenomena, whether as a scientist or practitioner (Chapter 10). In the closing chapter (Chapter 11), we come full circle and anchor the strategic implications we draw for OMB management in this extended framework.

3

ORGANIZATIONAL MISBEHAVIOR AND WORK CAREERS: THE TEMPORAL DYNAMIC CONNECTION

We argue that work careers in the twenty-first century cannot be fully understood if we continue to describe them as principally positive and attractive experiences, as the mainstream management and HRM literature has traditionally described them. Careers in organizations have been mostly branded and advocated as enticing, developmental and growth-enabling experiences (e.g., Hall, 1976; Schein, 1978; Vardi, 1980) with metaphors such as "ladder climbing," "executive suites," and "corporate stars." The leading paradigm has been the congruence model (e.g., job–person fit, person–environment fit), which emphasized matches at the expense of mismatches, fit over misfit, success over failure, movement over stuckness. We believe this paradigm no longer reflects the complexity and volatility of labor markets and career structures in postmodern economies.

This is because, generally speaking, the depiction of organizational life in management, careers, and organization studies literature has traditionally been positively and normatively biased (Ackroyd & Thompson, 1999; Vaughan, 1999) and thus unrealistic. In their critical review of the *Handbook of career studies* (Gunz & Peiperl, 2007), based on content analysis of the handbook chapters, Vardi and Kim (2007) affirmed that the majority of the contributions to the handbook conceived and portrayed careers as mostly positive, success-related, and personal, as well as organizational experiences. Consequently, they advocated a more balanced discourse and investigation of organizational career-related phenomena. As the nature of work and work organizations has changed in the beginning of this century, so have those work-related experiences we call organizational careers. These undoubtedly include not only the few orderly sequences of company promotions that exist in most places of work, but the vast variety of transitions and adjustments that reflect the changed organizational arena.

By emphasizing normative rather than controversial approaches and constructs, these fields of study and practice have become positively skewed in the way they portray organizations and organizational life. This should not come as a surprise because writers on careers (themselves probably successful academics and practitioners) tend to prefer writing about career success than about career failure, about promises than about disillusionments, about opportunities rather than obstacles. Despite this, a more balanced (i.e., transparent) view of organizations is sustained by a surge of interest in both prevalent macro-level organizational dark sides such as corporate corruption (e.g., Ashforth et al., 2008), and micro-level forms of potentially harmful (unethical) work-related behavior (e.g., Treviño et al., 2006). We believe that by relating organizational careers and organizational misbehavior, we contribute to a more balanced and more realistic view of organizations.

From a temporal and dynamic perspective of life within organizations, unfolding careers of organization members at all levels must influence, and be influenced by, many factors including prevalent "dark side" policies and activities (Baruch & Vardi, 2015). While unfolding careers are normally attributed to work behavior that conforms to prescribed performance rules and evaluated by employers as such, it is reasonable to argue that certain discretionary misdeeds also affect careers both positively and negatively. These effects have not been looked at in a systematic way by career and organizational behavior researchers. Vardi (2011), for example, has shown that past misconduct (both work-related and non-work-related) blocked leading candidates from being considered for top-echelon public positions (see below). Interestingly, those same forms of misconduct at earlier career stages were either instrumental in their promotion, or simply ignored as career criteria. We thus maintain that, in principle, from a temporal perspective, career aspirations and choices must affect the intentions to behave and misbehave, and the consequences of such choices and behaviors must in turn affect careers. Recall that for us, organizational misbehavior (OMB) refers to those discretionary acts by members of organizations that violate core organizational and/or societal norms that define proper conduct. As demonstrated throughout this book, this umbrella construct encompasses a full spectrum of phenomena of work-related misconduct present in every organization and experienced by most members throughout their careers. All such behaviors are considered prevalent workplace experiences and thus during their careers workers and managers experience them as witnesses, perpetrators, targets, or victims. We argue that they are inescapable and inevitable career-related experiences in work organizations. Behavior, and misbehavior, are part and parcel of organizational careers.

Promotions and the Dark Side

Vardi (2011) analyzed four cases of denied promotion that played an important role in the Israeli sociopolitical scene during the years 2010–11. The cases demonstrate the role of past misbehaviors as negative career determinants and the damage they can inflict. In three of the cases, the misdeeds, when committed, were not considered as negative behaviors by the candidates or by their organizations. These activities did not block the ascent of these individuals in their organizations up to that point. They were deemed improper only during the final stage of the selection process for a senior position. Not surprisingly, in the three cases, the top-notch candidates were caught off-guard, vehemently denied wrongdoing, and blamed others and the unfair change of promotion rules. They eventually lost the battle, and disappeared from the public eye.

By some strange coincidence, four top positions were open at approximately the same time in Israel's security branches: Head of Mossad (Israel national intelligence agency), chief of staff of the Israel Defense Forces (IDF), the head of Israel Police, and the head of the Israel Prison Services. As expected, the cream of the crop were enthusiastically "charging up-hill," competing for the top positions of Israel's four very powerful institutions. The competition was fierce, ambitions clashed, organizational politics materialized, circles of supporters engaged in open and covert smear battles. Ends seemed to justify all means. Both public and private mass media, consulting firms, and public relations specialists played an important role in the campaigns, producing unsavory stories and revealing hidden skeletons hidden in many a proverbial closet. This differs from internal promotion competitive processes in hierarchical organizations only in magnitude, viciousness, and public scrutiny.

In the Mossad case, past issues have not prevented the nomination of the new head, but in the case of the IDF chief of staff candidate, an ambitious reserve officer with a dubious past circulated a fake protocol that found its way to the (ever-ready for scandal) media to damage one of the leading candidates. Others dug out some old news about alleged past inappropriate real estate deals. The identity of the alleged faker was quickly revealed by people who just put two and two together, used personal networking ("it's a small country," "everybody knows everybody else," "there are really no secrets," as they say) and the man's pictures were all over the media. Some years later, the ambitious candidate who lost the race went into politics and became a government minister, past misconduct and scandals notwithstanding.

In the case of the police chief, one of the candidates was publicly charged with misconduct of a sexual nature. Although the alleged incidents occurred, if they did, several years in the past, as that officer had become a serious contender for the position of police chief, the charges and complaints were made public. Events unfolded quickly: One of the accusers disclosed her identity on camera and the aspiring officer announced the withdrawal of his candidacy through his articulate lawyer ("in order to protect the purity of the selection process and the integrity of the police force").

Careers have both collateral glory and, as the above cases reveal, collateral damage. When a career is "working well," all those connected seem to benefit from the glory (and perks) bestowed on the careerist. They therefore are motivated to protect him or her, conceal damaging information, and prepare the person for the next rung on the ladder, often ignoring potential collateral damage if failure occurs. Politicians, bureaucrats, and executives risk treading desperately in "career quicksand" on their self-motivated, high-visibility, high-investment journey to top echelon positions. This is in large measure due to the era of public exposure and transparency in which we now live. Secrets are a thing of the past and formal curricula vitae (CVs) can no longer cover up for dark alleys. Under conditions of competitive environments, boundaryless and borderless digital social media (Facebook, Twitter, WikiLeaks), the closer aspirants get to the summit, the higher the risks of defeat by past misbehavior, petty or grand, insidious or flagrant, job-related or otherwise. And the fall from such heights is very painful. Not only they, but also their families, past and present friends, and close supporters inadvertently become (oftentimes forced) players in their out-in-the-open campaigns. And thus, "collateral damage" could be quite significant to all.

Politicians (super-high-visibility careerists) are particularly vulnerable and have traditionally experienced this career predicament because they are elected to high office by the public and are closely watched and monitored by the media. Senior executives and high-level officials too cannot escape this fate, as selection decisions become more visible and more transparent. In 2011, the world was a captive audience to the highly publicized, highly embarrassing, and very salacious New York City arrest of French celebrity Dominique Strauss-Kahn, the head of the International Monetary Fund (IMF), when he was first accused of being an attempted rapist, then released by US authorities for lack of reliable evidence. He soon resigned his position. In 2011, in Israel, the country's former president, Moshe Katsav, was sentenced to seven years in prison for sexual misconduct while in office. In 2016, ex prime minister Ehud Olmert is facing jail time for his gross misconduct while in office. What allows individuals such as these to rise to the top while their transgressions are known to certain influential members of their political or organizational system? Could it be that such behaviors actually paved their way to the top? Are certain misbehaviors (OMB) instrumental in elevating certain officeholders' careers?

Ever since Tim Hall (1976) expanded the definition of organizational career to include all work-related experiences, many career researchers have enthusiastically adopted the notion that promotion is but one of the endless varieties of workplace career. Thus, by definition, all sequences of work experiences can be regarded as organizational careers. Certainly promotions are still important and meaningful career moves in most organizations and are aspired to by management-anchored employees (Schein, 1978). For organizations—corporations, governmental agencies, public service institutions—investing in and securing the promotion of the best managerial talents (dubbed "talent management") is still a high priority in HR planning and development agendas (e.g., Boudreau & Ramstad, 2007).

We contend that, both conceptually and practically, one cannot separate careers and misconduct because various forms of organizational misbehavior are an integral part of most people's work experiences, and are either detrimental or instrumental to their career management. All of us in academia have witnessed cases of both the admirable rise of stars and the agony of those blocked and harassed. All of us have written great letters of recommendations for colleagues and graduates. Have we always been telling the whole truth? Have we been objective? Have we always been neutral and unbiased? Vardi and Kim (2007) suggested that career research has traditionally emphasized a positively skewed view and discourse about careers at the expense of a more realistic (sometimes painful) approach. We have always preferred to talk about promotions and promotability than about demotion and demotability. We have focused on success and shunned studying career failure. But while high potentials are our heroes, low potentials actually do the mundane work. It is more tempting to follow those who "made it" and forget those who have lost the tournament, gave up the climb on the career ladder, or who tripped right before the last few rungs. Almost universally, we tend to hail the good traits of the chosen and ignore their negative ones.

Our OMB approach is useful because of its breadth and because it refrains from prejudging the effects and costs of these forms of job and career behavior, and does not subsume unintentionally inflicting damage or harm. The general integrative framework we proposed in the previous chapter outlines the concept in terms of OMB manifestations, antecedents, and mediators (i.e., intentions to misbehave). For example, at the individual level, experienced frustration of not being promoted as expected might affect the intention to misbehave and subsequently lead to "production misbehavior" in the form of intentional rule-breaking or sabotaging. At the same time, we acknowledge that individual differences means that certain people will be more vulnerable as compared with others, who may be more resilient, subject to personal sensitivity. By the same token, a strong organizational culture that "forces" career-minded employees to work long and hard may affect the intention to misbehave and lead to "political misbehavior," such as deception of management, in which employees manipulate office technology to create the false impression that work is being done when actually it is not. Thus, as part of the career and organizational socialization process, in addition to learning positive performance "ropes," employees must learn and internalize the rules of local deception (Shulman, 2007), possibly utilizing impression management tactics (Goffman, 1959) and internal politics (Vigoda, 2000) necessary for long-term success. These will be dealt with at length in the following chapters.

A Critical View

To promote realistic discourse about contemporary careers, Baruch and Vardi (2015) recently proposed that because of the present-day changing nature of organizations, labor markets, and career patterns, and the realization that misconduct is inherent in organizations, a framework that connects careers and misbehavior should be instrumental for generating conceptual, empirical, and practical thinking that may better account for learning about and managing careers in modern work systems. They present core career research constructs and show how they would look when dark-side arguments are added to them. We chose here just two of the leading career constructs in order to critically demonstrate the temporal and dynamic connection with OMB: The protean career and the boundaryless career.

Protean Careers and OMB

The "protean career" (Hall, 2004) is a career form in which the individual, rather than the organization, takes on the responsibility for enacting career paths and develops himself or herself according to his or her emerging and changing needs. The protean person's career choices and search for self-fulfillment are unifying and integrative elements in his or her life. This idea is insightful, but it overlooks the immense difficulty in developing such inner shifts of values and attitudes (Baruch & Quick, 2007; Nicholson, 1998). More importantly, not everyone has the practical ability to transform and adapt to his or her changing needs and values (Hall, 2004). Like many metaphors, the protean career suffers from certain limitations. Even the Greek god Proteus changed his shape only when he was faced with severe threat. While Proteus could initiate his own shape-changes, he apparently was not proactive in doing so, he did not engage in a planned and skilled manner but rather randomly and desperately when faced by a crisis and grave danger (Inkson, 2007). This would be fine if a person is willing and able to move (although the organization will incur loss in terms of human capital); however, it is not feasible if the person cannot move or has no will to do so, yet is forced to. Then the individual, for the sake of maintaining employability, is the one obliged to reinvent himself or herself despite inability or reluctance, which can lead to bitterness, inefficiency, and even to misconduct. The protean idea fits well with moves across managerial roles, or from professional roles to managerial positions. In most instances, however, it does not fit well with a transition from managerial to professional careers (e.g., even a very talented manager will find it challenging to transition to working as a medical doctor or accountant or lawyer). Some problems with Hall's conceptualization with the protean career include:

- The protean career mode actually fits only a minor segment of the labor market. The majority of change-averse individuals might regard it as a risky or even career-destructive *modus operandi*.
- Stress and ambiguity associated with frequent identity transformations could inadvertently produce inappropriate work-related impression management

behaviors, such as deceiving, faking, and politicking, which will eventually become career hindrances.

• Frequent transitions end in too many short-circled transitory career experiences, limiting the chances of reaching maturity and high-level achievements. For many individuals, excessive transformations may prohibit the crystallization of a solid and constructive career identity.

• Individuals who have gathered significant human capital might find it too hard and demanding to replace it and to capitalize on it in a new career. Thus, the costs attached to frequent career moves, whether voluntary or forced, may be significant indeed.

We propose that for organization members, the demanding experience of continually reinventing oneself may be related to increased intentions to engage in self-promoting and politicking forms of OMB, be they Type S or Type D.

Boundaryless Careers and OMB

The "boundaryless career" construct offers a positive perspective, depicting a transparent and open system that is flexible and full of opportunities (Arthur & Rousseau, 1996). This concept has attracted much attention in the career literature (Lee & Felps, 2013). In a boundaryless world, individuals can move across organizations and occupations to pursue the best opportunities for their personal and professional development without the negative stigma of failing in an organizational career. Career progress comes not only from intra-company hierarchical advancement but also, and even more often, from self-development. From this perspective, careers can be viewed as boundaryless as the borders between organizations and work environments become blurred (Ashkenas et al., 1995); yet the boundaryless career may also be accompanied by a loss of clarity and stability, growing ambiguity, job insecurity, and the need to readjust on a continual basis (Adkins et al., 2001).

Weaknesses in the conceptualization of the boundaryless career include:

• Careers cannot really or fully be boundaryless (Inkson et al., 2012). Some boundaries have become blurred, but most remain intact and help shape and direct people's career attitudes and aspirations as well as maintain organizational career systems. Boundaries are an inherent attribute of organizational and professional systems, and crossing boundaries is an integral part of careers. Such crossings may entail both positive and negative experiences for both the individual and the organization. In addition, many are unable to cross boundaries, or are unwilling to do so. Thus, the boundaryless career may be more rhetoric than reality.

• While for some people, in particular managers and professionals, boundarylessness may be a refreshing and challenging source of optimism (Arthur et al., 1999), for many it may create confusion, anxiety, and career despair. For such individuals, uncertain opportunities may actually induce stress rather than increase motivation.

- While for some organizations, the boundaryless career notion offers new structural and systemic solutions, for others it leads to the loss of some of the best people and possibly of their institutional memory and organizational learning. Newer practices such as talent management can be effective in this respect because they enhance adjustment competencies and the ability to cope with uncertainty.
- The climate of career boundarylessness may be interpreted by transient careerists as legitimizing low commitment to organizational norms of loyalty and proper conduct. Such an interpretation may be a precursor to engaging in career-related forms of OMB, such as deception, undermining, fraud, and abuse.

Thus, for organization members the experience of boundarylessness and career uncertainty may be also related to increased intentions to engage in self-benefiting forms of misbehavior (OMB Type S).

Implications

At the societal level, the dark side of careers might be reflected in the emergence of an alienated society. We may envisage, for example, a more complacent society in which there is a high focus on careers and careerism that lead to forms of workaholism, work overload, and consequent work–family spillover (Peiperl & Jones, 2001) alongside high unemployment, job insecurity, and withdrawal from the labor market, leading to a dependency on state benefits. In terms of diversity, the gap between rhetoric and reality remains wide, and the literature that emphasizes the need for equality neglects to identify the challenges (Bell et al., 2011; Yang & Konrad, 2011). High-talent female employees might find themselves totally immersed in their careers while forfeiting establishing their own families. Consequently, many choose to avoid having children altogether. Even when married, the "TINS (two incomes, no sex) syndrome" (Baruch, 2004, p. 116) implies that couples with the potential to deliver the best future talented generation avoid having children, because they are focused on career-related activities. Overall, the notion of gendered careers—the system that requires working women to be "superwomen"—has overloaded them with unrealistic expectations, leading to many opting out of the vicious cycle (Mainiero & Sullivan, 2006). Work–family stress most definitely spills over both ways and influences both career choices and actual job behavior (see discussion in Chapter 4).

The challenges for human resources practitioners in managing both careers and the many forms of OMB are many and varied (Benson et al., 2013). Those in charge must be well equipped to grasp the full spectrum of the realities of new careers, including the opportunities as well as threats that come along with them, their commonalities and differences. Not only savvy employees but practitioners as well must expand their repertoire of skills—competencies as well as their perspectives—to safely walk the darker and riskier career grounds. Many organizations indeed venture into OMB management by instilling codes of ethics and better monitoring employee and managerial conduct (e.g., Weitz & Vardi, 2008). At the practical level, organizational support (e.g., in the shape of coaching and mentoring) can be offered to individuals experiencing career difficulties. HR policies and practices need to be developed, adapted, or discontinued in line with their anticipated fit for the new shape of careers (Baruch & Peiperl, 2000). Our integrative model of OMB management (see Chapter 11, Figure 11.1) offers a strategic tool and guidelines, because it views careers as both antecedents of OMB and consequences of OMB. It has implications for employees and managers, it offers preventive and corrective interventions, and it is dynamic and temporal enough to be able to address such unfolding and interconnected processes.

Scholars of organizations and careers should portray the career accurately and realistically, providing a fair and balanced depiction of working life. Are not negative traits, attitudes, emotions, intentions, and behaviors important elements of people's career experiences? In our careers, we are both actors and spectators. A good drama (Nicholson, 2007) does not necessarily have a happy ending, and yet it receives both applause and criticism. We sometimes even choose to play the role of the "bad guys." Our premise is that without exploring the darker side of careers, even exposing intentional forms of related organizational misbehavior, a well-rounded, balanced, and comprehensive understanding of careers cannot be successfully attained. Acknowledging the negative aspects of careers and accepting the dark sides as significant and salient components of organizations can serve to encourage a balanced perspective in the study of careers and the complex interaction between person, work, and organization. By integrating the career in our OMB management framework, we begin to do just that.

PART II

OMB Manifestations and Antecedents

4

INDIVIDUAL-LEVEL
MANIFESTATIONS OF OMB

Men who are drunk are likely to prove a danger in dock work.

—Mars (1987)

Violence has been a recurring nightmare in organizations through the United States.

—Baron (1993)

How does OMB manifest itself in work organizations? What are the overt signs of OMB? What are the actual OMB phenomena? Members of organizations misbehave in every imaginable, sometimes unimaginable, ways. To cite one leading study, Analoui and Kakabadse (1992) identified 451 incidents of unconventional practices committed in a service organization over a period of about six years, and distinguished six major patterns: (1) pilferage and theft, (2) rule breaking, (3) destructive practices, (4) non-cooperation, (5) disruptive practices, and (6) misuse of facilities. These incidents were recorded for supervisory as well as non-supervisory employees, both overt and covert behaviors, and manifested not only by individuals but also by groups of employees.

Gruys (1999) took a different route. Based on the literature published between 1982 and 1997, he identified 87 different counterproductive behaviors—acts defined by Sackett and DeVore (2001) as intentional workplace behaviors that were viewed by the organization as contrary to its legitimate interests. By use of statistical techniques, Gruys grouped the items describing misbehavior into the following 11 clusters:

- Theft and related behavior (theft of cash or property, giving away goods or services, and misuse of employee discounts).
- Destruction of property (damaging, defacing, or destroying property and sabotaging production).
- Misuse of information (revealing confidential information and falsifying records).
- Misuse of time and resources (wasting time, altering time cards, and conducting private business during work time).
- Unsafe behavior (failing to follow safety procedures and failure to learn safety procedures).
- Poor attendance (unexcused absences, tardiness, and misuse of sick leave).
- Poor quality work (intentionally slow or sloppy work).
- Alcohol use (alcohol consumption on the job and working under the influence of alcohol).
- Drug use (possession, use, or sale of illegal drugs at work).
- Inappropriate verbal actions (arguing with customers and verbally harassing coworkers).
- Inappropriate physical actions (physically attacking coworkers and physical or sexual advances toward coworkers).

The ability of organization members to engage in OMB, despite the often intensive efforts of organizations to control it, is facilitated by the use of these verbal, behavioral, or cognitive techniques-neutralization techniques- which serve to reduce or eliminate the perceived discrepancy between a deviant action and the norms it violates. Drawing on existing literature from psychology, sociology, criminology, and organization theory, Sykes and Matza (1957) proposed a simplified typology of neutralization strategy and generate a number of hypotheses regarding the conditions or factors likely to determine their use and effectiveness. This is further discussed in Chapter 6.

To better understand the abundance and variety of dark-side activity following the OMB model presented in Chapter 2, we organized our review of OMB manifestations in three parts: Intrapersonal and interpersonal (Chapter 4); production and political (Chapter 5); corruption, unethical managerial behavior, and property manifestations (Chapter 6). Although we discuss possible causes, these three chapters focus on the behavior. In Chapters 7, 8, and 9, we examine the next key issue: What makes organizational members decide to engage in such behaviors? These chapters, therefore, explore the antecedents of OMB.

Figure 4.1 serves as a framework for the current chapter. Assuming that both intra- and interpersonal misbehaviors are intentional and a consequence of multilevel antecedent factors, we begin our discussion at the individual level of analysis.

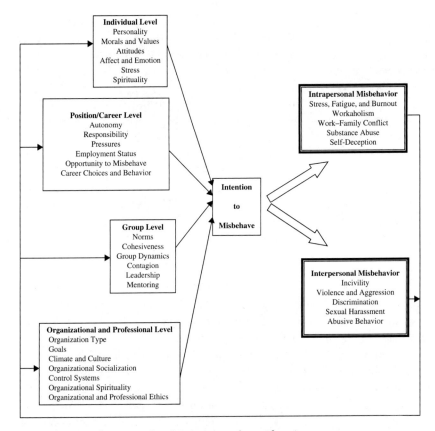

FIGURE 4.1 Intrapersonal and interpersonal manifestations

Intrapersonal Manifestations

Stress, Fatigue, and Burnout

Most work environments are perceived by many organization members—employees and managers—as stress-inducing because they experience excessive demands by rapidly changing technology, impatient colleagues and customers, unforgiving deadlines and competitions, conflicting internal and external demands, and so on. Certain sectors such as high-tech and various human services are considered especially stress-prone, and their employees are candidates for occupational chronic stress, fatigue, and burnout. In fact, stress is considered a significant workplace health issue in industrialized nations (Spector & Fox, 2002) and an important factor in explaining a variety of counterproductive work behaviors (Fox & Spector, 2005).

Stress is defined in terms of how it impacts physical and psychological health; it includes mental, physical, and emotional strain. Personal stress may occur in the workplace when an employee perceives a situation to be too strenuous to handle, and therefore threatening to his or her well-being. It may arise from the subjective appraisal of a situation as threatening or challenging and from the perception that adequate resources to cope with it are insufficient or unavailable (Beehr, 1995; Cohen & Edwards, 1989). Psychological stress, is the product of the perceived interaction with the environment and not necessarily the objective characteristics of the specific environment. Thus, two employees performing similar tasks side-by-side may perceive the situation differently because of personal circumstances, or attitudinal or personality differences. For one, the situation may seem quite benign, while for the other, the situation may seem unbearable and threatening—and stressful.

Because the work environment is complex, stress may originate from various sources. It may arise from the job itself (routine, fast-paced, difficult, repetitive, changing, isolate, restricting, ambiguous), from interpersonal relationships (lack of trust, discriminating, abusive, secretive, dishonest), and from the organization (unfair systems, over-controlling, lack of control, unethical climate). When such circumstances are perceived as stressful, individuals experience a three-stage psychological process of evaluating the situation: Primary appraisal—assessment of the significance of a potentially stressful situation for the person's well-being; secondary appraisal—assessment by the person of what can be done about it and the choice of specific coping adjustment; and reappraisal—re-evaluation of the situation and if further coping adjustment is called for (Lazarus & Folkman, 1984). Several researchers (e.g., Hobfoll, 2002) emphasize the negative effects of stress in terms of depletion of resources and loss of self-esteem. Others focus more on proactive adjustment reactions to stress such as engagement in misconduct (e.g., Fox et al., 2001). We suggest that among the adjustment mechanisms for coping with stress, the intention to engage in some type of misconduct is a viable option, and 'subsequently' the engagement in behaviors such as restriction of effort, excessive absenteeism, and substance abuse and so on (see review chapter on occupational stress and workplace deviance by Grant, 2013).

In this vein, Eschleman, Bowling, and LaHuis (2014) recently conducted a longitudinal study to ascertain the moderating effects of personality on the relationship between change in work stressors and counterproductive work behaviors. Over six months, increases in work stressors (interpersonal conflict and organizational constraints) were positively related to measures of counterproductive workplace behaviors. Two personality traits, agreeableness and conscientiousness, played a role in moderating these main effects. For employees characterized as low on agreeableness and low on conscientiousness, stress and misbehavior were strongly related. The researchers suggest that organizations and managers should be aware of the vulnerability of such employees to increasing levels of stress and perhaps assist them through training programs in coping with stressful situations.

Chronic stress is an acute intrapersonal work-related experience that is significant to the understanding of different types of misbehavior toward self and others. For instance, a person whose job competencies become obsolete because of neglect or burnout, when facing what is perceived to be a highly demanding task, may vent felt frustration and distress by harshly blaming or even confronting self and others. A fatigued intern in an emergency room may lose self-confidence and refrain from certain procedures, and a burned-out teacher may lose the will to confront students who misbehave. We thus view stress, fatigue, and burnout as potential antecedents, manifestations, and costs of OMB.

Workaholism

Individuals may also choose to abuse themselves at work in various ways. For example, they may exaggerate the role work plays in their lives. For different reasons, some become increasingly devoted to their jobs, work, and careers. Such over-commitment and over-involvement has been dubbed "workaholism" to denote a type of addictive behavior. The term *workaholism* is derived from another concept related to addictive behavior—alcoholism. The difference between the two concepts is that addiction to work, as far as the organization is concerned, is generally considered a virtue or positive attribute of the employee, whereas addiction to alcohol, or drugs, is considered a fault or negative characteristic, which could cause damage not only to the worker but also to his or her work environment. Although organizations recognize the need to combat substance abuse, they tend to encourage employees, managers in particular, to engage in excessive patterns of work (e.g., long and intensive hours) and often reward such devotion.

We tried to trace the phenomenon's genealogy. The very first usage of the term *workaholism* we found is in Oates' (1971) book, *Confessions of a workaholic: The facts about work addiction*. Oates treated workaholism as negative behavior, an addiction to work, and the compulsion of an uncontrollable need to work incessantly. Although workaholism has been considered to be a positive organizational phenomenon (e.g., Machlowitz, 1980), it has also been treated as a negative and rather problematic issue (e.g., Killinger, 1991; Porter, 1996). It is considered positive because, regardless of costs, such immersion in work may enhance productivity and organizational performance. However, workaholism may be equated with other addictions; employees afflicted with this addiction may be viewed as frustrated, unhappy, tense, uncooperative, troubled, and pressured individuals (e.g., Naughton, 1987). Assuming that in most cases workaholism is a habit of choice, it is regarded here as an intrapersonal expression of OMB.

A close examination of workaholism's negative aspects was undertaken by Porter (1996) who, like Oates (1971) and Naughton (1987), viewed excessive work as addictive behavior and suggested that, as such, it will have a negative impact not only on the setting in which it occurs, but on employees as well. To properly address dysfunctional behavior patterns that interfere with organizational operations, Porter called for a total change in perspective. For her, the similarities with other addictions include identity issues, rigid thinking, withdrawal behaviors, and denial. These factors influence the workaholic's decision-making and goals. They also interfere with effectiveness by distorting interpersonal relationships.

To better understand the phenomenon of workaholism, researchers have spent considerable resources mapping its dimensions. Scott, Moore, and Miceli (1997) suggested that, although much has been written about the phenomenon, rigorous research and theoretical development on the topic is in its infancy. In their groundbreaking article, they integrated literature from multiple disciplines and offered a definition of *workaholic behavior*. They identified three types of workaholic behavior patterns: Compulsive-dependent, perfectionist, and achievement-oriented. They also proposed a preliminary model that identifies potential linkages between each type of workaholism pattern and important outcomes such as performance, job and life satisfaction, and turnover. Scott et al.'s argument is that, depending on the type of workaholic behavior pattern, workaholism can be good or bad, and its consequences may be experienced or evaluated differently by individuals, organizations, and society at large. They concluded that researchers and managers should avoid making judgments about positive or negative effects of workaholism until more rigorous research has been conducted and published. We concur. OMB in general is a relative phenomenon; therefore one should refrain from making value judgments before assessing the long-term consequences for all parties involved.

Attempts have been made to operationalize workaholism (Cherrington, 1980; Machlowitz, 1980; Mosier, 1983). Some of the early definitions relate to the number of hours of work invested by the worker as a major characteristic of the addict (Mosier, 1983). Yet other studies have found that the amount of time devoted to work does not necessarily distinguish between the workaholic and others—not everyone who puts in many hours is addicted to work. Some work more hours than usual due to a temporary need (Helldorfer, 1987; Machlowitz, 1980), whereas others work more just to survive. A different definition refers to workaholics as people who always devote more time and thought to work than the situation requires. What distinguishes them from their colleagues is their attitude—the way they relate to their work rather than the actual time they spend working (Machlowitz, 1980).

Another way of defining the term *workaholism* and its measurement was offered by Spence and Robbins (1992). They noted that the addicted worker feels a strong inner urge to work, as well as guilt if he or she does not work. The workaholic is a person who exhibits three properties: He or she is highly work-involved, feels compelled or driven to work because of inner pressure, and is low in the enjoyment of work. Spence and Robbins chose to contrast the workaholic with what they labeled a *work enthusiast*, a person who, like the workaholic, is highly involved at work but, unlike the latter, is high in enjoyment and is not driven as hard. They identified three patterns of motives: Work involvement, drivenness, and work enjoyment. Hypothetically then, a workaholic is a person who "is highly work involved, feels compelled or driven to work because of inner pressures, and is low in enjoyment at work" (Spence and Robbins, 1992, p. 62). Yet there is also the work enthusiast (high on work involvement, low on drivenness, and high on enjoyment) and the enthusiastic workaholic (high on all three motives). For their validation study, Spence and Robbins developed questionnaires for all three patterns. These were sent via mail to a sample of male ($n = 134$) and female ($n = 157$) social workers. As predicted, those that fit the workaholic profile were higher than work enthusiasts (among other groups) on measures of perfectionism, non-delegation of responsibility, and job stress. Not surprisingly, they were also higher on a measure of health complaints.

The question of whether workaholism is related to the construct *meaning of work* (i.e., how central is work in a person's life) was examined by Snir and Harpaz (2000) in two samples of the Israeli labor force. Workaholics were higher on measures of work centrality and intrinsic work orientation. They perceive work as the most important facet in their lives and are constantly motivated to get more and more personally and directly involved in it. They also attribute less importance to interpersonal contacts at work.

To relate workaholism to personality, attitudinal, and affective measures, Burke (1999) collected data from 530 women and men in managerial and professional roles. Workaholism types were determined using Spence and Robbins' (1992) measures. Three personal beliefs and fears identified by Price (1982) in her cognitive social learning model of Type A behavior (we elaborate on this trait in Chapter 7) were assessed as well, suggesting a possible overlap between Type A personality and workaholism. Burke (1999) reported that most beliefs and fears measured were positively and significantly related to workaholism.

In a similar vein, Goldschmid-Aron (1997) conducted a field study among Israeli female directors of adult-education centers ($n = 93$) using Spence and Robbins' (1992) measures. She investigated the influence of three personal variables (Type A behavior pattern, work centrality, and career commitment) and perceived climate as an organizational effect. Goldschmid-Aron also found a positive relationship between Type A behavior pattern and workaholism. Furthermore, workaholism was positively related to the potential for hostility and irritability, perceived job pressures, and career commitment. That is, the more the managers perceived the work as pressured and overloaded, the more they reported work-addicted behaviors; and the higher the managers' commitment to their careers, the more they will be overly devoted to work.

We speculate that work environments saturated with overload and pressure may also be conducive to extreme modes of behavior, some of which may be defying organizational expectations of proper conduct. Different types of workaholic behavior patterns, each having potentially different antecedents (e.g., individual traits) and associations with job performance, work, and life outcomes, were also examined. For example, Naughton's (1987) classification is based on the two dimensions of career commitment and obsession–compulsion behavior pattern. We propose that such a classification may shed light on the variety of work and non-work behaviors expected from both workaholics and non-workaholics:

- Job-involved workaholics (high on work commitment and low on obsession–compulsion) are expected to perform well in demanding jobs, be highly satisfied, and have little interest in non-work activities. These individuals could easily engage themselves out of sheer commitment in committing acts of misconduct that benefit their employer (OMB Type O).
- Compulsive workaholics (high work commitment and high obsession–compulsion) are potentially poor performers (probably due to staff problems resulting from impatience and ritualized work habits). The behavior of these individuals may be characterized by harassment of others, rule breaking, and ignoring safety regulations (OMB Type D) when they become impatient with obstacles at work.
- Non-workaholics (low work commitment and low obsession–compulsion) spend more time on non-work interests. These employees may neglect important work-related duties, which could result in negative consequences for themselves or others.
- Compulsive non-workaholics (low commitment and high obsession–compulsion) are individuals who compulsively spend time in non-work activities. These individuals may intentionally sacrifice work performance and effort for the benefit of their outside interests and activities—a conflict of resources that could bear grave results for peers and the work process.

Peiperl and Jones (2001) elaborated on the distinction between *workaholics* and *overworkers* by proposing two underlying independent dimensions: Perceived effort and perceived return. Workaholics are those who work too much but feel the rewards arising from their work are at least equitably distributed between themselves and the organizations that employ them. Overworkers, by contrast, are people who work too much (in their own terms) just as workaholics do, but feel that the returns are inequitably distributed in favor of the organization. Workaholics have a clear reason to continue their extreme work behavior. Overworkers, by contrast, may be trapped in a pattern of work that is neither sensible nor equitable. In addition, two interesting categories of employees emerge: *Withholders*, those who work too little as their organizations reap most of the benefits, and *collectors*, those who reap relatively more rewards for less effort than their peers. The pathology, if there is one, is less about addiction among people who work too much but are satisfied with the outcomes and more about over-engagement, and possibly denial, among people who are not addicted to work but rather dissatisfied with its utility. Peiperl and Jones viewed workaholics as hard workers who enjoy their work and get a lot out of it, not as work addicts. They argued that, although there may be few people who are genuinely and pathologically addicted to work, they are the exception.

A recent meta-analysis details different correlations and outcomes to workaholism. At the individual level, it has been observed that Type A personalities, perfectionists, and extroverts are more likely to demonstrate workaholic tendencies. In addition, attitudes such as job involvement, work engagement, work enjoyment, and organizational commitment are positively related to workaholism. At the position and group level, it was found that managerial status, work overload, number of hours worked, overtime, time commitment to work, and role conflict are positively related to workaholism. More surprisingly, supervisory support is also positively associated with workaholism (Clark et al., 2014).

It is clear that management should pay closer attention to the overworked employees who continue to exhibit excessive work behavior while perceiving the balance of rewards they accrue as negative. We argue that such individuals are prime candidates for engagement in OMB Type S, attempting perhaps to purposely restore such perceived negative imbalances (e.g., by embezzlement or theft from their employers).

Work–family spillovers

Work-to-family and family-to-work conflicts are produced by simultaneous pressures from work and family roles that are mutually incompatible. These clashes may translate into conditions of stress and, as work–family boundaries become less distinct and more permeable, spillovers become inevitable (Duxbury et al., 2014). Consider, for instance, the continuous online availability and networking of family members during workdays that in and of themselves tend to become longer and more intensive, and that the work itself becomes boundaryless and transferrable. Work-to-family conflict, which represents the extent to which the work domain produces inter-role conflict in the family realm, can be divided into three dimensions: Time-, strain-, and behavior-based conflict (Greenhaus & Beutell, 1985). *Time-based* work-to-family conflict occurs when time devoted to the work role makes it difficult to fulfill family obligations. *Strain-based* work-to-family conflict represents the strain resulting from the work role spilling over into family roles. Finally, *behavior-based* work-to-family conflict occurs when individuals cannot adjust their work-related behaviors to meet their family role requirements.

Individuals who experience extensive work-to-family conflict may compromise either or both roles. Namely, work stresses may spill over to daily life at home and vice versa. One area where this is quite apparent is careers (Greenhaus & Foley, 2007). For instance, unfulfilled expectations for a promotion resulting in loss of self-confidence on the job and increased career anxiety may spill over into aggressive behavior at home. Conversely, marital strain may spill over to daily work, increasing abusive behavior toward subordinates. A study by Wu, Kwan, Liu, and Resick (2012) conducted among Chinese families demonstrated that employees who experience abusive supervision are likely to demonstrate aversive affect and behavior directed toward their family. These actions represent family-undermining behaviors. That is, subordinates of abusive supervisors may direct their displaced anger and frustration toward family members by engaging in family-undermining behaviors (e.g., Hoobler & Brass, 2006). Thus, spillovers work both ways. Here, however, we emphasize the possibility that family strains may spill over to job behaviors and intentionally to misbehaviors.

As the nature of work is continuously evolving, so too are work and family lives becoming increasingly intertwined, possibly creating strain for employees trying to function successfully in both domains. Now more than ever, a person's work role has the capacity to influence his or her family role and vice versa. The nature of this influence may be positive, thereby enriching both roles (Greenhaus & Powell, 2003), or negative, resulting in conflict (Byron, 2005). To be sure, this connected complexity of conflicts inevitably affects workplace behaviors among which OMB such as aggressive behavior toward others as well as production and property transgressions must be quite dominant.

When considering the intrapersonal domains, the maintenance of employee health and well-being becomes increasingly meaningful for both scholars and managers. For instance, emotional exhaustion, tension, and stress, as well as sleep deprivation, are not simply unpleasant states for employees to contend with at home after work; studies link them to key work outcomes such as increased job dissatisfaction (Scott & Judge, 2006), job stress (Hammer et al., 2004), turnover intentions (Kossek & Ozeki, 1999), deviant behavior (Christian & Ellis, 2011), and specifically excessive cyberloafing at work (Wagner et al., 2012).

Substance Abuse

One of the critical problems of intrapersonal misbehavior in the workplace is substance abuse—excessive use of alcohol, tobacco, and illegal drugs (Bacharach et al., 2002; Frone, 2013; Liu et al., 2015). These are addictive and harmful to the user; they usually have negative effects on the work environment and may be hazardous to non-users as well. Workers' drug abuse is perceived to be a growing problem for the labor force. Assembly line workers, long-haul truck drivers, and young professionals—disparate groups in terms of socioeconomic factors, education, income, and job conditions—are among those singled out most frequently for abusing illicit drugs on the job. The scant research available on the subject focuses on the role of the work organization in detecting and treating substance abuse through employee assistance programs, rather than focusing on the work context's role in alleviating the problem.

Mensch and Kandel (1988) investigated the relationship between job characteristics and use of illicit drugs in early adulthood. They wanted to determine whether certain ostensibly stressful features of the work environment contribute to substance abuse on and off the job. The relationships between job conditions and use of four classes of drugs (i.e., alcohol, cigarettes, marijuana, and cocaine) were investigated in 1984 among a nationally representative sample of young adults aged 19 to 27. Because the data failed to uncover any relationship between substance abuse and work conditions or occupations, the researchers concluded that workers' substance use is directly attributable to the workforce and less so to the conditions of the workplace.

In an investigation of alcohol abuse in the workplace through the Cornell University Smithers Institute for Alcohol-Related Workplace Studies, Bacharach et al. (2002) found that the costs of problem drinking (as a form of counterproductive behavior) in the United States are prohibitive to both employers and employees. These costs result from poor quality work, absenteeism, accidents, medical expenses, and so on. In 2006, estimates of the costs were close to $162 billion (Frone, 2013). Drinking per se is not necessarily perceived as evil or dysfunctional. In fact, some forms of drinking in the workplace are considered socially acceptable, such as during workplace parties, business dinners, and ceremonies. It is the excessive and irresponsible consumption that is bothersome to management and often damaging to drinkers, their families, and their peers. When such conduct is willful and drinkers are aware of the potential harm, problem drinking in the workplace is classified as OMB Type D.

Bacharach et al. (2002) collected data from thousands of union employees in order to identify the causes of problem drinking. They posited both organizational and personal antecedents: Workplace culture, policy enforcement, alienation, and stress. Problem drinking, the dependent variable, was measured by asking respondents a direct question adopted from Ewing's (1984) medical instrument for detecting alcoholism. The four-item question relies on honest self-reporting. The respondent is asked whether, in the last month, he or she felt that he or she should cut down on drinking, were annoyed by people criticizing their drinking, felt guilty about drinking, and had a drink first thing in the morning to steady nerves or to get rid of a hangover. The researchers found that, of the aforementioned antecedents, workplace culture (in terms of perceived permissive drinking norms) is the single most important risk factor that drives employees to drink. By implication, when employees perceive the organization to be permissive in terms of tolerating social drinking during and after work hours, the likelihood for drinking to become problematic and abusive increases.

Perhaps the best-known study of workplace drug use and its correlates was conducted by Mangione and Quinn (1975). They examined whether counterproductive behavior and drug use at work are symptoms of job dissatisfaction. Data were collected from a US national sample of 1,327 wage and salaried workers. Their findings show a significant negative association between job satisfaction and self-reported counterproductive behavior among men 30 years or older. For the same age group, similar results were found for drug use at work.

Harris and Greising (1998) presented a review of drug and alcohol use as dysfunctional workplace behavior. The authors first summarized the results of a survey of organizational practices regarding drug and alcohol abuse, followed by an overview of prior research on the topic. They then described two recent studies that examined the effect of drug and alcohol use on employee wages, reporting that individuals who are more likely to use these substances also tend to earn higher wages. Surprisingly, they found that the two variables, wages and drug and alcohol use, are indeed positively correlated. Harris and Greising noted several explanations for such relationships: (1) this is just a statistical artifact (spurious relationships); (2) for certain individuals, substance abuse offers a form of relaxation and diversion from job-related stress, which in turn contributes to better performance and income; and (3) certain users are also good performers.

An interesting question arising from the substance abuse literature relates to its nature: Is the use of alcohol and drugs in the workplace dysfunctional or merely behavior meant to be diversionary? Perhaps due to the negative connotations associated with alcohol and drug abuse, there is a tendency to group together different substances and thereby assume that the effects of use will be the same regardless of the substance. That is, there is often an implicit assumption that different drugs have similar effects for different users in the workplace. Most of the literature has focused on organizational outcomes such as accidents, absenteeism, performance, and turnover. However, it appears that substance abuse at work is a complex phenomenon not only because of the variety of substances involved, but because their use is associated with a wide variety of causes and outcomes. It also varies across different work environments and occupational groups (e.g., Shain, 1982; Sonnenstuhl, 1996).

A unique study of drug abuse within a specific occupational group was reported by Dabney and Hollinger (1999). They focused on pharmacists who, on average, spend six years in college studying the intricacies of prescription medicines and their effects on the human mind and body. After graduation, they embark on a career in which their expertise and familiarity with the proper use and dangers of prescription drugs continuously grow. Despite this wealth of experience and knowledge, pharmacists may become prescription-drug abusers. In order to understand the process by which these professionals come to abuse the tools of their trade, Dabney and Hollinger conducted in-depth interviews with 50 recovering drug-dependent pharmacists and concluded that, ironically, the knowledge and expertise may actually contribute to escalating prescription-drug abuse. They argued that being and becoming a pharmacist presents a paradox of familiarity, wherein technical knowledge and the built-in opportunity may actually delude pharmacists into believing that they are immune to the harmful effects of prescription-drug abuse to themselves and their careers.

Substance abuse and job behaviors such as psychological and physical withdrawal, positive work behaviors, and antagonistic work behaviors (a form of counterproductive and perhaps retaliatory behavior) were assessed in a sample of municipal employees in the southwestern United States (Lehman & Simpson, 1992). The employees who reported substance abuse at or away from work were found to more frequently engage in withdrawal activities and antagonistic work behaviors than did non-users, although users and non-users did not differ on positive work behaviors. Hierarchical regression models were used to determine whether substance abuse contributed unique variance to the prediction of job behaviors after controlling for the variance associated with personal and job background. Not surprisingly, the primary finding was that substance abuse added unique variance to the prediction of psychological and physical withdrawal behaviors.

The seemingly trivial question of whether workplace absenteeism and alcohol use are indeed positively related was addressed by McFarlin and Fals-Stewart (2002). They argued that nearly all investigations examining the link between alcohol use and absenteeism have been generally marked by three characteristics: (1) they have been correlational, cross-sectional studies examining the relationship between one or more global measures of alcohol use and absenteeism; (2) they have been cross-sectional in nature, with little to no information collected about the temporal relationship between alcohol use and absenteeism; and (3) they typically use samples consisting of problem drinkers. In their study, they selected a random sample of 280 employees of one of the three large companies located in the northeastern United States. Using psychometrically sound, semi-structured interviews, they gleaned information from employees about specific days of drinking during a one-month period and actually marked the day(s) on a calendar. Data about employee absences during the same target time period were collected from the firm's human resource department and were also marked on an actual calendar. A significant day-to-day relationship emerged between alcohol use and workplace absenteeism; workers were roughly twice as likely to be absent from work the day after they consumed alcohol. The researchers concluded that, given its staggering costs to business each year, identifying a powerful predictor of workplace absence is a necessary first step in developing proactive strategies to reduce alcohol-related absenteeism.

Drug testing may be one such strategy. Although management's use of drug testing programs is becoming a critical organizational issue, no systematic conceptual framework has been applied to the study of employee reactions to drug testing. Konovsky and Cropanzano (1991) dealt with this issue from the employee perspective. They focused on the way employees perceive drug testing programs and their fairness and on how this perception may influence both their job performance and how they feel toward their employer. They used an organizational justice framework to explain and predict the relationships between two types of justice (procedural justice and outcome fairness): Employee attitudes (satisfaction, commitment, and management trust) and behavior (turnover intentions and performance). Survey data from 195 employees in a pathology laboratory indicated that perceptions of justice predict employee attitudes and performance.

Certainly, when members of organizations behave in ways that are personally abusive in both intra- and interpersonal terms, employers must look for ways to monitor and curb such trends. This calls for three types of strategies: (1) formal management control—applying strict policy and discipline measures, (2) organizational redesign—restructuring work processes to reduce stress and isolation, and (3) cultural change—promulgating a normative value system that condemns abuse and condones proper behavior (Bacharach et al., 2002). These broad strategies are relevant to most other forms of misbehavior and should be considered relevant as we continue to explore other manifestations. How to apply them (as single strategy, in combination, at what level, etc.) is up to senior management because there is no single panacea. Local solutions should be a function of the specific diagnosed problems and the circumstances that naturally differ among organizations (see Chapter 11).

The reasons for substance abuse on the job may be summarized by three categories as follows:

1   *Social control*: A weakened work structure with limited supervision and low visibility may contribute to substance abuse on the job.
2   *Alienation*: Lack of interest on the job, absence of challenging work, and inadequate control over work may cause stress, which in turn may lead to substance abuse.
3   *Social availability*: Simply put, certain occupations or work environments encourage leisure-time drinking and drug abuse among employees.

Self-Deception

> Above all, don't lie to yourself. The man who lies to himself and listens to his own lie comes to a point that he cannot distinguish the truth within him, or around him, and so loses all respect for himself and for others. And having no respect he ceases to love.
>
> – Fyodor Dostoyevsky, *The Brothers Karamazov*

We regard self-deception as a form of intra-person misbehavior because it entails a cognitive activity that may be self-abusive. As a consequence, self-deception is the denial of truth and creation of a reality that masks a person's identity and by corollary may destroy trust and erode work relationships. Festinger (1957) treated self-deception as a kind of cognitive dissonance with behavioral consequences because in self-deception there is a gap between what individuals know about how they ought to or are expected to behave and how they intend to or actually do behave. This tenet is important because when we deceive ourselves at work, we may act toward ourselves and toward others in ways that may be harmful. Maslow (1962) also addressed self-deception as a defense mechanism we use when we are afraid of knowledge that would cause us to despise ourselves. As Peck (1983) articulated, self-deception is a denial of the duty we owe ourselves to refrain from avoiding the need to modify and adapt our behavior. Self-deception, he said, is a warping of perception that promotes a distorted view of reality and elevates self-interest above the desire for truth.

In his important review, Caldwell (2009) explicates the significance of self-deception in organizations and particularly in leadership. He observes that the ability of leaders to be perceived as trustworthy and authentic is often related to their own awareness about character flaws and weaknesses. When these are ignored or denied, leaders/managers tend to deceive themselves, and thus may act unethically toward themselves and toward others, subordinates and peers alike. Caldwell (2009) provides a useful summary of what Siegler (1962) identified as rationalizations that occur in the process of deceiving oneself:

- *A pretense (façade) to others*: Claiming prior knowledge about future outcomes or an attempt to look good by others.
- *Discount of a failure and articulation of past fears*: Claiming to have known in advance the likelihood of failure.
- *Inability to understand*: Failure to accept that a situation may really reflect something we do not comprehend.
- *Wanting reality to be different*: Personal biases that often lead to wishful thinking.
- *Intentional aversion of attention*: The tendency to avoid painful issues so that we do not have to confront them.

We too view self-deception as abusive in that it is distorting and misleading, it affects our perceptions of others, and therefore impacts our decisions and behavioral intentions. We believe that excessive self-deception on the job can become chronic and addictive and thus harmful to organization members. As with all addictions, it should be treated and controlled. We therefore adopt Caldwell's (2009) five ethical duties to oneself as a practical guideline to deal with self-deception, both as individuals and as management consultants:

- We owe ourselves the duty to understand how vulnerable we can be when we are unwilling to face incongruity.
- We need to identify and acknowledge those internal factors that cause us to deny and distort reality.
- We must continuously examine and reexamine our core beliefs.
- We must assume the responsibility for understanding and dealing with the stress causes of our self-deception and take corrective steps.
- We owe ourselves the responsibility to examine the consistency between beliefs and work behavior, and to confront incongruities when they occur.

Interpersonal Manifestations

Incivility

Interpersonal on-the-job misbehavior runs the gamut from minute and insignificant acts of incivility that could, by some measures, go unnoticed to blatant acts of violence and terror. Examples of incivility in the workplace abound: Answering the phone with a "yeah," neglecting to say "thank you" or "please," using voicemail to screen calls, leaving a half cup of coffee behind to avoid having to brew the next pot, standing impatiently over the desk of someone engaged in a phone conversation, leaving food trays behind for others to clean up, and talking loudly on the phone about non-work matters (Martin, 1996). Such conduct in the workplace is annoying, at the very least.

According to Baron and Neuman (1996), the business world was thought by many to be one of the last bastions of civility. For decades, the relationships among coworkers were characterized by formality, marked by collegiality, friendliness, and distant yet correct and polite interactions. However, the business world has started to reflect the casualness of society at large. Scholars (see Neuman & Baron, 1997) have cited employee diversity, re-engineering, downsizing, budget cuts, continually increasing pressures for productivity, autocratic work environments, the use of part-time employees, and contingent labor for the increase of uncivil and aggressive workplace behaviors.

We begin with the less pernicious aspect of interpersonal aggression, with what Andersson and Pearson (1999) so aptly called *workplace incivility*, but we stress that even minuscule expressions of impoliteness or rudeness may lead to more blatant aggression. Indeed, Andersson and Pearson explained at length how marginal manifestations of incivility could potentially spiral into increasingly aggressive behaviors. To gain a full understanding of the mechanisms that underlie the incivility spiral, they examined what happens at key points of this process, the starting and tipping points, factors that can facilitate the occurrence, and the dynamics of escalation from incivility to violence.

For Andersson and Pearson (1999), workplace incivility involves acting rudely, discourteously, or with disregard for others in the workplace in violation of workplace norms of mutual respect. Baron and Neuman (1996) found that a majority of the aggression in the workplace is actually relatively mild. These acts are mostly verbal rather than physical, passive rather than active, indirect rather than direct, and subtle rather than overt.

Incivility occurs when members of an organization knowingly engage in low-intensity behavior that violates local workplace norms. According to Andersson and Pearson (1999), such acts, although not necessarily aggressive, may initiate a tit-for-tat cycle that, beyond a certain tipping point, eventually becomes violent. Such incivility spirals in organizations were conceptualized by Masuch

(1985), who maintained that spirals are caused by organization actors because they are unwilling or unable to change their behavior. The escalation takes place when an action by an employee stimulates the negative action of another employee. The ensuing actions in a work setting constitute acts of misbehavior that violate norms of acceptable behavior. When they get out of hand, such interpersonal conflicts may result in extreme forms of violence—breaching not only local norms but also societal codes of behavior, as defined by the legal system. This would be the case when a simple exchange of insults turns into an aggravated assault.

Following this conceptual framework, Pearson, Andersson, and Porath (2000) conducted interviews and workshops across the United States with more than 700 workers, managers, and professionals representing different types of organizational and occupational environments. They accumulated a wealth of incidents of what they regarded as mild incivility, such as receiving nasty or demeaning notes, being treated as a child by others at work, being cut off while speaking, being berated for an action committed by another employee, being excluded from a meeting, and having one's credibility undermined in public. These are all minor offenses, but they are also perceived as ambiguous. This ambiguity, unlike cases of overt aggression or sheer vandalism, is open to interpretation by the target and may lead to the spiraling effect even when the actor did not originally intend to be derogatory.

A recent review of the literature dealing with incivility describes three perspectives: Experienced incivility, witnessed incivility, and instigated incivility. However, the majority of research focuses on experienced incivility—the frequency with which a target experiences uncivil behavior. Experienced incivility has individual-level antecedents such as targets' low agreeableness, low emotional stability, and younger age, and situational-level antecedents such as lower workgroup norms for civility and high role-stressors. Furthermore, studies indicate a wide spectrum of affective (e.g., emotional exhaustion), attitudinal (e.g., lower job satisfaction), and cognitive (e.g., lower perceived fairness) consequences for targets. Targets who experience incivility are also more likely to engage in counterproductive behaviors, retaliatory behaviors, and/or withdrawal behaviors, and to demonstrate lower levels of task performance and creativity (Schilpzand et al., 2014). Experienced incivility also predicts employees' perceived psychological contract breach and intentions to leave (Itzkovich, 2014).

Porath and Pearson (2010) emphasize the surprising costs of incivility to organizations and stakeholders in terms of not only lost profits, but also employees. They explicated how employees and managers intentionally decrease work effort and work quality because of experienced incivility, and lose work time as they worry about uncivil incidents and try to avoid the perpetrator. The flip side of incivility is the time spent on managing it. According to Porath and Pearson, HR professionals, managers, and executives report that they invest a great deal of time, energy, and money to amend and restore the effects and after-effects of incivility.

One interesting mode of incivility is using foul language at work, mostly among coworkers. Baruch and Jenkins (2007) discovered a silver lining in their investigation of swearing in British organizations: Cursing serves as a release mechanism in situations characterized by high tension. They developed a model for understanding the antecedents and consequences of using bad language in the workplace, and used a qualitative study to validate it. The 'swearing under focus' represented both social (to be socially accepted) and 'annoyance swearing' (to vent anger, frustration). Baruch and Jenkins (2007) found that employees use swear words on a continuous basis, but not necessarily in a negative, abusive manner. While most of the cases of using curse words involved employees at the lower levels of organizational hierarchies, executives too used such language, albeit less frequently. The primary issue for management is whether or not to maintain a permissive leadership culture at the workplace to deliberately allow swearing. In summary, research dealing with workplace incivility is rapidly growing (Francis et al., 2015). Prevalence rates and costs of incivility are rising as well (Porath & Pearson, 2010). We need to be on the alert when uncivil exchanges flare up in the workplace. While some of them might not be detrimental to the organization, when left undealt with, they can turn nasty or ugly, and may have damaging bottom-line outcomes.

Insults

One of the most common forms of workplace incivility is, without a doubt, insults. A unique insight into the social psychology of insults in organizations was offered by Gabriel (1998), who explored insults as a phenomenon that stands at the crossroads of emotion and narrative. Gabriel charted different forms of insulting behavior such as exclusion, stereotyping, ingratitude, scapegoating, rudeness, and being ignored or kept waiting. More potent insults may involve the defamation or despoiling of idealized objects, persons, and ideas. Obviously, people react differently to insults. Among the outcomes these experiences evoke are resigned tolerance, request for an apology, and retaliation. Gabriel, like Andersson and Pearson (1999), distinguished among insulting, bullying, and harassing behaviors, which are considered the accumulation, over time, of consistent and unrelenting insulting behavior. They are featured in organizational narratives whenever expressions such as "rubbing salt into the wound" or "adding insult to injury" are invoked. Insults may be verbal and gestural, consisting of rude or mocking diatribes, cutting remarks, negative stereotypes, or outright swearing. They can also be performed by deed, such as refusing an invitation or ignoring another person's presence. They may be subtle, residing in verbal innuendo or the facial expression of the actor, or they can be brutal, unambiguous, direct, and abusive as in cases of sexual, ethnic, or racial harassment. To supplement these propositions with empirical evidence, Gabriel cited insightful and emotional narratives generated by students who were asked to recall their own work internship experiences.

Insults are a form of aggression and serve to escalate conflict within the workplace (Calabrese, 2000). Buss' (1961) classification system for aggression effectively captures the complexity and variety of workplace aggression. Buss' (1961) system uses three dimensions to classify aggressive acts: (1) physical/verbal, (2) active/passive, and (3) direct/indirect. Physical acts involve deeds (e.g., kicking or shoving) while verbal acts involve the use of words to inflict harm (e.g., insults or harsh criticism). Insults are pervasive in the workplace. Berta (2003) reports that 22 percent of 600 restaurant workers in Texas and Florida reported calling coworkers insulting names, and 37 percent made fun of others' accents. Workplace insulting behaviors are an important organizational phenomenon because they evoke powerful emotions and often affect people's personal lives. Particularly convincing is the argument that insults frequently lead the targeted party to engage in retaliatory and vengeful acts. Such acts are consistent with our definition of OMB Type D—the intentional infliction of damage on others or the organization in general.

Revenge

Retribution and revenge are well documented in human history ("eye for an eye") and are, not surprisingly, prevalent in OB. McLean Parks (1997) wrote extensively about the *art and science* of revenge in organizations. She explored retribution from the perspective of internal justice, and the reciprocity norms on which assessments of organizational justice and injustice are based. She focused on retributive justice that is a form of justice available to those in organizations who are relatively less powerful but feel mistreated. She explained:

> As a justice mechanism available to the relatively powerless, retribution (as the broader construct, encompassing revenge, which generally has a pejorative connotation) can restore justice stemming from a variety of source of injustice: Getting less than expected or deserved (distributive justice), being the victim of unfair rules (procedural justice), or being ill treated as a human being (interactional justice).
>
> (McLean Parks, 1997, p. 114)

Following McLean Parks, there are three primary mechanisms of organizational retribution:

1   *Retributory recompense*: Based on inequity theory (Adams, 1965), this includes behaviors intended to balance the scales once an employee perceives or anticipates a wrong. It re-establishes a positive valence to individuals (who perceive themselves as victims) in exchange for what was lost. For example,

Greenberg (1990a) showed that employee theft is related to feelings of under-payment, and Boyd (1990) showed that thievery increases following mergers and acquisitions.

2   *Retributory impression management*: As shown earlier, impression management is a powerful tool individuals use to influence the way others perceive them and their behaviors. This form of retribution is quite subtle and can include both positive and negative impressions. On the one hand, tactics of flattery and ingratiation can be used to retaliate against figures of power in the organization, setting them up for future reprisal. On the other hand, individuals may apply revengeful acts while posing as victims and having no other way available to restore injustice. In any case, organizational avengers often use such tactics for deterrence purposes.

3   *Retributive retaliation*: This tactic adds the component of punishment; as the victim receives no recompense other than the simple satisfaction of know-ing that accounts have been settled ("don't get mad, get even"). To illus-trate, Sprouse (1992) recorded cases of retaliatory vandalism such as the one inflicted by a fired computer programmer who registered employees' names as historical figures in the *Encyclopedia Britannica*'s computerized system. We also know of a technician at a hospital who shut down the central oxygen flow to some units to avenge perceived mistreatment by his superior.

Such perpetrators of violence often see themselves as victims of injustice in the workplace. For example, Folger and Skarlicki (1998) suggested that interactional injustice (especially when perceived as a lack of interpersonal sensitivity) is partic-ularly important in predicting retaliation and aggression in the workplace. Before we discuss these manifestations, we need to understand the ideological underpin-nings of revenge in organizations. The current view of organizational revenge is biased: It is viewed as a destructive act committed by deviants and malcontents. Bies and Tripp (1998) discussed the ideological sources of this bias and the conse-quences of it for theory development and research on workplace revenge. When multiple actors involved in such incidents are considered—avenger, perpetrator, and bystander—revenge may be actually constructive. Their research offers ample evidence that avengers are often prosocially motivated, frequently effect positive outcomes, and consider multiple beneficiaries of their actions. This is in line with our premise that not all OMB manifestations are to be regarded as inherently dysfunctional to the organization.

Hostility, Aggression, and Violence

One of the main sources for assessing the extent to which organizational mem-bers are exposed to different forms of violence are surveys conducted yearly by the Society for Human Resource Management (SHRM) and the American Management Association (AMA). The cumulative data demonstrate how prevalent violence is in the workplace. For example, in 1993, the SHRM surveyed about 480 managers about violence in their companies. Seventy-five percent reported fistfights, 17 percent reported shootings, 7.5 percent stabbings, and 6.5 percent sexual assaults. One year later, the AMA found that of 500 general managers surveyed, about 10 percent reported fistfights and assault with weapons and 1 percent reported workplace rape (Denenberg & Braverman, 1999). Approximately two decades later, statistics have remained staggering. The 2011 SHRM survey indicated that of 267 organizations, 27 percent reported incidents of violence. Of these, about a third indicated that violence in the workplace affected employees in detrimental ways such as decreased morale, decreased sense of security, decreased trust among coworkers, and productivity deterioration (SHRM, 2011).

Today's complex organizations become an arena of not only productive behavior and individual excellence but also of enmity, hostility, and aggression. Although precise data concerning these attitudes and behaviors are not easily obtained, and because some of it highlights extreme forms of violent behavior such as homicide (Neuman & Baron, 1997), it appears that work-life has become more hazardous than before (Denenberg & Braverman, 1999). Human resource managers are increasingly expected to be familiar with the phenomenon and to offer diagnostic tools and interventions to cope with it. Literature on the violent workplace has become more available (e.g., Barling et al., 2009), as well as publications by government agencies such as the US Department of Justice (e.g., Bachman, 1994) and the US Department of Labor (2015).

Workplace violence became an important research issue in the last decade of the twentieth century and the first years of the new millennium. Incidents of work-related homicides often appeared in the media, citing emotional upheaval, stress, drugs, and layoffs as just a few of the factors that trigger such crises (Mantell, 1994). In the 1990s, incidences of workplace violence increased both in number and intensity and involve current and former employees as well as current and former customers. Some argued that one of the characteristics of modern society is that violence is moving from the streets to the workplace (Johnson & Indvik, 1994). It is not surprising that OB researchers' interest in these phenomena has been rising in recent years. A review of some of this conceptual and empirical work is presented next.

Many scholars of organizations (e.g., Greenberg & Barling, 1999; Johnson & Indvik, 1994; Martinko & Zellers, 1998) agree that aggression is more pervasive in modern organizations than it was in the second half of the twentieth century. Contemporary society is replete with examples of human aggression (individuals intentionally harming or injuring others). In less severe forms, it may involve verbal insults, sarcasm, spreading rumors, and withholding information—workplace incivility. The more extreme forms involve inflicting physical damage and causing workplace homicide (Neuman & Baron, 1997)—or as it came to be known following such incidents at the US postal service, *going postal*. This change may reflect cultural shifts within and outside organizations, which have coincided with economic and work environment upheavals of the latter part of the twentieth century. We believe external social pessimism has been matched by internal antagonism among individuals, groups, and subcultures, some of which is translated into hostile attitudes and aggressive behaviors.

Aggression in organizations can take many forms. It can be directed against the source of frustration either verbally or physically. It can also be directed covertly against a person; that is, an individual can secretly perform behaviors that can hurt another person. Aggression can also be directed against the organization. This organizational aggression, overt or covert, can be manifested as any behavior intended to harm the organization. Much of the recent treatment of workplace aggression emanates from Buss' (1961) classic typology discussed above. Neuman and Baron (1997) provide a comprehensive list of organizational acts of misbehavior organized according to Buss' typology. The examples included demonstrate the wide range of behaviors that can be construed as aggressive, some mild and passive (e.g., withholding pertinent feedback) and some extreme and active (e.g., inflicting bodily harm).

An extensive review of the organizational aggression literature led Beugré (1998) to conclude that, although many studies have underscored the multifaceted nature of workplace aggression, the vast body of research does not point to an integrative model of aggressive behaviors at work. He proposed that workplace aggression can be directed toward four targets: Superiors (upward aggression), peers (lateral aggression), subordinates (downward aggression), and the organization (systemic aggression). Beugré suggested an integrative model of workplace aggression that is much in line with our approach to OMB—that both misbehavior and behavior are products of the same forces. Beugré's (1998) model posits that workplace aggression stems from three sets of variables: (1) individual characteristics, including demographic variables (age, ethnicity, and gender), personality traits (negative affectivity, Type A behavior pattern, and the Big Five personality dimensions), and cognitive factors (hostile attribution bias and locus of control); (2) organizational factors, including socio-organizational dynamics (perceived fairness, organizational punishment, organizational frustration, and organizational stressors) and physical organizational environmental factors (lighting, temperature, and crowding); and (3) socio/cultural factors such as collectivism–individualism, power distance, and cross-cultural perceptions.

In a similar vein, by use of a cognitive appraisal perspective, Martinko and Zellars (1998) developed yet another conceptual framework for workplace violence and aggression. They suggested that numerous practitioner-oriented publications have documented concern about this issue and some practical suggestions have been offered, reflecting an increase in the number of violent and aggressive incidents perpetrated in the workplace. Their work places the extant empirical and conceptual literature relating to workplace violence and aggression within a social learning framework, emphasizing the individual cognitive appraisal as the key explanatory variable driving both affective reactions and aggressive behaviors. It offers valuable research propositions regarding the relationships among environmental variables, individual differences, attributions, emotions, and incidents of workplace aggression and violence.

Greenberg and Alge (1998) used an organizational justice perspective to explain workplace aggression. To them, aggressive acts are influenced by receiving unfavorable outcomes, as qualified by personal beliefs about the fairness of the procedures used to attain them. Aggressive reactions to unfair outcomes are believed to take more extreme forms of behavior, such as expressions of hostility, when unfair procedures (e.g., discrimination and favoritism) are used by the organization. The enactment of aggressive behavior, however, is moderated by the presence of various aggression-inducing and aggression-inhibiting psychological cognitions. These cognitions are considered primary when people focus on interpreting the fairness of what has already occurred (e.g., "Was it really unfair?") and secondary when people focus on deciding how to respond to unfairness that they already perceive (e.g., "Can I just forget about it?"). As a result, Greenberg and Alge advocate increased efforts at promoting justice in the workplace, which should serve as mechanisms for reducing workplace aggression. In other words, the more the organization is adamant about actually maintaining such systems, the more likely it is to be perceived by employees as a justice-prone workplace, and the better the chances that any intentions to act aggressively will be minimized.

A somewhat different approach was taken by Diamond (1997), who offered a psychoanalytic perspective of violence and aggression in the workplace, with particular focus on public sector organizations such as the postal service. Diamond posited that shame and injustice are at the core of the problem. Following a statistical summary of workplace violence and an overview of the relevant social and behavioral science research, Diamond provided a psychodynamic schema for analyzing the potential of violence at work. The model combines what he called a *toxic mix* of oppressive cultures and persecutory identities at work.

One particularly influential consequence of low organizational justice is frustration. Spector's (1978) important work on frustration in organizations promoted the plausible connection between the experience of frustration and the ensuing reactions of aggressive behavior. Behavioral reactions to organizational frustration (frustration occurs when an instigated goal response or expected behavioral sequence is interrupted or interdicted) include negative effects on job performance, absenteeism, turnover, organizational aggression, and interpersonal aggression. To the extent that these behaviors interfere with the organization's task, climate, or effectiveness, they may tangibly damage the organization. As such, they may be thought of as counterproductive, anti-role, antisocial, maladaptive, or dysfunctional behaviors. These behaviors may consist of attempts to find alternative paths to goal achievement, withdrawal from efforts to achieve organizational goals (turnover or absenteeism), interpersonal hostility or aggression, or organizational aggression.

A good example of this approach to the frustration–aggression connection is Fox and Spector's (1999) study, which investigated the situational, dispositional, and affective antecedents of counterproductive (i.e., aggressive) work behaviors. Fox and Spector treat any counterproductive behavior on the job as a form of aggression either against other persons or the organization, and they group together aggression, deviance, and counterproductive behavior. Frustration occurs when goal-oriented behavior is interrupted, foiled, or interdicted. When this takes place, the individual seeks ways to overcome this block. Organizational aggression is but one form of such behavior.

Fox and Spector (1999) collected data from 185 people from a variety of organizations. The dependent variable (aggressive behavior) consisted of four scales: (1) *minor organizational*, such as purposely wasting company materials or supplies, daydreaming rather than doing your work, or purposely doing your work incorrectly; (2) *serious organizational*, such as purposely littering or dirtying your work station or your employer's property or stealing something from work; (c) *minor personal*, such as failing to help a coworker or playing a practical joke on someone; and (d) *serious personal*, such as starting an argument with someone at work or being nasty to a fellow worker. A positive relationship was found between employees' experience of situational constraints (those events frustrating the achievement of organizational and personal goals, such as a dependence on untrained coworkers) and the behavioral responses (those personal and organizational aggressive acts). Most important, Fox and Spector clarified the role of felt frustration and dissatisfaction as affective reactions that mediate the relationship between event and act. They concluded that the initial tenet should be revised into a constraints–frustration–aggression model.

Finally, when it comes to analyzing and predicting organization-motivated aggressive behavior, O'Leary-Kelly et al.'s (1996) framework is at the forefront. Their review of the literature focuses on those aggressive actions and violent outcomes that are instigated by factors in the organization, which they termed *organization-motivated aggression* (OMA) and *organization-motivated violence* (OMV). O'Leary-Kelly and colleagues conceptually differentiated between the actions of an individual who attempts to physically injure a coworker (aggression) and the resulting injury to the coworker (violence). In formal terms, OMA is the attempted injurious or destructive behavior initiated by either an organizational insider or outsider that is instigated by some factors within the organizational context. OMV includes those significant negative effects on people or property that occur as a result of OMA. As intended activity on the job that seeks to inflict damage on others and to elements in the work setting, OMV is similar to OMB Type D. It may be instigated by individual, positional, or organizational factors and be motivated by either instrumental considerations (e.g., revenge) or normative beliefs (e.g., blind loyalty).

Bullying

Early research on workplace bullying is typically attributed to the work of the psychiatrist Heinz Leymann during the 1980s. Leymann borrowed the term *mobbing* from a Swedish physician who studied the destructive behavior of children in the schoolyard (Heinemann, 1972), and used it to describe one or a few individuals' systematic mistreatment of others in the same workplace (Einarsen et al., 2011; Leymann, 1996; Namie & Namie, 2009). During the early 1990s, the phrase *workplace bullying* was coined and popularized by the British journalist Andrea Adams, who contributed vastly to the widespread recognition of the phenomenon across the United Kingdom and co-authored the first book about bullying (see Adams & Crawford, 1992). During the mid-1990s, both terms—bullying and mobbing—became common in the European research community. Simultaneously, "public interest [in the issue] had spread from country to country" (Einarsen et al., 2011, p. 4), growing significantly among stakeholders such as organizations and trade unions (Agervold, 2007). Nonetheless, it was not until the late 1990s that the term *workplace bullying* was introduced in the United States (Yamada, 2008).

The most prominent American researchers of workplace bullying are Gary and Ruth Namie (Yamada, 2008). Namie and Namie (2004) describe Ruth's first encounter with bullying—a long period of time in which she endured constant harassment from her boss. Following this period, the couple decided to conjoin their disciplines of knowledge and previous experience as corporate counselors and founded the US anti-bullying movement. Namie and Namie's (2009) definition of workplace bullying is "unwanted, negative behavior unilaterally instigated by one or more perpetrators over a prolonged period of time, manifested as verbal and nonverbal behaviors or sabotaging tactics or a combination of all tactics that prevent the targeted persons from performing satisfactorily" (p. 203).

The Scandinavian approach, proposed by Ståle Einarsen—the head of the Bergen bullying research group in Norway—and associates (e.g., Hauge et al., 2009; Einarsen et al., 2011), defines bullying as a "situation in which one or more persons systematically and over a long period of time perceive themselves to be on the receiving end of negative treatment on the part of one or more persons, in a situation in which the person(s) exposed to the treatment have difficulty in defending themselves against this treatment" (Matthiesen & Einarsen, 2007, p. 735). In general, the European tradition has followed Leymann's conceptualization of bullying and its definitions are rather similar in nature (Keashly & Jagatic, 2003). The American literature is somewhat more fragmented and encompasses many definitions, such as workplace aggression (Neuman & Baron, 2005), emotional abuse (e.g., Keashly & Harvey, 2005), victimization (e.g., Aquino & Thau, 2009) and other terms such as workplace abuse, hostile behavior, and abusive supervision (Neall & Tuckey, 2014). Many of these terms usually refer to the general phenomenon of systematic mistreatment or harassment of an organizational member (Hauge et al., 2010; Neall & Tuckey, 2014).

In spite of scholars' different perspectives and definitions, there seems to be a consensus regarding several characteristics of bullying. First, it is a pattern of behavior, repetitive in nature, persistent, prolonged, and systematic (Baillien et al., 2014; Hauge et al., 2009; Harvey, 2009; Matthiesen & Einarsen, 2007; Namie & Namie, 2009; Vega & Comer, 2005). Second, it is always negative and mainly psychological/non-physical. Third, it is unwanted by the victim and characterized by an imbalanced power relationship whereby the targeted person is in an inferior position (Hauge et al., 2011; Privitera & Campbell, 2009). Last, bullying has a wide spectrum of consequences from the individual to the organizational level (e.g., Hauge et al., 2009; Salin, 2008).

To date, there is no definitive list of bullying behaviors (Nielsen & Einarsen, 2012), yet typical behaviors can be summarized as follows:

- Verbal abuse (Harvey et al., 2009; Hauge et al., 2009; Vega & Comer, 2005).
- Yelling or screaming (Yamada, 2008).
- Excessive, unjustified, and constant criticism (Salin, 2008; Vega & Comer, 2005).
- Gossiping, rumor spreading, slandering and social exclusion (Einarsen et al., 2009).
- Situating the employee as "the laughing stock of the department" (Nielsen & Einarsen, 2012, p. 310).
- Giving the "silent treatment" (Yamada, 2008).
- Accusations and public humiliation (Hauge et al., 2009).
- Threats and intimidations (Namie, 2007).
- Giving confusing and contradictory instructions and impossible deadlines, overloading with work, assigning meaningless tasks, or isolating from work activities (Vega & Comer, 2005).
- Undermining behavior or blocking promotions (Nielsen & Einarsen, 2012; Vega & Comer, 2005).
- Cyberbullying (Piotrowski, 2012; Privitera & Campbell, 2009).

Clearly, "bullying is not an everyday disagreement at work or the occasional loud argument, or simply having a bad day" (Yamada, 2008, p. 51) and yet it may originate from a coworker, a direct manager, or a subordinate. The organization's top management might also transgress rules of proper conduct and engage in bullying behaviors (Salin, 2008; Glambek et al., 2014). Hence, identifying the causes of bullying in the workplace is crucial. There are three main antecedents of bullying: (1) individual differences (perpetrator/target characteristics), (2) situational factors and work environments (e.g., Bowling & Beehr, 2006; Namie, 2007; Pilch & Turska, 2015). At the individual level, different personality variables may predict the likelihood of being a target of bullying, such as low levels of emotional stability and agreeableness; a tendency towards depression and anxiety; limited social skills and low self-esteem; insecurity, shame, and passiveness; poor performance rates or, alternately, being stigmatized as an overachiever (Matthiesen & Einarsen, 2007; O'Farrell & Nordstrom, 2013). Nonetheless, Namie and Namie (2004) maintain that perpetrators control all aspects of bullying, and that targets neither invite bullying nor seek to be abused – just as victims of sexual harassment or domestic violence do not generate their assaults.

At the situational level, interpersonal conflicts in the work-group may increase the likelihood of employees to become perpetrators (Hauge et al., 2009). Thus, an open process of negotiation during a work-group conflict might help restore and sustain respectful relationships among group members (Baillien et al., 2014). Moreover, it was found that fair and supportive leadership practices are negatively related to bullying at the departmental level (Hauge et al., 2011). At the organizational level, there are mixed findings. For example, it was found that employees who work in chaotic organizations—ones lacking transparency, accountability, and rules of proper conduct—are more likely to experience bullying (O'Farrell & Nordstrom, 2013). However, workers who perceive their employing organization to be a highly formalized place with a culture of rigidity might also be under increased risk of being bullied (Pilch & Turska, 2015). Other scholars argue that constant and rapid changes of organizational environments increase the likelihood of bullying to occur in the workplace (Harvey et. al, 2009). Therefore, a continuous effort is made by researchers and institutions to determine the phenomenon's magnitude across organizations in various countries.

Reports of the prevalence of bullying vary widely. In the US, the Workplace Bullying Institute (WBI, 2014) in partnership with the Zogby International Research Center surveyed 1,000 adult Americans and found that 27 percent of respondents were victims of bullying at work; 7 percent of them were being bullied at the time of the survey and 21 percent of the sample had witnessed bullying. Additional findings indicate that 56 percent of bullies are supervisors or managers, and in 61 percent of the cases, bullying stops only when the target loses his or her job (had been fired, forced out, or quit) (WBI, 2014). Prior to the 2014 WBI survey results, higher prevalence rates were reported in the US workforce. Wheeler, Halbesleben, and Shanine (2010) estimated a 50 percent prevalence rate of bullying among American employees and Schat, Frone, and Kelloway (2006) found a 41.4 percent prevalence rate in a 2,829 employee sample. Moreover, the previous Zogby survey (WBI, 2007) reported a 37 percent prevalence rate of bullied American employees based on a larger sample of 7,740 respondents (Namie & Namie, 2009).

In the European workforce, the prevalence of bullying has been estimated at between 9–15 percent, depending on cultural factors and operational definitions. In general, the rates vary from country to country. Agervold (2007), for example, conducted a study of 3,024 public-sector employees in Denmark and found a bullying prevalence rate of less than three percent. He compared these results to a study of a Swedish employees that indicated a bullying prevalence of 5 percent. In Norway, a sample of 2,539 employees reported a 6.8 percent estimate of workplace bullying (Nielsen et al., 2009). Rates in other countries vary as well; France 7.5–10 percent; Belgium 8–26 percent, Turkey 55 percent, etc. (see Nielsen et al., 2009, for an overview).

Addressing the issue more widely, Nielsen, Matthiesen, and Einarsen (2010) indicate how different measurement methods and sampling techniques contribute to the observed variation in prevalence rates of workplace bullying. Their meta-analysis indicates an average bullying rate of 14.6% across all studies, depending on measurement methods. Other variations emerge due to different sampling methods and the study's geographical area (as detailed above). Methodological issues may entail difficulties in determining the rate of bullying in work organizations, but one thing is certain: Workplace bullying exists and people and organizations face its consequences.

Since "bullies are cruelly inventive" (Namie, 2007, p. 45), they may use different technologies at work as a crafty path to target their victims (Privitera & Campbell, 2009). This phenomenon of *cyberbullying* in the workplace is defined as "inappropriate, unwanted social exchange behaviors initiated by a perpetrator via online or wireless communication technology and devices" (Piotrowski, 2012, p. 45). Victims of workplace cyberbullying may receive nefarious and humiliating e-mails, may be shouted at over the phone, and may be monitored excessively (Privitera & Campbell, 2009). Baruch (2005) found that of 649 employees, approximately 10 percent had experienced bullying through e-mail. This subtype of bullying and "shaming" is positively associated with undesired individual and organizational outcomes (i.e., intent to leave, absenteeism).

Workplace bullying is deleterious and ubiquitous. Many countries, therefore, have legislated, or are in the process of legislating, laws that provide protection for employees. Sweden has pioneered such advances with its anti-mobbing law.

It was followed by several European and Australian states, as well as Canada (Namie & Namie, 2009). In the United States there is currently no anti-bullying law, yet 31 legislators have introduced the Healthy Workplace Bill with the aim of counteracting bullying in workplaces (see The Healthy Workplace Bill, 2015; Yamada, 2004). This progression poses new challenges for organizations in their attempts to apply policies and sustain bullying-free environments (Salin, 2008).

Abusive Supervision

Over the past decade there has been an increased interest of the media (e.g., the recent film *Horrible Bosses*) and of academia (see Mackey et al., 2015) in the concept of 'bad bosses' (Hoobler & Hu, 2013). Much of the scholarly work focuses on the construct of *abusive supervision*, which was introduced and defined by Tepper (2000) as "subordinates' perceptions of the extent to which supervisors engage in the sustained display of hostile verbal and non-verbal behaviors, excluding physical contact" (p. 178). This definition entails several qualifying criteria that differentiate abusive supervision from other forms of supervisory and interpersonal mistreatment such as petty tyranny, victimization, and bullying (for an overview of related concepts see Schyns & Schilling, 2013). Abusive supervisory behavior is: (1) directed down the hierarchy, (2) non-physical, (3) sustained, (4) willful, yet (5) not necessarily intended to cause harm (Tepper, 2007). It is subordinates' subjective assessment (Tepper, 2007) of the extent to which their manager belittles and derogates their status, ridicules or humiliates them in the presence of others, gives them the "silent treatment," excludes them from group activities, invades their privacy, and avoids giving - or steals – credit for their work. Abusive supervision may also consist of behaviors such as angry outbursts, rudeness, undermining, withholding information, using non-contingent punishments, displaying little consideration, and coercing (Chan & McAllister, 2014; Neves, 2014; Tepper, 2000; Tepper et al., 2009; Xu et al., 2012).

Tepper's (2007) review suggests that early research on abusive supervision focused primarily on its consequences, including subordinates' work-related attitudes (i.e., job dissatisfaction, withdrawal behavior), low job performance ratings, psychological distress, subordinates' resistance behavior (i.e., refusal to perform supervisors' requests, problem drinking), and retaliatory behaviors. Moreover, studies typically considered two approaches to explain employee reactions to abusive supervision: The (in)justice perspective—in which employees perceive that they had been given an unfair treatment and react accordingly, or reactance theory—in which employees behave in different ways to regain a sense of personal control and autonomy as a result of their abuse (Mitchell & Ambrose, 2007). Other scholars draw heavily on social exchange theory—to explain subordinates' retribution patterns, and displaced aggression—to explain family and spousal consequences to abusive supervision (Carlson et al., 2012; Shoss et al., 2013).

Martinko, Harvey, Brees, and Mackey (2013) examined abusive supervision research published after Tepper's (2007) review, and found abusive supervision to be a rapidly growing field of inquiry; the number of studies published from 2008 to 2012 is three times as high as the number of publications released between 2000 and 2007. The flux of research may indicate a growing interest of scholars in expanding the field of abusive supervision. It may also represent a growing awareness for pervasive and miasmic workplace phenomena. Martinko et al.'s (2013) review indicates that subordinates' attitudes, attributions and perceptions, as well as situational moderators and organizational context, play a key role in the conceptualization of abusive supervision.

When employees attempt to determine the cause of their abuse, they make three types of attributions to their supervisors' behavior. First, they may perceive their supervisors to be mainly responsible for the abuse (external attribution). Second, they may believe that their own characteristics and behaviors led to the abusive treatment (internal attribution). Third, they may believe that no one else is treated poorly other than them (relational attribution). Each type of attribution generates different perceptual and behavioral paths. For example, external attributions are related to injustice perceptions, which in turn, are related to aggression directed toward one's supervisor (Burton et al., 2014).

The underlying processes that induce subordinates' reactions to abusive supervision were also examined by Chan and McAllister (2014). Their conceptual model suggests that when a subordinate perceives that he or she is being abused (moderated by individual, contextual, and relational factors) a state of paranoia evolves. First, extreme distrust, fear, anxiety, and threat-oriented emotions are evoked. Following this, paranoid cognitions such as hypervigilance, rumination, and sinister attribution tendencies are triggered. Having experienced paranoid arousal, employees may use coping strategies such as avoiding the supervisor, ingratiation, and following the supervisor. These potential reactions may prompt supervisors to increase their abuse, and ultimately exacerbate this vicious and pernicious cycle of abuse.

A reverse causal link was also reported in Lian, Ferris, Morrison, and Brown's (2013) study, whereby subordinates' deviant behaviors triggered supervisors to engage in abusive behaviors. Similar conceptions are documented in victimization studies indicating that provocative employees might signal supervisors to retaliate them (Lian et al., 2014). However, submissive employees might also trigger mistreatment from their supervisors (Lian et al., 2014), particularly those with low self-evaluations and low coworker support. This relationship was found to be stronger in post-downsized organizations, in which employees' vulnerability is higher (Neves, 2014). Overall, work environments character-ized by high uncertainty, stress and job insecurity may be breeding grounds for supervisory abuse.

In some cases, employees may hold the organization partly responsible for their being abused. When abusive supervisors are identified with the organiza-tion, employees may develop a belief that the organization cares little about their well-being and does not value their contribution. This, in turn, leads to lower per-formance levels, higher levels of production misbehavior (e.g., working slowly on purpose) and excessive criticism of the organization (Shoss et al., 2013).

Focusing on the perpetrator's perspective, Tepper, Moss, and Duffy (2011) examine how abusive supervisors perceive their victims, and whether these perceptions are associated with reports of abusive supervision by their sub-ordinates. Their model suggests that when supervisors perceive their subor-dinates to be dissimilar to them in terms of values and attitudes (deep-level dissimilarity), a perceived relationship conflict evokes and induces lower evalua-tions of subordinate performance. Consequently, unjustifiably low performance evaluations are associated with higher subordinates' reporting rates of abusive supervision. In addition, when supervisors experience a relationship conflict with their coworkers, subordinates with whom the supervisors have low quality LMX relationships are more likely to report abusive supervision. These subor-dinates display lower levels of work effort and organizational citizenship behav-ior (OCB) (Harris et al., 2011). The trickle-down process, whereby events or perceptions cascade to and from abusive supervision, resulting in negative indi-vidual and organizational outcomes, was aptly called the "kick the dog" phe-nomenon (Hoobler & Brass, 2006; Hoobler & Hu, 2013) which bears adverse implications for employees' family members as well. For instance, Hoobler and Hu's (2013) model of injustice and affect suggests that supervisors' percep-tion of interpersonal injustice is associated with increased levels of negative affect, which is positively related to subordinates' reports of abusive supervi-sion. Perceived abusive supervision, in turn, is positively related to subordinates' negative affect and to higher levels of work-family conflict, as reported by their family members.

A work–unit approach suggests that abusive supervisory behavior, experienced by either the employees themselves or by their coworkers, has detrimental effects on individual task performance and on helping behaviors in a workgroup, since it creates negative interpersonal dynamics not only between subordinates and supervisors, but also among peers (Peng et al., 2014). Similarly, personal experi-ence of abuse or belonging to a work unit with high levels of supervisory abuse is associated with higher reported rates of unethical acts and lower intentions to report other group members' ethical transgressions. This relationship is mediated by psychological states associated with low moral decision-making and low iden-tification with organizational values (Hannah et al., 2013).

Abusive supervision climate, defined as "the collective perceptions employees hold regarding abusive supervision in their work unit" (Priesemuth et al., 2014, p. 1513) is associated with social and task-related group outcomes. More specifically, the negative relationship between abusive supervision climate and group outcomes of OCB and cooperation is mediated through reduced identification with the workgroup. The negative relationship between abusive supervision climate and group performance is mediated through collective efficacy—a group's shared belief in its ability to perform its job tasks successfully.

Given that abusive supervision is "a reality of today's organizations" (Carlson et al., 2012, p. 849), one may wonder how employees survive in such hostile environments. Inevitably, employees use different coping strategies in their attempts to withstand destructive leadership. For instance, abusive supervision's effect on employees with high levels of social adaptability is less significant than its effect on employees with low levels of social adaptability, who experience more job tension, emotional exhaustion, and diminished job satisfaction (Mackey et al., 2013). Furthermore, employees' use of avoidance as a coping strategy, defined as mental or physical disengagement from the workplace, facilitates a negative relationship between abusive supervision and job performance (Nandkeolyar et al., 2014). Abusive supervision is also associated with employees' surface acting, defined as an attempt to hide emotions that are not considered acceptable to display on the job. Ultimately, when employees display surface acting they may experience higher levels of burnout (Carlson et al., 2012).

Organizations may benefit from selecting individuals with high levels of resilience (e.g., high adaptability, propensity for useful coping strategies; Mackey et al., 2013; Ong et al., 2006), yet supervisors should be sensitive to signs of employee distress (e.g., performance deterioration) that may exacerbate cycles of abuse (Chan & McAllister, 2014; Lian et al., 2013; Mackey et al., 2015). Most importantly, organizations should define high self-control as a key criterion when selecting individuals for supervisory/managerial positions. Finally, training supervisors in using their power and authority constructively (Lian et al., 2014), as well as promoting joint training programs for supervisors and subordinates, may facilitate and improve manager-employee relationships. Such trainings should therefore be embedded within organizations' human resource and career management practices (Mackey et al., 2015).

Workplace Sexual Harassment

In August 2002, the Academy of Management informed its thousands of members, academics and practitioners from around the world, about its credo (or code of ethics) in which it reiterates the commitment of its leadership and members to provide work environments free of sexual harassment and all forms of sexual intimidation and exploitation. Sexual harassment consists of unwelcome advances, requests for sexual favors, or physical conduct of a sexual nature. One of the inherent difficulties, of course, is to determine if a particular behavior is indeed a harassing one. Therefore, the credo specifies:

> The determination of what constitutes sexual harassment depends upon the specific facts and the context in which the conduct occurs. Sexual harassment takes many forms: Subtle and indirect or blatant and overt; conduct affecting an individual of the opposite or same sex; between peers or between individuals in a hierarchical relationship. Regardless of the intention of the actor, the key question is always whether the conduct is unwelcome to the individual to whom it is directed.
>
> (Academy of Management, 2002, p. 13)

Thus, the primary test in this case is not the intention of the perpetrator, but rather how the target *perceives* the specific behavior. This clearly exemplifies the difficulty in monitoring this type of OMB.

Flirting, bantering, and other sexual interactions are common in the workplace (Williams et al., 1999). Certainly not all social exchanges that have a sexual or romantic flavor constitute harassment or assault. Cleveland, Stockdale, and Murphy (2000) clearly differentiated between workplace romance and sexual harassment. *Consensual sexual relationships*, defined as those reflecting positive and autonomous expressions of workers' sexual desires, are also prevalent in the workplace. Nonetheless, our interest here is specifically on those overtures, gestures, contacts, and acts that defy organizational and societal codes of proper conduct and thus constitute harassment, bullying and abusive behaviors. As such, sexual harassment is a pervasive phenomenon in work organizations. Most American estimates indicate that 40–75 percent of women and 13–31 percent of men report some form of sexual harassment (e.g., Aggarwal & Gupta, 2000). According to Schneider, Swan, and Fitzgerald (1997), to cite just one credible source, close to 70 percent of female employees report that they had been objects of sexually harassing behavior in their workplaces. Estimates of the prevalence of sexual harassment in the workplace differ widely because of methodological issues such as sampled populations and industries, the way the concept is operationalized, and the retrospective timeframe specified (McDonald, 2012).

To a large extent, sexual harassment is regarded primarily as male misconduct. According to Welsh (1999), who took the legal perspective, regardless of gender, there are two forms of behavior which may be regarded as sexual harassment, and both are considered sexual discrimination: Quid pro quo harassment, involving sexual threats or bribery that are made conditional for key employment decisions (hiring, promotion, evaluation, and dismissal), and hostile environment harassment, involving acts that interfere with employees' ability to perform or are offensive to them, such as innuendo, lewd jokes, nasty comments, and physical contact. According to the definition set down by the Academy of Management code of ethics, an individual is considered to have been sexually harassed if he or she feels harassed, regardless of the legal definition (Academy of Management, 2002).

Sexual harassment is a relatively new concept. The term first appeared in a report Mary Rowe sent to the heads of MIT who went on to develop policies and procedures to curb it (Rowe, 1974). Around the same time, Lin Farley began teaching a course on Women and Work at Cornell University. She later termed the experiences described in her class "sexual harassment." Although she continued to hear it described by women from all walks of life, she discovered that the phenomenon of male harassment and intimidation of female workers had not yet been described in the literature and was not publicly recognized as a problem (Farley, 1978). In 1975, Lin Farley used the term publicly for the first time, as she testified before New York City Human Rights Commission Hearings on Women and Work. She defined sexual harassment as "unwanted sexual advances against women employees by male supervisors, bosses, foremen or managers" (1975). It was not until the 1990s that the phenomenon was acknowledged, and the term became widely known. This came about through the testimony of Anita Hill against a US Supreme Court nominee, Clarence Thompson. After her testimony in 1991, the number of reports of sexual harassment increased significantly and have been on the rise since (Bowers & Hook, 2002).

Systematic research on sexual harassment is still in its infancy (Welsh, 1999). Over the past 30 years, research has moved from prevalence studies to more sophisticated empirical and theoretical analyses of the causes and consequences of sexual harassment. For example, Cleveland and Kerst (1993) and Popovich and Warren (2010) examined the role of power in sexual harassment. Their review of the research suggests that the relationships among facets of power and types of sexual harassment are under-articulated. They viewed power as a multifaceted, multilevel construct. Men and women differ in both their use of power and their perceptions of power and powerlessness. Although power issues in sexual harassment have been discussed largely in the context of supervisory harassment, Cleveland and Kerst described the power concerns involved in both coworker and subordinate harassment. They concluded that to understand the role of power in sexual harassment, researchers need to consider the level of power, sources of power, context of the harassing situation, and reactions of the harassed victims.

Regarding the context that may give rise to sexual harassment in the workplace Rosabeth Moss Kanter (1977) argued that in firms in which males are a clear majority, working women are more visible and are more likely to be stereotyped and victimized. Studies have addressed the connection between gender representation in work organizations and sexual harassment. Kabat-Farr and Cortina (2014) found that underrepresentation of women in a workgroup led to the increased likelihood of gender harassment, but not necessarily sexual harassment. For men, underrepresentation did not increase the odds for either gender or sexual harassment.

Fitzgerald and her colleagues (1997a, 1997b) proposed and empirically tested an integrative model of sexual harassment in organizations. For them, both the organizational climate for sexual harassment and the job gender context are critical antecedents of harassment. The first variable taps the level of tolerance toward sexual harassment in an organization; the second variable assesses the gender ratio in a job class, as well as how recent women's entry is into the job class. The model proposes that sexual harassment consists of three facets: Gender harassment (crude expressions and offensive behavior), unwanted sexual attention (advances deemed unwanted and unreciprocated), and sexual coercion (quid pro quo harassment). It also proposes that perceived sexual harassment has negative consequences on job satisfaction and mental health, which in turn lead to withdrawal behavior.

The importance of organizational factors in predicting workplace sexual harassment was demonstrated by Willness et al. (2007), in their meta-analysis of 41 studies involving 70,000 respondents. They examined the manner in which a firm's organizational climate is perceived by its members, as well as the job gender context (composition of the workgroup, the ratio of males to females) and found that organizational climate and job context were both significantly related to sexual harassment. In organizations in which the tolerance for sexual harassment is low, as measured by the Organizational Tolerance for Sexual Harassment Inventory (OTSH; Fitzgerald et al, 1997a; Hulin et al., 1996), members believe that reporting harassment is risky, that those who complain will suffer for it, and that there will be no repercussions to perpetrators (O'Leary-Kelly, Bowes-Sperry, Bates, & Lean, 2009).

An integrative-interactive approach to sexual harassment as aggressive behavior was also employed by O'Leary-Kelly, Paetzold, and Griffin (2000b). Their model is interactive in that it elaborates on the effects of sexually harassing acts on the target's perceptions, motives, and behavioral response choice. They claimed that, quite surprisingly, researchers have given only scant attention to the study of sexual offenders. Therefore, they chose to present an actor-focused model of sexual harassment. In the model, which is based on interpersonal aggression research, the authors framed sexual harassment as one form of behavior an actor might choose for pursuing valued goals. That is, sexual harassment can serve a variety of goals, including emotional and self-presentational. To them, this type of behavior is goal-directed and chosen when it is believed to have a probability of success and low probability of punishment. Harassers are also influenced by moral intensity perceptions (O'Leary-Kelly & Bowes-Sperry, 2001). Moral intensity may be low when there is no social consensus regarding the act of harassment. If actors do not perceive sexual harassment to be an ethical issue, they will be more likely to engage in such behaviors.

Sexual harassment is viewed by many as counterproductive work behavior, akin to behaviors such as bullying, ethnic and racial harassment, verbal abuse, and other marginalizing behaviors. What sets it apart from other forms of abuse is that these behaviors may be excused by some as welcomed attention (Samuels, 2003). Wherever sexual harassment occurs, it is associated with additional dysfunctions. Reducing the occurrence of sexual harassment is not only a moral imperative; it is also the proper course management is beholden to pursue from a performance point of view. As Willness et al. (2007) show, increased incidents of sexual harassment may lead to decreased job satisfaction, decreased organizational commitment, work withdrawal behaviors, and decreased individual and workgroup productivity. Sexual harassment may also lead to physical as well as psychological symptoms; some victims may display effects of post-traumatic stress disorder.

Sexual harassment is also considered a workplace stressor with serious consequences for both individual members and their employing organizations. Empirical evidence from two organizations on job-related and psychological effects of sexual harassment in the workplace was presented by Schneider, Swan, and Fitzgerald (1997). Criticizing previous research, they argue that evidence regarding the outcomes of sexual harassment in the workplace has come mainly from self-selected samples and inadequate measures. They obtained sexual harassment data – experiences, coping responses, and job-related and psychological outcomes – from 447 private-sector employees and 300 university employees (all women). Discriminant statistical analyses indicate those women who had not been harassed and those who had experienced low, moderate, and high frequencies of harassment could be distinguished on the basis of both job-related and psychological outcomes. Overall, their results suggest that even relatively low-level but frequent types of sexual harassment can have significant negative consequences for working women.

Attitudes toward sexual harassment were examined in research conducted in Israel. By using in-depth, semi-structured interviews that permitted glimpses into rather personal and intimate experiences, Yanai (1998) found that most subjects encountered sexual advancements at work, although they had only seldom interpreted them as intentional harassment. Nonetheless, they were bothered by them and experienced concomitant negative emotions. Most of the victims tended to ignore the implications of the resultant feelings and tended to minimize the behavior of the harasser, including joking about the advances. Respondents tended to blame the harasser and his macho personality, as well as an organizational culture too tolerant of harassment.

Peled (2000) used questionnaires to ascertain the attitudes toward sexual harassment held by physicians and nurses in a large public hospital. Following the five-tier classification of sexual harassment (hints, seduction, bribery, coercion, and assault; see Fitzgerald et al., 1988), Peled asked subjects about their attitudes toward such acts and the frequency in which they take place in their departments. Her most striking finding was that, regardless of rank, position, and medical specialty, participants regarded all such acts as sexual harassment. However, some minor contextual differences did emerge: Women were stricter about any form of coercion than men were, nurses reported more harassment than physicians did, and smaller units (e.g., intensive care) displayed a more permissive attitude toward such behaviors. Such findings suggest that harassment on the job may be partially explained by work environment factors. This is consistent with Gutek's (1985) notions that work environments can indeed become sexualized (e.g., in male-dominated jobs) and that a sexualized ambience can strongly affect attitudes and behaviors. In addition, it supports findings reported by York (1989) who used a policy-capturing approach to ascertain the way organizational members conceive sexual harassment compared to its formal and legal definition. In that study, university equal employment officers were asked to judge 80 incidents of possible sexual harassment. Their inter-judge agreements as to what constituted harassment were indeed high, and they tended to agree on the type of action to be taken in such cases.

We cannot offer management a clear and universally accepted policy or procedures for minimizing the occurrence of sexual harassment in the workplace. Such policies differ across industries and cultures. There is no one best way (McCann, 2005). However, in large multinational firms, common elements such as a policy statement, a code of ethics, a grievance procedure, a sanctions policy, remedial measures, training and monitoring policies are beginning to emerge (McDonald, 2012). Fortunately, in many countries, workplace sexual harassment has come under the scrutiny of local and national laws, which make it unlawful and prosecutable. Both US state and federal laws protect employees from sexual harassment at work. Sexual harassment is a form of sex discrimination under Title VII of the Civil Rights Act of 1964. While Title VII is the base level for sexual harassment claims, states have sexual harassment laws that may be even stricter. In Israel, the 1988 Equal Employment Opportunity Law made it a crime for an employer to retaliate against an employee who had rejected sexual advances, and in 1998 the Israeli Sexual Harassment Law made such behavior illegal. The European Union Council and Parliament issued a directive making it a form of sex discrimination. The directive required all member states of the European Union to adopt laws on sexual harassment or amend existing laws to comply with its directive.

Organizations must do their utmost to curb these misbehaviors—not only because they face expensive legal charges, but because it strongly reflects on their standing as socially responsible agents of society. For a discussion of what types of interventions management can take to minimize interpersonal misbehaviors, see Chapter 11.

5

PRODUCTION AND POLITICAL MANIFESTATIONS

Many hands make light work!

— common knowledge about social loafing

In the previous chapter we discussed how individuals who engage in acts of misbehavior may harm themselves (e.g., by drinking or overworking) or abuse others (e.g., by manipulation or harassment) in their work setting. They may also choose to aim at their own job as well as the work of others. Furthermore, individuals may target the organization as a whole or any of its components—materially or symbolically. This chapter describes conceptual frameworks and empirical research dealing with work process misbehavior and the use of political means for promoting individual or group agendas. Again, we emphasize manifestations more than their causes. We also assume that such behaviors exist in all work organizations, albeit in different degrees of pervasiveness and intensity. We begin with what has been termed *counterproductive behavior* or *production deviance*. Then we delve into manifestations of misbehavior that are more political in nature. Figure 5.1 depicts such manifestations.

Counterproductive Behavior

Sackett and DeVore's (2001) review distinguishes between *counterproductive* behavior and *counterproductivity*. Counterproductive behavior is any intentional behavior that is deemed by the organization to run counter to its legitimate interests. This behavior is considered a facet of job performance. Counterproductivity refers to the outcomes of those counterproductive behaviors. Sackett and DeVore illustrated this distinction with the following example: Employees who intentionally

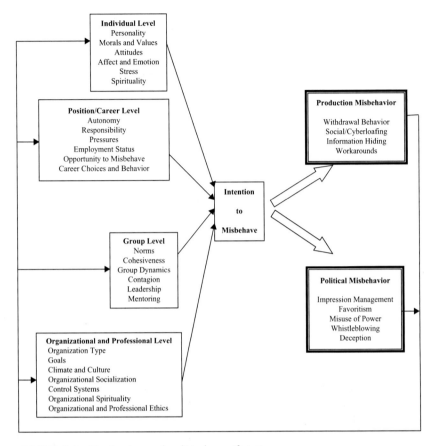

FIGURE 5.1 Production and political manifestations

ignore or violate safety regulations (regulations they know they should follow for their own protection and the protection of others) behave in a counterproductive way; the negative consequences that may arise from these behaviors—in this case, accidents and lost workdays—are regarded as counterproductivity. This definitional distinction has some merit but also poses some problems. Often, employees choose workarounds (Outmazgin & Soffer, 2013) to enhance their personal productivity or speed up their work while ignoring safety rules and regulations. In such cases, and if there are no clear negative consequences, the organization would not necessarily view this as counterproductive behavior or as counterproductivity.

Our approach is different. We suggest that a specific misbehavior be categorized as OMB if it violates the local core norms of behavior. Thus, regardless of the consequences, intentionally violating safety regulations constitutes OMB—in this case, OMB Type S—because the main motive is self-benefiting (i.e., higher earning, easier work). The difference between the two approaches is that we choose to focus on the actor's intention, whereas Sackett and DeVore take an organizational perspective.

Withdrawal Behavior

Behavioral violations at work were identified as production deviance by Hollinger and Clark (1983) because they interfere with local norms regarding work procedures and processes (sloppiness, low quality, slowdowns, and unjustified absence). Robinson and Bennett (1995) also treat work process misbehavior as production deviance (intentionally committed acts with the potential to harm the organization). In their four-type categorization, such behaviors are classified as minor and organization- (rather than person-) directed forms of misconduct. The most prevalent production-related misbehavior is the physical, as well as the psychological absence, or withdrawal from work. In human resource terms, we refer to these as *dysfunctional* lateness, absence, and turnover (we emphasize the term *dysfunctional* because certain withdrawal behaviors, e.g., turnover by unproductive employees ("deadwood"), may actually be regarded as desirable by the organization).

A thorough review of the literature on withdrawal from work (Johns, 2001) clearly indicates that a general construct of organizational withdrawal behavior does not yet exist, and thus it may still be more useful to distinguish between different expressions of withdrawal. There is no definite evidence indicating that lateness, absenteeism, and turnover are necessarily related behaviors. In some cases, employees who intend to quit may have high rates of absenteeism due to time spent on job searches or being psychologically less committed to the current workplace, whereas in other cases the intention to quit may lead employees to maintain regular work schedules and sustain good performance so as not to jeopardize their reputation and risk losing positive recommendations from superiors.

In certain organizations, especially where work arrangements are flexible and work processes are not sequentially dependent, lateness and absence may actually be quite acceptable. A good example of such units would be research and development settings that tolerate idiosyncratic work habits. Similarly, absenteeism is highly influenced by the social context. For example, group cohesiveness was found to be a major determinant of absenteeism rates (Gale, 1993; Johns, 1997). Organizational politics (discussed later) also play an important role in withdrawal behaviors, especially among employees whose relationship to the organization is not well-developed, such as new recruits.

Unjustified absence from work and excessive tardiness, if they run counter to organizational norms, regardless of their consequences, are indeed a form of production and work process-related OMB. The literature on withdrawal behavior in organizations is extensive, both in terms of conceptual models (e.g., Hanisch

& Hulin, 1991) and empirical analyses (e.g., Sagie, 1998). One clear conclusion from existing research is that it yields rather equivocal evidence for causes and consequences of withdrawal behavior. Simply put, the models, conceptualizations, and research into absenteeism and lateness offer little to further our understanding of the causal relationships or to increase our ability to predict these behaviors.

Withdrawal behavior, on the one hand, has been extensively documented and researched; on the other hand, relatively little is known about the intentions underlying the choice to be absent. In other words, we know withdrawal behavior is common; we do not know whether it is an intentional defiance of norms. Certainly, it is rarely intended to harm others or the organization. We believe it is most frequently a self-benefiting form of misconduct. Therefore, we chose to focus our attention on lesser-known forms of production-related misbehavior. Next, we explore the topics of social loafing, cyberloafing, knowledge hiding, and workarounds.

Social Loafing

Modern and humanistic management styles call for establishing various teams of workers in non-hierarchical organizational structures to psychologically empower workers and involve work teams in the processes of decision-making and production (see review by Guzzo & Dickson, 1996). Terms such as *product development teams, marketing teams, multidisciplinary teams, planning teams, project teams, ad hoc teams*, and *virtual teams* are fast becoming familiar to managers and workers alike. The prevalent view governing organizations' activities is that mutual learning and coordination and the team members' collective contribution to the final product's completion typify teamwork. Much emphasis is placed on the investigation of the qualities of the team and its contribution to the enrichment of workers' role and life. Teams have invariably been considered an asset (Blake & Mouton, 1964).

However, before deciding to redesign the workplace to allow for team empowerment, managers must also consider the quality and quantity of the collective output. For example, one needs to determine: (1) whether the team's output is in fact greater than the sum of individual members' inputs, and (2) whether the investment that members of the group are willing to contribute to the collective task is smaller, identical, or greater than that which they would otherwise make on their own. The importance of intrinsic and psychological needs of workers, partly satisfied by teamwork, should not be underestimated, and the actual output, productivity, and organizational efficiency should not be neglected.

Teamwork has many advantages, both from the point of view of workers and in terms of organizational efficiency. During the days of Frederick Winslow Taylor and scientific management, at the height of the efficiency craze that swept the United States in the first decades of the twentieth century, managers were thought to be capable of efficiently supervising 10–15 direct reports. Today it is clear that they can manage a much larger number of subordinates if the organization is properly structured, authority is delegated, and effective teamwork is facilitated. Moreover, enabling many groups to become self-managed grants the team members greater autonomy and opportunities to demonstrate their contributions to the organization. Modern communication and technology make it possible to distribute the tasks among individual workers and teams as never before. It is not unheard of to have a team of programmers work on a project in Silicon Valley during the day and go to sleep at night while another group of programmers, say in India, continues where their American counterparts left off. Therefore, it is not surprising that most research dealing with group work emphasizes such advantages. Human resource professionals and organizational consultants also stress the importance of teamwork in enhancing workers' role and their satisfaction, promoting solidarity among the workers and increasing organizational productivity.

Despite these organizational benefits, there is also a need to be aware of the difficulties within teams that may be detrimental to work processes. Through collective effort, teamwork may indeed ease the load and creatively enhance productivity. However, teamwork may also create conditions for certain individual members to exert less effort than they may otherwise. In the now classic experiments conducted by social psychologists at Ohio State University (Fleishman, 1953), *social loafing* was clearly evident. When subjects were asked to perform the simple tasks of hand-clapping and shouting, those in the group condition tended to decrease their individual efforts compared with when they performed them alone. The decrease in individual effort was interpreted by the researchers as loafing—a choice by an individual team member to reduce his or her individual contribution to the team's effort. These findings are consistent with the *Ringelmann effect*, which was first discovered by the French agricultural engineer Maximilien Ringelmann (1861–1931), and illustrates the inverse relationship that exists between the size of a group and the magnitude of each group member's individual contribution to the completion of a task. He found that when groups of coworkers pulled on a rope, their collective group performance was inferior to the sum of their abilities to pull it individually because some members of the team withhold effort (Kravitz & Martin, 1986; Latané et al., 1979).

A work team is characterized by ongoing interaction among its members to facilitate the attainment of a shared goal or execution of a collaborative project. That is, the emphasis shifts from individual to collaborative effort. Such effort calls for mutuality and full cooperation among the members, and the ability to contain and resolve personal and professional differences of opinion. The question, again, is whether all team members are willing and able to invest as much effort in the collective task as they would in an individual one. Will they feel committed to its success although they may not always be rewarded based on merit or effort? Are there workers who exploit their participation in a team? The answer to these questions is unclear because, unlike in a primary group (e.g., a family) where the relations constitute the aim of the group, the survival and success of a team are greatly dependent on members' belief that their participation is beneficial to them, more so than if they worked on their own. When this belief is lacking, the willingness of team members to contribute their relative share (sometimes more than their assigned share) to the success of the collective task diminishes.

OB researchers question whether, in fact, individuals working as a team experience full cooperation from their peers in the attainment of collective goals. Other possibilities do exist. Are they preoccupied with comparing their own efforts to those made by other participants and wonder whether they should make the effort while others may be loafing? Do team members really benefit from cross-fertilization and personal development, or are they more concerned about the manner of distribution of collective rewards? Should compensation be individually based or based solely on group membership?

Three main concepts used in the discussion and research of the phenomenon of withholding effort can be identified in the literature: *Shirking, social loafing,* and *free-riding.* Management scholars tend to treat them interchangeably. Researchers of organizational behavior recently suggested that it would be more productive to study the basic behavioral trait underlying all these concepts—namely, the propensity to withhold effort (e.g., Kidwell & Bennett, 1993). The distinction between these concepts is related to the cause or context of the occurrence of lack of cooperation or diminished effort. *Shirking,* usually defined by economists as an increase in an individual's tendency to invest less effort, may have a variety of causes such as lack of supervision, personal interest, and/or opportunism. The concept of *social loafing* is broader because it includes the social context. These processes may occur within the group framework because individual performance is less easily identifiable and the employee is less visible and identifiable in the crowd. *Free-riding* is usually defined as a passive reaction of individuals who want to benefit from the group but are unwilling to contribute their share of the costs. In this case, the individual makes a rational decision to withhold effort owing to the belief that even if the work is left to the others, he or she will enjoy the fruits of the final product (see Kidwell & Bennett, 1993).

The similarities among the three concepts—shirking, loafing, and free-riding—are evident: All stem from workers intentionally investing less than maximum effort, and they can be studied both experimentally and within the context of a work team, just as Ringelmann did in 1913. The distinction between them is mainly due to the researcher's specific point of view. For instance, economists tend to focus on shirking as an unproductive action, lowering the output of the group; social psychologists tend to relate to loafing within a social framework, stemming from the decreased likelihood of singling out the loafer; and sociologists emphasize the phenomenon of free-riding. Moreover, the models describing the phenomena of free-riding and shirking mostly use a rational analysis of cost-effectiveness to explain why workers avoid investing efforts. This emphasis led to neglect of social processes as probable contributive factors. However, many of the activities of teams working in organizations contain elements unexplainable by purely economic criteria: Accepted norms, behaviors and work patterns, feelings, and a sense of solidarity and esprit de corps develop among the group members, thus affecting their behavior in both positive and negative ways.

According to the rational choice approach, workers weigh the costs and benefits in material terms to maximize the gains accruing from their contribution. In this case, the workers adopt an effort level consistent with their belief that eventually the rewards will surpass their investment. Rational employees, in deciding whether to invest personal effort or avoid making it, will usually take into account such situational factors as the size of the group and whether the supervisor is able to discern the individuals' efforts or contributions to the task. They will consider to what extent they are dependent on the other group members in fulfilling the task, how dependent they are on this employment, and what the current conditions are of the labor market. The investment of effort is then a function of some or all of these factors (Knoke, 1990). Thus, in our framework, because social loafing is driven by instrumental considerations, it is regarded as a special case of OMB Type S (self-benefiting).

Unlike the economic approach, the normative approach maintains that individuals act in accordance with the values and social norms of the team. That is, if the norms relating to investment of effort, fairness, and distributive justice are high among the members of the group, they are more willing to invest effort and make individual contributions toward the attainment of collective output. Another approach, which attempts to explain why individuals contribute to collective activity in an organization, emphasizes the notion of emotional ties among team members. According to this approach, individuals' motivation to invest effort stems from their emotional ties with others in the team, and it increases as the group's identity develops. We return to the antecedents related to social loafing in Chapter 8.

Cyberloafing

Technology advances over the past few decades have been numerous and significant. Chief among them is the internet and its role in the conduct of business and the production of goods and services. And yet, alongside its many advantages, the internet is not without its downsides. Among other things, it provides employees with the ability to roam the globe, to pursue their various interests, including being in constant touch with family members, friends, brokers, etc. (Anandarajan, 2002). Employees surf the internet, regularly use private e-mail, access social media sites, as well as go shopping and job hunting on the web. Cyberloafing, also known as cyberslacking, is the term used to describe behavior by employees who use their organization's computing and internet resources for non-work-related activities during business hours. Cyberloafing includes activities such as internet browsing, online shopping and banking, social networking, e-mailing, and viewing online media such as YouTube or sporting events.

A *Forbes* article (Conner, 2012) reports that a majority of employees regularly spend significant amounts of time surfing the net on websites unrelated to work. Sixty-four percent do so every day. Of the younger members of the workforce, 73 percent of employees between the ages 18 and 35 report spending time inappropriately on the net at work on a daily basis. Lim and Chen (2012) cite several surveys that quantify the amount of time employees spend online for non-work purposes. The estimates they offer regarding American workers range from 61 percent of employees spending 24 percent of their work time surfing to 85 minutes per workday, to UK employees spending 40 percent (!) of their time cyberloafing. Lim and Chen (2012) found that when employees are asked to self-report their internet habits, the reported time spent is 51 minutes per workday.

The internet, then, has opened an avenue for employees to misbehave, to misuse company time by, among other things, cyberslacking. This is a form of production misbehavior. Lim (2002) argues that when employees perceive their work organization to be distributively, procedurally, and interactionally unjust, they will be more likely to cyberloaf. Cyberloafing, much like social loafing, meets the definition of a withdrawal behavior as cyberloafing reduces the amount of time an employee spends working to less than what is expected by the organization (Askew et al., 2014). As such, it is related to other withdrawal behaviors (absenteeism, tardiness, extended breaks, leaving early).

We feel it necessary to point out that although organizations are concerned with employees' productivity loss associated with cyberloafing activities, cyberloafing can serve as a way to cope with an unpleasant work environment and negative workplace experiences such as stress (e.g., Stanton, 2002; Oravec, 2002, 2004; Anandarajan & Simmers, 2005). Employees who are bored and stressed with their work are likely to cyberloaf to escape from mundane work (Anandarajan & Simmers, 2005). It may offer them a break, allowing them to refocus their attention on work demands. Such cyberloafing is likely to be beneficial as it allows employees to take an innocuous break from what otherwise would be a stressful environment. That is, some cyberloafing may indeed be a form of functional OMB.

Using evidence from experimental as well as survey data, Coker (2013) demonstrated that workplace internet leisure browsing (WILB) may have positive effects in restoring concentration and increasing vigilance, performance, and productivity, especially for the younger demographic in the workforce. Thus, whether cyberloafing results in gain or drain on work can be determined by understanding the context of employees' (mis)behavior (Lim & Chen, 2012).

Knowledge-Hiding

Organizational effectiveness relies on many contributing factors, of which the smooth flow of knowledge, knowhow, and information among members seems to be pivotal. Sharing these with no self-imposed restrictions seems essential in work-related exchanges between superiors and subordinates, as well as among peers. Yet, despite the efforts to enhance knowledge transfer in organizations by instilling values of trust and openness, success seems to be elusive. According to Connelly et al. (2012), it is becoming clear that in many instances employees are unwilling to share their knowledge even when organizational practices are designed to facilitate and encourage such transfer. They bring forth telling quotes from Schein (2004), which we would like to highlight as well, because they strongly support our view of OMB management. On one hand, learning "to withhold some versions of the truth is fundamental to the maintenance of the social order ... On the other hand, organizations have put enormous emphasis on 'openness,' 'information sharing,' 'knowledge management,' and 'telling it how it is' as part of a process of improving performance" (p. 261).

This illustrates the inherent tension between organizational values and practices of cooperation and mutual trust, and reality of embedded competition and distrust that exist as well. As Shulman (2007) has shown, deceptive behavior and deception learning are essential in organizations and in socialization processes. Knowingly withholding information from peers who may need it, and may depend on it, would fall under similar categories discussed here. While some writers (e.g., Takala & Urpilainen, 1999) view information-hiding not necessarily as an act of deception, we refer to these behaviors as OMB because they violate prevalent and basic organization norms of trust and sharing.

Connelly et al. (2012) conducted three studies to determine that knowledge-hiding does exist among employees. They also categorized the phenomenon and identified several interpersonal and organizational antecedents. They defined knowledge-hiding as an intentional attempt by an individual to withhold or conceal knowledge that has been requested by another person. Extending Pearson, Andersson, and Porath's (2004) conceptualization of incivility in organizations, Connelly and his colleagues mapped OMB manifestations in order to distinguish them from knowledge-sharing and hoarding, and relating them to knowledge-hiding. For them, the related manifestations are: Counterproductive work behaviors, harmful aggression, social undermining, incivility, and deception. Their empirical results suggest that knowledge-hiding is comprised of three related tactics: *Evasive hiding, rationalized hiding,* and *playing dumb.* These knowledge-hiding behaviors were related to interpersonal distrust, and to job and organizational predictors: Characteristics of the knowledge (complexity and task relatedness) and the knowledge-sharing climate.

As we suggested earlier, when it comes to work behaviors employees are as resourceful in adopting counterproductive forms of conduct as they are in adopting positive performance roles. A good example of this would be the three types of knowledge-hiding tactics mentioned above:

- *Evasive hiding* occurs when employees provide incorrect information or a misleading promise to give information in the future, while not intending to do so ("Told him/her that I would help him/her out later but stalled as much as possible," "Offered him/her some other information instead of what he/she really wanted").
- *Rationalized hiding* happens when the knowledge-hider offers a justification for failing to provide requested knowledge by either blaming another party or by just suggesting they are unable to provide it ("Told him/her that my boss would not let anyone share this knowledge," "Said that I would not answer his/her question").
- *Playing dumb* happens when the knowledge-hider pretends to be ignorant of the requested information ("Said that I did not know, even though I did," "Pretended I did not know what he/she was talking about").

Following Connelly and colleagues' research and drawing on social exchange theory (Blau, 1964) and Gouldner's (1960) norm of reciprocity, Cerne, Nerstad, Dysvik, and Skerlavaj (2014) conducted both field and experimental investigations to test the claim that interpersonal distrust may lead to knowledge-hiding, which, in turn, may start a reciprocal loop of distrust resulting in lowered creativity. They found sound support for their suggestion that "when a coworker is denied knowledge he or she needs to be creative, this person is likely to reciprocate by hiding knowledge from the initial knowledge hider. This behavior would successively impede the knowledge hider's creativity" (p. 186). Interestingly, they also found that when a mastery (or performance) climate exists, it can buffer the detrimental effects of knowledge-hiding on creativity. By implication, we can argue that this type of interpersonal OMB, which might negatively affect organizational effectiveness, if managed correctly (by for instance inducing a climate of performance motivation) may mitigate the potential damage caused by hiding knowledge.

A recent study by Kuchuk (2015) further elaborates this line of research in order to explore additional factors that may mitigate this dysfunctional form of misbehavior. Specifically, the study tested the hypotheses that personality traits—conscientiousness, agreeableness and honesty/humility—and some contextual variables as perceived by employees, such as organizational justice, will moderate the intentions to hide knowledge from peers. Kuchuk found that individuals with high scores on these personality traits are less likely to hide information. In addition, she found that justice perceptions also have a positive impact. Hence, in organizations where knowledge-sharing is highly important for efficient production or service, emphasis on these personality traits must be put in HRM employee selection, as a preventive measure. By the same token, improving interpersonal relationships and communication among peers (thereby enhancing perceptions of interactional justice), as a corrective measure, may also decrease the likelihood of such knowledge-hiding activities.

Workarounds

> For me, the first priority is to get the actual work done; following proce-
> dures is less important.
>
> (Anonymous employee)

Employees and managers may deliberately choose to ignore, circumvent or skip a work procedure for many reasons. Some could be positively motivated as to help a customer, cut red tape, speed up a service, and so on. Such work activities are known as business process workarounds (Outmazgin & Soffer, 2013). Workarounds are practical methods, often used temporarily, for achieving a task or goal when the regular method fails. In information technology settings, for instance, a workaround is applied to overcome programming, hardware, or communication problems. It can also be used by a conscientious service-giver to expedite a customer request. For example, in order to quicken the care, a nurse might administer a medicine to a patient in need, and only later fill out the necessary forms, all the while being fully cognizant of the hospital's rule that the form should be filled out, and approved, before administering the medication. Or, in a business environment, the merchandise distributor doing the morning round may first deliver the product to different sites in order to avoid traffic, and only later obtain customers' signatures. In both cases, the deliberate workaround, while not conforming to an organization-set rule or procedure, is goal-oriented without any intention to harm or inflict damage. Yet, in both scenarios, good intentions and non-compliant acts may backfire when things go wrong, when damage is done, and when losses are incurred.

According to Alter's (2014) conceptualization of workarounds, the term applies to cases when an employee perceives a specific (required) procedure as an obstacle and intentionally finds ways to work around it. Thus, workarounds, in general, are defined as any intentional deviation from preset strategies and procedures, intended to overcome an obstacle and promot some perceived goal (Alter, 2014; Poelmans, 1999). Such activities may be sporadic, on an ad hoc basis; some can become fairly prevalent and familiar to organization members. Some are viewed as harmless and opportunistic, some may be viewed as harmful. From an organizational perspective, such discretionary activities could be considered as non-compliance, as rule breaking, as counterproductive, because the procedures had been designed purposely, and installed, to facilitate standardized delivery of goods or services. Are workarounds manifestations of OMB? What would be the intentions of those who engage in them, of those who work around established procedures? Are they self-benefiting (OMB Type S)? Or organization-benefiting (OMB Type O)? Or perhaps sabotaging or inflicting harm (OMB Type D)?

Soffer, Outmazgin, and Tzafrir (2015) conducted an exploratory field study of business process workarounds, defined as intended defiance of required procedures in a business process. They applied and extended Vardi and Wiener's (1996) motivational OMB model to map and explain these behaviors both empirically and conceptually. Two principal questions led the investigation: How - and why - do employees engage in workarounds processes? Data were collected from five organizations representing different sectors and types: Documents pertaining to pre-set procedures (such as in purchasing and intake processes), system information, and interviews of managers and employees concerning local workarounds. Based on the data analysis, Soffer et al. (2015) derived several generic types of workarounds such as non-compliance to role definition, post hoc reporting and post factum information changes, and related them to both situational and motivational antecedents as posited in our OMB model (see Chapter 2). They concluded that, as their data indicate, workarounds persist over time and exist even in organizations where extensive managerial and disciplinary actions had been taken to prevent or curtail them. Apparently, strong underlying motivational forces exist in most organizations to fulfill job goals, forces that, perhaps inadvertently, facilitate business process workarounds as pervasive practices.

Political Manifestations

Whistleblowing

In the workplace, whistleblowing is an act undertaken by employees who decide to inform internal or external authorities, or members of the media, about illegal, unethical, or unacceptable practices. This is an extremely important issue because it can result in grave and sometimes tragic results for individuals who opt to blow the whistle, and may have serious consequences for organizations (Vinten, 1994). Vardi and Wiener (1996) viewed this phenomenon as a case of OMB because, in many settings, it may be considered by management a violation of core norms of duty and loyalty expected of members.

Blowing the whistle on the organization, or on specific members (e.g., superiors), would be considered OMB Type O if it is motivated by a strong sense of identification with organizational values and mission and, thus, by a genuine concern for the firm's well-being and success. However, acts of whistleblowing that are retaliatory and vengeful would be considered OMB Type D because they are intended to cause harm. Nonetheless, researchers suggest that whistleblowing is an act of good citizenship (Dworkin & Near, 1997) and should be encouraged and even rewarded. Proponents of this approach maintain that whistleblowers should be protected both by organizational sanctions and the law (Near & Miceli, 1995). Protection, they argue, is necessary because often the organization considers the whistleblower as an outcast—an employee who broke the ranks and who should be castigated.

In the US, two main laws deal with whistleblowing: (1) the Federal False Claims Act (FCA)—a cluster of laws that provide financial incentives for disclosure of wrongdoing, and (2) the Whistleblower Protection Act of 1989 (WPA)—a law that provides federal government employees protection from retaliation (Callahan & Dworkin, 2000). The WPA specifies:

> The purpose of this Act is to strengthen and improve protection for the rights of Federal employees, to prevent reprisals, and to help eliminate wrongdoing within the Government by (1) mandating that employees should not suffer adverse consequences as a result of prohibited personnel practices; and (2) establishing (A) that the primary role of the Office of Special Counsel is to protect employees, especially whistleblowers, from prohibited personnel practices; (B) that the Office of Special Counsel shall act in the interests of employees who seek assistance from the Office of Special Counsel; and (C) that while disciplining those who commit prohibited personnel practices may be used as a means by which to help accomplish that goal, the protection of individuals who are the subject of prohibited personnel practices remains the paramount consideration.
>
> (Library of Congress, 2015)

Whistleblowing is often viewed by some as misbehavior: Employers consider this practice as a subversive act and sometimes take vicious retaliatory steps against the perpetrators (Near & Miceli, 1986). Such employers may argue, for example, that even when instances of unethical behavior are discovered, they should be dealt with internally. In Near and Miceli's research, whistleblowers reported that they were more likely to suffer retaliation when they lacked the support of their superiors, when the reported incident was a serious matter, and when they used external channels to report the wrongdoing. Of course retaliation by the organization is even harsher if it is not highly dependent on the whistleblower, if the charges are deemed frivolous, or if there are no alternatives to the activity in question. We can clearly see a pattern of spiraling escalation of OMB: An improper act is committed in or by the organization, and a member decides to defy organizational norms of loyalty and discloses the wrongdoing to an external stakeholder. As a result, the organization commits further misbehavior by taking retaliatory actions against the whistleblower. Unquestionably, employees, more often than not, make critical career choices when they decide to blow the whistle on their employer.

Two of the most prominent researchers and writers on whistleblowing, Miceli and Near (1997), view whistleblowing as antisocial behavior. An early definition of *whistleblowing* is the disclosure by present or past employees of practices under the control of their employing organizations that they believe to be illegal, immoral, or illegitimate to persons or organizations believed capable of effecting action relevant to the disclosure (Near & Miceli, 1985). *Antisocial organizational behavior* is an act intentionally performed by a member of an organization directed toward an individual, group, or organization with the intent to cause harm. For whistleblowing to qualify as antisocial behavior according to this definition, it must be pursued with the intent to inflict damage or harm others. This behavior then is consistent with OMB Type D (Vardi & Wiener, 1996), and it is also regarded as an act of retaliation or revenge (Miceli & Near, 1997). We may expect that it is this type of whistleblowing that would be mostly met by reprisals or punitive action on the part of the employing organization. Such whistleblowers are considered to be dissidents rather than reformers raising a voice of concern and motivated primarily by pure intentions to help the organization improve itself (Near et al., 1993a). Moberg (1997) actually classified whistleblowing as a form of treason or betrayal.

The aptly titled volume, *Whistleblowing: Subversion or corporate citizenship?* (Vinten, 1994), accurately reflects the debate among scholars regarding the nature and moral justification of whistleblowing. Vinten provided a working definition for the act: "The unauthorized disclosure of information that an employee reasonably believes is evidence of the contravention of any law, rule or regulation, code of practice, or professional statement, or that involves mismanagement, corruption, abuse of authority, or danger to public or worker health and safety" (p. 5). Undoubtedly, there is a built-in asymmetry between the actor (the whistleblower) and the target (the organization). Thus, there is a greater need to protect the actor who, whether committing an act of citizenship or revenge, exposes wrongdoing, thereby contributing to the welfare of others often at great personal sacrifice. The organization, which is by far more powerful in every way, should accommodate this action, although at first it may be construed as misconduct or an act of disloyalty.

Organizational whistleblowing behavior is on the rise for the following reasons: First, shifts in the economy are closely related to the increase of more educated, more skilled, and more socially aware employees in the workforce. Second, the economy has become information intensive and data driven. Third, access to information and ease of disseminating it leads to whistleblowing as an unanticipated outcome of these shifts (Rothschild & Miethe, 1999). Furthermore, this type of disclosure by members represents a new and fast-growing form of employee resistance that can become quite costly for organizations, such as in the widely publicized case of exposing unethical addiction-producing practices in the tobacco industry.

Because of its nature, it is difficult to determine the prevalence of whistleblowing. Rothschild and Miethe (1999) provided some interesting information. Using a national sample of US working adults, they found that 37 percent of those surveyed observed some type of misconduct at work and that, of those, 62 percent blew the whistle. However, only 16 percent of the whistleblowers reported the misconduct to external stakeholders, whereas the vast majority elected to disclose the information only to the internal authorities. Rothschild and Miethe justifiably concluded that, when faced with clear incidents of organizational misconduct, the vast majority of members remain silent observers—only about 25 percent of the whistleblowers do so to external agents. Thus, in any organization, a sizable portion of employees are aware of, or at least have the potential of knowing about, substantial waste, fraud, and crime in the workplace. Whistleblowing is so unique and rare, and so likely to destroy careers, that when three persons did in fact blow the whistle in one year, all three were named *Time Magazine*'s Persons of the Year (Ashforth & Anand, 2003).

The dilemma facing the whistleblower was clear to De George (1986), who suggested three criteria for what he deemed morally justifiable whistleblowing: (1) the organization, left to its own devices, will inflict some damage on its employees or the public at large; (2) the wrongdoing should first be reported to an immediate superior, emphasizing the moral concern of the would-be whistleblower; and (3) if, after reporting the misconduct to superiors within the organization and exhausting internal procedures, the phenomenon persists and no action is taken, whistleblowing to external agents is regarded as good citizenship behavior.

A starker picture was portrayed by James (1984). He vividly and bleakly described the risks involved when employees choose to blow the whistle on their employers. His description supports the view that whistleblowing is considered an act of OMB by the organization. Whistleblowers almost always experience some form of retribution. In for-profit organizations, they are most likely fired. In addition, they are likely to be blacklisted and often leave their organization with damaging letters of recommendation. In not-for-profit organizations and public utilities, where management may not have the discretion to dismiss them, they are likely to be transferred, demoted, or denied promotions and bound to have their professional reputation shattered in the process. Worse yet, because employers perceive whistleblowers as a threat, they are often attacked on a personal basis, including threats to their families. Typically, they are branded and treated as traitors, receive negative publicity, and are framed as troublemakers, disgruntled employees, or publicity seekers. In short, we believe organizations do not go the distance against their own personnel unless they view their behavior as extremely damaging and a serious breach of acceptable behavior.

When faced with such high risks, two alternative propositions with regard to the motivational forces that affect an employee's decision to engage in this type of misbehavior (as viewed by the organization) should be evaluated. Somers and Casal (1994) suggested examining this issue from the commitment-behavior perspective. This allows for alternative propositions with regard to the expected relationship between organizational commitment and the propensity to blow the whistle. One alternative is that individuals who are highly committed (loyal) to their organization are less inclined to blow the whistle and thereby damage it. The second alternative is that committed employees identify strongly with their organization and are therefore more inclined to blow the whistle when they believe such an act benefits the organization. The results of the Somers and Casal study, drawn from about 600 management accountants, reveal an inverted-U relationship. Namely, individuals with moderate levels of organizational commitment are the most prone to act as whistleblowers.

Is the intention to blow the whistle predictable? An interesting attempt to answer this question empirically was reported by Ellis and Arieli (1999). Because of the unique military setting, in lieu of the term *whistleblowing*, the authors referred to this behavior as reporting administrative and disciplinary infractions. Conducted among male combat officers of the infantry of the Israel Defense Forces (IDF), the officers' conduct as information transmitters was assessed. Specifically, the researchers examined the extent to which organizational norms of conduct and individual attitudes toward these norms influence (predict) officers' decision to inform their superiors or remain silent and allow observed irregularities to go unchallenged. The military advocates reporting and promotes a culture that promulgates the need to and virtues of complete honesty and accountability; it also provides personnel with a number of official channels through which any individual can transmit such information. At the same time, the IDF also inculcates values of extreme loyalty to one's unit. Such strong values of loyalty often influence the intention to pass any information that might endanger the unit's reputation. Moreover, there are fairly strong social mechanisms in place that negatively sanction violation of such codes. Thus, any officer engaging in such conduct faces a dilemma between extreme feelings of loyalty to the unit and the moral obligation to divulge any knowledge of irregularity to the military authorities.

Using hypothetical scenarios, Ellis and Arieli (1999) tested assertions derived from Fishbein and Ajzen's (1975) reasoned action theory to predict officers' choice of conduct (see further discussion of the role of reasoned action in Chapter 7). It was expected that the intention to report would be predicted by the officer's attitude toward the act of reporting (a rational attitude based on instrumental considerations) and a strongly internalized norm of expected behavior (beliefs by significant others). Regression analyses indicate that the norms were stronger than the attitudes in accounting for whistleblowing. In simpler terms, this means that officers who intend to report irregularities do so because of strong identification with prevailing values.

In summary, social influence and organizational culture appear to be extremely important influences on whistleblowing behavior. For this type of job-related conduct to move from being considered as OMB to a normative form of conduct, it must first be integrated into the organization's value system and then become an essential part of the socialization process—of learning the ropes.

Deception

Two distinct forms of deceptive behavior in organizations can be identified: Personal and work-related. The former tends to produce deceptive behaviors that create energy in the organization and may be functional. The latter is a characteristic of power-acquisition behaviors designed to maintain an impression of rationality but they are really designed to cut corners to get things done or promote the well-being of one's own career or unit at others' expense. Viewing organizations as political environments, Schein (1979) examined the nature and function of deceptive behaviors. In particular, she stressed such concepts as the power-acquisition behaviors of individuals and the differential exhibition of these behaviors within high- and low-slack organizational systems. To Schein, deceptive behaviors are a function of three variables: The form of power-acquisition behaviors inherent in a given system, the potential benefits to the actors involved, and the potential benefits for the organization.

Machiavelli, while advising his prince, stressed the importance of deception in management. To him, the illusion of being honest, compassionate, and generous is important to gaining and maintaining power, but so is the necessity of breaking one's word, being cruel, and being parsimonious. Be a lion *and* a fox was his counsel.

Unquestionably, power-acquisition behaviors have many deceptive aspects. Deceptive behaviors are viewed as behaviors designed to present an illusion or false impression: Actions or appearances designed to present an illusion that belies the reality of the situation. Deception has more than one medium.

- *Communication*: May include false or partial information presented as full and accurate information.
- *Decision-making*: A manager may present an illusion of giving in to a demand when he or she was actually trying to gain something else.
- *Presentation of self*: Many managers exude confidence while masking a high level of uncertainty or insecurity.

David Shulman (2007), in his marvelous book *From hire to liar*, explored in depth what Vaughan (1999) described as "the dark side of organizations" but with a twist: Deception is actually functional and normal! The book relates the story of the under-organization where deception is as important to performance as organizational citizenship behavior (is OCB itself some subtle form of deceptive impression management?). Shulman anchors his exploratory investigation of the phenomenology of deception (from the actor's point of view) in the work of such leading scholars as Simmel, Goffman, Hochschild, and Granovetter, who had approached it from behavioral, dramaturgical, organizational, and economic perspectives. Of particular importance here are Goffman's seminal contributions. Goffman, with a keen eye for the less obvious facets of organizational behavior, regarded lies not as moral failings, but as routine requirements of social settings. In another odd twist of events, a controversy arose in the academic world regarding a researcher who is being blamed by her peers for publishing ethnographic work replete with misleading inaccuracies and what appears to be deceptive information. The scientist is Alice, Goffman's daughter (Goffman, 2014; see book review by Lubet, 2015).

Science magazine has just recently retracted an academic paper purporting to report that gay canvassers might cause opponents of same-sex marriage to change their stand against it (McNutt, 2015). The annual rate of retractions by academic journals, from 2001 to 2010, increased by a factor of 11 (Greineisen & Zhang, 2012). Fanelli's (2009) meta-analysis of retracted articles reports that about 2 percent of scientists admitted to having fabricated, falsified, or modified data or results at least once, and as many as a third confessed a variety of other questionable research practices. The apparent cause for such scientific and academic fraud—increased competition for academic jobs and research funding, combined with a "publish or perish" culture (Fanelli, 2011) as well as the autonomous nature of academic research with its lax (collegial) controls.

Shulman's book provides us with conceptual as well as anthropological-ethnographic tools to better understand how organizations accept deception, disseminate it, and institutionalize its dynamics so that when members join them, deception becomes a learned skill needed for survival and career success. On one hand, organizations depend on and require adherence to their role expectations as set by division of labor and responsibility. Thus, through various organizational socialization methods, mentoring and training processes, newcomers in particular, are educated about those expectations and are urged to adopt and internalize them. On the other hand, job realities, more often than not, require individuals to act as if they abide by and adhere to norm expectations, or behave "properly." Indeed, they *must* learn (e.g., Mars, 1982)—mostly through informal interactions, the skills necessary for pretending, for making the expected impression—how to manage in a world that demands an elaborate repertoire of deceptive acts and behaviors. In fact, one might add that deception too, albeit a wide array of job-related attitudes and behaviors, is just a part of the larger OMB arsenal of and a knack for unconventional (Analoui & Kakabadse, 1992) or political (Kacmar & Carlson, 1998) competencies new hires acquire as they are socialized into their work environment.

Early during his research, Shulman (2007) stumbled upon the notion that professionals lie when he realized that one of his subjects was deceiving him. This led him to investigate private detectives, whose job it is to discover the truth using techniques of deception as tools of their trade. After realizing that many "adversarial professions" (e.g., collection agents, insurance investigators, lawyers, law enforcement, military personnel, and public relations professionals) "incorporate morally contestable techniques, including deception, to accomplish their work" (p. 176), it was just a short leap to the realization that organization members, across the board, engage in some form of deceptive behavior, otherwise known as "impression management" (itself a deceptive construct, masking both intentional and unintentional acts of misleading others). Shulman then interviewed a sample of interns and employees from a variety of industries, from banking to entertainment, and found deception to be rampant. Shulman's conclusion is that organization members deceive themselves and others in order to survive in organizations: "Deception is a basic aspect of work" (p. 166). We tend to agree. However, we argue that being hired into an organization does not make one a liar, it requires that, in addition to developing positive work habits, one also needs to acquire or improve deception and lying skills.

Scholars, at times, exaggerate their arguments in order to publish, to increase their readership, and to advocate their claims. Publishers and editors use marketing deception to be competitive. We too, while trying our best to be professional, may have "sinned" just in the course of this treatise and used a bit of deception (for example, we stated that Shulman's is a "marvelous" book while thinking it is actually a "good" book), which leads us directly to the next topic: Impression management.

Impression Management

Consider the following scenario: Ron submitted his monthly report way behind schedule. It looked quite sloppy. To shift the blame from himself, Ron played down his own role in writing the report and placed the responsibility squarely on the shoulders of his new team members. He said that they were extremely unprofessional and uncooperative. He also implied that the computer program that they had installed failed to work properly. Based on this input (tardiness, sloppiness, and blame of peers and equipment), Ron's supervisor is now forming her judgment about this behavior. Moreover, she is going to follow this judgment with her own actions (feedback, evaluation, and sanctions). However, she should be aware that she might have been a target of deceptive impression management (IM) on Ron's part.

The study of IM in organizations is important in that self-representation may detract from or contribute to organizational effectiveness (Giacalone & Rosenfeld, 1991). IM by individuals in organizations consists of behaviors displayed by an employee with the purpose of controlling or manipulating the attributions and feelings formed of that person by others (Tedeschi & Reiss, 1981). It is defined as "any behavior that alters or maintains a person's image in the eyes of another and that has as its purpose the attainment of some valued goal" (Villanova & Bernardin, 1989, p. 299). Such behaviors, according to Gardner and Martinko (1998), may be regarded from the organization's perspective as dysfunctional IM. For example, Caldwell and O'Reilly (1982) studied the use of IM as a response to failure. They demonstrated that when confronted with failure, subjects may attempt to justify their position by manipulating the information that is presented to others. They also found that respondents who were more sensitive to social cues (known as *high self-monitors*) were more likely to engage in IM.

Erving Goffman identified the role of IM in management studies when he conceptualized this interpersonal phenomenon within his dramaturgical model of social life. Persons in social interaction, he posited, function as actors whose performances depend on the characteristics of both the situations and audiences at hand. The actors on life's stage strive to control the images and identities that they portray to relevant others to obtain desired end-states, be they social, psychological, or material. In this sense, IM is purposive and goal-directed presentation of self. It consists of strategic communications designed to establish, maintain, or protect desired identities.

Three key IM strategies—requests, accounts, and apologies—were observed by Goffman (1959). There are two types of accounts (statements that emphasize the role of certain personal or situational forces responsible for the failure): Excuses and justifications. Use of excuses typically entails an actor who recognizes that the act is improper but assigns responsibility to someone or something else. Justifications are made when a failing person attempts to convince others that although the act was inappropriate, certain conditions exist that justified it. Apologies or statements of remorse are viewed by Goffman as a gesture through which the individual splits him- or herself into two parts: One that is guilty of an offense and one that disassociates itself from the deceit. Apologies by a subordinate are usually expected to lead the manager to have lower expectations of future failures, thereby not necessitating close supervision. In addition, apologies imply remorse, which is a form of self-punishment or self-castigation. Thus, the apology lowers the likelihood of additional punishment.

To test the effects of subordinate IM on the appraisal and responses of a manager following an incident of poor performance, Wood and Mitchell (1981) conducted two classic experimental studies. Two common impression management tactics, *accounts* and *apologies*, were manipulated in each of the studies. On the basis of the discounting effect reported in attribution literature (Weiner, 1974), it was hypothesized that accounts of external causes for poor performance (excuses) would lead subjects—experienced nursing supervisors—to attribute less responsibility to the subordinate, be less personal in their responses, and be less punitive in their responses. Because of their equity restoration effects, apologies were expected to influence subjects' disciplinary responses to the poor performance without necessarily affecting their attributions of responsibility. Their data tend to support these hypotheses.

Similarly, another laboratory experiment (Wayne & Kacmar, 1991) was designed to tap the influence of subordinate IM on two aspects of the performance appraisal process: Supervisor rating of subordinate performance and supervisor verbal communication in a performance appraisal interview. It was hypothesized that subordinate IM would inflate performance ratings, and both

IM and objective performance would influence the supervisor's style of verbal communication during the interview. Subjects consisted of 96 undergraduate students who were assigned supervisory roles. Each subject interacted with a confederate subordinate who engaged in high- or low-level IM and performed at a high, average, or low level. Overall, the results support the positive influence of subordinate IM on performance ratings done by their superiors. In practical terms, this effect should be carefully considered when implementing any performance appraisal program in an organization.

A unique study of IM was reported by Becker and Martin (1995). The article's title piques one's interest: "Trying to look bad at work: Methods and motives for managing poor impressions in organizations." Drawing on the employment experiences of 162 individuals, the authors documented different forms of behavior such as purposely decreasing performance, playing dumb, or self-deprecating. Clearly, it is possible that people at times choose to intentionally look bad, inept, or unstable. Becker and Martin viewed intentionally looking bad at work as a form of IM, as self-handicapping behavior, whereby an employee purposely attempts to convey an unfavorable impression. For a behavior to be identified as such, the person engaging in the behavior must believe that a specific person or group will perceive the behavior as bad and the ultimate target of the behavior is that person or group.

It appears that the ways organizational members choose to create bad impressions of themselves are almost as varied as human nature. Becker and Martin generated the following classification to ascertain actual methods used at work:

- *Decrease performance*: Employees restrict productivity, make more mistakes than formerly, do low-quality work, or neglect to carry out their tasks.
- *Not working to full potential*: Employees feign ignorance of job knowledge or restrict quantity or quality of their work.
- *Withdrawal*: Employees engage in tardiness, faked illness, or unauthorized or long breaks.
- *Display of negative attitude*: Employees complain; act angry, upset, strange, or weird; or are hard to get along with or insubordinate.
- *Broadcast limitations*: Employees let others know of physical or health problems, errors, mistakes, or other personal limitations curtailing effective performance.

Bolino (1999) illustrated the consequences of dysfunctional effects of IM tactics by posing an intriguing question: Are members of organizations who are regarded as good citizens actually good at work or are they, in fact, good actors? Previous research on organizational citizenship behavior suggests that employees who engage in such behaviors are *good soldiers*, acting selflessly on behalf of their organizations (Organ, 1988). However, although such behaviors may indeed be innocent and even altruistic, they could also be manipulative and self-serving. This effect notwithstanding, we should consider that IM might actually lead organization members to engage in good citizenship behavior (Bolino, 1999).

More recently, Bolino, Kacmar, Turnley, and Gilstrap (2008) reviewed IM research published since 1988 and classified it into three levels of analysis:

1 *Individual-level IM*: This category consists of IM antecedents (e.g., self-esteem, job involvement), general evaluations that observers make about those who employ IM tactics, expressions of IM in selection processes and performance appraisals, and the effects of IM on career success.
2 *Organizational-level IM*: This category encompasses various IM tactics utilized by organizational representatives in order to influence others' perceptions of the organization (e.g., use of defensive IM in response to events that pose a threat to the organization's image).
3 *IM theories in organizational research*: This category refers to different IM motives, constructs and related concepts, such as feedback-seeking behavior, whistleblowing, OCB, professional image construction, and façades of conformity.

Subsequently, Bolino et al. (2008) suggested a typology of IM tactics. The first dimension entails an actor-versus-target perspective, and the second dimension—the goal of the tactic—entails four categories: To minimize (maximize) the perception of bad (good) in the target or the actor. For instance, if an actor seeks to minimize his or her good image, he or she may blur his or her connections with favorable others through strategic avoidance (blurring). Taking the target's perspective, if a person seeks to minimize his or her supervisor's positive impression of a coworker, he or she may explicitly help the coworker in an attempt to weaken his or her perceived abilities. Moreover, if a person strives to maximize his or her good image, he or she may use ingratiation tactics toward the target (e.g., supervisor), while intimidation tactics are used by actors who seek to establish a powerful and threatening position (maximizing bad). Given all of this, you will understand why we turn directly from IM to political behavior.

Political Behavior

Organizational scholars have pursued different avenues in their explorations of the intricacies of political action within work organizations. For most, the emphasis has been on the ways individuals and groups use power and influence in order to obtain desired resources. Some of the tactics actors choose are legitimate and are part and parcel of the normative system, and most are within the rules of the organization. At times, however, these tactics may be negative, manipulative, and exploitative. In this section, we explore those behaviors that are self-serving and manipulative and are not sanctioned by the organization. Such behaviors have many potentially negative consequences, including conflict and disharmony, which occur when elements in the organization are pitted against each other. The resultant work environments are typically replete with tension and hostility. Specifically, we explore both actual manifestations of organizational political behavior and the way political environments are perceived.

The nature of the organizational context offers numerous opportunities, rewards, and threats that provide individuals with circumstances and motives to manage the impressions that others form of them (by manipulating information, distorting facts, and withholding and filtering certain information; Fandt & Ferris, 1990). This formulation of IM is akin to the way we treat *organizational politics*, which has been defined as "opportunistic behavior engaged for the purpose of self-interest maximization" (Ferris & Kacmar, 1988, p. 4).

Research on organizational politics has dealt with the effectiveness of political behaviors, as well as on identifying the conditions under which employees behave opportunistically. Fandt and Ferris (1990) examined the effects of two situational conditions (accountability and ambiguity) and a personal characteristic (self-monitoring) on the management of information and impressions. They found that when accountability was high and ambiguity was low, there was greater use of defensive information and more emphasis on positive aspects of the decision than in any other condition.

From a theoretical standpoint, internal politics is all about the complex, often subtle forms of exercising power and influence in organizations. To examine the notion, Vigoda (1997) conducted a longitudinal investigation into organizational political behavior among public sector employees in Israel. He sought to ascertain the causes and consequences of employing political strategies on the job. Following the much-cited work of Mintzberg (1989) and Kipnis, Schmidt, and Wilkinson (1980), Vigoda viewed organizational politics as those intraorganizational influence tactics deliberately used by organization members to promote self-interests or organizational goals. He identified workplace behaviors that qualify as political strategies employees use to promote these interests:

- *Assertiveness*: Making demands, requests, and strict deadlines.
- *Ingratiation*: Satisfying the wants of others and making them feel important.
- *Rationality*: Planning ahead and using rational and logical arguments.
- *Sanctions*: Using protest, punishment, and negative feedback.
- *Exchange*: Tacitly bargaining for exchange of favors and mutual support.
- *Rank*: Pulling rank and position and appealing to higher-ranking superiors.
- *Blocking*: Putting obstacles in front of others and obstructing others' performance.
- *Coalition*: Obtaining the support of others against an organizational target.
- *Manipulation*: Controlling the flow of information, depriving others, and scanning.
- *Networking*: Developing informal social connections and recruiting supporters.

Analyzing close to 1,000 questionnaires collected at three different times, Vigoda (1997) found that: (1) men and highly educated employees tend to use these political tactics more extensively and frequently than women and less-educated employees; (2) use of political tactics is negatively related to job satisfaction and positively related to participation in decisions; (3) use of political tactics targeting subordinates and coworkers is much more than their use against superiors; and (4) managers use such tactics more frequently and more extensively than do non-managers.

Certainly, using political tactics to influence others is a legitimate and socially acceptable mode of behavior in work organizations. When such tactics involve the violation of core organizational or societal codes of proper conduct and acceptable human interaction, however, we regard them as OMB. Vigoda also found that employee perceptions of organizational politics were positively and significantly related to the intentions to quit and to misbehave. Interestingly, this measure of perceived organizational politics accounted for employees' job performance: The less employees perceived their work environment as political, the better was their performance (as appraised by their immediate supervisors).

We agree with Vigoda (1997) that although the measure of politics (the Perceptions of Organizational Politics Scale, adapted from Kacmar & Carlson, 1994) is limited to employee perceptions, the findings are valuable because individuals behave based on the way they perceive their environment. When employees feel strongly that the organization is characterized by favoritism, by a reward system not contingent on effort and performance, or that certain individuals or units always get things their way because nobody challenges their influence, they will act accordingly.

Generally speaking, organizations are social entities that, by their very nature, involve inherent struggles for resources and the use of different influence tactics by individuals and groups for obtaining them (Ackroyd & Thompson, 1999). In much the same vein, Ferris, Russ, and Fandt (1989) viewed organizational politics as behavior designed to maximize self-interest. When such behavior runs counter to organizational norms of proper conduct (e.g., peaceful, harmonious conflict resolution and compromise), we call it OMB Type S, because benefiting the person or group is the underlying motivation for the use of such political maneuvering.

Often, when employees are asked how they view organizational politics, they associate it with self-serving behavior, manipulation, subversive acts, defamation, and misuse of power and authority with no regard for others' welfare. Drory (1993) found that the negative effects of organizational politics are stronger for employees of lower status who are more vulnerable and more easily victimized by such manipulative behavior. Therefore, they exhibit more negative attitudes and behaviors toward the organization than higher-status employees.

Concluding Remarks

The view that organizations are actually political arenas, in a negative sense, was well articulated by Mintzberg (1983), who referred to organizational politics as individual or group behavior that is informal, ostensibly parochial, typically divisive, and, above all, illegitimate—sanctioned neither by formal authority, accepted ideology, nor certified expertise (although it may exploit any one of these). Other researchers such as Drory and Romm (1990) also viewed political behavior as self-serving activities that are contrary to organizational effectiveness designed to attain power at the expense of other stakeholders. Thus, when individuals resort to political tactics that are in violation of organizational codes of acceptable conduct, they clearly engage in acts of OMB. Moreover, when their work environment becomes too politically oriented or politicized, it may inadvertently become an arena for the kinds of manifestations of misconduct discussed here, such as social undermining and subversion, incivility and insult, and betrayal and revenge. The danger for the organization is not so much the existence of such conduct, some of it undoubtedly typifies any work organization, but in turning it into a way of life and making it normatively acceptable.

6

CORRUPTION, UNETHICAL ORGANIZATIONAL BEHAVIOR, AND PROPERTY MANIFESTATIONS

Malfeasance is usually just a matter of opportunity.

– Bliss and Aoki (1993)

Princeton pries into web site for Yale applicants
– headline in the *New York Times* (July 2002)

It should come as no surprise to those familiar with human nature and behavior patterns in the workplace that organizational members steal (take, pinch, borrow, lift, pilfer, filch, etc.) from their organizations almost any of their assets, material or intellectual. Employee theft is by far the most pervasive and intriguing form of OMB and one of the costliest (Cornwall, 1987; Greenberg, 1998). Employees at all levels take home some office supplies, misuse the office printer, return late from breaks, misuse computer time, falsify reimbursement requests, embezzle monies, cheat customers, and use a design idea for private business. We believe both employees and managers may not always be aware of the magnitude of theft around them and/or they may not always be willing to deal with it. By the same token, mainstream OB researchers have also shied away from including measures of theft in their field studies of workplace conduct and norms.

In addition to employee theft, we discuss other manifestations of misbehavior including corruption in organizations, cases of grand theft and fraud of enormous proportions, sabotage and vandalism, and we pay special attention to modern misbehavior such as data theft, cyberwars, piracy, and hacking. Figure 6.1 depicts the types of intentional property misbehavior we discuss in relation to the variety of possible antecedents that might account for them. In this chapter,

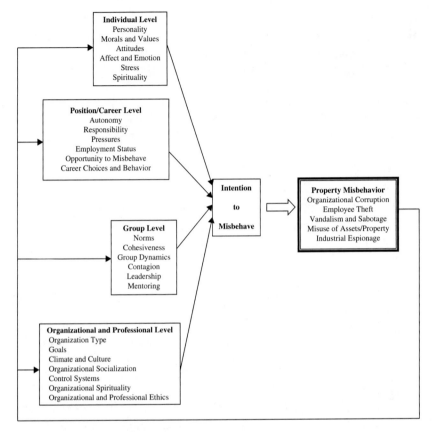

FIGURE 6.1 Property manifestations

the phenomenon (the behavior) is emphasized, and in Chapters 7, 8, and 9, some of its personal, positional, social, and organizational antecedents are explored. In Chapters 10 and 11, the focus shifts to measurement issues and overall managerial implications.

Physical Manifestations

As we begin to explore forms of OMB such as theft of organizational resources, we again approach the fine line between employee misconduct on the job and illegal, criminal activity. Although in managerial terms the distinction is important because it carries implications for formally dealing with specific cases of misconduct, from our theoretical perspective it is less crucial. Conceptually we regard theft, vandalism, corruption, or espionage as OMB when the act violates core organizational or societal rules. Thus, if a company specifies that using the company car for private use is not permitted, then its use may be regarded as OMB Type S if the purpose was to benefit from it.

Criminology is particularly helpful in clarifying some of the confusion in our domain. One such contribution is Clinard and Quinney's (1973) important work on criminal behavior. They posited that criminals differ by the type of crimes they commit, their social organization, their social background, their personal value system, and their self-image. They also developed a universal typology for criminal activity, which, over time, has gained prominence and support. It consists of eight categories arranged by degree of seriousness:

1   *Personal violence including some types of homicide*: In many cases, perpetrators are not criminals because they have no record, lead normal working lives, and identify with societal norms. Their crime is often a result of circumstances.

2   *Incidental property offenses*: Included are most individuals engaging in such acts as petty theft or vandalism of public property. These too would be considered crimes of circumstance.

3   *Occupational crime*: These are acts of theft, fraud, or embezzlement, ranging from a small business owner overcharging customers to a company's chief executive officer (CEO) who authorizes spurious accounting practices to deceive the authorities and investors and other stakeholders, or misuse of public funds.

4   *Political crimes*: These include actions that are politically or ideologically motivated. Many such activities are performed within formal institutions by individuals who strongly believe in what they do and what their organizations represent.

5   *Immoral crimes*: These acts are considered illegitimate as well as immoral because they may harm the public. For example, companies that conceal pertinent data about risk factors inherent in their products leave the public defenseless and exposed to danger.

6   *Conventional crimes*: This category consists of the typical crime activity (burglary, theft, and robbery) that is mostly carried out by career criminals. Such activity is often organized and planned, and in some cases involves acts of aggression and violence.

7   *Organized crime*: This is akin to any organizational activity because it is systematic, planned, coordinated, monitored, rewarded, and often competitive. It is also highly territorial and specialized and involves high levels of hidden networking, secrecy, and isolation from public scrutiny.

8   *Professional crime*: These include elite, professional, well-trained criminals who are regarded as real professionals. They are held in high esteem by criminals and authorities alike.

Organizational Corruption

Organizational corruption is defined as actions that violate organizational and or societal norms by misuse of organizational power or authority for personal or organizational gain (Aguilera & Vadera, 2008; Anand et al., 2004). That is, acts of organizational corruption run counter to societal or organizational norms, they are committed for the personal benefit of the actor, or for the gain of the subunit or the organization. The latter are classified as OMB Type O and the former as OMB Type S (Vardi & Wiener, 1992, 1996). While corruption is an abuse of office for personal or organizational gain, unethical behavior is "either illegal or morally unacceptable to the larger community" (Jones, 1991, p. 367). Corrupt acts within organizations do not happen in isolation. They require complicity of employees, who either go along with obviously unethical actions, or know about such acts but keep silent about them.

Corrupt acts include practices such as embezzlement and fraud—embezzlement is an act of deceit with the intent of illegally withholding entrusted assets without permission; fraud is an economic crime that involves deceit and personal gain—bribery, extortion, favoritism, nepotism, kickbacks, and the like. Luo (2005) argues that corruption is context-based—the political system and the social environment need to be examined in order to understand corruption. In general, corruption leads the corruptor to secure gains at significant public expense. Corruption is also power-based. The person committing the corrupt act is in a position of power that grants him or her discretionary authority. Because of its very nature, corruption is almost always covert. It is an informal, veiled system transforming benefits derived from one's role, power, and position to personal or organizational gain. It is a corrupt act as perceived by public and political authorities and therefore is dynamic and subject to changes in light of social and political ideologies. Anti-corruption laws in many societies have been changing to be in line with what is perceived to be ethically acceptable in the global economy (Luo, 2005).

Pinto, Leana, and Pil (2008) focus on two distinct dimensions of corruption in organizations. They seek to determine who is the primary beneficiary of the corrupt act and whether an individual or a group of actors undertake the act. At the individual level, one may expect to find a "bad apple" (Darley, 2005; Treviño & Youngblood, 1990), or one or more employees who personally engage in unethical behavior. The "bad apple" approach posits that seedy individuals, managers who typically score low on scales of moral development, self-worth and the like, and score relatively high on Machiavellianism and self-interest, commit corrupt acts. If, however, this "bad apple" type of behavior is rampant in the firm, it is more appropriate that the unit of analysis shifts from the individual or individuals, to the organization itself. It then becomes necessary to examine organizational phenomena—the "bad barrel"—that actually incentivize such behavior. These may include processes such as socialization, contagion mechanisms (see Chapter 8), as well as social identification defined as "the perception of oneness with or belongingness to some human aggregate" (Ashforth & Mael, 1989, p. 22).

Umphress and Bingham (2011) identify potentially unintended negative consequences of positive social exchange and organizational identification as unethical pro-organizational behavior. They define it to be "actions that are intended to promote the effective functioning of the organization or its members (e.g., leaders) and violate core societal values, mores, or standards of proper conduct" (p. 622). This definition is in line with what Vardi and Wiener (1996) termed OMB Type O. Ashforth and Mael (1989) define organization identification as an employee's sense and perception of belonging to and membership in his or her employing firm. Individuals who strongly identify with their organization, in order to benefit the firm's goals, may act in a corrupt and unethical manner and engage in OMB Type O, thereby overriding their own moral compass and value system.

A sense of unfairness may arise in workers who were confronted with an injustice or perceived inequity, which may give rise to distressing emotions. This sense of unfairness or injustice may spread throughout the workgroup and ultimately lead to organizational corruption (DeGoey, 2000). Williams and Dutton (1999) posit that emotions can permeate a social environment and actually characterize the organizational climate of a subunit or the whole firm. That is to say, emotions can, and do, diffuse throughout the workplace. In firms that place a premium on results, with senior management that places constant pressure on the "bottom line" and incentivizes results, one may find that subunits that are under-producing may engage in organizational corruption (Pinto et al., 2008).

Aguilera and Vadera (2008) also discuss corruption while using the organization as the unit of analysis. They posit that when employees are not mandated to follow ethical procedures, or if the organization lacks a set of uniform rules and regulations, workers may engage in procedural corruption. This occurs when there is dependence within groups or members of same status within the organization, and also when the firm's goals are clearly defined and hard to attain, while the means necessary to reach them are not clearly defined (Trice & Beyer, 1993). As more subunits use illegitimate means to achieve the goals set for them, the more the use of corrupt means to do so becomes the norm within the firm.

When corruption is present throughout the organization it is said to be schematic (Luo, 2005). That is, it occurs because of the simultaneous involvement of many levels of the firm in corrupt acts, and it happens repetitively. Howell and Shamir (2005) demonstrate that members of organizations with charismatic leaders behaving in response to collectivist motives are more likely to show blind faith in their leadership. Employees may engage in illicit activities due to their unquestioning belief in the leader and their assumption that it will benefit the organization. Leaders who implicitly approve corrupt behavior, even if they do not engage in illicit behaviors themselves, may encourage immorality in organizations. Leaders serve as role models for their workers; they model what is acceptable and what is not. By rewarding questionable practices, by holding employees accountable for performance goals but not for the manner in which they were attained, leaders may condone and actually foster corrupt practices.

The fact that an illicit act is repeated in the workplace is self-reinforcing. The past success of corrupt practices acts to validate them. Their resulting benefits become habit-forming and the organization comes to expect them and grow dependent on them. Its growing frequency makes it seem the norm and it becomes part and parcel of the organizational culture. Treviño et al. (2014) demonstrated that culture plays a significant and important role in determining ethical behavior. Culture impacts the way in which members perceive and interpret events and shapes their attitudes and behaviors (Kunda, 1992, 2006). Corrupt behavior is fostered when the organizational culture favors unethical norms and instills notions of amorality (McKenna, 1996). Amoral cultures are ones that do not encourage ethical behaviors, cultures in which illicit behavior may be implicitly or explicitly accepted. In organizations in which rules, procedures, directives, or suggestions from senior management are unethical or ethically ambiguous, corrupt acts are likely to be accepted and condoned and thereby become the organizational norm.

Corruption may be due to the environment in which the firm operates. For example, in some societies, the only way to do business is to engage in the illegal practice of bribery. In such a situation, the firm faces a stark choice, either to join in, as do other firms, or to exit the field altogether. In some global firms consisting of subsidiaries around the world, corruption may be found only in those business units located in countries in which unethical practices are the norm, the only way to conduct business. Such incidents of organizational corruption may be localized only to those subsidiaries. If and when such corruption is exposed, it may be that only the subunit will be vilified by the firm's home society and by the parent organization. That is, corporate headquarters may actually disown the corrupt subunit to protect the whole firm. Aguilera and Vadera (2008) call this *categorical corruption* and posit that senior management can actually keep this type of corruption in check, and that it is not, in this sense, contagious.

An intriguing issue raised by Darley (2005) is why are corrupt acts taking place in organizations that, we could safely assume, are staffed by decent moral people who are also rational and prudent enough to know that illicit acts are frequently detected. Darley argues that the "bad apples" approach is incorrect, and may even be damaging in that it allows researchers and senior managers to ignore wide-ranging effects of corruption. Screening out the occasional "bad apple" by putting in place better screening procedures and investing in more sophisticated training is much less taxing to the firm than thoroughly examining a system otherwise taken to be near perfect. Whether ethical decisions are undertaken depends on whether events trigger a person's reasoning system to generate an ethical check on courses of action that are generated from decision-makers' more intuitive perspectives. Many of the actions that begin cycles of corruption are products of intuitive judgments and, because of pressures to make fast decisions, are rapidly arrived at, without enough consideration for their legitimacy or morality. That is, they are not always subject to monitoring by our reasoning and rational system. A natural, intuitive decision may be a self-serving one, and an unethical one.

A corrupt action committed in an organization, if not criticized and labeled as such, may become the norm. While many, or even most of the employees may deem the act unethical and wrong, because of issues such as job (in)security, respect or fear of authority, they may opt to keep silent about it. One of the most famous examples of this mechanism is demonstrated by Hans Christian Andersen's (1837) fairy tale "The emperor's new clothes." He writes of a whole town fearing to talk of an unethical act out of dread that they would stand out, believing nobody else could see what they saw. Two strangers come to the emperor's kingdom and convince him that they will make for him the finest of all clothes, which can only be seen by those who are not stupid. All the while the two rob the kingdom blind... for the emperor's clothes. All the townspeople keep silent, and say nothing of the fact that they cannot see the clothes and that the emperor is naked. Only when a small child comes forth and says that the emperor is walking around naked the townspeople come forward and admit that the emperor has been tricked and that there was never an outfit being made. Allport (1924) termed this phenomenon *pluralistic ignorance*—a situation in which virtually all group members privately reject a particular group norm but believe that all others accept it.

Pluralistic ignorance may in fact explain that when an employee commits a corrupt act, if those around him are silent about it, the employee may conclude that that very act is an acceptable one and that is why no one says anything about it. This, then, may become the norm for what is acceptable in the organization. Tenbrunsel and Messick (2004) posit that past practices of the firm become a benchmark by which to judge new practices. If prior ones were deemed legitimate and ethical, similar practices are acceptable as well. And now we can start to understand how the workgroup begins to regard otherwise unethical acts as acceptable, and to gradually and incrementally become desensitized to corrupt acts without being aware of the unethicality of their new routines.

If, however, an unethical act has been committed and other employees in the workgroup in fact deem it as corrupt, the employee now needs to decide how to proceed. Since the act cannot be undone, the employee is faced with a decision—to either blow the whistle or let this course of corrupt action continue. Because of feelings of loyalty to the decision-maker, or the focal workgroup, or to other members of the organization, one may even assist in the perpetuation of such illicit actions. If the employee has become, over time, a committed member of the workgroup, it becomes his or her duty to help the group achieve its goals and to adopt the group's ethical and moral standards, even if they run counter to his or her own personal values (Abrams & Hogg, 1990).

Scholars make the case that corrupt and unethical acts in the workplace are typically committed by normative, upstanding members of the community (Darley, 2005; Ashforth & Anand, 2003; Anand et al., 2004; Ashforth et al., 2008) and seek to explain how it is that such upstanding folks engage in illicit and illegal activities at work. Ashforth and his colleagues make the case that individuals who engage in what the larger community views as corrupt acts—in what society deems to be corrupt—may view themselves as ethical within the context of the workplace. They posit that these employees use rationalization and socialization tactics to excuse their actions and thereby view themselves as not being corrupt. Rationalizations may be resorted to before committing the corrupt act, or after the fact to relieve guilt and misgivings (Staw, 1980). Rationalization not only eases the conscience but also acts to help categorize future unethical behavior as proper and acceptable.

Rationalization is an active self-justifying intensification of belief in an attempt to defend oneself against the implications of disconfirming information (Batson, 1975). In other words, rationalization is a defense mechanism employed by individuals in which controversial behaviors or feelings are justified and explained in a seemingly rational or logical manner to avoid the true and factual explanation, and are made consciously tolerable by plausible means. Rationalizations tend to account for lapses from normative behavior, thereby demonstrating the acceptance of organizational and societal norms of behavior. Pioneering work on rationalization, or techniques for justifying clearly criminal behavior, was done by Sykes and Matza (1957a, 1957b). They argue that humans are rational beings, and when we transgress, for whatever reason, we seek to justify our behavior, to neutralize our potential guilt. Copes (2003) has noted that for techniques of neutralization and rationalization to be applicable, it is first necessary for individuals to believe that there is something wrong with their behavior.

The way to deal with delinquent behavior, argue Sykes and Matza (1957a, 1957b), is to rationalize the behavior by means of neutralization techniques. They suggested five such means. The first technique is the denial of responsibility. Individuals who applied this technique of neutralization refused to accept responsibility for their actions. This denial goes beyond an initial belief that the behavior was the result of an accident, and extends into a belief that factors beyond their control were responsible for their behavior. For example, peer pressure, senior management orders, precedent, or financial pressures.

The second technique is the denial of injury; this is related to a belief that there was no injury or harm caused to anyone affected by the corrupt behavior. Further, if there was any harm then it was negated by the fact that the victim could afford the injury, and was therefore not an injury in the truest sense. For example, an employee who steals office supplies could justify, neutralize, his actions by saying that their monetary value is negligible to the firm. Greenberg (1998) showed that if the firm does not punish employees who steal from it, they effectively reinforce the belief that it is OK to do so.

The third technique of neutralization, the denial of victim, extends this concept. If there was a victim to the crime, it is justified because the victim was deserving of punishment or retaliation. The victim, the organization for example, actually deserves its fate because of its wrongdoing. The corrupt act may be viewed as revenge for unfair treatment by employers (Hollinger & Clark, 1983).

The fourth technique of neutralization was termed by Sykes and Matza (1957b) as the *condemnation of the condemners*. In this case, the individual is clearly aware that the act chosen is corrupt, but let themselves off the hook by accusing the condemner, by justifying the behavior on the basis that those who were victimized were not real victims because they were hypocrites, or that the victims would have engaged in the same activities if they were provided with the opportunity. This may stem from a rejection of the firm's rules and procedures, or considering a bothersome law as being vague or simply wrong.

The fifth technique of neutralization is the appeal to higher loyalties or superordination. This technique of neutralization is often applied when an individual recognizes that perhaps an act was inappropriate but justifies the behavior on the grounds that their immediate workgroup or the firm needed their behavior at the time. Employees may justify wrongfully using company funds by arguing that they were helping those in dire need (Sykes & Matza, 1957a, 1957b).

Subsequent research projects developed five additional techniques of neutralization. Klockars (1974) proposed the metaphor of the *ledger technique*, which is used when an individual argues that the unethical behavior was acceptable because the person is a morally decent one, and has a track record of continuously doing good deeds. In other words, they developed a reserve of good deeds that overshadowed their one corrupt one. Coleman (1994) suggested three techniques of neutralization: The denial of the necessity of the law, the claim that everybody else is doing it, and the claim of entitlement. The denial of the necessity of the law argues that the law has nothing to do with the greater good of people. As a result, the law is perceived to be inappropriate and therefore it is not necessary to obey it. The claim that everybody else is doing it is one often used when individuals feel that there is so much disrespect for a law that the general consensus is that the law is nullified or deemed to be unimportant. The claim of entitlement is used by individuals who feel that they are entitled to engage in an activity because of some unique consideration in their life (Coleman, 1994) or special status in society. Minor (1981) suggested a different technique - the defense of necessity - which means that while the behavior may be inappropriate, it is also necessary in order to prevent an even greater or harsher corrupt act from taking place.

Employees have at their disposal a series of rational strategies to choose from to cognitively justify their misbehavior. Neutralization and rationalization techniques play an extremely important role in helping individuals to engage in corrupt acts, to misbehave, to engage in wrongdoing or unethical behavior at work, in spite of the great expense and intensive effort of organizations to curtail OMB.

A Framework for Unethical Managerial Behavior

The ethical dilemmas facing managers are well elucidated by Ferrell and Fraedrich (1994). They viewed ethical dilemmas as situations, problems, or opportunities that demand that the manager choose among alternatives evaluated in moral terms of good or bad and correct or wrong. Hosmer (1991) viewed the conflict between economic goals and human concerns as ethical dilemmas, and Treviño and Nelson (1994) focused on conflicts among basic values as the source of ethical dilemmas. According to Toffler (1986), managers face three major issues that create moral dilemmas for them: Human resource issues make up 67 percent of these dilemmas, 27 percent are related to suppliers and customers, and, to a much lesser degree, 6 percent are pressures from superiors to act in ways that are contrary to one's personal values.

In many cases, managers must choose between different modes of operation. Sometimes the choice is between ethical and unethical solutions. If the choice is clear-cut from a moral standpoint, there may not be an ethical dilemma. A manager faces a dilemma when he or she is confronted by two ethically acceptable solutions—when the implementation of one could benefit some but cause harm to others. This type of dilemma is surely exacerbated when the needs of varied stakeholders are in conflict. For example, managers who debate whether they should divulge information concerning certain shortcomings of a product may be pressured by their own values (concern for the safety of the public), on the one hand, and by the interests of the stockholders or other managers in the company (dividends, profit, and market share), on the other.

Treviño and Nelson (1994) defined *business ethics* as behavior based on principles, norms, and business standards about which society is in agreement. Brummer (1985) viewed the discussion of ethics at two levels. Dilemmas on the micro-level focus on conflicts between the person's job demands and the person's moral judgment and values—workers' loyalty to the organization and management versus their conscience, values, and principles. At the macro-level, most dilemmas pertain to matters of strategy and organization policy. Petrick, Wagly, and Thomas (1991) also dealt with the concept of ethics in business. They suggested introducing the philosophical level in addition to the micro- and macro-levels. The micro-level deals with individual and interpersonal issues regarding ethical dilemmas whereas macro-level issues involve businesses, markets, and publics. Such issues as the definition and dimensions of morality and moral principles are debated at the meta-philosophical level.

Three historical approaches to business ethics were reviewed by Bowie and Dunka (1990). The early approach (e.g., Carr, 1968) argues that there is no such thing as business ethics—business profit is clearly the name of the game, moral standards are immaterial. The second approach (e.g., Carroll, 1978; Friedman, 1970) posits that, although the ultimate goal of a business organization is profit maximization, the firm must go about its business ethically and morally. In fact, the welfare of society and the success of a business are not in conflict, but ultimately go hand in hand. Thus, managers should exercise ethical judgment when making organizational decisions, taking into account the needs of the firm and the public as well. A more recent approach—the stakeholder approach—goes one step further (see Freeman & Gilbert, 1988), arguing that the consideration is not only sufficient, but is a necessary condition for business success. For instance, Allinson (1998) suggested that ethics and ethical considerations are an integral element of business. They should be regarded as a contributing rather than a constraining factor ("Good ethics is good business"). Therefore, this approach puts ethics at the core of management and managerial decision-making processes (Green, 1994; Welch, 1997). We thus consider unethical managerial conduct as a special case of OMB because, when committed, it violates a clear-cut norm of what is right and what is wrong.

Models of Ethical Decision-Making

Making strategic and tactical decisions is the primary and most significant activity conducted by managers in all types of organizations and at all levels of management. It is the prototypical function of managers, and it distinguishes between them and non-supervisory employees. Not surprisingly, the importance attributed to ethical and unethical decision-making in management is reflected by the extensive literature dealing with ethical decision-making in business and the various models developed by researchers, each focusing on different analytical frameworks and variables. The extensive literature on the topic reflects the many dilemmas routinely facing managers and the factors likely to affect their decision-making processes.

Ferrell, Gresham, and Fraedrich (1989) presented an integrative model of ethical decision-making in business, creating a synthesis of the three historical approaches described earlier. Their integrative model relates to both cognitive influences and social learning. The cognitive model comprises five stages: The first stage is the identification of the moral dilemma by the individual; the second relates to the effect of the individual's moral development on the decision-making process; the third deals with the cognitive stage and the individual's moral assessment, his or her perception of the situation, affecting his or her judgment. The individual's moral judgment then affects the willingness to engage in a certain behavior or to make a decision on the basis of the preliminary decision, which is the fourth stage. The decision leads the person to the fifth and final stage—executing the decision, which can be perceived as either ethical or unethical.

Ethical decision-making, as Rest (1986) showed, is comprised of a number of elements: Awareness and recognition of the existence of a moral problem, enactment of moral judgment, establishment of a moral intention, and carrying out a moral action. Based on Rest's findings, Jones (1991) proposed a model based on two external variables affecting the decision-making process. The first variable relates to organizational factors, including group dynamics, group cohesion, authority structure, and socialization processes. The second variable is the moral strength of the decision assessed on six dimensions: Significance of the outcome, social consensus, likelihood of outcome, frequency, closeness to decision, and concentration of results.

A breakthrough was made by Treviño (1986), who developed an interactional model of managerial decision-making. Her model posits that ethical decisions in organizations can be explained by the interaction of individual- and situation-level variables. Treviño drew on Kohlberg's (1969) model of cognitive moral development and argued that the individual's stage of moral development affects his or her perception of the moral dilemma and determines the decision-making process regarding what is right or wrong in a certain situation. The perception of right and wrong cannot adequately explain ethical decision-making because moral judgments occur within a social context and may be affected by both situational and personality variables. The situational variables that may influence the process are job context, cultural orientation, and organizational context. Personality variables—ego strength, field dependence, and locus of control—also affect the likelihood of distinguishing between right and wrong. Treviño's model provides a theoretical and practical basis for understanding managers' way of thinking when faced with moral dilemmas, and it shows that unethical managerial behavior is affected by factors at the individual, organizational, and environmental levels.

A cognitive model of ethical and unethical decision-making by managers relates to two main variables—individual characteristics and influence of the environment—affecting the decision-making process (Bommer et al., 1987). It does this by way of the individual's decision-making process, which is affected by variables such as available information, whether the information contains hard quantifiable or soft variables, individual attributes, managers' cognitive ability, perception of the results, risk inherent in the decision, and value or effectiveness they attribute to the outcome. The individual attributes are the level of moral development according to Kohlberg's model; personality traits such as locus of control, authoritativeness, and neuroticism; demographic variables such as gender, age, and education; motivation (self-esteem and confidence); personal goals; values; and additional variables such as life experience and intelligence. The situational variable is the five different social contexts: The personal environment, comprising family, peer group, and professional environment, reflecting codes of behavior; the work environment, presenting an explicit policy, collective culture, and influence of shared goals; the governmental and judicial environments, including laws, administrative offices, and the judicial system; and the social environment, including the religious, humanistic, cultural, and social values of the individual in the process of making ethical and unethical decisions.

Dubinsky and Loken (1989) developed a model based on the theory of reasoned action (Fishbein & Ajzen, 1975; reviewed in Chapter 7). Their model describes four stages in ethical and unethical decision-making. The first stage relates to four concepts: Beliefs about behavior, assessment of the outcomes, normative beliefs, and motivation to comply. The next stage includes two variables: (1) attitude toward the behavior, affected by beliefs about behavior, and (2) assessment of the outcomes and subjective norms relating to ethical and unethical behavior, affected by normative beliefs and motivation to comply. The third stage is influenced by the last two variables—intentions to behave in an ethical or unethical way. These intentions determine the fourth (final) stage—the actual ethical or unethical behavior.

Focusing on managers, Izraeli (1994) developed a model of stakeholder-circles, which situates the manager within five spheres of environmental factors: Social, business, professional, intraorganizational, and personal. The first four circles include factors of the organization, whereas the fifth is indirectly affected through the managers' interactions with their personal environment. Each circle includes varied types of stakeholders who influence the organization and are influenced by it. Thus, Izraeli's model assumes that behavior of senior managers, who are affected by all five spheres, is influenced (because they represent the organization and liaise between it and the environment) by the social, cultural, and political constraints of their environment and the value system and cultural norms derived from it, as well as by the economic constraints (the state of the market, the competitors, and the company's financial balance), which are in fact the sources of legitimization and the motivation for their ethical or unethical behavior. At the same time, they are influenced by the specific characteristics of their organizational environment: The role structure that gives them broad autonomy in decision-making, and the ability to influence many stakeholders in their organization and immediate environment.

Finally, Schminke (1998) developed a non-rational model of ethical decision-making based on the classic garbage can model (Cohen et al., 1972) called the *magic of the punch bowl*. The underlying idea is that four components—problems, solutions, participants, and choices—are constantly mixed and circulated in management's proverbial punch bowl. For an organizational decision to be ethical, all four components must somehow come together. This model highlights the fact that the decision-making process in organizations is almost never orderly, rational, and linear as we sometimes imagine it to be, but rather an outcome strongly influenced by human limitations, bounded rationality, error, hidden individual and group agendas, and organizational politics (e.g., Allison, 1971). Like the punch we sometimes drink, the quality is not only a function of the caliber of its components, but of the unique way the ingredients are prepared and mixed.

An OMB Perspective of Unethical Decisions

We chose Treviño's (1986) interactional model of unethical managerial decisions to serve as a conceptual basis for further theoretical developments. Her model aptly combines antecedents of decisions that represent the wide range of influences beginning from personality traits through positional characteristics to critical organizational constraints. In addition to being comprehensive, the model and its propositions offer an interactional thinking aspect that we find useful. This does not mean that other models (e.g., Bommer et al., 1987; Ferrell & Gresham, 1985; Hosmer, 1987; Jones, 1991; Schminke, 1998) are less valuable or that they should not be consulted as well.

Treviño and her colleagues (e.g., Kish-Gephart et al., 2010; Treviño et al., 2014) maintain that ethical issues are ever-present in the uncertain environment in which modern organizations exist—with their varied stakeholders, conflicting interests, and values. Sometimes they may collide. Because their decisions affect the lives and well-being of others, managers engage in discretionary decision-making behavior that often involves ethical choices: "Their decisions and acts can produce tremendous social consequences, particularly in the realms of health, safety, and welfare of consumers, employees, and the community" (Treviño, 1986, p. 601). Treviño's model posits that ethical and unethical decision-making in organizations is explained by the interaction of individual and organizational components, not by a single dominant characteristic of either the manager or company. Any such decision stems from the need to personally resolve an ethical dilemma and act on it. What mediates the dilemma–decision linkage is the person's moral development. The manager reacts to the dilemma with personal cognitions determined first and foremost by his or her moral development stage. Kohlberg's (1969) notion of cognitive development was deemed relevant because it posits that a person's level of cognitive moral development strongly influences the perception of what is right and wrong as well as of the rights of relevant others. It is a useful conceptual tool for explaining how managers think about ethical dilemmas and what additional factors influence how they decide what is the right thing to do in a particular organizational situation (see Treviño, 1986).

Ethical judgment and reasoning at work are principally predicated on a person's moral development, which involves the individual's orderly passage through developmental stages. At the early, pre-conventional stage, the individual is preoccupied with personal interests and the actual consequences of his or her deeds. At the conventional level, the individual is guided by expectations of others—society at large or closer affiliation groups including peer and family groups. At the principled stage, the individual upholds values and higher order principles, including social contracts, ideologies, and religious beliefs. For example, Manning (1981) used the model to explain how different managers reacted to decreases in productivity among salespersons who had experienced emotional problems. It was suggested that a principled-stage manager, when appraising such performance records, would consider the mutual obligations that the organization and employees hold. For example, he or she would recommend that professional help be given in light of a previous good record. However, a pre-conventional manager would focus on his or her own job, reasoning that failing to penalize the employees would harm his or her own position and career.

Obviously managers enter the organization with a previously determined level of moral development. Over time and with increased experience, they may continue to develop morally. Moreover, organizational characteristics and processes, such as technology and culture, also influence moral judgment. At any time, decisions are not only a function of personality traits (e.g., locus of control and ego strength) and the specific stage the person is in, but of their interaction with situational attributes such as normative and authority structures characteristic of the organization's culture. Thus, unethical decisions, which by definition are intentional and purposeful choices, may be explained by self-benefiting considerations (OMB Type S), organization-benefiting motives (OMB Type O), or destructive aims (OMB Type D). How, under different conditions, specific internal and external forces that affect such considerations are formed remains an empirical question.

Property Manifestations

Employee Theft

> *Miss Behavior*
> The good-old waitress in a blackish dress
> at the Inn's decorated friendly café
> was attentively busy fulfilling
> her customers' wishes for extra this or that,
> all the while keeping on her famous smile
> and civil manners, but when quickly turning
> the corner on her way to the bustling kitchen,
> I could unobtrusively observe her
> stuffing a dark blue bag from the Gap
> with leftover rolls and silverware,
> and hurriedly sipping red wine
> from a third-filled carafe
> off her cluttered tray…
> And I, empirically delighted, tucked in
> my dim-lighted booth in the rear,
> awarded myself with a personal toast
> and a big expert grin…
>
> (Vardi, 2007, p. 24)

According to the National Council on Crime and Delinquency (1975), employee theft is a "rational crime of opportunity, done as an intentional act that involves a breach of trust, resulting in a direct economic benefit to the actor, against the employing organization, within varying degrees of localized tolerance" (p. 7). That is, certain acts (e.g., unauthorized consumption of food and beverages by workers in a restaurant) may be perceived differently by owners and employees and in other ways at various locations. Sennewald (1986), a former president of the International Association of Professional Security Consultants, offered some insights into the realm of employee theft, referring to them as theft maxims. No business, industry, institution, or enterprise is immune to internal theft:

- Employee theft is a social disease and, as such, is contagious.
- Many organizations protect their property against theft by outsiders, but they neglect to protect it against theft by insiders.
- Theft is a combination of attitude and act. Organizations tend to emphasize dealing with acts rather than attitudes.
- Forgiving theft because of severity of damage or because of rank or seniority is tantamount to licensing more theft.
- Organizations lose more from embezzlement and fraud than from armed robberies.

Other maxims pertain to the employees:

- Everyone who is caught stealing says he or she is stealing for the first time.
- Theft in organizations is often a retaliatory act against management.
- Success in stealing often becomes addictive.
- Employees who are known to lie are also prime candidates to steal.

These maxims bear some important theoretical significance for any student of OMB and attest to the phenomenon's pervasiveness.

Buss (1993) is frequently cited for estimating that organizations in the United States lose $120 billion annually to employee theft. Losses from employee theft play a major part in the bankruptcies of 30–50 percent of all insolvent US businesses yearly (Greenberg, 1997; Greenberg & Barling, 1996; Hollinger, 1989). Furthermore, despite what many may think, in the United States, employees steal more from their employing organizations than America's shoplifters. By some counts, employees account for 43 percent of lost revenue while shoplifters account for 37 percent (Pinsker, 2014). The numbers themselves are not really critical because it is impossible to precisely calculate such damages on the national level. What is important is the message. Employee theft is a pervasive and a daily workplace behavior (Delaney, 1993).

It is estimated that 75 percent of organizational members steal something of value from their workplace at least once, and that most damage is not due to isolated grand theft cases, but to the accumulation of petty theft (Lipman & McGraw, 1988; McGurn, 1988). According to Halverson's (1998) survey of the retail industry in the United States, which covered 29 retailers with more than 11,000 stores and close to two million employees, 1.76 percent of sales income was lost because of employee theft ($4.4 billion for one year). More than 780,000 employees were caught stealing an average of $903.18 worth of merchandise. About 40 percent of the workforce admitted the temptation to steal, and 20 percent admitted taking some cash from stores. Using direct and experimental measurement techniques to elicit valid reports of past theft behavior, Wimbush and Dalton (1997) questioned approximately 800 employees and ex-employees of theft-prone workplaces such as stores and restaurants. The direct questions elicited a positive response from 28 percent of the employees, whereas the more subtle, indirect methods revealed that 58 percent admitted to stealing from their employers.

The Association of Certified Fraud Examiners (2014) found that the typical US organization loses 5 percent of its revenues to fraud each year; more than one-fifth of the cases caused losses of at least $1 million. Perpetrators with higher levels of authority tend to cause much larger losses. The median loss among frauds committed by owners or senior executives was $573,000, the median loss caused by managers was $180,000, and the median loss caused by employees was $60,000. The longer a perpetrator had worked for an organization, the higher fraud losses tended to be. Perpetrators with more than ten years of experience at the company caused a median loss of $229,000. By comparison, the median loss caused by perpetrators who committed fraud in their first year on the job was $25,000. Most are first-time offenders with clean employment histories. Nearly half (40–50 percent) of victim organizations never recover any losses due to fraud.

Estimates of employee theft, and its effects, vary widely because figures are reported across different economic sectors, different parts of the world and the use of a variety of calculation methods. Wimbush and Dalton (1997) concluded that estimates of losses due to employee theft range from $6 billion to $200 billion. Their best estimate is approximately $40 billion. They also estimate that it accounts for 30 percent of business failures.

No matter the precise numbers and percentages, it is exceedingly clear that a significant portion of the workforce steals from their employers and that the cumulative economic implications of this are enormous. Employee theft is clearly illegal. It is also perceived to be unethical behavior, not only by those victimized but also by perpetrators themselves (Sauser, 2005). We acknowledge the pervasive existence of employee theft and need to articulate ways to observe, measure, and control its various manifestations. Indeed, organizations have become more aware of this phenomenon; with the advancement of technology, many attempt to use increasingly more sophisticated digital surveillance methods to thwart or catch perpetrators or monitor computer abuse. Others use selection testing such as honesty and integrity tests (see A in Figure 11.1), to identify theft-prone candidates before they enter the premises.

Establishing the base rate is difficult and related to the problem of defining the theft phenomenon. The term *theft* is not limited to stealing hard equipment or property. Merriam (1977) defined *employee theft* as unauthorized taking, control, or transfer of money, goods, or services of an employer committed during the work-day. Greenberg's (1995) definition is more inclusive: "any unauthorized appropriation of company property by employees either for one's use or for sale to another. It includes, but not limited to, the removal of products, supplies, materials, funds, data, information, or intellectual property" (p. 154).

"Unauthorized" is a hard concept to define organizationally. In restaurants, for instance, employees who consume unauthorized quantities of food or drink may actually be stealing from the owners. However, they may believe, perhaps coached by peers and others, that these are customary job perks, not theft. Furthermore, a lax atmosphere may exist that creates a sense among employees that such behavior, if not condoned, is at least not frowned upon. Such an atmosphere, of course, may be reflected in employees' ambivalence as to what is considered theft and what is not. When the norm is not clearly defined and communicated, it is hard to distinguish misbehavior from acceptable behavior (Rubin-Kedar, 2000). We recently overheard a hushed debate among some university administrative employees in the cafeteria during lunch. Apparently some employees come in early in the morning, clock in, and then leave the workplace to carry out personal errands without clocking out. The hushed debate was about the legitimacy of this misconduct. When one person said that it is improper, the others agreed, but how can they know? How can those in authority find out? And besides, many people do it.

In their practitioner-oriented book entitled *Are your employees stealing you blind?* Bliss and Aoki (1993) argue that most people do not look for ways to cheat, but when an opportunity presents itself, they may not be quick to brush it aside. The authors illustrated this with a list of some remarkable white-collar thefts recorded by a fraud investigator: A bookkeeper in a doctor's office had been skimming over $250,000 a year in payment to a fictitious supplier; an apartment building manager found a way to pocket most of the cash received as rent by adjusting the books to conceal the theft; a partner loaned himself nearly $800,000 of partnership funds without the knowledge of the other partners, eventually forcing the firm into bankruptcy; a bookkeeper embezzled more than $300,000 in five years by using the company president's signature stamp to sign checks made out to nonexistent firms and cashed them with the help of a bank teller.

These cases may sound like rare instances of big-time theft. They are. Yet we regard the daily misuse of organizational resources in the same category—theft—and therefore as OMB. This may include the vast majority of organizational members who take time off from work, use equipment for personal use, or consume goods that should be sold. You may regard this as petty. Yet if it violates any rule or norm, by definition it is OMB. Thus, we discuss employee theft as a common and prevalent form of organizational behavior.

Employee theft has been a concern to owners, managers, and labor representatives from the beginning of productive systems (Horning, 1970). Although practitioners such as security officers, insurance agents, and arbitrators have been burdened by the problems arising from theft and its damages, academic interest has lagged. Horning suggested that, despite its costs and prevalence, theft has not been accorded much attention by either students of deviant behavior or organizational analysts, stating that "Even sociologists, with their empirical, analytical, and theoretical interest in normative behavior, have been conspicuously neglectful of the non-legal activities of industrial operatives" (p. 46).

The many references to theft—pilfering, misappropriation, peculation, filching, mulcting, poaching, embezzling, stealing, petty thievery, petty larceny, grand theft, and purloining—illustrate the range of acts in question. However, they do not reveal the nature of the relationship between thief and victim, and they do not tell us anything about the motivation behind the acts or whether they were committed to inflict damage or benefit the self, group, or organization. Horning (1970) thus laid the foundation for the present distinctions among OMB types. For example, an employee admits in an interview: "Occasionally I'll bring something home accidentally. I'll stick it in my pocket and forget it and bring it home. I don't return that 'cause it's only a small part and I didn't take it intentionally" (p. 55). How should one characterize such behavior? What is the motivation? Benefiting self? Inflicting damage? Doing what is customary? Is it a prosocial or an antisocial activity? We turn to the individual-level antecedents of theft in the next chapter. Suffice it to say that employee theft could be regarded as both prosocial behavior when it is motivated by a desire to adhere to some group norms and antisocial when it is motivated by some desire to harm and inflict damage.

Horning (1970) proposed some important conceptual distinctions between white-collar and corporate crimes and between blue-collar crime and blue-collar theft. The categorization of white-collar crime should be reserved to acts by salaried employees that victimize the organization, whereas corporate crime pertains to acts that benefit the organization. Blue-collar crime includes all illegal acts committed by rank-and-file employees (non-salaried) that involve the organization's assets (e.g., theft and destruction of property) or the misuse of the location for engaging in such acts as gambling on company premises during work hours. Specifically, Horning defined employee theft as the "illegal or unauthorized utilization of facilities and removal and conversion to one's own use of company property or personal property located on the plant premises by non-salaried personnel employed in the plant" (p. 48).

Employee theft is considered a major component of what is known as shrinkage (the totality of goods and materials missing due to shoplifting, vendor theft, misplacement, accounting or bookkeeping manipulation, or error as well as employee pilferage). Rosenbaum (1976) studied employee theft and tried to find ways to predict its occurrence. He suggested that worker theft, especially in the private sector, is largely undetected, unreported, and under-prosecuted. Based on data on employee selection and theft data collected from two samples drawn from privately owned merchandising companies, Rosenbaum concluded that organizations might be able to use data from employment application blanks to distinguish between employees who may pose a risk (and thus would need more surveillance on the job) and those who pose less threat of stealing (and thus do not require special surveillance).

Humphreys (1977) harshly criticized this study for failing to account for the base rate for theft in these organizations, which renders such conclusions and implications premature (see further discussion of methodological problems in OMB measurement in Chapter 10).

Understanding the pervasiveness and importance of this form of behavior, Hollinger and his colleagues (Hollinger & Clark, 1982, 1983; Hollinger & Davis, 2006) studied employee theft quite extensively, and their research is frequently cited. They analyzed questionnaire data from more than 9,000 employees representing retail, hospital, and manufacturing organizations. They operationally defined theft as the unauthorized taking of organization property by employees who generally have a non-deviant self-concept. They also assumed that for most employees, theft is a function of perceived deterrence. Lax controls, they argued, lead to more prevalence of theft. Using direct questions, Hollinger and Clark (1983) asked their respondents to anonymously report their past year's level of participation in thefts of merchandise, supplies, tools, equipment, and other material assets belonging to their employers. Retail sector employees were asked about the frequency (from daily to 1–3 times a year) of misuse of discount privileges, taking store merchandise, receiving pay for hours not worked, borrowing or taking money without approval, claiming false reimbursements, and damaging merchandise to buy it on discount. In all, 35.1 percent of 3,500 individuals admitted being involved in theft. Of the 4,111 hospital personnel, about 33 percent were involved in such acts as taking supplies, misusing medication intended for patients, and taking hospital equipment or tools. About 28 percent of the 1,497 manufacturing sector employees admitted to taking raw materials used in production, taking finished products, taking precious metals, and receiving some undeserved pay. Such questions, although pertaining to stealing from the organization, may not be interpreted that way by employees who may regard their behavior as quite acceptable.

A fascinating discussion of the fine line between taking and stealing is offered by Greenberg (1998), who wrote on the geometry of employee theft that there is a cognitive "grey area" regarding what various members of the organization considered theft. He presented a conceptual analysis to explain this ambiguity following two lead questions: (1) When do members take company property? And (2) when is taking such property regarded as theft? His goal was to develop a framework for theft deterrence.

Although managers tend to frequently complain "everybody's stealing the company blind," workers tend to conceal or deny knowledge of it. This gap could be attributed to two sources. One is the actual difference in day-to-day experiences among job holders at different levels. Another stems from the ambiguity inherent in the way different individuals interpret their own behavior and that of others. Thus, what constitutes theft may be subjective. Greenberg (1998) cited a legal definition of employee theft that helps explain this issue.

Following Lewin's (1951) force-field theory, Greenberg (1998) suggested that taking behavior be conceived as resulting from the net strength of individual, group, and organizational-level forces that both encourage and inhibit acts of taking. Greenberg proposed that employee theft may be deterred by efforts to counter these cognitive strategies as well as attempts to strengthen inhibiting forces and weaken encouraging forces. To the extent that people desire to present themselves as behaving in a morally appropriate manner, they attempt to negotiate the legitimacy of their acts of taking with others who threaten to impose labels (e.g., thief) that challenge their moral self-images.

Can we indeed predict engagement in theft activity? It is hard to say, but some attempts have been made. For example, Jones and Terris (1983) designed a predictive validity study to test the claim that employees with dishonest attitudes who heavily employ neutralization and rationalization to justify their behavior engage in counterproductive activity and theft in particular. They used the Personnel Selection Inventory—Form 1 (London House Press, 1980) as a measure of workplace dishonesty; it assesses perceptions and attitudes toward theft. The measure presumes that theft proneness is exhibited by (1) more rumination over theft activities (e.g., "How often in recent years have you simply thought about taking money, without actually doing it?"); (2) more projection of theft in others (e.g., "How many executives steal from their companies?"); (3) greater rationalization of their acts (e.g., "Will everyone steal if the conditions were right?"); (4) less punitive attitudes toward thieves (e.g., "A young person was caught stealing $50,000 in cash from an employer. If you were his employer, what would you do?"); and (5) more inter-thief loyalty (e.g., "If you were caught stealing, would you tell on the people who helped you?"). They found that employees with higher dishonesty scores were also rated higher by their supervisors on counterproductive acts. Additionally, units with the highest theft records were staffed with personnel with higher dishonesty scores. Thus, tolerant personal predispositions toward this misbehavior and its justification may well be predictive of actual conduct and could be utilized in the design of personnel managerial tools, such as selection tests.

Some of the behavioral signs to look for when monitoring employee theft are signs often ignored by both superiors and peers (Bliss & Aoki, 1993). In fact, "when embezzlement or some other internal rip-off is discovered, management's usual response is an embarrassed confession that certain early warning signs were ignored, that a 'hunch' that something was wrong was shrugged off" (Bliss & Aoki, 1993, p. 23). Such signs can be an abrupt change in lifestyle, excessive use of alcohol or drugs, close social ties with suppliers or customers, refusal to take a vacation, unusual and obsessive neatness, and frequent borrowing from other employees. Obviously, this approach addresses management concerns about subordinates. However, with the growing evidence that managers and senior executives are also prone to engage in improper behavior that amounts to large-scale theft and fraud, employees should be aware of the early warning signs for organization members at all levels, such as a sudden sale of company stocks and options.

In summary, corruption in organizations and employee theft cannot be totally eliminated. Senior management is beholden to its stakeholders to devise the ways and means for keeping them at a minimum. It is incumbent on management to create a culture of trust, to instill in its employees the sense that the organization is a good place to work. While firms need to be results- and bottom-line-oriented, it is management's responsibility to ascertain that the means to achieve organizational goals are both ethical and proper and do not run counter to workforce's moral codes of behavior. Senior management needs to put in place a code of ethics that specifies what is expected of its workforce in terms of proper conduct and what is unacceptable. It also needs to put in mechanisms for training and sanctions for breaching the code. Most importantly, management needs to lead by example.

Sabotage and Vandalism

Based on the literature dealing with sabotage (e.g., Dubois, 1976; Giacalone & Rosenfeld, 1987; Linstead, 1985; Sprouse, 1994; Taylor & Walton, 1971), Giacalone, Riordan, and Rosenfeld (1997) stipulated that deterrence or apprehension of employees engaged in sabotage require specifying (1) a proper definition of what it is, (2) the number of perpetrators and the internal organizational support for sabotage, (3) the history of sabotage in the organization, (4) the provocation of the acts, (5) the targeting of the acts, and (6) the extent of damage done.

Definition of the Act of Sabotage

There is an inherent difficulty in defining an act of misbehavior as sabotage because there is no consensus as to exactly what it is, and because it may apply to a wide variety of actions such as the damage done to equipment, spreading a virus over the internet, stealing goods or knowledge, harming products or services, vandalizing property, and so on. Scholars have offered different classifications. In addition to Dubois' (1976) typology, Strool (1978) identified the following types of sabotage: Informational, chemical, electronic, mechanical, fire-related, explosive, and psychological. Giacalone and Rosenfeld (1987) proposed four groups: Slowdowns, destructiveness, dishonesty, and causing chaos. Obviously one major problem is distinguishing between intentional (e.g., spilling coffee on your computer on purpose) and accidental sabotage (e.g., spilling coffee on your computer by accident); although the outcome may be the same, qualitatively these should be construed as different behaviors. It is important to correctly identify the act, because inaccurate assessments often lead to improper management reactions, which not only may be unfair to the employees, but could actually exacerbate the situation and indeed cause retaliatory sabotage.

Who is or are the Perpetrator/s?

It is important to ascertain whether sabotage is an individual or group act because this determination may lead to different interpretations and reactions. Individual sabotage (usually committed covertly) is regarded and treated as such, but collective sabotage is different. Giacalone et al. (1997) proposed three types: (1) independent group sabotage is performed by a number of individuals in the organization who may not be aware of each other's activity, (2) conspiratorial group sabotage is committed as a result of a specific group decision, and (3) blind-eye group sabotage occurs when a number of individuals know of or witness an act of sabotage and choose not to inform management about it. This complicity is sabotage as well.

What is the History of Sabotage in the Organization?

Occasional sabotage is certainly important. Yet a pattern of sabotage behavior is consequential for both perpetrators and organizations because they indicate that there may exist a persistent and most probably unresolved problem. Thus, both the extent and history of the observed phenomenon should be examined. This knowledge is bound to make the organization's reaction less haphazard and more effective.

Was the Act Provoked?

It is extremely important to understand that there is a vast difference between acts of sabotage perpetrated by employees identified as suffering from personality or emotional disorders and acts perpetrated by employees motivated to engage in them for reasons such as defiant reaction to managerial control or abuse. Sociopaths or psychopaths should obviously be treated as employees in need of help. However, the personal or organizational causes of such behavior of psychopaths, which make up the lion's share of saboteurs, require careful investigation.

Who is Targeted?

It is important to distinguish among personal, group, and organizational targets. Often the results of sabotage or vandalism can be deceiving. Although the consequences could be organization-wide, the intended target could be a specific manager or decision. This distinction is important because again a misreading of the situation might lead to inappropriate action such as removing the cause of the activity from the scene.

What Type of Damage Was Done?

Aggressive acts of sabotage or vandalism, in addition to causing physical damage, may spill over to indirect, long-term psychological effects such as increased stress and uncertainty (e.g., Painter, 1991). Therefore, it is useful to identify both types of consequences—personal and organizational—because this sometimes leads to the identification of hidden motives for aggressive sabotage acts.

The most blatant manifestations of employee misconduct that targets the organization's products and property with an implicit intention to inflict some damage are vandalism and sabotage. These fall within the realm of workplace aggression, but are often not considered violent behavior. Giacalone and Rosenfeld (1987) suggested that employee sabotage occurs when people who are currently employed in an organization engage in intentional behaviors that effectively damage that organization's property, reputation, products, or services. Some mild forms of sabotage and vandalism, such as graffiti or spreading rumors maligning the employer, are quite often dismissed by management and may at times even be tolerated. The question, again, is where should one draw the line between acceptable and unacceptable damaging behavior. As we pointed out, any act that purposely inflicts some damage on the organization as a whole, its assets, or its stakeholders is regarded as OMB Type D—damaging, destructive, or disparaging behavior committed intentionally.

Vandalism at work is not a newly discovered phenomenon. It may take on new forms because of technological advances and changes, but employees' physical tampering with their work environment is well documented. Crino and Leap (1988) offer several basic reasons why employees engage in workplace sabotage:

- to make a statement or send a message to others
- to take revenge
- to have an impact on a large faceless system
- to satisfy a need to destroy
- to seek thrills
- to avoid work

A fascinating depiction and analysis of industrial sabotage was presented by the French sociologist Dubois (1976) in his book *Sabotage in industry*. Dubois distinguished between two prototypes of sabotage: Instrumental and demonstrative. Instrumental sabotage is aimed at a limited or total transformation of the present situation. Demonstrative sabotage is an expression of protest, dismay, or rejection of management values, policies, or actions; it is not aimed at achieving certain demands. That is, it is by and large political in nature. To illustrate an industrial context that enhances such actions, Dubois, akin to Blauner's (1964) depictions of mass production settings that produce worker alienation, vividly described the plight of a quality control worker in a tire factory:

> Tires by the thousands. Fifteen thousand a day. Several hundred pass the quality controller in every eight-hour period, one every forty seconds. His job is to examine and test each one for faults: Any tire that is defective must be set aside. Suppose he does not do his job properly—what then? ... It is easy enough not to check: Just a matter of doing nothing.
>
> (Dubois, 1976, p. 13)

If, Dubois (1976) remarked, in this type of setting many individuals engage in such behavior and the organization is forced to increase the means and resources devoted to control it, this could be "the first indication that sabotage is going on" (p. 13). Dubois further demonstrated that destructive sabotage, such as the machine-breaking phenomenon in industrializing societies during the eighteenth and nineteenth centuries, is mainly a defensive reaction by employees resisting the mechanization of their work. Similarly, Ackroyd and Thompson (1999) viewed vandalism and sabotage as a form of resistance to managerial control.

For example, F. W. Taylor (1911) identified management's responsibility for the go-slow type of sabotage. His logic was that such employee behavior is a direct result of the piece-rate method of pay. Intuitively, such a method should increase productivity because of the clear effort-to-pay contingency. However, the reality is different: Employees restrict their performance for fear that, as a result of their productivity, management will redesign work or establish new, yet higher standards. Deliberate absenteeism (i.e., absenteeism not justified by illness, family obligations, etc.) is typically an intentional act in which the employee rejects a given work situation. In another classic portrayal of industrial organizations of the mid-twentieth century, Turner and Lawrence (1965) showed that absenteeism was the highest in settings where jobs had little or no variety, were not intellectually stimulating, and demanded low levels of personal responsibility. Such absenteeism is regarded as sabotage because when it persists over time and spreads through the organization it may cause substantial disruptions, actual losses, and a possibility for some kind of chaos.

Angry, bitter, bored, frustrated, envious, and resentful employees are the ones sabotaging employers' equipment and operations in increasingly sophisticated and creative ways. Employees and managers often use sabotaging tactics (e.g., agreeing to carry out a task, but then stalling) when they covertly resist imposed changes (Laabs et al., 1999). The variety of options seems endless. Sabotage can range from simple pranks to the most sophisticated financial fraud. The media has reported numerous cases in which angry employees tampered with products in unimaginable ways—from putting rodents in food products to needles in baby food, set their company on fire, or wiped out entire databases. Sabotage is taking on new forms as computer networking is now available to most employees. Workers are overtly and covertly setting computer bombs, viruses, worms, and more; erasing databases such as customer lists; or tampering with personnel files. Writers on sabotage behavior (e.g., Analoui & Kakabadse, 1991, 1992; Skarlicki & Folger, 1997) claim that sabotage is the tool of the disgruntled employee who feels discriminated against, taken advantage of, and ignored by the organization. They see it mostly as retaliatory behavior whereby members, alone or in groups, take revenge on the system.

In an *Industry Week* article, Caudron (1995) illustrated what he called *get even* employees—a breed of workers who will do anything to sabotage the company, be it by antagonizing customers, assaulting the computer system, or damaging critical pieces of equipment. These, he assumed, are employees who react strongly to their feeling resentful, alienated, or fearful about job security and being wary of management. He presented the following cases:

Case 1: Tired of constant overwork and lack of management appreciation, employees at an industrial plant punch a hole in a drum of toxic chemicals. Slowly the air seeps into the drum, pressure builds, and the drum explodes, spewing dangerous chemicals into the workplace. Work comes to a standstill until the hazardous substance can be cleaned up. The perpetrators, hiding a smile, head home for a much-needed day of rest.

Case 2: Disgruntled over the lack of recognition of his work and fearful of an impending layoff, a computer programmer for a major defense contractor plants a logic bomb in the information system. His plan is to destroy vital data on a rocket project and then, in the event of a layoff, get hired as a high-priced consultant to reconstruct the lost information.

Case 3: Angry over reconstructing, reengineering, and never-ending management platitudes, a hospital employee infects the computer system with a virus that destroys the last word in each file. The problem is, once the virus works its way through the system, it turns around and starts all over again. Slowly but surely, each file is erased from the end to the beginning. Managers seldom scroll all the way to the bottom of their documents. Volumes of data are damaged before the virus is detected.

Morin (1995) portrayed a rather bleak picture of the corporate world, which is inflicted by what he termed *silent sabotage*. He blamed the spread of sabotage on a valueless society and a sense of anomie, and he urged organizations to instil value systems and codes of ethics with which employees can better identify. We cannot agree more!

Intellectual Manifestations

Modern OMB

One of the most frightening documents we read on computer-related misbehavior is Cornwall's (1987) book, *Datatheft*. It chillingly describes the endless opportunities to misbehave, the unlimited possibilities that computer and telecommunication systems provide, and the incredible repertoire of activities they generate. Cornwall richly illustrated types of activities relevant to OMB researchers:

- Crimes made easier by the computers—fraud (false inputting, fake inventorying, and fake outputs), forgery, impersonation, information theft, and eavesdropping.
- Crimes not possible without a computer—computer manipulation (data files, application software, expert and system programs, attack on hardware, compromised hardware, compromised measurement devices, and vandalism/sabotage), theft of software, theft of hardware and peripherals, theft of computer resources, and hacking (by employees and by outsiders).

One of the reasons that computer systems have made misbehavior so easy is their nature: (1) there is a general absence of direct human involvement; (2) most, if not all, of the organization's assets are computerized or at least managed through the system; (3) contents of files are invisible; (4) managers and administrators tend to trust experts in handling computers and data not realizing the level of risk to which they are exposed; (5) raw data, such as documents, are mostly handled by non-experts and are mostly unprotected while being processed; and (6) basically all systems are breakable and, because they are ever-changing, never becoming fully protected. Certainly with the internet's infinite capabilities of handling data, the opportunities to steal and manipulate other people's information and intellectual property have risen significantly.

Espionage and cyberwars also appear to be fast growing due to global computer interconnectedness (Crane, 2005; Holt & Schell, 2011). The academic world received a firsthand reminder of the potential threat of internet espionage right at the heart of one of its most respected Ivy League institutions. Apparently the Yale University admissions office website was breached by an outsider who scanned through 11 files of applicants. The spied-on files were placed in a special site that could be accessed by applicants checking on the status of their applications. Entry was possible by using birthdates and Social Security numbers. One month later, in a meeting of Ivy League admissions officials, the story broke: Curious about whether certain applicants had been rejected by their rival, the Princeton University admissions director visited the site and examined files he was not supposed to see. This was no complicated hacking job: He simply used the numbers of students who had registered at both universities. The director was removed, and Princeton hired the services of a Newark law firm to investigate. Mr. D. G., dismayed by this scandal, wrote a letter to the editor: "As a member of Yale's class of 2006, I am appalled by Princeton's violation of fundamental privacy of its applicants… it is plausible that Princeton changed the admissions status of prospective students based on whether or not those students were admitted to Yale" (*New York Times*, July 28, 2002). The director's misconduct would be classified as OMB Type O if his primary motive was to spy on behalf of his organization, OMB Type S if the motive was to gain some personal benefit, and OMB Type D if the intention was to harm the competition.

On November 24, 2014, Sony Pictures Entertainment was hacked by a mysterious group calling itself the "Guardians of Peace". Sony's confidential data was obtained; embarrassing e-mails of employees, Hollywood stars, and executives were exposed; and five Sony films were leaked online. Many have speculated that North Korea was responsible for the cyberattack because Sony was about to release its upcoming comedy *The Interview*, a movie that involves a plot of an assassination attempt on Kim Jong Un, ruler of North Korea. About a month later, the FBI confirmed these speculations (BBC News, 2014; Grisham, 2015). In general, the FBI reports a steep rise in cases of economic (international) espionage targeted at US companies. Incidents such as theft of trade secrets have led to losses of hundreds of billions of dollars within just one year (Bruer, 2015).

The internet has made industrial espionage, misinformation, and subversion big business. Well-paid hackers are often the brains and soldiers in these wars among corporations. Hacker newsgroups have emerged as communities of experts who generate, shuffle, and disseminate important information. This is now called *espionomics*. If one knows how, one can find almost any pertinent information needed to make strategic and tactical decisions for any company—who filed the most recent patent on polymers, how project teams are operating in your competitor's research and development units, what they publish and what they hide, where certain executives traveled recently, or how the weather in Colombia affects the quality and quantity of coffee beans next year. With the availability of information, a whole new counterespionage and protection industry has emerged as well. Big Brother has become a world giant, albeit taking different shapes in different countries. In France, for instance, financial documents pertaining to the state of business organizations are available for public or private scrutiny, whereas information pertaining to individual citizens is not. In the United States, it is pretty much the other way around (Guinsel, 1997). What worries most countries and institutions is the relative ease with which subversive individuals and organizations can penetrate information networks and use them for illicit purposes.

One of the most harmful and dangerous forms of modern misbehavior is known as *internet piracy*. In 2002, Mr. John Sankus, a 29-year-old computer technician, was sentenced to 46 months in prison. He was charged by the US Customs Services with being the ringleader of an international gang of software pirates that deprived companies of millions of dollars through illegal distribution of copyrighted software, games, and movies on the internet. His group, known as DrinkorDie, is just one of thousands that engage in such piracy. Many operate from within their work organizations, using company resources to download and distribute protected material. What seems especially interesting about the new-age pirates is their motive. Many of them, Mr. Sankus suggested, are not out to cheat anybody or benefit financially. Some do it for fun, for the challenge, for the competition, or because they cherish the feeling of mastering the technology. Nonetheless, according to the Business Software Alliance, software internet piracy costs about $10 billion per year in lost sales worldwide (*New York Times*, July 11, 2002). Software worth a whopping $59 billion dollars was stolen worldwide in 2010 according to the Business Software Alliance. In the US alone, 20 percent of all software installations in 2010 were pirated copies that cost the software industry $9.5 billion dollars (Webroot, 2015). During the past few years we have also seen large-scale data theft by people such as Edward Snowden who released to the public stolen documents from the US National Security Agency and Julian Assange of WikiLeaks who similarly releases secret documents to the public.

Why do the new-age pirates, hackers, and saboteurs do what they do? Using qualitative research techniques of observation and interviewing, Turgeman-Goldschmidt (2001) penetrated the hackers' culture in Israel and studied, from their own stories and accounts, not only how they operate, but also how they justify and rationalize their misbehavior. She contacted 54 hackers who were located through a snowball networking process and interviewed them at length. All fit a particular profile: Young men around 24 years old, single, educated, working in the computer industry, above-average income, secular, and urban. They all presented themselves as non-conformist, computer freaks from a young age, who were talented and smart. Contrary to the public image of the lone hacker and his computer, it appears that these hackers and their colleagues use their network for social bonding. What starts as a virtual contact often develops into close, collegial, and professional friendships.

Hackers' illicit activities can be divided into three categories: (1) misconduct related to breach of copyright regulations (duplicating, disseminating, and trading protected programs); (2) misconduct related to hacking (breaking into, browsing and using protected data banks or internet sites, using internet services without pay, writing and disseminating viruses, stealing information, retrieving or changing official documents, causing the collapse of computer systems, and misusing credit card information); and (3) misconduct known as *freaking*. Hackers rationalize their misconduct by using self-benefiting rationalizations. Unlike other offenders who use economic deprivation reasons (e.g., Analoui & Kakabadse, 1992; Greenberg, 1997), hackers claim they use computers for competition, kicks, fun, thrill, satisfying curiosity, and control. They steal because they can and because they enjoy the excitement. They do, however, use neutralizing tactics (Sykes & Matza, 1957b) such as denying responsibility, denying damaging the victim, blaming the accusers for creating the opportunity, and resorting to higher values.

What we know about cyber-OMB is only beginning to emerge and may be just the tip of the iceberg of endless opportunities for untold individual and organizational forms of misconduct. One reason that this and other forms of illegal and immoral forms of misconduct are spreading so rapidly is the perpetrators' ability to live with it.

A Final Observation

We offer a rather humorous depiction of the same manifestations so tediously described in the preceding section. To do this, we consulted *The Dilbert principle*

(Adams, 1996). We seriously consider it an important and insightful explication of the modern workplace. The definition of what Adams so vividly described as the *virtual hourly compensation* is the total amount of compensation one receives per hour including:

> Salary, bonuses, health plan, inflated travel reimbursement claims, stolen office supplies, airline frequent flyer awards, coffee, donuts, newspapers and magazines, personal phone calls, office sex, telecommuting, illegitimate sick ˙ days, internet surfing, personal e-mail, use of laser printer for your résumé, free photocopies, training for your next job, cubicle used as a retail outlet.
>
> (Adams, 1996, p. 92)

This reflects the kind of property misconduct we encountered in our own research and careers. Furthermore, Adams (1996) commented on the public astonishment at the discovery that giant corporations collapse or file for bankruptcy because some CEOs engage in gross misbehavior. People seem surprised that captains of industry are stealing vast amounts of money at every opportunity. He suggested, again using his unique sense of corporate humor, that we put things in perspective: "Every employee I ever worked with in my cubicle-dwelling days was pillaging the company on a regular basis, too. But the quantity of loot was rarely noteworthy... The CEOs aren't less ethical than employees and stockholders; they're just more effective" (p. 92). We cannot refute Adams' astute observation.

Acts of OMB are committed intentionally by members of work organizations. Thus far, our goal was to venture into the darker side of these organizations and enumerate and describe the many forms and manifestations of OMB. The repertoire is indeed impressive. In Chapter 7 we begin to address the inevitable questions: Why do employees intentionally misbehave? What motivates them to violate accepted norms and standards of proper conduct—to intentionally inflict damage and take advantage of resources that belong to others? How can we account for this conduct? Earlier we suggested that any explanation for unacceptable work behaviors has to be as complex and multidimensional as the explanation of behavior designed to directly contribute to the well-being of the organization and its stakeholders. Our goal is to gain a better understanding of the phenomenon and generate plausible propositions for future research, anchored in a solid theoretical statement that captures the essence and complexity of OMB, its manifestations, and antecedents.

7

INDIVIDUAL-LEVEL
ANTECEDENTS OF OMB

Aggression is not anger, but it often accompanies anger.

– Allcorn (1994)

We now turn our attention to possible causes for misbehavior at the individual level. In order to do that, we need to consider that any human behavior can seldom be accounted for and explained by a single direct cause. For example, to predict ethical and unethical decisions by managers, Treviño et al. (2014) enlisted a number of personality, job, and organizational variables that may interactively account for the dependent variable—the type of decision made. Because of this multidimensionality, and for the sake of effective presentation, we begin our discussion about the causes of OMB, following our model (Figure 2.2) by levels of analysis. In this chapter, we identify selected individual-level antecedents; in Chapter 8, we discuss position and group-level influences; and in Chapter 9, we identify organizational-level antecedents.

We believe that the ability to predict intentional misbehavior patterns would be an important contribution to OB research. However, empirical research on misbehavior in general, and its temporal aspects in particular, is still lacking, mostly because of management's hesitancy to provide researchers full access to systematically observe misbehavior and researchers' reluctance to engage in long-term investigations. It is also difficult because most misconduct is often a low base-rate phenomenon, and much of it is hard to observe. Such obstacles often require indirect, subtle observation methods. For example, we can measure OMB directly or by means of its proxy - the intention to misbehave. Dalton, Johnson, and Daily (1999) discussed at length both the limitations and usefulness of using intent-to variables in OB research. These variables are useful in misbehavior research because such conduct is mostly the type of low base-rate behavior that presents problems of sampling and limited range on scales. For example, in their research of organizational whistleblowing, Ellis and Arieli (1999) and others (e.g., Near et al., 1993b; Somers & Casal, 1994) used the intention to blow the whistle as a proxy for actual reporting of irregularities. Because of the complexities of OMB research we devote Chapter 10 to the measurement dilemmas involved.

In this chapter, we present selected theoretical contributions, as well as evidence from empirical studies, that suggest ways in which personality traits, predispositions and attitudes, and affect may contribute to the intention to misbehave. Clearly, the number of individual-level antecedents of misbehavior is large, and it is impossible to discuss all of them here. Therefore, we selected antecedents that adequately represent them: Personality, morals and values, attitudes, affect and emotion, and others' behavior. The overall scheme is depicted in Figure 7.1.

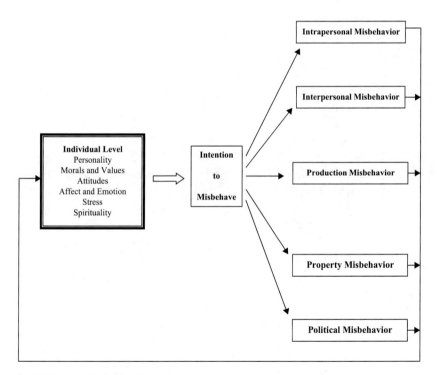

FIGURE 7.1   Individual-level antecedents

Personality Traits

Personality in Organizational Behavior

Although personality variables played a fundamental role in the research of attitudes, feelings, and behaviors from the mid-1960s through the early 1990s, in theories of OB they gained only minor importance (Mount & Barrick, 1995; Murphy, 1996; Weiss & Adler, 1984). For example, Mitchell (1979) emphasized that personality variables in studies of OB mainly serve to minimize the connection between a situational variable and other criteria. Although his survey indicates that personality characteristics predict attitudes, motivation, and leadership, he pointed out that the studies' main foci are attitudes, motivation, and leadership, not personality attributes. Weiss and Adler (1984), much like Mitchell (1979), concluded unequivocally that, although personality measures appear to be related to behavioral outcomes, they do not play a leading role in OB research.

Neglect of personality research during this period, described by Hough and Schneider (1996) as "the dark period" of OB, apparently stemmed from the dominance of the situational approach, which maintains that personality characteristics are illusive and personality can account for only a small part of the variance in OB, compared with situational factors (Guion & Gottier, 1965). Studies carried out from the 1960s to the 1990s, explaining the variance of some behavioral outcome criterion by means of these two components, almost always highlighted the weight of situational variables (Mitchell, 1979; Vardi, 1978). Naturally, this led many OB researchers to focus on situational factors as having the greatest influence on attitudes and behavior in the workplace. The evidence provided by Landy (1985) is that, in the course of 20 years after Guion and Gottier's conclusions were published, only a small number of studies related personality measures to performance at work. This can also be attributed to personality research, its slow and inadequate conceptual development, and the poor quality of the methodology employed (Weiss & Adler, 1984). Ozer and Reise (1994) suggested that OB researchers have not invested sufficient effort in conceptualizations and theories defining the psychological elements that comprise the human personality. That trend has led to long-term disagreements among researchers regarding the definition of *personality* and the ways it differs from values, interests, and emotional responses (Murphy, 1996).

Nevertheless, researchers and practitioners in the field of industrial and occupational (I/O) psychology made use of personality variables in empirical research, particularly for the purpose of employee classification selection. Hough and Schneider (1996) claimed that I/O practitioners have played an important role in the eventual revival of personality research. In the 1990s, we saw changes in both OB and personality research. Students of OB started to explore OMB, deal with its domain and dimensions, and carry out empirical studies (e.g., Giacalone & Greenberg, 1997; Robinson & Bennett, 1995; Vardi & Wiener, 1996). Concurrently, a renewed interest in personality variables occurred, attributed by many researchers to the emergence of a wide framework for the examination of personality, called the *Big Five personality traits* (see Chapter 2; also see Judge et al., 1997; Mount & Barrick, 1995; Seibert & Kraimer, 1999). This led to the publication of numerous studies examining the validity of predicting workplace behavior by means of personality measures (Hough & Schneider, 1996). In the next section we further explore the personality–OMB relationship.

The Big Five Personality Traits and OMB

Personality traits are commonly conceived as those inner structures directing an individual's behavior in a relatively stable manner (e.g., Allport, 1961). Such hypothesized structuring requires that we find parsimonious ways to organize traits conceptually. Otherwise, identifying personality characteristics and using them to explain behavior becomes tedious and Sisyphean. A good example of this potential confusion may be borrowed from Moberg (1997). In trying to describe *employee vice*, Moberg generated a list of 32 terms that purport to be a variety of similar traits such as: Cowardice, lawlessness, dishonesty, disloyalty, insincerity, unreliability, callousness, lack of civility, indecency, uncooperativeness, bluntness, intolerance, and selfishness. To avoid cumbersome lists, social scientists prefer to organize countless specific traits into clusters that tap some logical commonality.

One such clustering is the Big Five personality traits categorization, which stems from studies using a variety of questionnaires with both self-reports and descriptions of others, in different languages and cultures (Digman, 1990; Mount & Barrick, 1995). The core Big Five personality traits literature (Digman, 1990; Mount & Barrick, 1995; McCrae & John, 1992) provides us with accepted definitions of the basic dimensions of human personality:

Extroversion includes traits such as sociability, talkativeness, assertiveness, adventurousness, daring, vitality, and drive. At the other end of the spectrum are people described as *introverted*—shy, quiet, inhibited, and reserved.
Agreeableness consists of traits such as courtesy, friendliness, and flexibility. Agreeable individuals are described as trusting, cooperative, forgiving, considerate, and tolerant. This dimension thus comprises the more humane aspects of personality, such as altruism and caring for others as opposed to hostility, apathy, and lack of compassion (Digman, 1990).
Emotional stability represents differences in people's disposition to feel tense, anxious, depressed, angry, excitable, insecure, nervous, and fearful. People ranked high on this scale are characterized as emotionally stable. Neurotic individuals typically score low on this dimension.

Conscientiousness is defined by traits such as responsibility, trustworthiness, and efficiency. People who score high on this dimension are regarded as well-organized, good planners, and achievement-oriented. Some researchers maintain that this dimension typifies persons who are reliable, prudent, methodical, efficient, and good planners, and others stress ambitiousness and competitiveness. In several surveys, researchers (e.g., Mount & Barrick, 1995) concluded that conscientiousness consists of both aspects: Self-discipline and competitiveness. McCrae and John (1992) argued that this is the most value-laden dimension, describing good persons (as opposed to bad ones)—those highly desired by work organizations.

Openness to experiences represents individuals with a wide range of interests who are receptive to new experiences, imaginative, curious, responsive to the arts, and intellectually stimulated. Researchers (e.g., McCrae & John, 1992; Mount & Barrick, 1995) pointed out that this dimension is the most controversial of the Big Five personality traits. Although some define it as culturally based (e.g., Norman, 1963), others view it as more intellectual (e.g., John, 1989). Following Costa and McCrae (1988), there is a growing consensus that this dimension comprises traits such as: Imagination, inquisitiveness, originality, aesthetic sensitivity, and wide horizons (Hellriegel et al., 2001). People ranked low on this scale are characterized as dogmatic.

Extroversion

Most of the studies attempting to predict behaviors by means of the extroversion trait report a positive relationship between extroversion and positive behaviors or attitudes in the workplace. These may range from a high level of performance to career success and satisfaction at work. Barrick and Mount (1991) examined the predictive validity of the Big Five personality traits and work performance among five different occupational groups. Extroversion predicts work performance characterized by a great deal of interaction with others, such as managers and salespeople. The researchers concluded that traits such as sociability, zestfulness, and assertiveness, which are included in the dimension of extroversion, contribute to success in these occupations. Vinchur, Schippmann, Switzer, and Roth (1998), who focused on salespeople, reported that vitality (also a sub-trait of extroversion) has the highest predictive value for success at selling. An additional positive criterion related to extroversion is career success. Seibert and Kraimer (1999) found that personality traits explain additional variance in career success apart from situational variables. They stressed the positive relationship between extroversion and an inner sense of success (satisfaction) and external career success (pay and advancement). Furnham and Zacherl (1986) also reported a positive relationship between satisfaction and extroversion—namely that extroverted people tend to report greater work satisfaction, especially with regard to pay, and a high level of overall satisfaction from work.

These studies demonstrate that extroverts (i.e., active, assertive, energetic, and sociable individuals) tend to report a higher level of satisfaction derived from their work and career, and they also tend to display higher levels of performance especially in occupations demanding interaction with others (managers and salespeople). Nonetheless, some studies report a positive relationship between extroversion and misbehavior in the workplace. For instance, Collins and Schmidt (1993) found that the personality profile of white-collar offenders (convicted of offenses such as fraud, embezzlement, and forgery) was typically more extroverted, compared with employees in similar hierarchical levels who were not convicted of such acts. Judge et al. (1997) reported that a significant positive correlation between extroversion and absenteeism. They qualified this finding by saying that this relationship can only be confirmed if situational variables, such as the type of occupation or its characteristics, are controlled because they may affect the willingness of an extrovert to invest in work.

Agreeableness

According to Graziano and Eisenberg (1997), one of the components of agreeableness is a prosocial disposition or voluntary behavior directed toward the well-being of others. Being agreeable is also referred to as being likeable, generous, pleasant, and considerate (Goldberg, 1992). Employees ranked high on this trait are more likely to perform well at work (Tett et al., 1991), and display less hostility and aggression toward others (Graziano & Eisenberg, 1997).

Agreeableness is positively related to work performance (Tett et al., 1991). Yet in occupations characterized by a high level of autonomy, less amiable managers (those ranked lower on agreeableness) display a higher level of performance compared with more amiable managers (Barrick & Mount, 1993). A possible explanation for this is that in such positions overly amiable managers are perceived negatively by their supervisors. Another possibility is that managers, tending to cooperate and assist others, perform better in the less vague and more structured aspects of their roles (Barrick & Mount, 1993). Additional studies show that the traits characterizing an amiable person are related to teamwork (e.g., Hough, 1992). That is, the more employees tend to cooperate, help, and behave pleasantly with others, the better they are suited to teamwork and the more likely they are to succeed in it. This explains why friendly, agreeable, and sociable workers are less prone to delinquent behavior such as theft, absenteeism, vandalism, substance abuse (Ashton, 1998) and vindictive behavior even when they feel that organizational justice has been breached (Skarlicki et al., 1999).

Emotional Stability

A person characterized by low emotional stability tends to experience tension, anxiety, depression, anger, and insecurity and is more nervous and highly strung than others. Research examining this trait shows that employees with low emotional stability tend to feel dissatisfied with their work and career, perform at somewhat lower levels than others, and at times behave vindictively toward their organization. More specifically, people ranked low on emotional stability tend to be less satisfied with the amount of work demanded of them, their fellow workers, and their salary. Reinforcing such findings, Seibert and Kraimer (1999) reported a positive correlation between emotional stability and internal (subjective) career success. Overall, according to Tett et al. (1991), emotional stability is positively and significantly related to performance.

Skarlicki et al. (1999) examined the relationships among negative affectivity, perceptions of organizational justice, and vindictiveness. Negative affectivity was measured on a scale composed of six personality traits (calm, apprehensive, tense, nervous, depressed, and irritable) also included in the emotional stability dimension of the Big Five personality traits (Goldberg, 1992). Their findings show a relationship between negative affectivity and organizational vindictiveness. They also show that the tendency to act vindictively is high when the level of negative affectivity is higher and the perception of justice is lower. Because of the way negative affectivity is measured, it may be possible to project these findings onto people describing themselves as low on emotional stability. It is reasonable to suggest that the lower people are ranked on the emotional stability scale, the more likely they will be to act vindictively, especially when they also perceive low levels of organizational justice (e.g., discrimination, favoritism, and inconsistency).

Conscientiousness

Many researchers have pointed out that, among the Big Five personality traits, conscientiousness most effectively predicts a variety of criteria in the workplace and its environment (Barrick et al., 1993; Hough & Schneider, 1996; Mount & Barrick, 1995). Some researchers (see, e.g., Schmidt & Hunter, 1992) have gone so far as to argue that conscientiousness plays an important and central role in determining performance levels at work. Therefore, this trait must be taken into consideration when attempting to predict and explain factors related to this criterion. OB researchers who focus on personality variables conclude that there is a positive relationship between conscientiousness and work performance (e.g., Barrick & Mount, 1991; Fallan et al., 2000; Hough et al., 1990; Tett et al., 1991; Vinchur et al., 1998).

The most comprehensive research on this topic, conducted by Barrick and Mount (1991, 1993), indicates that conscientiousness consistently predicts a higher levels of performance across different occupational groups such as professionals, policemen, managers, salespersons, and trained or partially trained workers. Whereas Barrick and Mount (1991) examined the level of performance according to workers' professional skills, guidance skills, and the way they were assessed according to labor force data, Vinchur et al. (1998) took a different approach. They studied workers' performance according to supervisory reports (calling this criterion *objective success*) and arrived at similar findings. More specifically, they found that achievement orientation is the main component of conscientiousness in predicting objective success. However, Fallan et al. (2000), who examined the relationship between the Big Five personality traits and the performance level of cashiers in a large organization, found that the general conscientiousness scale better predicts work performance than each component of this trait separately (pride at work, perfectionism, accuracy, and diligence). In the wake of these studies, Fallan et al. (2000) concluded that this personality trait—describing a person with achievement orientation, commitment, responsibility, and perseverance—is indeed conducive to task performance in all types of occupations.

The predictive validity of the conscientiousness trait was also examined in relation to additional criteria, such as tests of integrity and teamwork, irresponsible and non-functional behavior, replacement, and absenteeism. Ones, Viswesvaran, and Schmidt (1993) reported a particularly strong positive relationship between conscientiousness and integrity tests. For instance, they found that people who are responsible, compliant, and reliable (i.e., conscientious) also tend to be graded high on integrity, sincerity, and trustworthiness. Hough (1992) argued that conscientiousness is the personality trait with the strongest relationship to teamwork. She also examined a negative aspect of workers' behavior—irresponsible behavior—and found that two facets of conscientiousness (achievement orientation and dependability) were most highly (negatively) correlated to workers' irresponsible behavior. Additional studies support the claim that the less conscientious workers are (i.e., the lower they score on traits such as responsibility, compliance, achievement orientation, organizational ability, and orderliness), the more they are prone to exhibit dysfunctional behaviors in the workplace such as delinquent activities and substance abuse (Sarchione et al., 1998) or theft, vandalism, and absenteeism (Ashton, 1998). Moreover, negative relationships were found between turnover (Barrick et al., 1994) and absenteeism (Judge et al., 1997) and workers' scores for conscientiousness.

We propose, as did Hogan and Ones (1997), that conscientious workers (responsible, achievement-oriented, and dependable) tend to be good corporate citizens and invest exceptional effort at work without expecting rewards because they care. Conversely, workers low on this personality trait do not perform well at work and may be more inclined to get involved in a variety of behaviors that may be dysfunctional or even harmful to the organization.

Openness

People in this category actively seek out new and different experiences. Openness is comprised of inquisitiveness, aesthetic sensitivity, intellectual curiosity, wide-ranging imagination, and originality (McCrae & Costa, 1997). Studies have shown that people open to new experiences tend to support liberal parties and social causes, which is consistent with their quest for knowledge and natural inquisitiveness. Their willingness to question existing values and seek out the unfamiliar (McCrae & Costa, 1997) leads to the development of high moral values. In light of this, we presume that people holding such values will be less prone to behave in unethical ways and actively participate in misbehavior in the workplace (Treviño, 1986). Tett et al. (1991) reported a significant relationship between openness and performance at work. However, studies (e.g., Hough, 1992) show that openness (termed *intelligence*) is positively related to workers' irresponsible behavior apparently due to their inquisitiveness and originality, which at times may lead to irresponsible actions.

In summary, most of the studies attempting to predict behavior at work by means of the Big Five indicate that conscientiousness (i.e., responsibility, accuracy, and achievement orientation) is highly appreciated in the world of work. Apparently, workers ranked high on this trait perform their work better, are valued by their supervisors, tend to display good citizenship behavior, and are less prone to engage in some forms of OMB. As in the case of conscientiousness, the studies examining the predictive validity of agreeableness report stable relationships with positive behaviors at work (e.g., satisfaction and performance, teamwork, and career satisfaction) and negative relationships to misbehaviors (i.e., delinquent behavior and organizational vindictiveness). Likeable, generous, and amiable workers are less prone to misbehave toward the organization or its workers. Workers low on emotional stability, who appear to experience high levels of tension, anxiety, depression, nervousness, and anger, perform less well on their professional tasks, are less satisfied with their work, and are more likely to behave in vindictive ways.

In their review and meta-analysis of the research dealing with misconduct, Berry et al. (2007) found that deviance has a strong negative correlation with agreeableness, conscientiousness, and emotional stability. Specifically, agreeableness is strongly (negatively) associated with deviance toward others in the workplace (e.g., gossip), while conscientiousness is strongly (negatively) associated with deviant behaviors targeted toward the organization (e.g., damaging company property). Other studies also indicate that agreeableness, conscientiousness, and emotional stability are the strongest negative predictors of misbehavior (e.g., Jensen & Patel, 2011; Le et al., 2014; Mount et al., 2006). Openness and extroversion predict different manifestations of OMB. Higher scores on openness to experience may increase the likelihood of production misbehavior and lower scores on extroversion may increase acts of theft (Bolton et al., 2010).

In sum, the emergence of personality traits approach, and the broad consensus regarding its effectiveness, prompted many researchers to conduct empirical studies to examine its validity as a predictor of behavior. The early studies were mainly directed at clinical assessment of flawed personality (Wiggins & Pincus, 1992). With time, a great deal of research was conducted with the intention to predict a variety of work behaviors. Traditionally, the main criterion variable was performance, subsequently a variety of other criteria came under scrutiny, such as job satisfaction, career success, and some forms of misconduct. To further demonstrate research opportunities inherent in the search for the role of personality in explaining and predicting OMB, we turn to the Ashton Study.

The Ashton Study

To test the predictive power of personality traits, Ashton (1998) conducted a study of 50 male and 77 female undergraduate students with summer job experiences. This study is of special interest because, unlike most research into the predictive validity of employee selection measures, Ashton used a measure of OMB as a job performance criterion. The study comes in the wake of the methodological debate (e.g., Ones & Viswesvaran, 1996) known as the *bandwidth-fidelity dilemma*. The issue involved is the utility of using broad personality traits (e.g., each of the Big Five or a general integrity factor) rather than narrower, more specific traits (i.e., particular scale components) in predicting workplace behavior. Ashton sought to determine whether narrow, rather than broad, traits better account for what he called *workplace delinquency*.

Ashton (1998) asked participants to recall their recent summer work as waiters, fast-food servers, messengers, and the like, and to relate their actual work behavior. The students were advised that, because the responses are completely anonymous, there is no need to try and make a good (or bad) impression. (A discussion of impression management and the problems researchers face when seeking to obtain data regarding sensitive issues such as stealing from or vandalizing one's workplace appears in Chapter 10.) Ashton's Workplace Behavior Questionnaire contains behavioral, direct, self-report, and quantitative questions that tap the following behaviors: Unjustified absenteeism, lateness, alcohol use, safety violations, goldbricking, theft, freebies (the total dollar value of goods or services that you have given to your friends or relatives for free), and vandalism. Most of the respondents indicated some involvement in misbehavior. Also, as in Vardi and Weitz's (2002c) study, some gender differences emerged: The mean score for male students was significantly higher than that for female students. This may indicate that either the male students committed more OMB and/or they were more willing to admit to such conduct.

Two of the Big Five traits—conscientiousness and agreeableness—were found to be negatively and significantly correlated with misbehavior. Of the narrow traits, risk taking and irresponsibility correlated with misbehavior, and these relationships were stronger than the two predictive broad traits. Yet the somewhat equivocal findings, the ambiguity of currently available personality measures, and the limited validity of the criterion measure only underscore the difficulties of obtaining hard empirical data on real workplace misbehavior. Nevertheless, these findings reinforce our conviction that further systematic investigation of the impact personality traits have on the intentions to engage in different types of OMB is needed.

Integrating Personality, Organizational Justice, and OMB

To demonstrate a potentially interesting research direction, we suggest that OMB be studied as a function of the interaction between the Big Five and the three types of perceived organizational justice, the former representing the personality and the latter the situation. Assuming that the strength of the relationship between personality and actual behavior is influenced by situational factors, this model regards *organizational justice* as a moderator variable. Organizational justice reflects a person's evaluation of the kinds and levels of equity existing in the employing organization (Greenberg, 1990b). Three types of justice are proposed following the justice literature: (1) *distributive justice*—employee perceptions concerning equity of the organizational reward system, (2) *procedural justice*—employee perceptions concerning equitability as reflected in organizational policies, and (3) *interactional justice*—employee perceptions concerning the quality of interpersonal treatment by authority figures within the organization.

Researchers investigated these variables in relation to a variety of work behaviors including improper behaviors. For example, Greenberg and Alge (1998) discussed extensively the relationship between organizational justice and aggressive behavior. Skarlicki et al. (1999) tested the role of personality as a moderator of the perceived justice–misbehavior relationship. Our rationale is that, given certain personality traits, a person's inclination to engage in a certain type of OMB (especially Types S and D) might change as a result of perceiving different levels of justice. As may be seen in Table 7.1, organizational justice perceptions serve as a moderating effect on the relationship between personality traits and OMB. We argue, for instance, that the relationship between agreeableness and OMB toward others will be strengthened when the person perceives a violation of interactional justice. Similarly, the tendency of a person with low emotional stability to engage in organizational misbehavior (OMB Type O) will be mitigated when the person perceives that procedural justice is strictly maintained.

The potential of this framework, and additional propositions derived from Bennett and Robinson's (2000) distinction between workplace misconduct aimed at others and misconduct aimed at the organization, are presented in Table 7.1. The terms specify probable interactions among the three types of justice perceptions and each of the five personality traits. For instance, we may expect that individual employees who score low on emotional stability will be inclined to

TABLE 7.1 Research propositions for the moderating effects of perceived organizational justice on the personality–OMB relationship

	Justice perception		
Personality traits	Violation of distributive justice	Violation of procedural justice	Violation of interactional justice
Emotional stability (low level)	OMB toward others	OMB toward organization	OMB toward others and organization
Agreeableness (low level)	OMB toward others	—	OMB toward others
Conscientiousness (low level)	—	—	OMB toward organization
Extroversion (high level)	—	—	OMB toward others
Extroversion (low level)	OMB toward organization	OMB toward organization	—

misbehave toward the organization (e.g., steal, loaf, and be counterproductive) when they perceive low distributive, procedural, and/or interactional justice. We might also expect such persons to target other individuals in their work setting (e.g., undermine, insult, harass, and manipulate) when they perceive low distributive and/or interactional justice.

Intentions and Attitudes

Predicting the Intention to Misbehave: An Investigation

Unquestionably, for employees and managers, the decision to deal with ethical dilemmas in a certain way is a complex cognitive process (e.g., Treviño et al., 2014). We conducted a study designed to specifically test hypotheses regarding the prediction of the intention to engage in different types of OMB (Vardi & Weitz, 2002c). Here we briefly report the rationale, method, and findings of this study to illustrate the need to better understand the kind of cognitive calculations one makes when an intention to act in a way that violates organizational codes of proper behavior is formed.

Individual behavior follows a cognitive process that leads to the formation of behavioral intentions (Fishbein & Ajzen, 1975). By understanding how such intentions are formed, one may be in a position to explain and predict behavior. The theory of reasoned action (TRA) is predicated on several basic assumptions: (1) the individual is an organism that utilizes available information to form opinions and values and make judgments and decisions; (2) most behaviors are voluntary, and thus controlled by the individual; and (3) in most cases, individual attitudes and behaviors are in congruence. Hence, a negative form of behavior toward a person or an object follows a negative attitude toward that person or object. Accordingly, the factor that determines whether a person will or will not engage in a particular behavior is the behavioral intention to carry it out, which is determined by the person's attitude toward the behavior and his or her subjective norm—the person's belief about whether significant others think that he or she should engage in such behavior.

Significant others are individuals whose expectations and preferences in this particular domain are important to the focal person such as family members, colleagues, or superiors at work. Hence, the behavioral intention is considered to be a linear regression function of attitudes toward the behavior and the subjective norm. The weights of the two predictors are determined empirically. According to Fishbein and Ajzen, attitude toward behavior is a function of the individual's important behavioral beliefs that represent the perceived consequences of the behavior and the value he or she attaches to those consequences. The subjective norm is a function of the individual's beliefs about the degree to which referent others believe that he or she should carry out the behavior weighted by his or her motivation to comply with the referent's opinions (see Ajzen, 1985; Ajzen & Fishbein, 1980; Fishbein & Ajzen, 1975). This theory is useful in explaining most social behaviors, including both functional and dysfunctional work-related behavior (Ajzen & Fishbein, 1980; Kurland, 1995; Sheppard et al., 1988; Vardi & Wiener, 1992; Wiener, 1982).

Vardi and Wiener (1996) postulated that the intention to misbehave, which is the immediate cause of an eventual act of misbehavior, is formed differently when the psychological forces that precede it are primarily instrumental or normative. Specifically, OMB Type S (self-benefiting misbehavior) is assumed to be mostly motivated by an instrumental judgment as to the utility of engaging in such an act for the individual, the positive and negative values accruing from it, and eventual personal consequences (attitude according to the Fishbein and Ajzen's (1975) theory of reasoned action). OMB Type O (organization-benefiting misbehavior), in contrast, is primarily motivated by affective as well as normative forces within the person. For instance, strong affective or normative commitment (Meyer & Allen, 1997; Wiener, 1982) to the organization may lead an individual member to engage in forms of misconduct to protect it. Thus, the theory of reasoned action would suggest that, in this type of misbehavior (e.g., an unethical decision), the subjective norm has a higher weight in determining the preceding intention. Finally, OMB Type D (intentional acts that inflict damage) is assumed to be motivated by either attitude or subjective norm. At times, it may be motivated on a calculative basis (e.g., getting even), and at times it can be a result of an ideological identification with a cause or group. Three research hypotheses follow these suppositions:

- The weight of a person's (instrumental) attitude toward OMB Type S is higher than the subjective internalized norm toward such conduct in predicting the intention to engage in such behavior at work.
- The weight of the subjective norm toward committing OMB Type O is higher than the person's instrumental attitude when predicting the intention to engage in OMB Type S.
- There are no differences in the weights of attitude and subjective norm when predicting the intention to engage in OMB Type D.

Intentions to Engage in OMB

To measure the intentions to perform Types S, O, or D acts of OMB, we presented three different hypothetical scenarios accompanied by this question: If you were in that situation, would you have acted similarly or differently? We generated 12 narratives representing workplace circumstances and specific behaviors that supposedly deal with them, designed to represent the three OMB types. These were then submitted to eight participants in graduate seminars who were asked to read all the stories and identify the primary motivation behind each behavior. The three stories selected were those receiving the most votes as representing Types S, O, or D intentions. The students were also presented with the methodological dilemma of whether it would be preferable to ask a direct question (how would you handle the situation?) or an indirect question (how would the person in the story handle the situation?). After discussing the pros and cons of each approach, the group voted for the direct approach, which was adopted for the study. This scenario-based measure is presented in Appendix 3.

Attitudes Toward OMB

Based on Fishbein and Ajzen (1975), we also hypothesized that individuals evaluate the eventual consequences of certain behaviors, as well as their importance and significance. Thus, each scenario was followed by a list of potential positive and negative outcomes: I will gain financially, I will feel guilty, my actions will lead to my dismissal, I will be appreciated by my family, my colleagues will follow my lead, I will feel that I betrayed my values, and my reputation might be tarnished. For each outcome, the respondent was asked to assess how certain he or she is that these outcomes would follow the described act. Scores were calculated for each of the three types S, O, and D.

Subjective Norm

After listing positive and negative outcomes, we suggested to the subjects seven significant others (spouse, relative, immediate superior, manager, colleague, customer, and friend). Each respondent was asked to consider how three of the most important of the seven figures suggest he or she would behave in the described situation and to what extent he or she would be willing to adhere their suggestion. The computation of scores followed the same procedure as before. The more positive the score, the more the respondent internalized a tolerant subjective norm toward the misbehavior and vice versa.

The strength of the intention to misbehave differs by type in a descending order: Self-benefiting > organization benefiting > damaging. All six correlations (three OMB types and the two precursors) are moderate and significant, supporting the proposition that both the attitude toward the behavior and the subjective norm may be conceived as precursors of the intention to misbehave, tapping related but different psychological decision-making processes. All three regression models in which intention is predicted by both attitude and subjective norm were found to be significant. The variance explained by the two predictors is substantial—ranging from 15 percent to 24 percent. However, only the intention to engage in OMB Type S was predicted as hypothesized. That is, the (instrumental) attitude had a higher weight in forming the intention than the (normative) subjective norm. Type O was predicted by both precursors, whereas the Type D intention was mostly accounted for by the attitude towards the act of inflicting damage.

Because the sample included a majority of female (65 percent) employees, we decided to test an a posteriori hypothesis that TRA scale predictions will not differ between the two groups. Men's intentions to perform acts of misbehavior on the job were higher than women for Types S and O. Most important, women's subjective norms appear to be much less tolerant toward any type of OMB than among the working men in this sample.

Our results confirm the TRA-based prediction that each one of these behaviors would be predicted by the instrumental considerations with regard to such an act, as well as the internalized subjective norm reflecting the assumed values of significant others. In addition, the separate regression models for each of the three types provided some support for the supposition that the relative weights of attitude and subjective norm depended on the specific stimulus or situation.

This finding sheds light on the cognitive processes involved in making decisions to behave in two distinct manners that knowingly violate organizational and/or societal norms: Choosing to act within the work environment in a way that enhances personal or organization-wide outcomes and choosing to purposely inflict some damage on elements of the work environment such as other individuals, the work itself, or organizational resources. It appears that Types S and D intentions to misbehave are more heavily influenced by the person's assessment of both positive and negative eventual consequences than by the internalized subjective norm.

The theory of reasoned action, as its name indicates, is primarily rational. In order to enrich it, we need to incorporate into this line of research personality and affect variables to better understand workplace behavior (George & Brief,

1996; Fisher & Ashkanasy, 2000). Strong emotions such as anger, envy, and jealousy (Smith & Kim, 2007; Vecchio, 2000) play a significant role in provoking job-related misbehavior (Duffy et al., 2012; Khan et al., 2014). For instance, some scholars integrate Weiss and Cropanzano's (1996) affective events theory to study how different patterns of misbehavior emerge, and demonstrate that the intentions to misbehave have both cognitive and affective antecedents (e.g., Lam et al., 2009; Rodell & Judge, 2009). It stands to reason that OMB Type S may be better predicted by intentions that emanate from cognitive instrumental considerations and OMB Type O is motivated by affective states such as strong identification with the organization's goals and culture.

Affect and Emotion

Understanding the causes, characteristics, and implications of various emotions emerging in the workplace constitutes an important, yet relatively neglected aspect of OB (Muchinsky, 2000). As Lazarus (1991) pointed out, despite the assumptions expressed throughout the ages by philosophers, theologians, and writers as to the role of emotions in the human experience, the study of emotions as a component of academic research is a relatively new phenomenon (see Fitness, 2000; Weiss & Cropanzano, 1996). Over the past three decades, affect and emotions attracted the attention of researchers interested in the social psychology of the workplace, an environment typified by complex power structures and dynamic relationships and saturated by emotions (Barsade & Gibson, 2007). At the same time, the rapid advent of emotional intelligence literature provided an additional impetus for OB researchers. The studies by Salovey and Mayer (1990) and Gardner (1983) popularized this notion, and Goleman (1995, 1998) and his colleagues (Goleman et el., 2013) published bestsellers by that name. Goleman and Cherniss (2001) expanded emotional intelligence to include work-related behavior, selection, and employee development. Zilberman (2002) found empirical support for a negative relationship between emotional intelligence and OMB among managers. Jung and Yoon (2012) reported similar results among hotel employees, whereby emotional intelligence had a significant negative effect on counterproductive behaviors in the workplace.

We believe that emotions are an integral component of daily organizational life. Work experience is permeated by feelings ranging from moments of frustration or joy, through sadness or fear, to an enduring sense of dissatisfaction or commitment (Ashforth & Humphrey, 1995). Research has shown that affect (emotion) influences motivation, performance, satisfaction, commitment, and other organizational outcomes (George, 1989; Lewis, 2000). There is ample evidence that negative emotions have an important detrimental effect on employees, including absenteeism and dissatisfaction (George, 1989; Staw et al., 1994). Despite the prevalence of emotions in the workplace, researchers have just begun to study and form theories on the subject. This dearth of empirical studies coupled with the important role played by emotions in affecting behavior act as powerful motivating factors promoting research on the phenomenon.

The starting point of current research on emotions in organizations is Hochschild's (1983) book *The managed heart*, which skillfully and artfully deals with what she termed *emotional labor*. Hochschild studied the work of flight attendants and maintained that wearing the mask dictated by the organization—smiles, pleasantness, cordiality, and neatness—actually required a real emotional effort. She found that obeying the organization's emotional rules, as learned and internalized during socialization and training processes, can have a deep emotional impact. Some flight attendants adopt a pattern of naïve enthusiasm for their work, yet they may feel and behave differently after work. Others define their emotional role as "being on their best behavior": They smile, laugh, and express concern in a persuasive manner when it is required—in other words, they expertly manage the impression they wish to make. With the passing of time and the mounting pressure, emotional labor extracts a price: It may cause burnout and, at times, authentic emotions penetrate through the mask in the form of irritability, anger, or actual revolt.

Hochschild's (1983) canonical work inspired OB researchers. Rafaeli and Sutton (1987, 1989) focused their attention on the expression of emotions as a component of the role played at work. Staw, Bell, and Clausen (1986) studied *dispositional affect* to predict work satisfaction. Their work soon promoted the adoption of *trait affectivity* as a useful variable in the study of organizations. Isen and Baron (1991), dealing with the influence of moods, turned the attention of researchers to more transitory aspects of emotions in the workplace.

Interest in emotions in the workplace gained momentum during the past three decades. Although the body of research is still not fully developed, it is promising and has enriched the understanding of human behavior in organizations (Fisher & Ashkanasy, 2000). George and Brief (1996) maintain that emotions are central to our understanding of motivation in the workplace. Persistent negative emotions such as anger (Allcorn, 1994), frustration (Spector, 1978), and fear (Burke, 1999) no doubt exert a strong influence on both employees and organizations. For instance, employees may act in ways that harm the organization or coworkers. It is important, therefore, to better understand the role of affect in determining the intentions to misbehave.

Emotions are easy to comprehend intuitively, but they are difficult to define. Van Brakel (1994) provided a list of 22 definitions of the term *emotion*. Ashforth and Humphrey (1995) simply defined emotion in broad and comprehensive terms as a subjective feeling state. This definition includes basic emotions (e.g., joy, love, and anger) and social emotions (e.g., guilt, shame, envy, and jealousy), as well as related concepts such as affect, sentiments, and moods. The difficulty in developing a definition stems from the awareness that an emotional response is a combination of related reactions. Several researchers (e.g., Lazarus, 1991) stressed that the best way to relate to emotions is to perceive them as temporal processes, as opposed to states, because emotional responses develop with the passing of time and usually include a sequence or series of emotional reactions. Plutchik (1993, 2001) proposed a serial model of human feelings in which specific factors generate the sequence of events we call emotions. Human feelings are indicators of evident or unconscious judgments as to the importance of events. Emotions provide information about responses to situations we would otherwise not be aware of, and they reveal needs, worries, and motives.

The conclusion that may be drawn from the discussion thus far is that an emotion is a response to an event (Weiss & Cropanzano, 1996). It is not a personality trait, although there may be different levels of affect that chronically accompany responses to specific events. As pointed out by Frijda (1993), emotions always have an object; they are related to something. There is a reason why a person is happy, angry, or frightened. For example, if someone threatens me, my emotional response may be fear. Similarly, if someone abuses my trust, my response may be anger, which can engender a desire to retaliate. If a hungry person sees food he may be happy. If a peer gets a promotion, I may become envious, and my jealousy will perhaps lead to attempts at discrediting the person. From a temporal perspective, such a definition poses interesting questions about the dynamic relationship between emotional responses and misbehavior.

Jealousy and Envy at Work

We first distinguish between jealousy and envy. The terms *jealous* and *zealous* are both derived from the same Greek root meaning an enthusiastic devotion and care for a person or an object. Jealousy relates to a concern that what was attained or cared for is in danger of being lost. The term *envy* is derived from the Latin *invidere*, meaning to look at a person maliciously. In this sense, envy represents the desire to possess the assets or qualities of another (Bryson, 1977). We may compare it to *rivalry*, from the Latin *rivalus*: The person competing for access to the same source of water. The *Oxford Dictionary* uses these Latin roots to define the term *jealous* as troubled by the belief, suspicion, or apprehension that the goods one seeks to preserve for oneself will pass to another, and anger toward another person because of existing or suspected rivalry. *Envy* is defined as a feeling of dissatisfaction and resentment aroused by another person's possession of coveted benefits such as greater happiness, success, prestige, or possession of anything desirable. Although the concepts of jealousy and envy are distinguishable, we often find that they are used interchangeably, with *jealousy* often used to describe both situations.

On the basis of the theoretical work carried out by White and Mullen (1989), Vecchio (1995, 2000) viewed jealousy as a pattern of thoughts, feelings, and behaviors stemming from a blow to a worker's self-esteem due to a loss of outcomes related to workplace relationships. An important aspect of workers' jealousy is the real or imagined threat. This threat identifies jealousy at work as a type of reaction to stress (e.g., a strong emotional reaction, including the wish to behave defensively or withdraw). Unquestionably, firms and organizational careers are replete with such stress-producing, jealousy-provoking situations.

Although jealousy can be defined in general terms, a different conceptualization is called for when dealing with workers because of the unique nature of social relationships at work. For instance, the norms prevalent in social relations in the workplace differ from those within a family unit and between two people who love each other. In the work setting, the difficulty inherent in breaking off a relationship is not so great, and the degree of acceptability of the use of physical violence is generally lower than elsewhere, whereas social pressure to deliberately ignore rivalry is greater (Gayford, 1979). Such differences in norms limit acceptable responses to the experience of jealousy. Moreover, the types of rewards implemented at work differ from those used in other social situations (Foa & Foa, 1980).

Because envy and jealousy are emotions with negative social connotations and may constitute sources of stress, there is a tendency to perceive them as dysfunctional. However, in a certain sense, these emotions among workers may be functional in that they may in fact promote specific behaviors and act as discriminating cues, resulting in healthy competitive responses. Nevertheless, reports of a rise in workplace violence (including the murder of workers and their supervisors) and harassment of rivals show that work situations are not exempt from pathological responses to envy and jealousy (Sprouse, 1992). Apart from responses considered pathological (e.g., obsessive thoughts), envy and jealousy tend to create cognitive dissonance, producing adaptive coping behaviors (Festinger, 1954). Envy can arouse a range of reactions, ranging from adaptive responses to destructive or pathological reactions.

Based on the model of affective events proposed by Weiss and Cropanzano (1996) and Vecchio's (1995) model of envy and jealousy in work situations, we posit that events in the course of work arouse feelings leading to both proper behaviors as well as OMB. Vecchio (1997), for example, showed that coping with envy and jealousy encompasses a wide range of behaviors along two dimensions: A constructive–destructive continuum and an assessment of the extent to which others are involved. People may respond to envy and jealousy in a destructive way and, within the context of the workplace, engage in OMB. Not surprisingly, there is a growing interest in the way negative emotions trigger aggression (Barling et al., 2009). In this context, envy and jealousy are especially relevant to the workplace: Interpersonal misbehavior and undermining behaviors are triggered by workers' feelings of envy and jealousy (Duffy et al., 2012;

Khan et al., 2014). People motivated by envy and jealousy may harm their rivals, for instance, by subverting their careers, embarrassing them or spreading malicious rumors and shaming them.

Employees may also respond to envy and jealousy by being hostile, cynical, angry, sabotaging their rivals' work, and ostracizing them. Such responses are motivated by the desire for revenge against the rival. They stem from people's need to preserve their perception of the organizational world as a familiar, just, and fair world (Lerner, 1980). When something occurs that threatens this perception (e.g., an event arousing envy or jealousy), it motivates people to restructure such occurrences and assists in reaching psychological closure (Janoff-Bulman, 1992). People are motivated by the need to preserve their positive personal and social identity, and their sense of control over their world. When events threatening their self-esteem occur (e.g., episodes arousing jealousy), they act to confirm their self-worth and preserve their sense of control. Such actions may be channeled into harmful directions. Revenge as a response to jealousy or envy may be directed against the rival, but it may well be against the organization perceived as responsible for unfair treatment (e.g., unfair distribution of rewards), and may take the form of sabotage or theft of the organization's resources. In work organizations, employees may respond to jealousy and envy with misbehaviors. Hence, we formulate the following proposition: Overall, there is a positive relationship between jealousy and OMB and between envy and OMB. Jealousy is more strongly related to OMB Type O, and envy is related to both OMB Type S and Type D.

Others' Influence

OMB may originate from personality traits, attitudes, and emotional states. Yet we should also consider the conduct of other persons with whom we interact at work as a major individual-level determinant of misbehavior. (Group-level effects are explored in the next chapter.) We have already considered effects such as envy and jealousy when we discussed emotional reactions. We now seek to explore what others actually do that triggers intentions to misbehave. We have chosen three unique constructs that represent powerful behavioral effects: Cynicism, breach of the psychological contract, and social undermining. All three have the potential to generate intentions to misbehave at work, effecting one's and others' careers.

Cynicism

Attitudes toward work are reflected in the way individuals act on their jobs. The OB literature, as shown in Chapter 1, has paid a great deal of attention to the relationship between attitudes and behavior in the workplace (e.g., O'Reilly, 1991). Thus, we have a relatively good understanding of how job satisfaction (e.g., Spector, 1997a) and commitment (e.g., Meyer & Allen, 1997) effect work-related behavior (Wiener, 1982). We refrain from delving into those well-documented work attitudes, but note that we also found overall satisfaction (Yosifon, 2001) and organizational commitment to be important determinants of misbehavior. Cohen (1999) found that they negatively correlate with self-report measures of workplace misconduct. We now discuss a less researched, yet prevalent attitude—cynicism at work—to represent a key attitudinal OMB antecedent.

Cynicism is a form of disparagement of others, inherent in many organizations (Kanter & Mirvis, 1989). Like most other complex attitudes (e.g., its counterpart, trust), it has affective, cognitive, and behavior intention components. Cynicism is both a general and specific attitude characterized by frustration and disillusionment, as well as negative feelings of contempt and distrust towards a person, group, ideology, social convention, or institution (Andersson, 1996). Not surprisingly, cynicism is described in various studies as a personality trait, an emotion, a belief, or attitude. Some argue that it reflects a basic philosophy about human nature, an antithesis to idealism, or a general attitude that one cannot depend on other people to be trustworthy and sincere. A cynical person may consider his or her work as oppressive, unrewarding, and unworthy of effort. For instance, if the firm does not truly care about its employees, it does not actually merit their commitment to it.

Whitener (1999) reported an interaction of employee cynicism and managerial behavior on how employees trust their superiors. Reichers, Wanous, and Austin (1997) examined employee cynicism about formal organizational change and argued that although such change is necessary in most organizations as a condition for their survival, many of its targets (i.e., the affected personnel) tend to remain cynical about both its importance and effectiveness. Cynicism about organizational change, they maintain, often combines pessimism about the likelihood of successful change, accompanied by casting the blame for the current and future bad fortunes on the incompetent or lazy managers responsible for the change.

Data from their study, and previously published research, suggest numerous factors that foster cynicism. These include a history of change programs that were not successful, a lack of adequate information about change, and a predisposition to cynicism. Cynicism regarding organizational changes has negative consequences for commitment, satisfaction, and motivation of employees. We consider cynicism behavior as an important precursor of all types of OMB.

Cynicism about organizational change is distinct from skepticism and resistance to change (Reichers et al., 1997). Skeptics doubt the likelihood of success, but they are still reasonably hopeful that positive change will occur. Resistance to change may result from self-interest, conservatism, past experience, misunderstanding, and inherent limited tolerance for change. Yet cynicism about change involves a real loss of faith in the leaders of change, and it is more often than not a response to a history of change attempts that have not entirely or clearly been successful. More important, cynicism frequently arises, despite the best intentions of those initiating and managing the change process. It can actually become a self-fulfilling prophecy if cynics refuse to support change. Cynicism is recognized as an important barrier to change and has the potential to spill over into other aspects of work and personal life, such as OMB.

To determine the causes and consequences of cynicism in the workplace, Andersson and Bateman (1997) conducted a scenario-based experiment. Their results reveal that high levels of executive compensation, poor organizational performance, and harsh immediate layoffs generate cynicism among white-collar workers. They believe that cynicism relates negatively to intentions to perform good citizenship behavior, which is conceptualized (as noted earlier) as individual behavior that is discretionary, not directly or explicitly recognized by the formal reward system, and that, in the aggregate, promotes the effective functioning of the organization (Organ, 1988). These behaviors (1) do not explicitly lead to rewards or punishment, (2) are not part of an employee's job description, and (3) do not require training to perform. Yet Andersson and Bateman also proposed that cynicism is positively related to employee intentions to comply with requests to engage in unethical behaviors. Cynicism may result in OMB Types S, D, and O.

Breach of the Psychological Contract

Making and keeping promises are the heart and soul of any mutual voluntary interrelationship. This is the basis for trust in any relationship in general and at work in particular. These simple and fundamental precepts underlie the psychological contract approach. Although its sources can be traced to early OB literature (Argyris, 1960) and research (Kotter, 1973), it was Rousseau's work (e.g., 1989, 1990; Rousseau & Parks, 1993; Rousseau & Tijoriwala, 1998) that elevated the idea to a solid, universally accepted, theoretical framework. The theory is fully described in Rousseau's (1995) influential book, *Psychological contracts in organizations*.

Psychological contracts are implicit, unwritten agreements between agents who wish to be connected in some kind of social exchange (e.g., employee–employer, supervisor–subordinate, and mentor–trainee). The contract enumerates, negotiates, specifies, and communicates mutual expectations to give to and receive from each other (Kotter, 1973) or specific mutual obligations and promises (Rousseau, 1995). Although such an implicit understanding may not be legally binding, it is believed to be a strong antecedent of any social exchange within the organization.

The problem begins when one or both parties to a contract sense a violation—a reneging on promises or a breach. Unlike the concept of unmet expectations (Porter & Steers, 1973), which denotes, for example, a new employee's frustrations because real promises are not actually delivered by the organization, a psychological contract violation occurs when one party perceives that its counterpart is unable or unwilling (or both) to keep its promises (Robinson, 1996; Rousseau, 1995; Turnley & Feldman, 1999, 2000). The psychological effects of breaking promises in organizations are often exacerbated because the contract comes with a sense of entitlement. This develops because temporally the psychological contract becomes more and more emotionally binding: "I have taken your word for a promotion as a promise, so now I feel I am entitled to it." Such implicit entitlements, of course, make feelings of contract violations more pronounced (Setter, 2001).

Violations of psychological contracts in organizations are not the exception, but the rule, as demonstrated by Robinson and Rousseau (1994). They are often associated with negative outcomes (Robinson, 1996) which range from disappointment and dissatisfaction to reduced trust, withdrawal, turnover, and decreased efforts (Rousseau, 1995). This comes as no surprise in the rapidly changing organizational world in which we live. In fact, these changes enhance the likelihood that organization members increasingly realize that their implicit agreements about work and careers are being violated (Rousseau, 1998). As these personal (basically cognitive) experiences become acute, we can expect negative emotions to follow: Frustration, disappointment, cynicism, anger, feeling let down, and betrayal. These emotions amount to a fairly strong affective reaction of being mistreated or even violated. Hirschman (1970) predicted that such emotions push individuals to react by both passive resignation and active protest. Robinson and Rousseau (1994) found empirical support for such reactions. In their study of 128 management alumni who were surveyed at graduation and a year later while already employed, they found that the occurrence of a psychological contract violation correlated positively with turnover and negatively with job satisfaction.

We extend these ideas and findings to predict that contract violations will also affect members' intentions to engage in OMB. The more and longer organization members perceive their implicit psychological agreements with a relevant agent of the organization (a colleague, supervisor, human resources representative, senior management) as breached, the stronger will be the negative emotional reaction, and the higher the likelihood that they will engage in OMB (Type S and/or Type D).

As discussed in previous chapters, both self-benefiting and damaging misbehaviors can manifest themselves in a variety of ways and levels: Intra- and interpersonal, property, production, and political. For example, one can suspect that a strong sense of frustration about entitlements will lead to thoughts about getting even (retribution), which might in turn lead to the intention to inflict some real damage on those perceived as breaking a promise. Research provides a better understanding of the specific effects that varying degrees of perceived contract violation may have on the intention to engage in OMB (e.g., Bordia et al., 2008; Chiu & Peng, 2008; Jensen et al., 2010).

Social Undermining

Despite the emotions described in previous sections, interpersonal relationships at work, we contend, are mostly quite congenial. When you ask employees about their reasons for coming to work, almost invariably you hear about how friendly and helpful people are around them. Moreover, employees tend to recognize the importance of being cooperative as part of the reciprocal relationships that are so necessary for their own task performance. Yet employees are also aware of the flip-side of the coin: Negative exchanges, interference, hindrance, cover-ups, rumor-mongering, and back-stabbing. Organizational realities are replete with both types of interpersonal exchanges.

Duffy, Ganster, and Pagon (2002) reported an investigation of social undermining in the workplace conducted among Slovenian police officers. Participants were asked about the behavior of their supervisor and coworkers. With regard to the immediate supervisor, they were asked: How often has your supervisor intentionally hurt your feelings? Put you down when you questioned work procedures? Undermined your effort to be successful on the job? Belittled your ideas? Did not defend you when people spoke poorly of you? Concerning their peers, the subjects were asked: How often has the coworker closest to you intentionally insulted you? Spread rumors about you? Delayed work to make you look bad or slow you down? Talked negatively about you behind your back? Gave you incorrect or misleading information about the job? A statistical analysis of the items revealed that the first set of questions indeed clustered as supervisor undermining and coworker undermining. Duffy et al. (2002) defined the overall construct of *social undermining* as "behavior intended to hinder, over time, the ability to establish and maintain positive interpersonal relationships, work-related success, and favorable reputation" (p. 332).

Undermining can evidently take different forms. It can be a direct act, such as saying derogatory things and rejecting or belittling somebody's well-intended offer, or it can be done passively by withholding something desired by the other party, such as concealing information (Kuchuk, 2015), not revealing a plan, excluding the person from important engagements, and so on. By the same token, undermining may be explicit, verbal, or physical, such as a vocal refusal to give assistance, or it may be more passive, by avoiding contact and giving the silent treatment.

As expected, Duffy and his colleagues (2002) found that high levels of perceived undermining were related to measures of active (e.g., stealing) and passive (e.g., absence from work) counterproductive behaviors (Raelin, 1994; Robinson & Bennett, 1995; Skarlicki & Folger, 1997). This is quite consistent with similar conceptions of antisocial behavior at work (Giacalone & Greenberg, 1997), workplace deviance (Robinson & Bennett, 1995), and workplace aggression (Neuman & Baron, 1997). Therefore, we view willful and intended undermining as OMB Types S and D because, like violation of psychological contracts or cynicism, it too may trigger processes of negative affect, aversive emotions, retaliatory sentiments, and, consequently, a decision to engage in different forms of OMB.

8

POSITION-LEVEL AND WORKGROUP-LEVEL ANTECEDENTS

Lead us not into temptation.

– New Testament

Conditions that affect members' behavior at work are found at the individual, group, and organizational levels. In this chapter, we explore how the characteristics of the job and how membership in a specific workgroup may increase the intention to misbehave (see Figure 8.1). Job characteristics play an important role in enhancing good performance, as well as creating crucial forces that stimulate misbehavior. In the first part of this chapter, we will argue that lax controls may be construed by employees as an organization's weakness or indifference, which in turn may be interpreted as a license to misbehave. To support some of our claims, we present data from field research designed to test such suppositions especially as they pertain to job-level attributes as antecedents of OMB. In the second part of the chapter, we will shift our focus to the group level of analysis by looking at the way certain group dynamics, such as the strengthening of internal cohesiveness and the group pressure to conform, also influence how individual team members operate. For example, workgroups, by pressure or modeling, may induce and enforce social loafing and withholding effort or damaging manifestations such as theft and aggression. Recall that in the previous chapters we discussed some of these as manifestations. Now we look at them as antecedents. We start with the job itself as a potential antecedent of OMB.

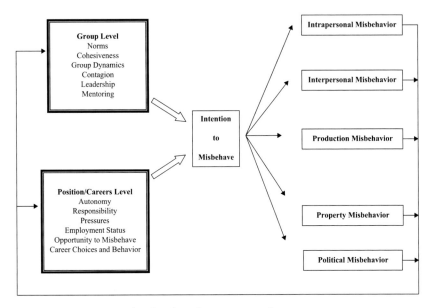

FIGURE 8.1 Position-level and workgroup antecedents

Job-Level Antecedents

Our readers probably do not recognize the names Terry Lynn Barton and Leonard Gregg, but both received a great deal of media attention during the hot summer of 2002. Ms. Barton was a seasonal employee of the Colorado State Forest Service for 18 years. Mr. Gregg was a part-time firefighter from Cibecue at the Fort Apache reservation in Arizona. These two individuals, federal employees paid to control forest fires, were both charged with actually igniting them, generating wildfires that went out of control causing extensive damage. On June 18, 2002, federal investigators concluded that ten days earlier, while alone on routine patrol, Ms. Barton intentionally started a fire that eventually burned nearly 120,000 acres in central Colorado. Fueled by temperatures in the mid-90s and swirling winds, the fire went out of control, burning in its wake 25 homes and forcing thousands to flee (*New York Times*, June 19, 2002). Investigators concluded that the fire was deliberately set and had been staged to look like a campfire gone wild. They did not buy Ms. Barton's story of innocently burning a letter from her estranged husband at the campsite. Ms. Barton was sentenced to 12 years in prison for damaging federal and private property, as well as misleading investigators. Mr. Gregg was charged with setting a blaze that burned vast lands of natural vegetation and more than 400 homes and was sentenced to ten years in prison. Prosecutors argued that he purposely started the fire to make money fighting it (*Wikipedia*, July 20, 2015).

Both cases of misconduct on the job are certainly extreme and very serious because of the disastrous outcomes. However, it is important to account for job factors that contribute to this kind of behavior. We now focus on the role that job autonomy plays in presenting employees with opportunities to carry out damaging acts such as the ones just described. In these two cases, performing their jobs in isolated areas and having the knowhow and means to set the fires are important contributing factors to the employees' decision to engage in such acts.

The Job Autonomy Study

One of the factors conducive to misbehavior is the actual opportunity to engage in it (i.e., the degree of freedom or latitude allowed for individual members to intentionally act in ways that violate core organizational norms that specify what is considered proper work conduct). The level of prescribed job autonomy, although designed to create a structure of opportunity that facilitates desirable and normative behaviors, may also contribute to people's engagement in misbehavior. Paradoxically, this may be an unanticipated consequence of management's good intentions. Most research on the effects of job autonomy on employees has focused on examining its link to positive work outcomes such as performance, satisfaction, and creativity (e.g., Volmer et al., 2012). We identified few studies that dealt with negative outcomes and therefore decided to explore this issue ourselves.

We examined the possible negative effects of job autonomy on work-related behavior among Israeli employees (Vardi & Weitz, 2001), we sought to determine whether employee-perceived autonomy should be regarded not only as a positive aspect of their job but also, under certain conditions, as an opportunity to defy norms of proper conduct. We asked 250 managers and non-managers from different organizations, occupations, and ranks to fill out questionnaires concerning their own as well as their colleagues' actions on the job that are considered to be OMB. Our findings indicate that autonomy and its subcomponents were positively related to both self and others' reported incidents of OMB. In addition, we tested hypotheses concerning the role of autonomy in explaining OMB relative to selected individual and organizational variables. We found that certain personality (Type A), attitudinal (job satisfaction and professional identification), and organizational (position) variables were directly and indirectly related to OMB.

The literature on job autonomy as an organizational variable can be divided into two domains: Control theories and job design theories. Control theories treat organizational control as a factor that influences worker's attitudes and behavior. Because researchers view autonomy as a type of control, they attempt to understand its effect on employee behavior (Ganster, 1989; Karasek & Theorell, 1990; Spector, 1986; Thompson, 1981). The job design theories regard autonomy as part of work enrichment (Abdel Halim, 1978; Lee et al., 1990; Pines, 1981). Job autonomy has been conceptualized primarily as a characteristic that elicits positive work attitudes and behaviors. Our research has unveiled a dark side of job autonomy – that for organizations it could be a double-edged sword.

The Job Characteristics Model (Hackman & Oldham, 1976) is by far the best-known model relating job design to employee attitudes and behavior. One of the core job dimensions that contributes to motivation and satisfaction in a specific position is *autonomy*. This dimension is viewed as the way in which the position provides individuals with meaningful discretion, independence, and personal initiative in organizing their work and controlling performance. Autonomy is assumed to engender a certain critical psychological state (experienced responsibility for results of the work), which, in turn, may contribute to the coveted work outcomes: High internal work motivation, high-quality work performance, high satisfaction with the work, and low absenteeism and turnover.

Most researchers who study the negative effects of job autonomy have attributed their results to differences in the need for autonomy (Harrell & Alpert, 1979; Langer, 1983). For people with a low need for autonomy, a job characterized by a great deal of autonomy will create a sense of tension, overload, and at times decline in their work satisfaction. Moreover, autonomy may decrease their sense of control and arouse a feeling of confusion. In other words, autonomy is a positive job characteristic only if and when the individual is interested in and capable of handling it. Hackman and Oldham (1976) considered personal growth needs as having a moderating influence on the worker whose job is enriched. Yet they did not raise the possibility that an individual with low growth needs may react to autonomy—not only by a decline in motivation or satisfaction, but also by venting frustration and misbehaving. Spector (1997b) showed how such job context frustrations can lead to antisocial work behavior.

Combining the job design and control theories, Breaugh (1985) defined *job autonomy* as workers' level of freedom to decide on work methods, schedules, and the criteria for evaluating their work. To assess these characteristics, he developed a research instrument that measures the degree of judgment the individual has with regard to various dimensions of his or her work as follows: (1) autonomy in work method—the degree to which individuals are free to conduct and choose processes and methods for performing the work, (2) autonomy in scheduling—the degree to which workers feel that they have control over their schedule, and (3) autonomy in performance criteria—the degree to which workers are able to set or choose the standards for evaluating their own performance. We adopted this definition for our study, and explored the role of autonomy, hierarchical level, and type of job as antecedents of OMB.

Autonomy and OMB

To date, very little has been written about job autonomy as a possible cause of OMB (Lu et al., 2016; Vardi & Weitz, 2001). Those researchers who did so (e.g., Allen & Greenberger, 1980; Wortman & Breham, 1975) posited that a low level of job autonomy is likely to increase the tendency for misconduct. For example, Analoui and Kakabadse (1992) noted that one of the motives for unconventional practices they observed both managers and subordinates commit was the desire for more autonomy. In another study, Molstad (1988) found that, when faced with routine work and micro-management, workers developed various action strategies to give themselves a sense of control and autonomy. For example, they created an impression among the managers that they were working hard and were not free to take on more work, or they developed a private language that the managers could not understand. This "autonomous" behavior gave the workers a sense of control despite the attempted management supervision.

Yet, one might argue that a great deal of job freedom is precisely what might lead to misbehavior. Extensive job autonomy may actually create opportunities for OMB. For example, Mars (1982) found that differences in the level of supervision over employees' attendance at work were related to the opportunity structure for deviance. Similarly, Bukowski's (2009) *Post office* provides a vivid account of a postman's trials and tribulations on the dangerous and challenging mail delivery routes of Los Angeles in the 1970s, serving as a very realistic example. According to Vardi and Wiener (1996), organizations with sensible control systems are more effective in controlling their employees' behavior than organizations with either very restrictive or very flexible systems. The latter, they proposed, are liable to increase the motivation for exhibiting OMB Types S and D. We suggest that both high and low autonomy might, albeit inadvertently, increase improper conduct on the job. These job characteristics, along with their known positive effects, may also enable manifestations of OMB. Autonomy, by definition, gives the worker a great deal of latitude in performing tasks, scheduling, and evaluation of output. When employees perceive their positions as autonomous, such perception may facilitate misbehaviors such as working slowly, stealing time, engaging in private activities during working hours, and abusing other organizational resources. Based on this assumption, we hypothesized that job autonomy and OMB are positively correlated: The higher the job autonomy, the stronger the intention to misbehave (Hypothesis 1).

Hierarchical Level

There is no doubt that employees, at various hierarchical levels, differ in terms of work needs, motivation, expectations and aspirations, and the degree to which they desire job autonomy. More specifically, differences were found in the ways employees at different job levels cope with autonomy and job pressures (Greenberg & Strasser, 1986; Savery, 1988; Westman, 1992). Salancik (1977) argued that employees at more senior levels develop a higher sense of responsibility than lower ranking individuals. Steers and Spencer (1977) and Schein (1978) suggested that a higher ranking manager is more involved in decision-making and identifies more with the organization and its core values. Thus, although managers are more exposed to temptations by virtue of their formal position, greater independence, contacts with external agents, broader knowledge of the organization, and easier access to resources, the inherent responsibility, moral development, authority, and observance of rules and procedures should mitigate tendencies for misbehavior. Additionally, managers are expected to adhere to the normative system to which they subscribe and serve as role models for others, especially their own subordinates. Therefore, we hypothesize that the tendency for OMB is lower for those in a managerial role than in a non-managerial role (Hypothesis 2).

Type of Job

Following Schein's (1978) model of organizational careers, Gaertner (1980) characterized the types of jobs in an organization by the extent to which they permit examination of the employees' skills and attitudes. She defined an *assessment position* as one that requires great administrative and managerial responsibility and exposes the individual to various career management bodies in the system. Thus, the performance of these role holders is under greater scrutiny. For example, Holtsman-Chen (1984) examined career progression in a governmental security agency. She found that service in field positions increased workers' chances of advancing in the system because agents' behavior was closely monitored. In contrast, Vardi and Wiener (1996) noted that in many peripheral jobs, it is difficult to supervise and control workers' behavior. For instance, messenger services or services at the client's home are jobs with built-in opportunities for misbehaviors such as cheating, loafing, and stealing (e.g., Rubin-Kedar, 2000). That is, these types of jobs are liable to increase the tendency for misbehavior (particularly OMB Type S). Therefore, we hypothesized that in field positions, there is a greater tendency for OMB than for employees located in company headquarters (Hypothesis 3).

To test these hypotheses, data were collected in a private personnel placement center in the greater Tel Aviv area. The sample comprised employees from various organizations and diverse jobs. The research instrument was a self-report questionnaire especially designed for this study.

OMB

We used items characterizing production deviance for this scale that were adopted from Robinson and Bennett (1995). In addition, we included two types of lead questions—one pertaining to behavior by others and one to behavior of the subject. In this part of the study, the items were presented as projective questions, relating to other people in the organization. For example, "To what extent do workers at your workplace lie about their work hours?" In a separate section, we presented the same items as direct questions relating to the employee and his or her behavior at work.

Job Autonomy

Job autonomy level was examined by the subject's self-report about his or her last job. Items were adopted from a questionnaire by Breaugh (1985). The first three items relate to the work methods (e.g., "I could decide how to do my work"), the next three items examine the degree of autonomy in setting work schedules (e.g., "My work allows me to decide when to do each action"), and the last three items refer to autonomy in evaluating the outcomes (e.g., "I could choose what goals and tasks to accomplish and complete").

Job Type

Job type was examined by this question: "Did you perform your job in the office (staff position) or outside the office (field position)?"

Job Level

Each subject was asked two questions pertaining to whether they had been in charge of other people. Those who answered positively were coded as *managers*, whereas others were coded as *non-managers*.

To test the main hypothesis, we correlated OMB with job autonomy and found a positive correlation both in reporting on others and on the self. Therefore, we consider that job autonomy is an antecedent of OMB because it is a structural feature of the job. In addition, a positive correlation was found between each individual dimension of autonomy (in the "general autonomy" variable) and OMB reported of the self and others, with the exception of the relation between autonomy in scheduling and OMB reported of others, which was not found to be significant. We also found a positive correlation between hierarchical level and reporting OMB of others. That is, managers who are responsible for other employees report on others' misconduct more than non-supervisory employees. However, no correlation between job type and OMB was found.

Finally, to test the assumption that job autonomy is a predictor of OMB, we regressed the misbehavior measures on job autonomy while controlling for some attitudinal measures we collected. As expected, job autonomy, employee satisfaction, and professional identity explained about 16 percent of the variance of the self-report OMB variable. Does all this make sense? Some possible explanations for the positive correlations found between job autonomy and OMB are discussed next.

Opportunity to Misbehave

This concept relates to the characteristics of the job or the organization that pave the way for deviance. The positive correlation between job autonomy and OMB described earlier supports the hypothesis that the structure of opportunity, availability of varied avenues for action, and extensive freedom on the job may increase the tendency for OMB (Vardi & Wiener, 1996). Moreover, if autonomy is perceived by subordinates as the absence of close supervision or, alternatively, as managerial weakness, it may actually increase the tendency to commit OMB.

Sense of Inequity

A job characterized by a great deal of autonomy inevitably entails more tasks and personal responsibility. Individuals who think they are not adequately rewarded for their great investment in the job may feel a sense of inequity that may lead to an increased tendency for OMB. They may attempt to compensate themselves in more creative ways, such as workarounds, decreased output, slow work, resting, and taking care of private business and behaving unethically on the job. The freedom of action they possess may enable them to adopt these behaviors. Research on inequity and distributive injustice support this claim (e.g., Greenberg, 1990a, 1993). In addition, Ackroyd and Thompson (1999) suggested that most OMB is driven by employees' sense of organizational and managerial maltreatment. When despair and opportunity coexist, misbehavior may emerge.

Managerial Responsibility

A significant positive correlation was found between managerial role and OMB (reported of others). Managers report more OMB (of subordinates, colleagues, and other managers) than do workers in non-managerial roles. The hypothesis regarding the negative correlation between managerial role and OMB was not supported. By virtue of their role, managers are responsible for enforcing the rules, regulations, and procedures; are more involved in decision-making; are required to prevent employee OMB; and identify more with the organization and its values (e.g., Salancik, 1977; Savery, 1988; Steers & Spencer, 1977). Indeed, they are expected to be role models for proper behavior.

The Fast-Food Study

Supermarkets, home appliance businesses, cellular companies, personal computer stores, credit card companies, and fast-food chains offer home deliveries and messenger services. Although the number of jobs involved is growing, there are few studies of the behavior of employees working outside the organizations' physical space. Therefore, we sought to examine the relationship between various types of jobs, including those of messengers, and OMB and conducted a field study using an ethnographic approach. Following Kunda (1992, 2006) and Analoui and Kakabadse (1992), qualitative data were collected through observation and onsite interviews (interview citations that follow are adapted from Rubin-Kedar, 2000).

The study was designed to examine on-the-job behavior characterizing fast-food employees. It distinguishes between levels of OMB of various groups of employees within the organization and investigates how the organizational values of these groups affect their tendency toward engaging in OMB. The Burger Farm franchise in Israel has more than 70 branches, 40 of which provide home deliveries. Branches providing home deliveries employ, in addition to the messengers, a person responsible for this service and telephone operators receiving the orders. Although the performance of branch employees is closely monitored by the manager and deputy, the behavior of the messengers working outside the branch is of great concern to the chain's management, who are apparently aware of the difficulties in directly supervising the behavior of these employees.

Participating branches had approximately 40 branch workers (i.e., employees working within the branch precincts, among them cashiers, telephone operators, and kitchen staff). In addition, they employed some 20 uniformed messengers on scooters. The cashiers' job included dealing with the customers, receiving orders and payment from the customers, and handing them food; kitchen staff were responsible for preparing the food and bringing it to the cashiers; telephone operators received orders from customers wishing to have food brought to their homes or workplaces and passed the orders to the kitchen staff.

Messengers, all young men mostly employed right after their military service, hold a coveted position at Burger Farm. They are responsible for checking the order before leaving for the designated address to ensure that the food prepared in the kitchen matched the order received by telephone. Then they rush through the city traffic, deliver the order, and receive the cash payment. It is not surprising that messengers' conduct outside the branch is of great concern to management. For example, the manager responsible for delivery countrywide explained:

> We operate covert customer services in order to check the behavior of the messengers when they are outside the branch. Sometimes we also receive information from customers who complain about unsatisfactory service by a messenger, or people report reckless driving. But apart from these measures, it is difficult to determine how they actually behave; the fact that they work outside the branch reduces the possibility of supervision.

As we examined the information that was collected, we began to suspect that the tendency toward engaging in OMB is higher among messengers than branch employees. Our findings indeed support this notion, particularly when it comes to self-reported OMB. This is consistent with theoretical propositions made by a number of researchers regarding the relationship between the job type and OMB (Hollinger, 1986; Van Maanen & Barley, 1984). These researchers related the built-in opportunities provided by the job as a factor likely to explain OMB. According to Vardi and Wiener (1992, 1996), the concept of *built-in opportunity* refers particularly to activities that are difficult for the organization to control, such as home deliveries, cashier work, and food service, which make misconduct relatively easy.

Such delivery messengers apparently have many more built-in opportunities for OMB than other workers because they spend most of their time outside the branch and are not closely supervised. Therefore, they may think that they "can do whatever they feel like." One participant remarked that sometimes there are no deliveries during his shift ("down time") so, "why not go and see friends, instead of vegetating at the branch. No one can find out, and if they do ask questions, there are plenty of excuses for the boss: 'There were traffic jams,' 'I couldn't find the house,' 'they didn't give me the correct address,' and a lot of things like that. Sometimes we fix up beforehand to meet with friends, when there is no work—that's what everybody does."

Taking a break between deliveries is just one example of the variety of misbehaviors the messengers mentioned. "It's much better to be a messenger," one of them said. "They don't push you around all the time. For instance, it's different for the cashiers—they [supervisors] stand beside them every minute insisting about cleanliness, 'put your cap on,' and so on. I am away most of the time. Who'll tell me off if I don't put my cap on? We don't bother about such nonsense."

Our conclusions from this study can be summarized as follows:

- Among messengers there was a greater tendency to engage in OMB as compared with branch workers.
- Among branch employees there was a greater tendency to adopt positive organizational values as compared with messengers.
- Managers were more likely to adopt positive organizational values than subordinates.
- An increase in the adherence to organizational values led to a decrease in OMB.
- Managers reported a greater tendency to engage in OMB against property as compared with subordinates (when reporting about others).
- No moderating influence by organizational values was found on the relationship between organizational rank and OMB.

Furthermore, we may begin to draw some implications, at least in terms of increased managerial awareness, to job-level antecedents of OMB. To enable organizations to influence managers' and employees' intentions to engage in OMB, organizations must be aware of the following factors:

- The differences between groups of workers and their differing perceptions of what is considered OMB.
- The importance of organizational values in affecting the employees' behavior positively or negatively.
- The possibility that conflict between core and subculture values may encourage adoption of certain patterns of OMB.
- The need to maintain consistency between codes of behavior and managerial practice.

Group-Level Influences

The Importance of Teams

The efficiency of most of work processes in organizations depends on workers' willful collaboration (Porter et al., 1975). In an increasing number of organizations, planning and decision-making processes, as well as the actual work, are carried out by teams of workers. This has many advantages, in terms of job satisfaction and productivity. By definition, a *team* is characterized by ongoing interaction among its members to facilitate the attainment of a shared goal or the execution of a collaborative project (Tziner & Vardi, 1982). The emphasis shifts from individual work to interdependence, which calls for mutuality and full cooperation among the members, tolerance, and the overcoming of personal and professional differences of opinion. The following questions arise: Are all team members willing and able to invest as much effort in the collective task as they would in an individual one? Will group members' negative attitudes and behaviors towards work influence others? Will they feel committed to its success although they are not always rewarded accordingly? Are certain workers taking advantage of others in the group? The answers to these questions are not clear because, unlike in a primary group (e.g., a family) wherein the relations constitute its aim, the survival and successes of a team are greatly dependent on the individuals' belief that their participation in the group will be personally beneficial to them—more so than if they worked on their own. When this belief is lacking, the willingness of team members to contribute their relative share (and more than their share) to the success of the collective task may diminish.

The Contagion Effect

The study of group behavior typically focuses on members' actions as a function of processes such as groupthink (Janis, 1982), conformity to group norms (Asch, 1956), and social learning (Bandura, 1973). As early as the turn of the last century, Le Bon (1908) explained the conduct of the mob by proposing that emotions and behavior in a crowd are contagious, that individuals will subjugate their own interests to those of the group. Social contagion occurs when individuals change their behavior as a result of their contact with others (Latané, 2000). More succinctly, social contagion "is the spread of behavior from one person to another through the social information an imitator (or focal individual) has of the behavior of a referent other" (Ferguson, 2007, p. 32). That is, the contagion effect occurs through the transmission of social information and learning (direct observation, indirect knowledge, verbal and non-verbal cues) of behavior among workgroup members.

Social contagion is a powerful medium. The social group influences the individual's cognitions and perceptions regarding her work environment and thereby shapes proper behavior or misbehavior. Seeing a colleague at work intentionally misbehave for personal gain, or to harm the organization, and learning that the misbehaving actor is not reprimanded for his misdeed may create a contagion effect.

While similar, social learning and social contagion are not the same. In the latter, employees who are inclined to misbehave perceive others around them misbehaving, which may prompt them to intentionally misbehave. In social learning, however, the misbehavior is reinforced by external stimuli and the employee's OMB is learned through observation (Bandura, 1973). Some researchers call this type of behavior "copycatting" (Robinson et al., 2014, p. 131). That is, employees who see fellow employees engaging in OMB and being rewarded for it are more likely to engage in OMB. In social contagion, the copycatting employee would be motivated by an internal factor such as his perception of justice as well as by external factors such as seeing OMB being rewarded. Internal as well as external factors are predictors of social contagion (Ferguson, 2007; Robinson & O'Leary-Kelly, 1998). The social contagion logic posits that an employee may desire to misbehave, but because of inner tensions such as a sense of justice and personal moral code may resist acting upon the impulse. Employees with low moral standards, in a workgroup in which OMB is rewarded, rather than punished, may misbehave as well.

We recently conducted a study to explore the role of social contagion in the spread of OMB in organizations (Vardi et al., 2014). We examined whether misbehavior of workgroup members influences the misbehavior of a single group member in order to determine if individual-level factors such as personality traits and organizational justice perceptions moderate this influence. The model we proposed is a rather simple one:

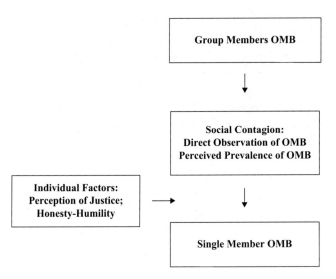

FIGURE 8.2   Contagion model of OMB

To test our model, we used a self-report questionnaire to collect data from 147 employees belonging to 26 work teams, employed for more than six months. The represented organizations were diverse (high-tech companies, government offices, telecommunications firms, academic institutions, etc.) with 50 employees and more. Each work team consisted of at least three team members.

We found a positive relationship between OMB of group members and OMB of a single group member as well as a positive relationship between social information (direct observation and perceived prevalence of OMB) and OMB of group members. We also found that social information (direct observation and perceived prevalence of OMB) mediates the relationship between OMB of group members and OMB of an individual group member. Regarding internal factors, we found a negative relationship between employees characterized by being low on the trait of honesty-humility (being truthful, loyal and sincere; Ashton et al., 2000) and OMB. Similarly, we found a positive relationship between low-level justice perception and OMB.

The STEAL Motive (to Steal)

Greenberg (1997) offered an insight into the role of groups in explaining employee theft, which may be expanded to other forms of OMB as well, especially those classified as Type S. He found that "employee theft is a behavior that is carefully regulated by organizational norms and work group norms and that stealing is an effective way of supporting these norms" (p. 89). This may sound quite surprising at first. However, this contention becomes clear as he clarified the STEAL motive—STEAL stands for *Support, Thwart, Even the score,* and *ApprovaL*—these are the four types of motives for stealing. The two dimensions that produce them are (1) the intention—whether the act is motivated by prosocial or antisocial considerations, and (2) the target—whether the act targets the organization or coworkers.

Support is a prosocial behavior because the employee steals to adhere to his or her group, which condones and may even encourage the act. *Thwart* applies to the situation in which the motive to steal assets from the employer is in defiance of group norms—stealing actually thwarts the group's attempts to control the employee's behavior. Stealing to *even the score* (as revenge or retaliation) occurs when an employee violates the organizational norms. In contrast, *approval* occurs when an employee steals to gain favor by a supervisor known to condone and encourage such acts. From any vantage point, the group plays an extremely important role in either increasing or limiting employee theft behavior (see detailed explanations in Greenberg, 1997).

Withholding Effort in Teams

As suggested in Chapter 5, researchers are becoming more interested in team effects and have begun to explore whether individuals working as a team experience full cooperation among its members for the attainment of collective goals. The literature dealing with social loafing suggests that members are preoccupied with comparing their own efforts to those made by other participants. They often wonder whether it is worth making an effort because, as far as they can judge, the others are loafing. Kidwell and Bennett (1993) developed a construct that focuses on the propensity to withhold effort, denoting the probability that the individual will invest less than maximum effort in a group task. We follow their thinking and suggest a number of conditions that may facilitate the propensity to engage in loafing in work teams.

The Reward System

One of the effects of the economic approach to the issue of withholding individual effort within an organizational or team framework is the emphasis on a reward system, which is considered likely to counteract the tendency to withhold effort. That is, rewards, and the fear of losing them, create motivation to refrain from counterproductive behavior (Cappelli & Chauvin, 1991). This approach perceives workers to be rational thinkers who are preoccupied by their own interests and evaluate the costs incurred by withholding effort. Under conditions of widespread unemployment, workers are afraid they would be made redundant as a result of them withholding effort, and therefore they refrain from shirking and unproductive behavior. Nonetheless, when the perceived cost of dismissal is low, such as in conditions of full employment economy, team members may be more inclined to withhold effort.

Group Size

As discussed in Chapter 5, Ringelmann found that when people work together as a group, their collective performance is lower than the expected sum total of their individual performances (cited in Kravitz & Martin, 1986). He also found that the larger the group size, the corresponding individual contribution is less pronounced and the individual worker may exert less effort. The larger the group, the greater the anonymity of the worker, and the possibility to supervise individual performance decreases. This, in turn, diminishes the ability to recognize individual effort. Such a situation appears to lead rational individuals to reduce their efforts because these are not sufficiently appreciated by the supervisors. In contrast, smaller groups may succeed in generating greater individual effort because they permit supervision of the individual's behavior, thereby promoting effort and collaboration. Moreover, in a small team, each member's contribution is more critical for the completion of the collective task than in a large group. Taken together, the characteristics of the small team encourage the members to invest additional effort.

Turnover Rate

Collaboration among team members may be influenced by long-term preservation of an accepted effort level. It is easier for team members to refuse to collaborate and withhold effort if their participation is temporary or if they are not well acquainted with other team members. Therefore, the level of collaboration also depends on the turnover rate of team members. When that rate is low, there is a good chance that the relations among the team members will be more personal and will involve deeper emotional ties (Granovetter, 1985), which may affect their willingness to invest effort. However, when the turnover rate is high, workers' ties to the group are weak and temporary, and their motivation to collaborate and invest a great deal of effort may decrease. Emotional ties, developing through sustained interaction and going beyond rational cost-effectiveness analysis, are therefore likely to affect individual effort.

Length of Service

A demographic variable that may play an important role in strengthening the emotional ties developing among team members is the similarity of the team members' tenure or *homogeneous length of service*. The importance of this type of homogeneity lies in the socialization process the team members undergo; it may foster the development of stronger emotional ties among the members. For example, when all participants begin working together as a team at approximately the same time, have similar experiences, and arrive at shared perceptions of norms of satisfactory behavior, they are more likely to identify with the group and be committed to the attainment of its goals. Such cohesiveness may constitute an important factor affecting the decision of team members to invest maximum effort, thus fulfilling their obligation to the other team members. Therefore, the longer the time team members spend together, the more likely each member is to invest individual effort because of feelings of mutual obligation and commitment to the collective task. Conversely, heterogeneity in the length of service decreases the possibility of the group identity. Therefore, group members who have spent less time together, or joined the team at different times, are less likely to develop a sense of mutual obligation and more likely to withhold personal effort.

Contribution to Task

What is the point of investing great effort if it is not duly acknowledged and appreciated? The perception of relative individual contribution to group performance is the worker's belief that his or her manager is aware of his or her personal efforts. Apparently, a necessary precondition for shirking and withholding effort is the lack of awareness and recognition of worker's individual contributions by those in charge. Indeed, the assumption underlying research on social loafing is that the larger the group size, the less motivated individuals are to invest effort, among other things, because they believe they can hide in the crowd or because they know that the person responsible cannot identify their personal efforts and achievements. Thus, if workers believe that their manager encounters difficulties in supervising the task and identifying individual performance, they will be less willing to waste their efforts for nothing and tend to withhold them. In group tasks, based on complex technology, *interdependence* among the team members grows, supervision of performance decreases, and, as a result, workers' motivation to invest personal effort is low. However, when mutual dependence among team members is low and supervision is easier, workers are more willing to invest personal effort during the performance of a collective task.

Social Norms

Consensus within the group with regard to social norms may reduce the worker's utilitarian self-interest. This means that if there is a consensus in the team, most of the members will be willing to forego their personal gain and focus on the task and collective interest. It has already been shown that the individual is more influenced by the desire to act according to normative social standards than on the basis of cost-effectiveness. Obviously, people may differ in this respect, but it is to be expected that, when the prevalent social norms emphasize investment of effort, team members will act accordingly even if it is not for their own benefit. Teams of volunteers provide a salient example of this phenomenon. Conversely, when individual loafing and withholding effort are the prevalent group norm, its members will join in and withhold effort even if exerting effort is likely to be beneficial to them.

Perceived Fairness

Do individuals reduce their personal effort because they expect their colleagues to slack off and they wish to achieve equity? Indeed, research indicates that employees prefer to reduce their effort so as not to feel they are giving others *a free ride*. Workers' marked tendency to withhold effort is due to their being perturbed that others will withhold effort and enjoy their contribution to the task. However, this *sucker syndrome* is rejected by some researchers, who maintain that individuals decide to withhold effort simply because they believe that other team members intend to do so. Research reveals that under conditions of collective reward, individuals decide on the amount of effort in line with their subjective perception of the situation's fairness. This means that, to the extent that workers believe that other team members invest equal effort, and that they are not the only "suckers," they will invest personal effort to achieve the collective task. However, if they feel that other team members receive the same reward for less effort, they will avoid exerting effort in the collective task (Kidwell & Bennett, 1993).

Perceived Altruism

Altruism is expressed in two types of contributions in an organization: (1) prosocial behavior—workers' behavior within or beyond their role, helping individuals, groups, or organizations, not necessarily profitable for the organization; and (2) good citizenship—an informal contribution that workers choose to make, or withhold, regardless of formal rewards and sanctions. Altruistic behaviors, such as helping others with difficult tasks, instructing new workers, and helping those temporarily absent, may stem from inner moral principles or merely from friendliness or reciprocity among colleagues involving empathy and sympathy for others. If workers feel that most team members behave in an altruistic way toward each other, their own motivation to help and invest effort may grow. However, to the extent that they feel that the behavior of others in the team is not altruistic, they will presumably tend to behave similarly and reduce their own individual effort. This provides additional support to the contagion effect we discussed earlier.

9

ORGANIZATION-LEVEL ANTECEDENTS

The principal assumption underlying most scholarly work on the management of OB (e.g., March & Simon, 1958; Weick, 1979) is that work organizations affect the particular ways their members choose to behave on the job. The classical organization theory writers provided numerous frameworks designed to illustrate, explain, and provide the logic for these influences. We know that individual behavior is affected by a whole range of macro-variables such as the organization's environment (e.g., Aldrich, 1979; Katz & Kahn, 1978), the firm's strategy (e.g., Miles & Snow, 1978), the organization type (e.g., Etzioni, 1961), the organization design (Galbraith, 1977), the technology (e.g., Perrow, 1986; Thompson, 1967), the form and structure (Hall, 1976), and the organization's culture (Schein, 1985). A decade later, researchers began to explore organization-level effects on members' work-related misconduct (e.g., Ackroyd & Thompson, 1999; Vaughan, 1999).

We now focus on selected organization-level characteristics that are, to a large extent, defined, designed, and managed by the organization: Type and primary mission, culture and climate, and behavior control systems. Because these characteristics are accepted as important antecedents of members' work conduct (e.g., Johnson & Gill, 1993; Kunda, 1992, 2006; Nadler & Tushman, 1980), we suggest that they may also be useful in predicting and managing patterns of OMB. This perspective is depicted in Figure 9.1.

Before proceeding, we explain our point of view, noting that our main interest is in understanding individual work-related behavior. More precisely, we now identify macro-level antecedents that may account for the formation of implicit intentions to engage in OMB. We study the organization—a plausible antecedent for OMB. This approach differs from that of writers who choose to view misbehavior as an antecedent affecting the well-being of the organization as a whole. Consider, for example, the quite disturbing case-based book by Mitroff

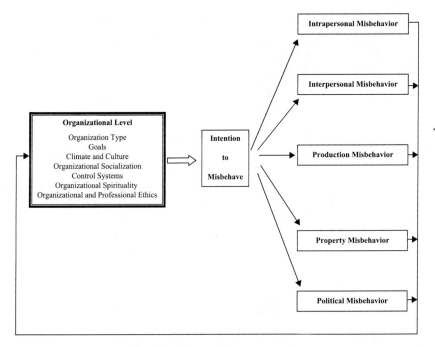

FIGURE 9.1 Organizational-level antecedents

and Kilmann (1984) aptly entitled: *Corporate tragedies: Product tampering, sabotage, and other catastrophes.* The authors discuss five types of organizational calamities, some of which are caused by internal sabotage, others by external tampering with products, and yet others are basically an inevitable misfortune when products just malfunction. First, we focus on the motive, not the consequences. Second, we pay more attention to sabotage and tampering by members of the organizations. We feel that it would be more useful for an organization to manage OMB perpetrated by members of the organization than to concentrate on external threats, some of which may be just plain *normal accidents*, to borrow Perrow's (1984) term.

Organization Type

Organizations are regarded by most theorists as formal social systems designed to produce goods and services through continuous exchange with their environments. In modern societies, they are formed, exist, and developed because of the effective and efficient manner in which they utilize resources, operating under various conditions of uncertainty, and handling large volumes of information processing to solve complex problems. Because of these capacities, work organizations come in different shapes and sizes representing countless possible combinations, permutations, and interactions. It is useful to categorize them so that scientists can draw some generalizations and provide predictions as to how they might resolve their unique sets of problems in terms of both business strategy and human resource management (see general reviews in Hall, 1999; Scott, 1998; Usdiken & Leblebici, 2001).

Proposing organizational typologies is an important step in furthering our understanding of the complex social phenomena called *work organizations*. The many classifications that have emerged over the past decades from this scientific effort allow for a large variety of theoretical explications of the organization–behavior relationship in which we are particularly interested. However, here we focus on high-tech firms, on the one hand, and public-service organizations, on the other. We examine the effects of organization type on misbehavior through the intervening role of positional and individual-level variables such as experience, autonomy, pressure, stress and burnout, and pay.

High-Tech

High-tech organizations employ, design, and/or manufacture software and hardware for advanced communications and computer technologies. Many firms devote their resources to technological advancement in the form of intensive research and development efforts. At times, development of sophisticated technology may outpace the development of the hardware necessary for their application (Moore, 1995). Their added value as an organization is the unique knowledge and novelty of the ideas their employees successfully generate. Because they face high levels of uncertainty, high-tech organizations attempt to recruit and select talented individuals who can effectively operate under such conditions—people who are creative, can produce new concepts, break new ground, raise substantial resources, and market their product in the highly competitive global market.

One can identify the following core features that characterize high-tech organizations.

Risk and uncertainty: High-tech organizations, especially start-ups, operate in turbulent, high-risk, extremely competitive environments. Such external conditions are often reflected in internal work environments saturated with a high degree of pressure and stress to meet deadlines, internal inter-project, inter-team competitions, as well as extremely demanding and unstructured work schedules (Ganot, 1999; Reshef-Tamari, 1999).

Attitude toward time: Time is of the essence in any high-tech organization because the fast pace of product development often renders even new ideas obsolete as they enter the market. Time seems to constantly be in short supply. Misuse of company time is considered extremely detrimental. Work is often not subject to normative time schedules—time zones in different parts of the world often govern local employee performance. Workers are continuously at the beck and call of their projects, firms, and clients.

Competitiveness: High-tech employees believe that a firm's success is directly tied to high-stake personal rewards and future options. This belief, in turn, leads to competitive behavior on the personal level and may lead to internal politicking and a jungle-fighting mentality at the firm level. Such beliefs, however, may contribute to a high attrition rate and burnout.

Structural flexibility: As a result of external turbulence, the internal designs of high-tech organizations are fluid. This environment is necessary for survival, and theorists have described this responsiveness with novel terms such as the *intelligent* (Arthur et al., 1995), *boundaryless* (Ashkenas et al., 1995), *virtual* (Cooper & Rousseau, 1999), *lean* (Holbeche, 1998), and *agile* (Gobillot, 2007; Gothelf, 2014) organizations. Although these terms hint at somewhat different organizational forms, all allude to work environments that are highly volatile, organic, and dynamic, with two related and distinct common denominators—uncertainty and pressure—directly impacting members' attitudes, behaviors, and careers.

Successful high-tech firms, as they grow and reinvent themselves, expend considerable effort to attract managers and employees, assimilating them into a culture that encourages and rewards non-conformist and, at times, esoteric behaviors. At the extremes, such behaviors may also include phenomena such as bootlegging (Augsdorfer, 2005), business process workarounds (Outmazgin & Soffer, 2013), subtle industrial espionage (Crane, 2005), skunkworks (the term refers to technology projects developed in semi-secrecy) (Rich & Janos, 1994; Daft, 2013), and informal head- and talent-hunting (Michaels et al., 2001). Indirectly, this employment culture rewards job-hopping and high personal career commitment at the expense of the more traditional job or organizational loyalty. Kunda (1992, 2006) observed that, in this atmosphere, there is a constant tension between employees and management, which engineers the local culture as a control-enhancing mechanism. We suspect that the manipulation of employees by means of such tacit strategies may backfire. Fimbel and Burstein (1990), for example, found that in high-tech organizations, employee misconduct is indeed strongly related to such organizational strategies and traits. When employees receive a message from management that coming to market early is an important goal, they may release their product although they know full well it is not yet of proper quality—that it is not free from programming or hardware deficiencies.

Public Service Organizations

Although service organizations do not share the same features with high-tech firms, both operate in highly stressful environments. Lovelock (1983) and Danet

(1981) elaborated helpful methods for classifying service organizations. Lovelock's method lists the following lead questions:

Who or what is the direct receiver of service? Services can be aimed at people's bodies (e.g., health facilities), people's minds (e.g., education institutions), material and equipment (e.g., maintenance services), or non-physical assets (e.g., financial services).

What kind of relationship exists between the customer and the organization? Some contacts can be permanent, such as the services given by an insurance company; others are per transaction, such as theater transcription rights. Some can be given regardless of any membership, such as police protection, whereas others require some type of affiliation, such as a community center or church. Some can be just a one-time contact, such as an international call serviced by a long-distance phone company.

What is the discretion given to the service provider? The major question here is the extent of leeway or degrees of freedom in responding professionally by matching appropriate responses to problems. For example, how much discretion is given by the organization to a team of experts in spending public resources on any given case?

What is the level of demand for the service relative to its supply? How do fluctuations in the demands for particular services relate to the organization's ability to provide services? In particular, the impact of limited resources on the quality of the service rendered may be worrisome.

What are the methods used in providing the services? Does the service require direct contacts with employees? Is the service to be delivered on-site or by means of remote communications? Is the service provided at the customer's location? Is the service concentrated in one locale or is it distributed?

In our studies of work-related misbehavior in public service organizations, we distinguished different organizations by the type of customer serviced (Danet, 1981): Welfare agencies, general hospitals, schools, and postal services. These organizations trust their employees to provide customers with the quality service they are socially obligated to render. This is because, in most cases, service is delegated to individuals or groups that play the role of *boundary spanners.* That is, they represent the organization at the contact point with external clients or customers. Such are the roles of the nurses, welfare agents, and teachers whom we surveyed. Boundary spanning presents problems for both the position holders and their employers (e.g., United States Post Office code of ethics; see Bukowski, 2009). The primary problems are the direct encounter with customers and their expectations, the relative isolation in which the contact takes place, the duality of caring for the client while representing the organization, and working for bureaucratic systems, such as public social welfare agencies (Vardi & Weitz, 2002a). It is not surprising that these employees often feel pressure, stress, and have higher degrees of burnout. In addition to being the good service providers they are trained to be, some tend to engage in various manifestations of OMB. We attempt to propose some possible explanations for such contrasts in behavior from an interactional perspective.

Organization Type, Experienced Stress, and OMB

Both high-tech and service organizations are stress-inducing work environments (Briner & Hockey, 1988). In high-tech organizations, perceived stress may result from the fast-paced, competitive, deadline-targeted atmosphere, whereas in the service environment, stress may result from the constant demand for ethical decisions, caring for the needy, and economic constraints limiting performance. Stress exists regardless of the specific source. In a study of the research and development (R&D) section of a large high-tech firm, Ganot (1999) and Reshef-Tamari (1999) found evidence that high levels of job ambiguity, job uncertainty, and a highly charged atmosphere (all components of stress) contributed to the variance in production-related misconduct. They measured high-tech misconduct using production deviance items found in Robinson and Bennett's (1995) questionnaire and additional items pertaining to computer-related misconduct, such as *cyberloafing* (for a discussion of this phenomenon, see Chapter 5).

In public health services, work stress may bear negative influences on caregivers and thus harm both their employing organizations and their clients. In general, it may negatively affect the quality of service rendered to clientele. Wolfgang (1988) suggested that chronic stress among health care workers decreases their level of concentration in solving problems and their obligation to provide high-level treatment. It may also increase incidence of substance abuse, as well as increase the likelihood of mental health problems, divorce, and even suicide. Ravid-Robbins (1999) investigated OMB among registered nurses in three Israeli hospitals. She identified stress as a major antecedent of both OMB *Types S* and *D*. Similarly, Levin (1989) and Kantor (1999) found that social workers who suffer from work overload behave less professionally, their motivation to work with clients decreases, they become less empathetic and more apathetic, and they report misbehavior toward their welfare agency as an employer.

Nurses occupy extremely vulnerable boundary-spanning positions in hospitals: They are in constant contact with patients who depend on their professionalism and compassion. Nurses working long shifts in intensive care units or emergency rooms are exposed to pressure-cooker work situations, must deal with doctors' demands and pressures from worried family members, and treat critically ill patients as well. In many cases, they are also financially undercompensated. These inherent conflicts present additional stress (Gray-Toft & Anderson, 1981). Stressful work environments affect employee behavior because they may become the sources for frustration, annoyance, irritation, impatience, and intolerance. Such emotional states, in turn, may lead to various forms of improper conduct.

We therefore draw the following observation with regard to the roles that organization type and character play in inducing employee misbehavior: In both high-tech and public service organizations, the higher the perceived stress in the work environment, the higher the extent of employee burnout, and the higher the probability for employees' intentions to engage in OMB Types S and D. Such intentions may be manifested in intra- and interpersonal, property, and production misconduct.

The next section is devoted to field research. We report at some length a number of studies conducted in different types of work organizations to explore antecedents of various measures of OMB. Although we emphasize macro-level factors, we also include variables that are typically measured at the group and individual level, such as management style and organizational commitment.

Field Studies in Public Service and High-Tech Organizations

We conducted four different cross-sectional, exploratory, studies in four organizations—a national utility company (Study 1), a group of hospitals (Study 2), a postal service unit (Study 3), and a high-tech R&D unit (Study 4)—selected to represent a variety of work organizations in different sectors: Private and public, utilities and health care, and mediating and intensive technologies. We searched for statistically significant relationships between selected antecedent variables and perceived or reported expressions of misbehavior. Thus, we do not report a unified set of hypotheses and variables, but rather those to which these organizations gave us access due to the sensitive nature of the topic under investigation. In the first study, we posed three research questions: What is the relationship between the manner in which managers act (lead) and the misbehavior of their subordinates? Is the level of dissatisfaction with work reflected in reported misbehavior? Is misbehavior reported differently for the self and others (colleagues and peers)?

The interest in managerial leadership has traditionally tilted toward the search for effectiveness, with emphasis on positive work outcomes such as performance, organizational citizenship behavior, commitment, and attachment (House & Podsakoff, 1994), whereas managers' effects on subordinates' misconduct have been conspicuously neglected. Traditional research notwithstanding, it stands to reason that as much as managers influence normative behavior such as adequate level of work performance, managers' attitudes and behaviors should also influence subordinates' intentions to misbehave. For instance, Greenberg (1990a) demonstrated in a quasi-experimental study that the type of information managers provided their subordinates concerning change in pay is directly related to employee theft. We assumed that employees reciprocate considerate managerial behavior by refraining from behaving in a manner detrimental to their manager, whereas a more restrictive style may lead to mistrust resulting in more revengeful intentions (Bies & Tripp, 1995). We hypothesized that OMB is related to leadership style: The more a manager employs a considerate style toward subordinates, the lower is the subordinates' misbehavior.

Based on previous findings of employee misconduct research (Hollinger & Clark, 1983; Mangione & Quinn, 1975), we suggested that feelings of frustration and job dissatisfaction are important affective forces that should increase people's intentions to engage in misconduct in much the same way that they increase withdrawal behaviors such as tardiness and absenteeism. We expected the employee's level of job satisfaction to be negatively related to OMB: The lower the level of job satisfaction, the higher the OMB.

Work environments in general, and human service organizations in particular, often pose extremely demanding contexts for their employees. Such demands may be especially acute in jobs in which service providers directly interact with clients or customers (Schneider & Bowen, 1995). Although they strive to provide quality service, we expect such settings to also induce work-related misbehavior among their staff. Hospital nurses (Study 2) serve as a good example of workers who are subjected to demanding organizational environments because of the crucial service they perform to their patients, their boundary-spanning role, and the inherent conflicts with other stakeholders (physicians, administrators, and patients' families). Their behavior (and misbehavior) is determined by their attitude toward the work, level of responsibility and authority, and the manner in which they perceive organizational and professional obligations. Specifically, we expected nurses' misbehavior to be related to how they perceive their unit's service climate, their own attitude toward providing health care service, and the level of their job and professional commitments. For example, we expected nurses in supervisory roles to relate to misbehavior differently from staff nurses. That is, OMB is negatively related to employee orientation toward service and perceived service climate, employee attitudes of organizational commitment and professional involvement, and level of job responsibility.

The traditional assertion posited in the mainstream OB literature has been that employment status (Archer, 1994), as well as the design of one's task (Hackman & Oldham, 1980), influence attitudes and behaviors toward both work and employing organization (Steers & Mowday, 1977). We now extend these assumptions and argue that these factors also bear on employee misbehavior. For example, in Chapter 8 we addressed the issue of job design and OMB, suggesting that it may offer built-in opportunities to misbehave and thus be an important antecedent of OMB. Although job autonomy can enhance performance, it might also offer employees the opportunity to misbehave (Vardi & Weitz, 2001). Similarly, temporary employees can be expected to feel less attached to the organization and more inclined to engage in OMB than full-time, permanent employees.

The Israeli Postal Service was selected for Study 3 after some incidents of mail theft in several distribution centers were discovered and reported in the local media. This particular work environment is characterized by relatively lax controls, little monitoring, and obvious temptations (employees physically handle mail containing goods, cash, and checks during the night shift), with full-time, part-time, and temporary employees performing similar work side-by-side. We agree with previous findings that temporary employees engage in OMB more than full-time permanent employees, and that job satisfaction, work commitment, and career opportunities moderate the relationship between employment status and OMB.

The possible effects of the work environment on OMB were investigated in Study 4—a high-tech setting. Extended work hours, extremely heavy workload, competitiveness, unrealistic deadlines, high levels of turnover, and the pressure to excel characterize the high-tech culture. Furthermore, the work atmosphere is characterized with underlying tensions between individualism and managerial controls (Kunda, 1992, 2006). Reports (e.g., Fimbel & Burstein, 1990) indicate that the high-tech industry is replete with employee misconduct (e.g., concealing bugs in software from customers). We sought to identify some of the determinants of OMB (e.g., time wasting, internet surfing, quality compromising, bootlegging, and substance abuse) in such a stressful work environment. Based on mainstream stress literature (e.g., McGrath, 1976; Shirom, 1982), we assumed that the subjective pressure that emanates from a job environment characterized by ambiguity, role conflict, and overload (Kahn et al., 1964) may not only enhance excellence, but OMB as well.

In high-tech work environments, the intention to misbehave could be related to the employee's affective state, such as satisfaction from work and the organization as a whole (Vardi & Wiener, 1996). Specifically, job satisfaction is postulated to play a mitigating role between the level of subjective pressure and misbehavior because for professionals pressure is not necessarily a negative motive (Meglino, 1977) and because positive affect toward the organization may inhibit thoughts of revenge or malice aimed at the work, colleagues, or the employer (Spector, 1997a). Therefore, we expected a positive relationship between OMB and perceived work-related job pressure (ambiguity, role conflict, and overload), and that job satisfaction moderates the relationship between stress and OMB.

Study 3: Public Postal Services

This research was conducted in the central mail-sorting unit of the Israeli Post Office, a governmental agency similar to the US Postal Service. We randomly selected 160 employees to represent full-time, permanent, and temporary employees doing different types of jobs such as manual sorting clerks, mechanized sorting typists, bulk mail handlers, and third-shift workers. Following Analoui and Kakabadse's (1992) model for qualitative field research on employee misconduct, the methodology for the study included 11 months of participant observation by a graduate student who was also a personnel contractor for the unit, a follow-up using formal and informal interviews, and self-report questionnaires that were distributed at workstations during shift hours (morning, afternoon, and night). One hundred and twenty-one questionnaires were collected (61 temporary and 60 permanent employees). The response rate was 75 percent.

Study 4: High-Tech

This study was conducted in the R&D section of one of Israel's leading high-tech firms located in an industrial park in Tel Aviv. The company deals with data transmission and communication and employs 650 persons. All 200 members of the R&D group received questionnaires via interoffice mail. The sample included 73 men and 22 women, with an average age of 31; a majority (84.3 percent) were trained professionals in computers and electronics, 60 percent with a Bachelor's degree and 11 percent with a Master's; and the rest identified themselves as students. Most of them (67 percent) were in the software area, and 30 percent held supervisory positions.

As a caveat, we find it necessary to remind the reader that the measurement of sensitive issues in organizations is quite problematic, especially when it comes to behaviors that are deemed by employers as unhelpful, counterproductive, or dysfunctional (Bennett & Robinson, 2000; Sackett & DeVore, 2001; Skarlicki & Folger, 1997). To avoid respondents, discomfort and to lower the effect of social desirability, researchers may use non-direct language when asking individuals to report the misconduct of others (rather than themselves). Based on attribution theory (Weiner, 1974), we expected that, as a rule, when reporting misbehavior, both managers and employees tend to minimize their own misbehavior while perhaps exaggerating that of others. Therefore, we argue that organization members tend to attribute more misbehavior to others than to themselves. For a discussion of measurement issues regarding OMB research see Chapter 10.

Conclusions from the Four Studies

The four studies should be evaluated both separately and integratively. They are exploratory in nature and begin to converge toward a systematic conception of the antecedents of OMB. We discuss the results and their empirical and practical implications from both perspectives. Undoubtedly, further research on OMB should be of a more comparative nature and should utilize both qualitative and quantitative methods to encompass and account for more of the variance.

The results of Study 1 suggest that there is a significant negative correlation between considerate leadership style and self-reporting of OMB. We can ascribe this finding to the influence managers have on their subordinates' attitudes and behavior, which can either enhance normal conduct, good citizenship behavior (Pillai et al., 1999), or misbehavior. This finding provides additional confirmation of studies that report negative correlations between considerate leadership style and physical withdrawal from work (e.g., turnover and absenteeism). However, consideration could be interpreted by subordinates in a variety of ways. Although most employees take it for what it is—considerate treatment—some view such style as a sign of weakness and may take advantage of a lax manager. However, many interpret consideration as an expression of trust and reciprocate by abstaining from misconduct.

Our data also indicate that there is a negative correlation between initiating structure, leadership style, and OMB. This finding runs counter to our initial assertion, which was based on the literature that establishes a positive correlation between this kind of leadership style and employee grievances and turnover rate (Fleishman & Harris, 1962). This may be explained by the fact that when managers provide stricter and less ambiguous supervision, there is actually less built-in opportunity to misbehave (Vardi & Wiener, 1996). Alternatively, although some withdrawal behavior may be related to more strict control, it may not necessarily lead to misconduct.

The relationship between work satisfaction and misbehavior is more complex than the straightforward negative correlation we expected. For example, satisfaction with the work and satisfaction with the supervisor were more strongly related with self-reported OMB than with OMB reported about others. This finding supports Locke's (1968) contention that job-related satisfaction, perceptions, and behaviors are interconnected in significant and often instrumental (and perhaps even causal) ways. However, we failed to find empirical support for the claim that misbehavior is related to dissatisfaction with pay. Again, we may conclude that such a relationship is not a simple one. It may be mitigated by both internal and external factors. Kraut (1975), for example, failed to show that changes in pay satisfaction and voluntary withdrawal behavior were related, whereas Greenberg (1990a) demonstrated that dissatisfaction with company pay policy was related to employee theft.

We found significant differences between OMB Type O and OMB Type S reporting, for both minor and major misbehaviors. Minor misbehaviors were more frequently reported than major ones. This is consistent with Hollinger and Clark's (1982) findings that more than half of the subjects who participated in their research reported that they were involved in production deviance (considered minor), but only one-third reported property (major) deviance. The reason for this pattern may be that minor misbehaviors are perceived as less critical to the organization's well-being than major misbehaviors.

Caregivers, such as hospital nurses (Study 2), are expected not only to demonstrate compassion and empathy, but also to perform their duties professionally and efficiently. In carrying out their demanding work, they may earn a patient's gratitude, but they are also held accountable for mistakes that may be costly as well as fatal. Yet, quite often, nurses find themselves between a rock and a hard place because of their relatively low professional status and their boundary-spanning employee–client role. In many cases, their level of responsibility far exceeds their level of authority. Nurses have been shown to be prime candidates for occupational stress and burnout (Pines & Kanner, 1982). When coupled with the highly intense 24/7 work environment and the continuous sense of emergency, such conditions may also trigger misbehaviors that run counter to organizational and professional codes of proper conduct.

Reports on OMB also differed by rank and formal education. Nurses with academic backgrounds and nurses who hold supervisory positions reported higher levels of misbehavior. This may be related to a major limitation of this study. Originally, we designed the OMB measure to explore personal engagement in such activities as proposed by Robinson and Bennett (1995), but this was vetoed by the HMO's director of human resources because some questions were perceived to be too intrusive and politically sensitive. Only a non-direct approach was approved. The data may therefore be contaminated by the participant's position and responsibility to report as well as by social desirability. These limitations notwithstanding, this study may still imply that instilling a service orientation, creating and maintaining a quality-service atmosphere, as well as encouraging personal identification with the hospital may help in two complementary ways: Enhance service and its gains, and reduce misconduct and its costs.

We assumed that temporary employees would identify less with the organization and therefore be more inclined to engage in OMB than permanent employees. In fact, the results of Study 3 reveal some differences between the two groups. As expected, tenured postal workers scored significantly higher than the temporary ones on all attitudinal measures (satisfaction, commitment, and perceived opportunities). The groups also differed on several human capital characteristics—the tenured employees were older, less educated, and less skilled than the temporary employees, many of whom were college students. However, contrary to the main hypothesis, there was no difference in both observed and reported misconduct between the two groups of employees.

Among the R&D professionals participating in Study 4, misbehaviors were positively related to stress, whereas stress was negatively related to job satisfaction. Stress was also positively related to important job attributes such as seniority and rank. However, contrary to our expectations, misbehavior was unrelated to both these attributes and job satisfaction. Of the three dimensions of perceived stress regressed on OMB—overload, conflict, and ambiguity—only the latter contributed significantly to the variance explained in the OMB dependent measure. This may allude to the complexity of the high-tech experience for individual employees.

In intensive high-tech environments such as competitive R&D units, employees are exposed to high levels of stress that emanate from high job demands, expectations to innovate and solve non-routine problems, and expectations for quick solutions. Both role overload and role conflicts are prevalent. In fact, new R&D employees are selected for their ability to thrive in such work environments. Moreover, employees are probably attracted to this type of work setting because they find it not only non-threatening, but actually challenging. This kind of self-selection into specific organizational environments was discussed by Schneider (1987) in his now famous attraction–selection–attrition model. For our subjects, overload and conflict may not be stressors at all. However, role ambiguity appears to be a stressor because it primarily manifests itself in uncertainty about resource availability. If such ambivalence causes frustration, it may lead to misbehavior on the job.

Spirituality and Misbehavior

Scholars report a steady increase of interest in spirituality at work among management researchers, especially during the last two decades (Giacalone & Jurkiewicz, 2003; Tischler, 1999). The organization studies literature suggests that spirituality enhances employee well-being and quality of life, that it provides employees with a sense of purpose and meaning at work and a sense of interconnectedness and community (Karakas, 2009).

Spirituality, although sometimes critically regarded as defining a new movement or culture of secular, eclectic "new age" theology, or the adoption of a perennial philosophy (Hicks, 2003; Gotsis & Kortezi, 2008; Lynn et al., 2009), is typically considered to be a human experience that is pervasive and yet has nothing to do with specific religious faiths or traditions, and is beyond the dogma of religion (Guillory, 2000). In the organizational spirituality literature, it is customary to refer to what Schmidt-Wilk, Heaton, and Steingard (2000) call "applied spirituality," and Dehler and Welsh (1994, 1997) as simply "spirituality," which are the practical implications and measurable outcomes that arise from the inner experience. Organizational spirituality (OS) may be defined as "organizational culture guided by mission statement, leadership and business practices that are socially responsible and value driven, that recognizes the contributions employees make to the organization, that promotes individual spiritual development and well-being" (Kinjerski & Skrypnek, 2006, p. 262).

Pandey and Gupta (2008) describe seven variables of the spiritual climate of the organization: Meaningful work that is for life, and not only for living (Ashmos & Duchun, 2000); hopefulness, the belief that organizational goals can be achieved; authenticity, the alignment of people's actions with their core values and beliefs; the employee feeling as whole human being; a sense of community, of interconnectedness and interdependence, care for the world at large, for the social and natural environment; respect for diversity; and work that has a meditative "flow," being at one with the activity (Jurkiewicz & Giacalone, 2004; McCormick, 1994; Zohar & Marshall, 2004). Pawar (2008) suggested integrating the term with four other existing organizational behavior terms—transformational leadership, organizational citizenship behavior (OCB), organizational support and procedural justice. In their pioneering book, Mitroff and Denton (1999) showed that employees seek this climate of spirituality (not religion) in their organizations, and Kolodinsky, Giacalone, and Jurkiewicz (2008) found that workers desire workplaces perceived as exuding spiritual values, even if the workers themselves are not personally spiritual.

The impact of spirituality, whether personal or organizational, in the world of work has two dimensions: On the employees' values, beliefs, attitudes, behaviors and their very well-being, and on the overall functioning and performance of the organization. Intuitively, one would expect spirituality in organizations to be positively related to various workplace attitudinal and performance outcomes. Indeed, many studies provide support for this notion. Several scholars contend that spirituality can lead to improved employee performance, to better functioning employees in terms of their overall contribution to the work organization, to higher productivity, better decision-making, greater creativity, higher intuitive capacities, and increased problem-solving capabilities and overall more efficient use of material and human resources (Burack, 1999; Cash & Gray, 2000; Guillory, 2000; Karakas, 2009; Krishnakumar & Neck, 2002).

It has also been observed that stronger spiritual beliefs can lead to a greater sense of control, meaning, and deeper intimacy (Tedeschi & Calhoun, 1996). Spirituality might contribute to employees' sense of security in a holistic sense, even if the organizational environment is not stable. Many values-based spiritual organizations have made honesty and integrity their credo, their prime focus (Burack, 1999; Wagner-Marsh & Conley, 1999). Ethical mindset is also related to spirituality (Issa & Pick, 2010). Moreover, mutual trust may lead to better organizational performance through effective decision-making processes, more open and frank communication between key organizational actors, greater focus on customer issues, and greater innovation (Kriger & Hanson, 1999).

An interesting study was conducted in a police force (Adebayo et al., 2007), and another other in an educational setting (James, 2005). In both, workplace spirituality significantly moderated the relationship between perceived justice and cynical behavior. With reference to organizational cynicism, a spiritual approach can be helpful in restoring hope, and acquiring a more balanced view about justice and injustice, safety and danger, and good and malevolence (Drescher & Foy, 1995). It is commonly believed that spirituality will buffer the effects of negative organizational perceptions, and be associated with more positive attitudes and outlooks.

As we began to link the OMB and spirituality domains, it appeared to us that the latter might serve as a force that moderates the intentions individuals develop towards engaging in acts of misconduct. We posit that certain perceived job and organization attributes may intensify such intentions, as will personality traits and frustrations related to the person–organization interaction. Following this assumption, we argue that spiritual individuals should react differently to such antecedent factors than non-spirituals, that for the spirituals, these factors will have a smaller impact on behaviors that might harm the work, peers or the organization at large. Because spirituality is both a personal and an organizational characteristic, it is thought to moderate the relationship between negative perceptions of the organization and organizational misbehavior. Therefore, we should find that employees who perceive the workplace to be characterized by excessive politics, injustice, lack of support, and organizational violations are more likely to develop negative (e.g., cynical, contemptuous) attitudes and intentions towards the organization.

However, for individuals with a strong sense of spirituality, such attitudes and intentions may be attenuated because of an internal sense of purpose surrounding their life, and the belief that there is higher meaning for the events that occur in all aspects of life, work-life in particular. Weitz, Vardi, and Setter (2012) explored this very notion. They examined the link between OMB and spirituality—the negative impact of spirituality on employees' intention to misbehave—and found that individual spirituality and organizational spirituality are negatively related to OMB and that this relationship is moderated; that is, job design dimensions such as autonomy and interdependence, personality factors such as conscientiousness, and organization justice facets such as procedural, rewards, and distributive justice moderate the relationship between OMB and spirituality. Weitz and his colleagues (2012) also found that employees who perceive themselves as low in spirituality are less influenced by external, contextual variables, whereas highly spiritual people are more affected by them. For example, highly spiritual people scored higher on the OMB index in negative situations than non-spiritual ones. This sensitivity to context is quite surprising, as it could be theorized that spirituality would yield an unwavering moral streak that will not budge, that would be unbending, even in the most dire circumstances.

Organization Culture and Climate

Culture has been a central research topic in sociology and anthropology and was gradually integrated into organization analysis. Its inclusion in organization theory broadened the scope and depth of our understanding of organizational dynamics. It has made our perceptions more holistic and articulate. Adopting organizational culture as a key construct has brought researchers closer to understanding the intricacies of the human condition in formal systems and allowed for legitimizing ethnographic methodology as a viable research approach (see a thorough review by Ashkanasy & Jackson, 2001). We now know that members of organizations are not only reacting to the complexity of specialized formal arrangements that make up the organization's structure, but also to factors such as values, codes, language, cues, symbols, and so on (Trice & Beyer, 1993; Wiener, 1988). Our ability to study organizational culture has made it possible to understand how members comprehend their organization and how, for instance, they develop, assimilate, and adjust their organizational identity (Ailon-Souday, 2001; Kunda, 1992, 2006).

Schein's (1985) organizational culture model elegantly captures these notions. He viewed organization culture as the pattern of common fundamental assumptions that helps members cope with both internal and external problems. He defined *organizational culture* as

> a pattern of basic assumptions invented, discovered, or developed by a given group as it learns to cope with its problems of external adaptation and internal integration—that has worked well enough to be considered valid and, therefore, to be taught to members as the correct way to perceive, think, and feel in relation to those problems.
>
> (Schein, 1985, p. 9)

Schein identified culture at three levels: Artifacts, espoused values, and basic underlying assumptions. As behavior, patterns of OMB are such artifacts; they are rooted in the espoused values and basic paradigms underlying cultural precepts. By communicating expectations and role modeling, managers transmit these cultural precepts to members with regard to desirable and acceptable behavior, as well as to misbehavior.

Others view organizational culture more narrowly, emphasizing its function as a bonding mechanism holding the organization together (Tichy, 1982)—a local value system crystallizing the core beliefs of the organization's founders, owners, or principal stakeholders (Wiener, 1988). Daft (1995) added the notion that culture represents the emotional, less definable, and less discernible aspects of the organization. Often, culture is taken for granted because it is unobtrusive by nature. Its presence is subtle. It may become prominent when change takes place: When one enters a new organization, when strategic shifts are planned, and when mergers and acquisitions become a reality. Then culture takes on a unique role—a sense-making role to help understand the ramifications and meanings of the change.

Some distinguish between weak and strong cultures by the strength of members' normative commitment toward the organization (e.g., Wiener, 1988). In organizations with strong cultures, employees feel a deep sense of normative commitment the more they identify with their goals. Moreover, in these environments there is a strong and clear relationship between goals and means, missions and strategies, and aims and actions. This type of coherence between intentions and deeds makes people highly committed to both. According to Wiener, such systemic congruence enhances employees' duty and loyalty, as well as their willingness to sacrifice their own interests for the organization. Meglino et al. (1989) defined *strong culture* by the high level of unity among members in terms of common beliefs, values, and norms. For them, this sense of unity is the very source of positive motivational, affective, and behavioral outcomes at work. Wiener and Vardi (1990) and Kunda (1992, 2006) also suggested that under such cultural influences, employees' motivation and performance might be positively charged, and increased efforts on behalf of the organization may be observed. Such efforts, we argue, may not only manifest themselves in positive energy (e.g., extra-role citizenship behaviors of not-for-reward contribution), but also in negative, potentially destructive energy (manifested in OMB Type O) or in cases of blind loyalty (Wiener, 1988).

We now present another field study conducted in an Israeli company designed to examine our proposition that organizational culture and climate are contextual variables that are closely tied to OMB. The study demonstrates the empirical usefulness of an integrative approach to the observation of OMB patterns (see Vardi, 2001).

Effects of Organizational Climate on OMB

OMB is a product of the interaction between factors at the individual and organization levels; its frequency and intensity vary under different contextual circumstances. Initially, Vardi and Wiener (1992) proposed a motivational framework for OMB, which delineates individual and organizational antecedents of the intention to misbehave. At the individual level, they included personality, person–organization value congruence, generalized values of loyalty and duty, personal circumstances, and lack of satisfaction of personal needs. The organizational level included such factors as built-in opportunities to misbehave, control systems, goals, culture, and cohesiveness. Several other scholars also emphasized the effects that organizational factors have on employee misconduct in work organizations. Some of the factors suggested were organization values (Kemper, 1966), organization culture and climate (Boye & Jones, 1997; Hollinger & Clark, 1983; Kemper, 1966; Treviño, 1986), organizational socialization (Kemper, 1966), ethical climate (Carr, 1968; Jones, 1991), and built-in opportunity (Hollinger & Clark, 1983; Kemper, 1966; Treviño, 1986). In line with these observations, we chose to further examine the role that specific climate perceptions (i.e., ethical climate) may play in affecting reported incidents of OMB in a given organization.

The Ethical Climate Study

The study was conducted in a metal products company in northern Israel that employs 150 persons, of whom 138 worked at that particular location. They belonged to four departments: Production, production services, administration, and marketing. From the 138 individuals contacted, 97 returned the research questionnaire (for a 70 percent response rate) distributed on an individual basis at the workstation or office. The sample included 81 percent men with an average of 11 years of work experience. Their ages ranged from 24 to 60 years, and the average level of formal education was 12 years. Twenty-five individuals were classified as managers and all others (74 percent) as subordinates. Due to the sensitive subject matter, participants were promised full confidentiality and anonymity. No raw data were made available to the company, and feedback was given only at the aggregate level.

This study was designed to test the proposition that OMB is in large measure influenced by perceptions related to organization-wide and/or unit-specific climates. It follows a line of conceptual and empirical research that has established the role of organizational climate as an antecedent of employee unethical behavior (Victor & Cullen, 1987, 1988). The principal tenet underlying this line of research is twofold: (1) climate perceptions reflect some commonality in or sharing of some core impressions about the organization and its components, such as the human resource systems; and (2) such shared beliefs are espoused by members independently of individual attitudes and intentions. Thus, climate perceptions may be viewed as correlates (antecedents or outcomes) of other role- and organization-related variables. For example, Victor and Cullen (1988) posited the following claims: (1) organizations and subgroups within organizations develop different normative systems; (2) although these are not necessarily monolithic or homogeneous, members know them well enough to be perceived as work climate; and (3) these perceptions differ from affective evaluations of the work environment. This line of research originates from Schneider's (1980) suggestion that various types and facets of climates are embedded in perception of an overall organizational climate.

In our view, ethical climates are embedded in an organizational climate, which in turn is part of the organizational culture. We believe the difference lies in the level of specificity of the observed criterion. Organizational culture pertains mostly to overall shared values (Wiener, 1988), climate relates to systems and subsystems (Schneider, 1975), and ethical climate reflects local constraints and guidelines of individual decisions and behavior. This assumption merits further investigation using a multilevel, multi-company research design—a design that was unfortunately beyond the scope of this study.

Organizational culture, as suggested earlier, is one of the principal factors affecting individual motivation and behavior in general (Kunda, 1992, 2006; Wiener & Vardi, 1990) and misconduct in particular (Hollinger & Clark, 1983; Kemper, 1966; Treviño et al., 2014; Vardi & Wiener, 1992). Organizational culture plays an important role in affecting motivation at work. In an organization with a strong culture, one in which the values and norms are directed toward deviance, OMB becomes normative and may endanger the organization's existence. Treviño (1986) also indicated that the organization's culture provides the collective norms that guide behavior. Norms regarding what is and what is not appropriate behavior are shared and used to guide behavior. In a weak culture, the values, goals, purposes, and beliefs of the total organization are not clear, and therefore diverse subcultures are likely to emerge (Trice, 1993; Trice & Beyer, 1993). Members' behaviors are then likely to rely on norms generated by their referent groups or relevant subcultures (Schein, 1984). Hence, exploring the role of subcultures in an organization may be important in creating different value systems with regard to both normative and non-normative behavior.

Organizations are also believed to have ethical climates (Victor & Cullen, 1988) that reflect common perceptions and beliefs concerning organizational expectations of proper conduct. Albeit "in the eye of the beholder," climates are considered as more discernible, measurable organizational attributes than cultures. Such beliefs are considered more manageable because a specific climate (e.g., service climate) is closely related to manager–employee interactions, performance, and effectiveness (see Isaac, 1993). In addition, the promotion and management of ethical climates has received considerable empirical attention (e.g., Cullen et al., 1989; Petrick & Manning, 1990), emphasizing their importance. We expected that the more the overall organizational climate is perceived as positive, the lower will be the level of reported intentional OMB.

We found OMB to correlate with reward climate ($r = -0.24$, $p < 0.05$) and support climate ($r = -0.24$, $p < 0.05$). Thus, the more positively organizational climate is viewed, the less the reported misbehavior. We argued that managers view the organizational climate as being more positive than their subordinates. Supporting this hypothesis, for managers the mean was 3.08 ($SD = 0.28$) and for workers 2.91 ($SD = 0.27$; $t = 2.26$, $p < 0.01$).

Conclusions

As opposed to many studies that use data from random individuals from different organizations and industries, this study was conducted onsite. The sample represented the behaviors and perceptions of the workforce of this particular company; it reflected both managerial and rank-and-files employees and the functional structure of the company. Thus, we believe that, given certain field research limitations, the data present an authentic assessment of both climates and misbehaviors in the plant. We found that there was a significant negative relationship between organizational climate and OMB, and between organizational climate dimensions (warmth and support, and reward) and OMB. This supports the theoretical supposition that climate has both a positive and negative effect on members' intentions to behave on the job. The overriding implication for management is that it must be aware of the differential impact of climate dimensions on employee attitudes and behavior. More important, certain climates may encourage patterns of misbehavior.

Behavior Control Systems

The popular media outlets often report cases of large-scale fraud and embezzlement (e.g., Enron, Tyco, World-Com, Bernie Madoff). These raise some inevitable questions: How is it possible that such large-scale, long-term misconduct goes unnoticed in a system based on integrity and accountability? How do large-scale pernicious activities go on undetected by any number of control and regulation mechanisms? These are obviously issues of organizational and behavioral controls. We refer to both physical means used for control and surveillance (e.g., closed-circuit television, digital control systems) as well as managerial systems (e.g., rules and regulations, auditing, and disciplinary means) whose aim is to monitor, detect, penalize, and are used to decrease improper conduct. In the following section, we discuss the role of management control systems in monitoring OB and OMB.

Johnson and Gill (1993) entitled their book *Management control and organizational behavior* to denote the importance they explicitly attached to control as the quintessential task of management. In their words: "Control means making potential labor power real, and it also entails controlling and manipulating the non-human resources that make this power possible" (p. viii). They suggested that if managerial work is concerned with controlling human resources, all managers must cope with the vagaries of OB and OMB. This includes understanding and predicting both pro-normative and counter-normative behaviors (i.e., both standard and expected modes of conduct and misbehavior).

According to Sewell (1998), the use of control systems spread to many work organizations following World War II, when the concepts of command and control were tested and implemented by the huge military organizations that took part in the war. These concepts pertain to managerial functions that monitor the execution of plans, evaluation of their success, and the feedback needed for taking corrective measures for failures. Despite the popularity of these concepts among managers, it appears that it is difficult to determine the effectiveness of organizational control systems.

This may be due to the view of many organizations that publicizing data about their control systems may be construed as an admission to the existence of counterproductive and dysfunctional activities within their boundaries. Although from a public scrutiny perspective such information should be desirable and welcome, from a business perspective it may be construed as damaging the firm's reputation (Rosenbaum & Baumer, 1984; Sackett & DeVore, 2001).

The current integrative view of organizational control, to which we too subscribe, has its roots in the early (1950s) psychological approach described by Argyris (1957) and the classical organizational sociology works of Gouldner (1954), Merton (1953), Selznick (1957), and Etzioni (1961). Argyris studied how budgets affect organization members' behavior from an individual, psychological perspective. His sociological counterparts showed that members react to hierarchical control systems both favorably (demonstrating compliant behavior or, in their language, anticipated consequences) and unfavorably (unanticipated consequences). From a sociological point of view, these non-conformist reactions by organizational members were interpreted as people's natural resistance to formal control, on the one hand, and the inability of managers to mobilize members' motivations and commitments, on the other hand.

An example of a formalistic approach to management control that ignored the human side was the Management Accounting School at Harvard University advanced by Anthony and Dearden (1976). This highly technical approach to control puts the burden on managers because it holds them accountable for executing plans on a daily basis. For them, control is proper and necessary. However, such a conceptualization of organization control, although elegant and appealing, is too narrow because it tends to ignore the complexities and uncertainties inherent in OB. We add that accounting alone cannot explain many of the darker-side realities discussed so far in this book. We agree with Johnson and Gill's (1993) framework because they too viewed control as an organization process that is ongoing and includes various facets of managing human OB such as the effects of organizational socialization, the deliberate manipulation of culture, and the effects of different management styles.

Such an approach was taken by Leatherwood and Spector (1991) in their study of employee misconduct. They integrated two theoretical models (organizational control and agency theory) to explain misuse of company resources such as taking kickbacks, vandalizing equipment, unauthorized markdowns, and theft of cash, merchandise, and time. Such deliberate misconduct is referred to as *moral hazard* (traditionally associated with more benign misbehaviors such as free-riding, social loafing, and shirking) because it threatens the implicit delicate contractual relationship between organizations and members. The two models (see Eisenhardt, 1985, 1989) suggest that there are two main conditions that may increase the likelihood of misbehavior. One is the existence of significant divergence in preferences between agents and their principals (agency theory). The second is the existence of concrete opportunities to pursue self-interest (control theory). Thus, when opportunities to engage in misconduct are constrained (controlled) or when interests are better aligned, misbehavior decreases. To constrain agents' opportunity to engage in misbehavior, we can use inducements to participate in proper and desirable (i.e., aligned) modes of performance by offering incentives, stock options, and competitive packages of pay, profit-sharing, and bonuses. Such privileges must be contingent on proper conduct. We can also use systems designed to constrain opportunities like forming a policy or method to thwart probable misconduct: Inventory control, internal and external auditing, and monitoring and disciplining improper activity.

The Role of Sanctions

In addition to monitoring and deterrence functions, organizational control mechanisms provide management with specific information necessary to activate disciplinary action when warranted. This leads us to the role of sanctions, of punishment, in the management of OB. Punishment is no easy task because our cultural upbringing immediately conjures up images of corporal and physical modes of discipline, which by and large are viewed negatively and are prohibited. It also brings up images of totalitarianism or coercion (Goffman, 1959), in which compliance is based on strict adherence to institutional rules and regulations, and any deviance is punishable. In many non-Western societies and in some religions, refraining from harshly disciplining a naughty child, a deviant citizen, or a straying believer would be considered a weakness and bad control strategy. In organizations, punishment is typically discouraged because quite often it may actually generate undesirable affective, attitudinal, and behavioral reactions that could outweigh the intended benefits (e.g., Luthans & Kreitner, 1985).

Some form of disciplinary systems must exist in any organized social endeavor, both within and outside formal organizations (family, community centers, work teams, and departments). It is necessary because most social entities are predicated on implicit trust; when trust is breached, they must react to restore authority and accountability and, in turn, restore trust. Moreover, discipline is certainly essential in the dyadic (one-on-one) work relationship between authority figures such as teachers, commanders, and supervisors and their students, soldiers, or subordinates. Following Treviño's (1992) justice perspective of punishment in organizations, we also suggest that the value of maintaining a viable and relevant disciplinary system lies in the effects it should have on the observers (third-party organization members), not only on the penalized perpetrator of misbehavior.

According to Treviño (1992), "punishment is defined as the manager's application of a negative consequence or the withdrawal of a positive consequence from someone under his or her supervision" (p. 649). Punishment follows acts of misbehavior or misconduct viewed as such from the agent's (i.e., the manager's) perspective. It is likely to be witnessed, observed, or at least heard of by observers in the immediate work environment. Thus, *misconduct* is defined as "behavior that falls short of the agent's moral or technical (work) standards" (p. 648). It would almost invariably include instances of employee theft, harassment and bullying, unjustified absence, insubordination, vandalism, and purposeful substandard performance. Arguably, in most work environments, there is reasonable agreement between agents and observers that such behaviors are not condoned by either side, are unacceptable, and thus are punishable. In this case, we can expect a direct and positive effect of the punishment event on the observers, namely because of social learning processes, observers of credible punishment are likely to learn from it and be deterred from engaging in similar acts. At the same time, failure to punish may result in increased misbehavior. Whether the punishment is effective in reducing future misbehavior also depends on people's perceptions of the events and their evaluations of whether justice was done. Specifically, the model suggests punishment will affect third-party members when they evaluate it positively in terms of retributive, distributive, and procedural justice.

Retributive justice is a fundamental social belief in the function of punishment and its necessity for the maintenance of social order (Blau, 1964). In organizations it may translate into the notion that "here people get what they deserve" when they misbehave. Perhaps even more important is the notion that punishment is required to "hold the organization together." Treviño (1992) developed the following proposition: When observers agree with the supervisor's definition of a coworker's behavior as misconduct, they expect and desire punishment and evaluate it as just. To stress the point, she also suggested that when observers agree with the supervisor's definition of a coworker's behavior as misconduct, they evaluate management's failure to punish the individual as unjust.

Because sanctions are related to work outcomes, it is certainly related to two other types of organizational justice: Distributive and procedural (see Chapter 7 for a discussion of organizational justice in the context of employee personality and OMB). To recap: Distributive justice (e.g., Deutsch, 1985) taps the process of subjectively evaluating the fairness with which organizational resources are allocated to different members. Procedural justice (e.g., Lind & Tyler, 1988) concerns the perceived process of allocating the resources (policy, decisions, and implementation). Hence, researchers proposed that these fairness perceptions are essential in making any reward and punishment system effective as an antecedent of actual work behavior. For example, Treviño (1992) suggested the following: Observers' attitudes such as commitment, loyalty, satisfaction, trust, and consequently work performance are associated with their evaluations of the punishment as just and fair. Undoubtedly, such a proposition can be expanded to include predictions about OMB. For example, we argue that observers' OMB Types S and D increase when they perceive the organization as unjustly and unfairly treating coworkers who are blamed for some form of OMB. One viable explanation would be that this increase demonstrates a retaliatory or revenge behavior on behalf on the perpetrators who, by the justice perceptions of their observing peers, were wrongly treated by management. This would be the case when some are more harshly punished than others for committing the same type of misbehavior under similar circumstances.

PART III

Implications for Research and Management

10

MEASUREMENT DILEMMAS IN OMB RESEARCH

For more than 100 years, the behavior of people in organizational settings has been the subject of some of the most interesting research published by sociologists, anthropologists, and occupation and organization scientists. Undoubtedly, what makes this research both challenging and frustrating is the absence of a single unique formula that would provide a perfect solution to problems arising in organizations (Porter et al., 1975). Each academic discipline focuses on different aspects of behavior and implements various measurement strategies; almost all of them are valuable and contribute to the growing body of knowledge commonly known as *organizational behavior* (see Chapter 1). Yet, as Daft (1980) so cogently argued, the various methods of research use and create a limited view of reality and offer an incomplete description of the phenomena under study. Both the organizational world and human behavior are complex. Furthermore, as already shown, turning our research agenda to work- and job-related misbehaviors makes our investigation of organizations even more complex and challenging. Our challenge, then, is not to decide which approach is the best, but rather, to eclectically, and by design, incorporate a variety of methods, tapping and reflecting complex realities (Jick, 1979).

The purpose of this chapter is to highlight key dilemmas inherent in the current investigation of OMB that runs, as demonstrated throughout this book, a whole spectrum of behaviors from relatively minor misbehavior (minor incivilities, ignoring rules, and undermining behavior) to the most serious (theft, violence, harassment, and destruction). Certainly, no specific approach is perfectly suited for such variety and complexity; the choice of strategy mainly depends on the goals of the study, the particular research population, the site and setting constraints, and the researcher's training and preferences. As with all social and behavioral science research, identifying the pertinent dilemmas facing the researcher is a good starting point. In the following sections, we characterize various research methods and review strategies for the study of OMB.

Dilemmas Pertaining to Measurement Strategy

When embarking on the study of people's behavior in organizations, a strategy must be adopted. We organize the dilemmas facing researchers, following the logic of the now classic bipolar scheme proposed by Porter et al. (1975). To illustrate each dilemma, we refer to research mentioned in earlier chapters.

Theoretical Versus Empirical

The first dilemma, relevant to any scientific endeavor is the choice between an empirical and a theoretical approach. In organizational behavior, the tendency has been to focus on empirical research rather than theoretical issues. Perhaps one of the reasons for the emphasis on empirical research is that this field has its roots in industrial psychology (Porter & Schneider, 2014; also see Appendix 2). Because industrial psychologists focused mainly on empirical testing aimed at developing instruments to be used in the selection and assessment of employees, they were preoccupied with research methodology. Organizational psychology—the apparent heir of industrial psychology—still emphasizes rigorous measurement because of practicing psychologists' felt need to rely on precise data to make decisions about their clients (Aguinis et al., 2001). Nonetheless, the importance of developing conceptual frameworks for OB has been widely recognized, as evidenced by the status that theory-oriented periodicals such as the *Academy of Management Review*, alongside the more empirically oriented journals such as the *Academy of Management Journal* and the *Administrative Science Quarterly*, have achieved.

In their survey of the business ethics literature, for example, Randall and Gibson (1990) found that of 94 empirical studies examining the beliefs and ethical behaviors of employees, 64 percent did not present any theoretical framework serving as a basis for their research, and 75 percent of the studies did not propose any hypothesis to be examined. They therefore called for special efforts to improve research methodology that would enable the building of a solid theoretical basis with which to (1) predict the types of behaviors we may expect under different conditions, (2) develop logical research designs to examine our assumptions and/or predictions, and (3) interpret findings in the light of specific theories. If the need arises, theories may be reformulated. Indeed, some important insights regarding organizations can be obtained when predictions based on a theory are rejected. The following points should be considered when developing meaningful and useful OB theories, and OMB frameworks as well:

- A strong OB theory is interdisciplinary, combining both micro- and macro-levels of analysis (Rousseau, 1997). Daft and Lewin (1993) shared this view and maintained that the science of OB must develop and maintain interdisciplinary research. They pointed out that environmental, technological, and economic changes create new organizational realities to which previous explanations may not be relevant. Thus, continuous theory construction is required if we are to better comprehend such realities.

- Collecting empirical data is critical for the evaluation of a specific theory's validity. A specific theory indicates what is supposed to be taking place, and empirical information demonstrates to what extent these relationships do in fact exist (Porter et al., 1975). According to Bacharach (1989), one of the critical criteria for evaluating theory building is *empirical adequacy*: "If a theory is operationalized in such a way as to preclude disconfirmation, then it is clearly not falsifiable" (p. 506). Therefore, for the measurement to be valid, it is essential that the instrument used be based on at least a tentative theoretical model guiding the development of the measurement scale (Bennett & Robinson, 2000). Yet without proper measurement, we cannot accept or reject a theoretical interpretation of the phenomenon.

- Premature adoption of a theory should be avoided (Spector, 2001). That is, a theory may be a useful tool; but to be a truly efficient one, it must be solid, and based on conceptual and empirical studies. Studies invariably supply the best raw materials for the construction of a theory. Daft (1980) maintained that one of the main problems of the models in the field is the dearth of adequate terminology. In his study of the complexity of organizational models and the lexis and language used to report the observations conducted in organizations, a low variance in the terminology was revealed, leading him to conclude that only simple, quantifiable relationships had been examined. He also pointed out the need for a greater variety and specificity of the terminology used for the definition of phenomena to enable researchers to analyze more complex organizational models. More perspectives and variables should be incorporated into OB research to create more complex models. This change must be accompanied by a significant modification of models, such as the conversion of static relationships into dynamic ones and the use of specific human attributes rather than general terminology.

- Recent developments in management studies call for using more dynamic frameworks to describe the dynamic and temporal nature of individual and organization interactions. For example, organizational career research is beginning to recognize the need to apply time-series analyses and causal loops in which career experiences and job behaviors are interrelated (e.g., Baruch & Vardi, 2015).

A solid theoretical base and sound empirical research are of critical importance for the development of the scholarly study of OMB. Although misbehaviors constitute an integral component of the variety of behaviors in the workplace, the science of OMB lags behind with regard to the collection of empirical data and the development of a broad theoretical framework. Both are necessary to further the understanding of the phenomenon and to pave the way for future research and theory building. Bennett and Robinson (2000) draw our attention to the *conceptual confusion* we face when we use the terms *deviance, antisocial behavior*, and *aggression*. In addition, and perhaps related to this confusion, the measurement of misbehavior is difficult (for detailed discussions of measurement issues see Bowling & Gruys, 2010; Hershcovis, 2011; Tepper & Henle, 2011). First, commonly used instruments cannot adequately capture manifestations of nearly invisible misbehavior (small effect size; Cohen, 1992) such as loafing or making negative impressions. Second, the measurement may not reflect the actual frequency of phenomena such as theft by employees (e.g., inventory shortages may be due to either errors made purposely or to theft). Third, determining the degree of employee theft by the number of employees caught stealing or by those who willingly admit stealing does not reflect the full extent of the phenomenon. It is difficult to determine the ratio of reported to unreported OMB.

During the 1990s, we witnessed significant developments in the knowledge about OMB—in both theoretical and empirical terms. A number of researchers have developed theoretical frameworks with different emphases. Vardi and Wiener (1992, 1996) proposed a motivational approach to misbehavior using a deductive approach (building on previous theories and constructs); Robinson and Bennett (1995), using an inductive methodology, generated a typology of employee deviance; Griffin et al. (1998b) proposed a process model for describing dysfunctional workplace behavior; Ackroyd and Thompson (1999) emphasized organizational misbehavior as a form of employee resistance to managerial control; and Sackett and DeVore (2001) reviewed the emerging knowledge and developed a comprehensive framework for the understanding of counterproductive work behavior. Following their 1995 model, Bennett and Robinson (2000) developed a research instrument measuring OMB. They maintained that, despite the phenomenon's pervasiveness and cost, our current understanding of misbehaviors is still limited, and there is a need for extensive empirical research. Such research is possible only if a valid measure of deviance in the workplace is available. They provided an instrument of great importance for future studies in the field (this and other instruments are discussed later in this chapter).

On the empirical side, studies have attempted to assess OMB and account for the variance. For instance, since Greenberg's (1990a) findings of the relationship between employees' sense of having been treated unfairly and theft in the workplace, organizational justice has come to be known as a prominent antecedent of workplace misconduct (for reviews and meta-analyses see Berry et al., 2007; Cohen-Charash & Spector, 2001; Colquitt et al., 2013). Similarly, since Baron and Neuman's (1996) work on workplace aggression, the aggression literature has indicated various individual and situational predictors of interpersonal and organizational aggression (see Barling et al.'s, 2009 review; see also Hershcovis et al., 2007, for a meta-analysis). Other scholars have provided important insights on the effects of individual, job, group and organization-level precursors of withdrawal behavior (e.g., Eder & Eisenberger, 2008; Fugate et al., 2012; Howard, & Cordes, 2010; Sliter et al., 2012; Somers, 2009; Way et al., 2010). Vardi and Weitz (2002c) used the model of reasoned action for the prediction of misbehaviors, Duffy et al. (2012) suggested a social context model of envy and social undermining, and Bakker, Demerouti, and Dollard (2008) used the spillover-crossover model in order to explain how job demands generate work–family conflict, to name just a few.

Descriptive Versus Prescriptive Studies

The second dilemma facing the researcher is whether to take a descriptive or prescriptive approach. In reality, the relationship between description and prescription can be symbiotic (Porter et al., 1975). In fact, both are essential for in-depth analyses of organizational life. Those who formulate prescriptions are in need of insights and information gleaned from descriptive studies (i.e., adequate descriptions that provide the basis for any prescription). OB researchers are greatly tempted to move from describing phenomena to prescribing solutions and remedies. We are often quick to assert how much better it would be "if the employee had more autonomy" or "if only supervisors were more considerate," "if only our workers would be more spiritual." Although it is usually quite easy to arrive at a consensus regarding how things should be, we believe ready-made prescriptions and panaceas must be avoided. For instance, we found that consideration, autonomy, and spirituality might actually increase the intention to misbehave (Vardi & Weitz, 2001, 2002b; Weitz et al., 2012). When solid theoretical grounding is lacking, recommending interventions may be premature and, at times, risky. Even after conducting an empirical study that has applicable elements, recommendations based on such findings must be given with utmost caution and awareness of the limitations.

The apparent preference for a prescriptive approach stems from the congruence paradigm described in the beginning of the book:

- *At the subjective level*—Kotter (1973) maintained that the manager has three objectives vis-à-vis the employee: Attachment, satisfaction, and performance. The management of OB attains these when there is greater congruence between the expectations of both parties, when the psychological contract is not breached. Congruence leads to outcomes desirable for the organization.
- *At the job level*—Hackman and Oldham (1976) argued that a well-designed and a properly aligned job produces positive outcomes such as motivation, satisfaction, and long-term employee commitment.

- *At the occupational level*—Holland's (1985) model presents states of congruence between the occupational environment chosen by individuals and their personality traits. There are six basic personality types, and it is possible to match each one of them to a different occupational environment that is the most suitable and in which individuals can fulfill their potential and find satisfaction.
- *At the career level*—Schein (1971) proposed that individuals and organizations are two entities with different sets of needs. The individual needs to develop and feel secure, whereas the organization has the need and resources to meet those needs. If an organizational career incorporates the individual's needs and the organization's, the results will be positive—development, success, and high morale. According to Schein, congruence between the two entities constitutes the ideal, desirable situation.
- *At the organizational level*—Nadler and Tushman (1980) and Peters and Waterman (1982) posited that the most successful organization is one that displays congruence and alignment among its organizational components; the greater the fit, the better the organization functions.

Models and conceptual frameworks such as these raise several important questions with regard to the sole desirability of states of congruence: Are they indeed functional for the organization? Are states of incongruence necessarily dysfunctional for the organization? Will states of congruence necessarily lead to functional behavior? Researchers of OMB should assume that both *congruence* and *incongruence* might lead to proper behaviors *and* misbehaviors. For example, consider the effects on the worker of an unchallenging job that is perfectly aligned, or how creative employees can become disaffected when friction and uncertainty exist in their job. Furthermore, before offering sweeping recommendations, we need to ascertain that misbehaviors we wish to control are indeed dysfunctional for the organization and its members.

Macro-Level Versus Micro-Level

The third dilemma facing researchers is whether to focus on the macro or micro levels (Porter et al., 1975). The macro-level of OB has its origins in sociology, political science, and economics; it deals with organizational structures, planning, and activities within the general social context. The micro-level has its origins in psychology and social psychology; and it deals with individuals and groups and how they affect and are affected by the organizational system (O'Reilly, 1991; Staw, 1984). Macro-level researchers are interested in broad theories explaining the functioning of systems and the commonalities and differences among organizations. They often use descriptive empirical studies and pay relatively little

attention to practical implications. Micro-level studies mostly ascertain commonalities and differences among individuals and groups using survey and experimental methods for precise hypothesis testing (O'Reilly, 1991). In this book, we
discussed antecedents of misbehavior and distinguished between levels of analysis: Organization at the macro-level and group, task, and individual at the micro-
level. Sackett and DeVore (2001) proposed a similar classification of antecedents
with regard to counterproductive behavior. We recommend that researchers of
OMB utilize *multilevel*, dynamic, and interactive designs when possible. This would
allow for better control of background characteristics in multivariate analyses.

Structure Versus Process

The fourth dilemma facing researchers is whether to adopt structural or process
perspectives. Structure comprises the type of arrangements among the various
components of the organization and their interrelationships. Formal organizations may be viewed as structured social systems, which are a matter of choice
and, therefore, may be changed. A study with emphasis on structure typically deals
with the way the various components form part of a coherent framework and
how they affect individual and group behavior. Process studies focus on dynamics,
activities, and experiences such as socialization, communication, leadership, and
careers. From an analytical point of view, it is essential to emphasize structure as
opposed to function. An approach combining the two generally provides the best
explanation of behavior in organizations.

Our research on organizational structures and their effects on misbehavior
has dealt with questions concerning the relationship between employment status
(temporary and permanent) and misbehavior (Galmor, 1996), the role of organizational climate (Vardi, 2001), and the influence of job autonomy on misbehavior
(Vardi & Weitz, 2001). Using a macro-historical perspective, Vardi, De Vries, and
Gushpantz (2000) examined the bank-stocks regulation affair in Israel utilizing
system and organizational levels of description and analysis. The system level of
analysis dealt with the contribution of mechanisms and processes pertaining to
the social, cultural, political, and economic environments. The organizational level
examined the influence of structure and culture on the misconduct patterns of
the bankers and managers involved.

A process perspective on misbehavior can best be exemplified by Andersson
and Pearson's (1999) research on incivility in the workplace. They posited a spiraling effect of uncivil OB and maintained that, although an accidental expression
of incivility may not strongly affect what goes on in the organization, a spiraling
process may lead to significant manifestations of aggressiveness. Robinson and
O'Leary-Kelly (1998), Ferguson (2007), and Vardi and Weitz (2015) explored the
spread of organizational misbehavior as a social contagion process.

Formal Versus Informal

The fifth dilemma involves the decision of whether to focus on the formal or informal aspects of organizational life (Porter et al., 1975). Complex organizations involving people at work constitute structured social systems that are usually called formal organizations because they include specific and well-defined relationships and functions. However, any formal organizational system generates an informal set of behaviors and relationships that reflects the dynamics emerging as a result of the social and interpersonal interactions among members. Metaphorically, one may view the formal aspects of an organization such as size, form, and rules as the observable tip of the proverbial iceberg and the informal relationships, value systems, interactions, and dependencies as the voluminous unseen part of the iceberg.

In the past, OB studies tended to focus on the formal organizational structure. They mostly dealt with ways the organizational structure can be made more rational and, therefore, more efficient. In the 1930s, researchers noted that focusing on the formal organizational structure is not the only means to explain organizational behavior or to change it. The now famous Hawthorne studies were the first to incorporate the informal dimension into organizational research, including group dynamics and the influence of team members on one another's productivity and OMB (e.g., goldbricking), social status, informal communication, norms, and so on. Since then, there has been an increasing tendency to focus on the informal aspects of organizational life (see Appendix 2). OB researchers encounter a variety of structures, relationships, and actions requiring research that combines both formal and informal facets. Thus, OMB researchers should examine formal codes of ethics, rules and regulations, and management control systems, on the one hand, and the dynamics of behavior, such as social loafing, impression management, retaliation, or undermining, on the other hand. Eventually, we should be able to combine both perspectives to form more viable accounts of why and how individuals misbehave.

Objective Versus Subjective

The choice between a subjective and an objective observation is our sixth dilemma (Porter et al., 1975). Researchers go to great lengths to produce reliable and sound data that can be validated and generalized. Although, to many, science strives to be as objective as possible, this does not reduce the importance of subjectivity as a source of valid information. After all, the organizational behavior of individuals stems, to a significant degree, from the subjective world from which it is formed by perceptions, intellect, values, predispositions, and attitudes. The so-called *real features* of the situation are not those that influence the specific behavior; it is the way we grasp, interpret, perceive, and are influenced by them that leads us to action. In fact, this very gap between objective circumstances and individuals' perception of that reality is an important source of unexpected behaviors. Take, for example, the notion of *stress*. In many types of organizations (e.g., high-tech, hospitals, and law firms), work, objectively speaking, is loaded with stressful elements (Westman, 1992). Yet individuals working under such conditions perceive them differently. For some these are considered challenges and opportunities (e.g., Type As and workaholics); for others they are a source of personal tedium, anguish, and strain that affects their personal well-being (e.g., burnout and physical symptoms). To truly comprehend misbehavior, we need both phenomenological observations and hard objective data. Conclusions based on just one or the other are bound to lead to erroneous and lopsided conclusions.

Cognitive Versus Affective

The seventh dilemma is the choice between cognitive- and affective-focused research (Porter et al., 1975). Our OMB perspective—and research—originates from the idea that misbehavior is internally motivated by both cognitive and affective subjective processes (Vardi & Weitz, 2002c). Cognition relates to the individual's thought processes, such as decision and choice-making, whereas affect refers to the individual's emotional world. People express both thought and emotion at work. For example, when things seem under control or have little direct effect on the individual, he or she might rely on cognitive, rational processes. Yet when the individual senses pressure or is directly affected by the events, he or she will have more affective reactions. Behavior is the result of cognition, affect, or both. Unquestionably, OMB researchers must account for both. We showed that OB literature presents promising cognitive and affective models that can be utilized in OMB research (e.g., see Fishbein & Ajzen, 1975, for a cognitive model; Weiss & Cropanzano, 1996, for an affective model). Models that include both cognitive and affective variables will offer better explanations of misbehavior variance than either model separately.

Direct Versus Indirect

Our eighth research dilemma is the choice between direct and indirect measurement. The ideal strategy is to measure every form of misbehavior objectively, but this type of research necessitates the existence of visible, easily measurable behaviors, such as absences, as opposed to a variety of concealed behaviors that employees (and management) may not wish to reveal, such as theft and sexual harassment. The instruments at our disposal are either direct, such as self-reports, or indirect, such as reports about others. There are difficulties in interpreting both direct and indirect reports. For example, the data in self-reports may be biased due to the effect of social desirability, and ranking by superiors may be affected by the halo effect. Both of these problems are discussed in detail later; here we merely point out that these strategies are not ideal.

Although there is evidence supporting the validity of self-reports in general, and although they provide accurate assessments of deviant behavior in particular, this method has limitations. First, respondents tend to create a more positive impression of themselves, possibly distorting the results. However, a meta-analytical study by Ones, Viswesvaran, and Schmidt (1993) showed that self-reports provide more valid results than external measures of deviance. They explained this by the fact that many deviant behaviors are concealed; therefore, external measurement is not as effective. Second, there is significant evidence that the correlation between admission of the misbehavior and the actual behavior is high. Therefore, researchers believe that self-reports can serve as a valid instrument for the assessment of a great variety of misbehaviors in the workplace, especially when the respondents' anonymity is ensured. Slora (1989) designed a study to determine the rate of employee deviance based on Hollinger and Clark's (1983) typology and concluded that the use of anonymous surveys may be efficient in determining the base rate of deviance. The high response rate to the surveys and frequency of admitting misbehavior revealed that employees are willing to report their own deviant actions.

Similarly, Fox and Spector (1999) argued that if the research objective is to understand what employees feel and perceive, and how they respond, the method of self-reports might be effective. This conclusion stems from the difficulty in obtaining solid and objective data on criteria such as delinquent behavior, theft, and damaging the organization's property while the respondents are employed by the organization (Hogan & Hogan, 1989).

Despite the advantages of self-reports, most researchers emphasize their limitations. Lee (1993) pointed out that this method leads to incomplete data. The respondents' tendency to report less misbehavior than that which actually occurs may stem from their fear of being discovered and may result from social desirability. Distorted responses may also result from research reports of false relationships among variables (Zerbe & Paulhus, 1987). This may have a significant effect on research because incomplete reports may reduce the range of the variables and weaken the correlation of the relationship examined. According to Lehman and Simpson (1992), these shortcomings of self-report questionnaires may have a detrimental effect on the reliability of the information obtained.

The second strategy to measure OMB relies on information obtained from relevant others in the organization, such as co-workers. Utilizing an indirect strategy, Hunt (1996) conducted a large-scale study and obtained data for more than 18,000 employees in 36 firms. From those, five types of misbehaviors were effectively derived: Absence, misbehavior while on the job (unauthorized breaks or conducting personal affairs during work hours), unruly behavior, theft, and substance abuse. Thus, projective questionnaires—ones that ask about others' behavior—may reduce the lack of reliability typical of direct reports, particularly when dealing with unconventional organizational behavior (see OMB questionnaire in Appendix 1). Social projection (Allport, 1924) denotes the tendency of individuals to attribute their own personal attitudes to others around them. This method is based on the (somewhat naïve) assumption that others feel or respond the same way as we do. Ross, Greene, and House (1977) maintained that individuals tend to (1) be affected in their thinking by false consensus, (2) perceive their own judgment and behavior as common to everyone, and therefore (3) reject alternative answers that may seem atypical. People tend to deem their own behavior as acceptable and widespread, otherwise it would be deviant. We used both direct and projective questionnaires to obtain data on OMB and found it to be methodologically justified to employ the different methods (Vardi & Weitz, 2001, 2002a, 2002b, 2002c).

Quantitative Versus Qualitative Research

The final dilemma concerns the choice between qualitative and quantitative methods. Quantitative measurement deals with the assignment of numbers to qualities or properties of people, objects, or events based on a given set of rules (Stevens, 1968). Spector (2001) posited that the field of I/O psychology tends to be a statistical science (i.e., the type of data gathered makes possible the use of statistical methods). When hundreds and sometimes thousands of observations take place, there is a need for a variety of statistical methods and tests to draw sensible conclusions (e.g., Hollinger & Clark, 1982). These tests make it possible to determine whether variables are related and, in some cases, to infer causality. The statistical methods commonly used in the OB field include correlational analysis, multiple regression, various analyses of variance, and factor analysis (see Aguinis et al., 2001).

Van Maanen (1979) convincingly argued that qualitative research is more suitable than quantitative research for the description and analysis of the dynamic of social processes, whereas the quantitative approach is more appropriate for the analysis of a situation and social structures. The qualitative approach is better suited for analysis of complex events. He maintained that the quantification of measures and analysis of the relationships between variables might shed light on only a small part of the overall picture because the picture is greater than the sum of the elements composing it. Social relationships have deep underlying structures, which may elude research using the analytical method.

Qualitative research methods include use of participant observation, non-participant observation, interviews, and archival research (Analoui & Kakabadse, 1992). Qualitative measurement has also been applied for the observation of OMB. Dabney and Hollinger (1999) used interviews in a study on pharmacists' illegal use of drugs. The data were collected from 50 pharmacists recovering from the misuse of drugs. The information was recorded, and a thematic analysis was carried out. Results reveal that the face-to-face interviews, planned to examine the personal histories of a random sample of pharmacists, provide firsthand information about the attitudes and behaviors of pharmacists using drugs. Yanai (1998) investigated sexual harassment in the workplace by means of in-depth interviews with 18 working women. She obtained rich information about guarded, personal experiences, feelings, personal interpretations, and retrospective rationalizations.

Another method used in qualitative research is unobtrusive observations of individuals going about their normal practice. Typically, one or more observers are instructed on how and what to look for in the workplace setting, or the observations may be completely unstructured (Ailon-Souday, 2001). An alternative method is participative observation—facilitating the documentation of behavior in the most natural setting possible (Analoui & Kakabadse, 1992). Although ethnographic methods are used more in anthropological research, this method can also be used in OB research to assess employees' behavior without the observer's presence affecting the subjects' behavior (see Kunda, 1992, 2006). Because of ethical considerations and the need to safeguard the rights of the individual employees, the use of this method is mostly limited to behavior in public research sites.

When the researcher's goal is to examine the underlying processes leading to sensitive and controversial misbehavior, the participative observation approach offers appropriate tools and techniques that may yield explanatory insights. Using such methods, whether overtly or undercover, has the potential to generate rich, firsthand impressions. Analoui and Kakabadse (1992) implemented a qualitative, long-term research design using direct observations in a particular service organization. They emphasized the great importance of choosing the method and instruments of data collection. They posited that subtle forms of unconventional behavior, such as when subordinates are dishonest with their supervisor, cannot be studied the same way as behaviors such as unauthorized strikes and absences. The dilemma is this: Any attempt to question the participants or ask them to describe and explain their motives by means of common research methods, such as questionnaires and structured interviews, will actually call for less than honest replies. The simple labeling of certain behaviors as *unconventional* or *deviant* would make sharing innermost thoughts with an outsider undesirable. Therefore, Analoui and Kakabadse opted for participative observation. One of the researchers spent six years posing as a regular employee while taking notes about incidents in which he judged some misconduct was involved. This procedure enabled him to overcome problems of physical access to information with no disruptions in the work environment. The collected data—about rank-and-file as well as supervisory personnel—were then carefully analyzed, and theories to explain them were proposed.

Historical archival research is another type of qualitative, unobtrusive study. Historical analysis is clearly an important method of investigation of organizational misconduct at both the individual and organizational levels (Vardi et al., 2000). In such studies, questions on past phenomena are answered by means-selected facts and organized in explanatory patterns that emerge from the data. Obviously a historical perspective attempts to view the past through the eyes and representations of those who lived and acted at the time. Thus, it depends on the quality and extent of evidence left behind. One advantage of a historical investigation lies in the ability of the social scientist to anchor the observations in a larger picture—the social, cultural, and economic conditions prevailing at the time. Another advantage lies in the possibility of examining and analyzing behavioral processes and phenomena without relying on the faulty memory of subjects or their tendency to tell what they want you to know.

The conclusions drawn from qualitative data collected by means of interviews, observations, historical records, and case studies depend on how well they are analyzed. Content analysis is a technique aimed at drawing inferences by means of systematic and objective identification of defined attributes and messages embedded in written material (Holsti, 1968). These qualitative methods were employed by Sukenik (2001) to learn about airline pilots' safety culture; by Ofer (2003) in her study on OMB socialization in a commercial airline; by Shechter-Shmueli (2005) in her study of whistleblowing in an operating room of a public hospital; and by Turgeman-Goldschmidt (2001) to delve into the world of computer hacking.

In summary, we propose that OMB researchers consider the following. First, due to the sensitive nature of OMB, the unwillingness of management to let academicians research the phenomenon, and the reluctance of employees to divulge information regarding it, we recommend the use of both direct and indirect measurement methods. Integrating both methods within one study is invaluable—it contributes to both construct validity and reliability of the data. Second, one of the most effective methods for the study of OMB is the implementation of qualitative research by means of systematic observations. Participative observation is efficient because it reveals behaviors people usually prefer not to report. By being just another member of the organization, the researcher has a far better chance to identify manifestations of misbehavior without encountering apprehension or attempts to conceal or distort them. Third, experimental research designs and longitudinal studies may reveal causal relationships.

Problems Affecting the Measurement of OMB

The difficulties in measuring OMB may be roughly classified from the most general to very specific problems. The most general problems are related to the macro-level of measurement, including difficulties stemming from cross-cultural data, effects of the measurement methods and the observation of low base rates, and limited variance behaviors. Specific micro-level problems pertain to the respondents and include issues of social desirability, impression management, halo effect, and cognitive dissonance. In this section, we discuss micro-level problems first, and follow up with macro-level issues.

Social Desirability

Social desirability is defined as respondents' tendency to appear in a favorable light, whatever their feelings, opinions, or behaviors may be in a particular context (Crowne & Marlowe, 1960). To be perceived in a positive way, subjects tend to reply in a way they assume is preferred by the researcher even if their answers may not reflect their real opinions. Thus, correlations resulting from self-report questionnaires may be biased and should be interpreted with caution.

The contaminating effects of questionnaire answers in the OB field are evident in the work of Golembiewski and Munzenrider (1975). They were especially concerned with the influence of social desirability because high grades on the scale measuring social desirability suggest that respondents faked their answers to appear in a favorable light. Distortion of the answers may lead to the appearance of a false, non-existent relationship between variables (Zerbe & Paulhus, 1987) or the omission of sensitive behaviors, attitudes, or feelings untapped by the range of actual answers. Lehman and Simpson (1992) also raise doubts as to the reliability of information obtained by means of self-report questionnaires. Moorman and Podaskoff (1992) examined how social desirability had been researched in OB, and how it had affected research results. Their meta-analysis of 33 studies that examined the relationships between patterns of social desirability responses and OB variables indicated that social desirability is significantly related to commonly used variables such as locus of control, overall job satisfaction, role conflict, role ambiguity, and organizational commitment.

Social desirability creates methodological difficulties when attempting to expose misbehaviors, as evidenced in empirical studies. We argued that almost all OMB research focuses on the less severe aspects of misbehavior. Most of the research in the field deals with relatively minor behaviors such as faking illness, arriving late and leaving early, attending to personal matters at work, and so on. When it comes to more serious misbehaviors (e.g., interpersonal aggressiveness, verbal abuse, and sexual harassment), the range of the variables examined is often limited, precluding it from rigorous statistical analysis. We may attribute some of this restriction of variance and data skewness to the effects of social desirability.

Impression Management

This concept is commonly defined as any behavior designed to enhance a person's image in the eyes of another with the intention of attaining personally valuable goals (Villanova & Bernardin, 1989). Zerbe and Paulhus (1987) viewed impression management as a subcategory of social desirability responses. Such behavior is geared toward the control of the perceptions of others regarding one's behavior, both in a positive and negative way (Becker & Martin, 1995; Wayne & Kacmar, 1991). Because individuals in an organization are naturally reluctant to admit to have engaged in OMB due to its often sensitive nature and the fear of being branded as deviants, they may choose to create a positive impression. However, as suggested, impression management may not necessarily be due to a desire to please the researchers or other interested parties (Zerbe & Paulhus, 1987). For different reasons, employees may want to make bad impressions (self-handicapping) as well. For instance, they may want to avoid extra responsibility, be left alone, withdraw into more passive positions, and so on (Becker & Martin, 1995). It stands to reason that such tendencies may also be reflected in research surveys especially when subjects suspect research results will be reported to superiors on whom they wish to make a bad impression.

Halo Effect

This bias is defined as the tendency of a general impression of a person to affect the way specific traits are evaluated (Greenberg & Baron, 1997). A positive impression leads to the appraisal of additional positive traits, and a negative impression results in the assessment of additional negative traits. The underlying assumption is that individuals construct a specific image of one's personality on the basis of a presumed relationship between traits. Thus, if a person is perceived as diligent, he or she is also considered to be thorough and meticulous. Halo effect most certainly impacts the measurement of reported OMB, especially when the scales are based on reports about others (coworkers, subordinates, or superiors). For example, when superiors evaluate and report work performance of subordinates whom they consider efficient, their initial opinion will affect their attribution of misbehaviors to these subordinates. Conversely, we found that managers tend to report higher levels of OMB about subordinates who also had lower levels of organizational commitment and job satisfaction. We interpreted this finding as a possible result of the influence of negative halo effect on managers' assessments.

Cognitive Dissonance

Festinger (1957) defined *cognitive dissonance* as the state in which an individual simultaneously holds two conflicting positions. Holding contradictory cognitions may cause some psychological tension and discomfort. The individual would then naturally seek to reduce this uneasiness and resolve the dissonance. For example, a sense of dissonance leads the person to justify behaviors devoid of any obvious logical basis and to find reasons reinforcing choices made in the past (known as *post-decision dissonance*). Hence, once an individual has chosen to behave in a certain way, he or she will seek to justify and endorse the decision. If the decision appears justified, a state of dissonance will not ensue; if the justification does not appear satisfactory, a feeling of dissonance will develop and the person will attempt to reduce it. Therefore, when observing OMB, we should take into consideration the respondents' tendency to reduce the feeling of cognitive dissonance if it exists. Because OMB is intentional and involves the violation of acceptable norms, it is quite natural for individuals engaging in such conduct to experience dissonance. To cope with dissonance, they may rationalize their choice, deny it, or use neutralizing tactics (Sykes & Matza, 1957a, 1957b). We now turn to some macro-level research problems.

Low-Base-Rate Behaviors

Although OMB is a widespread and costly phenomenon, researchers need to be aware that they deal with what is known as *low-base-rate behaviors*. In relative terms, OMB—like its counterpart organizational citizenship behavior (OCB)—is the exception, not the rule, in our everyday work-life experience. Although serious misbehaviors such as sabotage or sexual harassment do occur, at any given time in any given sample, they may be relatively infrequent, and therefore not every respondent may be in a position to provide the information required. As Roznowski and Hulin (1992) argued, the problem in the study of low-base-rate behaviors is particularly evident when we research an isolated behavioral manifestation of a widespread phenomenon (e.g., theft). The low base rate of an isolated binary variable creates an abnormal distribution, and therefore relating to such distributions as if they were normal is problematic. An attempt to turn a distribution into a normal one by collecting data over a longer period of time or generalizing individual rating to the group level may be only partially successful at best.

To cope with the problem of low-base-rate behaviors, a wide conceptual framework should be developed encompassing clusters of misbehaviors (Roznowski & Hulin, 1992). However, Robinson and Greenberg (1998) maintained that one of the improper ways to cope with this phenomenon is to create a wide and sometimes unsuitable conceptual framework encompassing a number of deviant behaviors, thereby raising their overall rate. This method replaces one problem with another—an unreliable measurement with a more fundamental problem, the degree of construct validity. From our own research experience, we conclude that dealing honestly and ethically with the concerns of management, and guaranteeing strict anonymity and confidentiality, improves the chances of gaining access, obtaining truthful answers, and receiving reports of sensitive attitudes and behaviors.

Measurement in Different Cultural Settings

Such measurement involves two main problems. First, due to rapid globalization and the creation of a world economy, there is a growing interest in extending the research base from a limited number of English-speaking countries to other parts of the world (Spector, 2001). Second, as the scope of research widens to include many nations and cultures, the problem of transferring research instruments from one culture to another (and the comparisons among cultures) becomes more acute (Aguinis et al., 2001; Riordan & Vandenberg, 1994). The issue of what is considered deviant is culturally dependent: Employees' behaviors breaching multinational norms, or organizational norms breaching those prevalent in specific societies in which they operate (Bamberger & Sonnenstuhl, 1998).

The main methodological problem, of course, is the transfer of measures from one culture to another without first adjusting them to suit the existing culture. Researchers have wondered whether what has been developed and learned within the framework of one culture may be used effectively in another (Hofstede, 1993). Consider what may happen to the validity and reliability of measures of aggressive behavior originally developed in the United States in English, when employed in countries where English is not the native language (Spector, 2001). It is necessary to determine to what extent an instrument developed in one culture is valid in another to ensure that the conclusions drawn from it are indeed valid (Aguinis et al., 2001).

The first step in transferring instruments to other cultures is to translate them to the target language and then translate them back into the source language. This method of *retranslation* can ensure that the two versions of the instrument are well-matched content-wise (Spector, 2001). Considering that many words in one language have additional meanings and connotations—different from those intended in the original—requires that one person translates the instrument into the target language, and another, who has not seen the source, translates it back. The second version of the instrument is compared with the original one, and any mismatch is discussed and dealt with. The discrepancies between the two versions may be removed by a reformulation of the item in the target language and re-examination of the match. This process, as thorough as it may be, does not ensure that the transfer of an instrument to another culture will be completely valid. Yet such systematic steps may increase its validity.

How to Measure OMB

Firstly, it is necessary to precisely define what the researcher wishes to measure. Appendix 4 enumerates the variety of behaviors and various definitions the literature provides. Although this wealth of information might be a discouraging factor to some, we prefer to look at it positively—many more options may become available as we search and explore phenomena of OMB. Whatever method we choose in view of the dilemmas presented earlier—whether a theoretical or an empirical study, qualitative or quantitative research, direct or indirect reports, micro- or macro-levels—the choice will have a critical and decisive effect on the selection of the instrument to be used, the items to be included, and the way the results are interpreted. Furthermore, when using self-report scales to elicit evidence of personal misbehavior, we have to include a measure of social desirability to partial out its influence on the way respondents report their behavior.

Now that we have presented dilemmas associated with measuring OMB, we argue that sound and rigorous research is necessary and possible. First, we need to properly define what it is we wish to accurately measure. Second, we need to search for instruments designed to capture the phenomenon of interest.

Consider the measures of production and property-oriented misbehavior. The first instrument we may consider is Hollinger and Clark's (1982) scale of workplace deviance. It includes a list of misbehaviors divided into two categories: Property deviance, including damage to tangible property or the organization's assets; and production deviance, including breach of norms set for the performance of work, detrimental to quality and quantity of output. The measure's empirical advantage is twofold. First, it distinguishes property deviance items from production deviance items. Second, it allows for industry sector differences (retail, manufacturing, and hospitals). Property deviance includes such items as misusing discount privileges, damaging merchandise, taking store merchandise (retail); taking precious metals, taking raw material, taking finished products (manufacturing); taking hospital supplies, and taking or using medications (hospitals). Production deviance consists of items such as taking long lunch or coffee breaks, being under the influence of alcohol or drugs, and taking unjustified sick leave.

Following Vardi and Wiener (1992) and Robinson and Bennett (1995), Bennett and Robinson (2000) defined *workplace deviance* "as voluntary behavior that violates significant organizational norms and, in so doing, threatens the well-being of the organization or its members, or both" (p. 349). They developed an instrument for measuring workplace deviance and described in detail the theoretical basis for the instrument and the specific steps they took in deriving the items from different groups, the item selection processes, and the construct validity study they conducted to test the instrument's theoretical rigor. The instrument subsumes that workplace deviance can be captured by two general variables: Interpersonal and organizational, each ranging from very minor to severe deviance.

Additional measures of misbehaviors include. Griffin et al.'s (1998a, 1998b) classification of dysfunctional organizational behaviors. Their scale distinguishes between behaviors detrimental to the well-being of the self and those harming the organization. Moreover, they emphasized the importance of measuring outcome variables and further distinguished between outcome variables resulting in a specific cost (absences, theft, and sabotage) and those with general consequences (impression management and political behavior). They maintained that research is more productive if it is not limited to variables such as satisfaction, and can be expanded to include a wide range of functional and dysfunctional behaviors.

Skarlicki and Folger (1997) developed an instrument to measure organizational retaliatory behaviors. They maintained that such behaviors increase in response to injustice and unfairness and treated misbehavior as a reaction to critical events and not as personality traits. The items pertain to various OMB manifestations, such as damaging equipment, wasting company materials, disobedience, impression management at work, gossiping, spreading rumors, giving the "silent treatment," and working slow.

Research Guidelines

- When measuring misbehaviors as an overall phenomenon, a comprehensive instrument should be used to measure a composite of (mis)behaviors defined by the researcher.
- When measuring particular misbehaviors, it is crucial to ensure that the instrument is appropriate not only for the population under study, but also for the behaviors specified.
- To ensure efficient measurement of OMB, a combination of methods should be used. Triangulating questionnaire data with observations, interviews, and unobtrusive measures is recommended.
- When using an instrument originally formulated in a different language, an accurate translation that is faithful to the original and culturally relevant is necessary for both validity and reliability.
- To ensure efficient and comprehensive measurement of OMB, it is advisable to include direct (self-) and indirect (projective) techniques. This helps respondents overcome inhibitions and reluctance to report about behaviors they may initially prefer to keep to themselves.
- Measurement by means of direct reports of misbehaviors should include a valid and reliable instrument measuring social desirability.
- Because employees can exhibit positive extra-role behaviors and also engage in misbehavior, using both OMB and OCB scales increases our understanding of the full extent of work-related behavior. The use of both scales to measure these independent behaviors by reverse scoring may contaminate the data and conclusions drawn from them.

Our own research and the extensive review of other studies enhanced our initial thinking that the dark side of organizational life is indeed fascinating and in need of further exploration. As we become more aware of the antecedents and manifestations of OMB and of how they relate under different circumstances, we are in a position to think about strategies for managing these behaviors better. Our next and concluding chapter develops a comprehensive framework for the management of OMB.

11

A MODEL OF OMB MANAGEMENT

In recent years, the study of OMB has emerged as an important field of inquiry within OB (Barling et al., 2008; Ivancevich et al., 2014; Richards, 2008). Based on our experience and numerous discussions with practitioners, it remains uncharted territory for most managers. Hence, this chapter has two main goals: To propose a general integrative framework for the management of OMB and to draw managers' attention to the phenomenon, its social consequences, and steep financial costs. The dynamic model we present deals with the key question of why employees misbehave and what are the temporal consequences to consider strategically: It describes the varied processes, at different levels, that may lead employees to engage in different kinds of OMB and suggests guidelines for the management of organizational misbehavior (see Figure 11.1).

Recall that we define organizational misbehavior as any intentional action by members of organizations that defies and violates the shared organizational norms and expectations and/or core societal values, mores, and standards of proper conduct. It is a motivational process in which the intention to misbehave mediates the relationship between its antecedents and manifestations. The intention to misbehave and the decision as to which form of misbehavior one will engage in is assumed to be influenced by two independent forces: An instrumental force reflecting beliefs about personal interests, and a normative force reflecting internalized organizational expectations. These two forces are a function of one or more antecedents acting collectively or separately at varied levels: Individual, task/position, group, and organization. OMB often comes with a hefty price tag (personal, social, and financial), and these costs determine, to a large extent, the type, timing, and scope of the preventive and corrective interventions to be applied by management.

The proposed integrative model of OMB posits four key points of intervention through which management may act to lower the probability of OMB, thus controlling for costs and other negative consequences. These four action levers differ with respect to their focus and call for different types of corrective measures. One important implication derived from the model is that OMB management is not a linear, but an iterative process (i.e., dynamic, temporal, continuous, and repetitive). Our model is dynamic, not a static one. We view OMB not only as a consequence of certain contextual factors but also as an occurrence with effects and ramifications for the future of the organization and its workforce. For example, we showed that OMB may result in stress and burnout and affect the unfolding careers of organizational members. Because the model deals with antecedents, manifestations, and costs of OMB, the organization may apply preventive strategies or responsive tactics. The key issue is to what extent the selected interventions succeed in altering behavioral patterns of its targets so that the frequency and severity of OMB are decreased. Organizational misbehavior will always be with us. Management is beholden to do its outmost best to minimize it and its pernicious effects. Furthermore, management needs to be aware that some types of OMB may actually benefit the organization (e.g., whistleblowing).

To cope with OMB, one must be familiar with the dynamics of this phenomenon. That is, management needs to understand why employees intend to misbehave and to be aware of different processes, in varied levels and settings, that lead certain individuals to engage in specific forms of OMB. Management should also be aware of the forces that influence (increase or decrease) the intention to misbehave, and what possible expressions and costs are to be expected. However, keep in mind that there are possible beneficial as well as adverse consequences of the intervention(s) designed to control these behaviors.

We do not intend to provide the reader with a complete one-size-fits-all remedy for OMB management. We do not believe such panaceas exist. After all, work organizations have different goals, values, culture, rules, norms, and design, as well as different control systems and built-in opportunities to misbehave; employees have different personality traits, needs, attitudes, emotions, intentions, and desires. The varieties of possible forms of misbehavior, as well as the ways to deal with them, make it impossible to cover the whole range of probable antecedents and expressions of OMB and to develop and implement a unified and generic solution. Rather, we offer a strategic model, assistance to decision-makers, and organization development practitioners in their attempt to cope with the phenomenon, and we present the reader with guidelines for dealing with the relevant issues and for devising proper alternatives for action. A word of caution: Interventions designed to prevent OMB may have an adverse impact on the level of OMB if not designed and implemented carefully and sensitively. For example, surveillance cameras (CCTV) may serve management as a control system to monitor their employees, and at the same time challenge workers to beat the system.

Toward OMB Management: Prevention Versus Response

Researchers debate whether organizations should focus their efforts on preventive activities such as the use of selection procedures to screen potential troublemakers, and design the job a priori so it does not allow autonomy-related misbehavior, or responsive activities such as the termination of employees caught stealing. Several models (e.g., Neuman & Baron, 1997; O'Leary-Kelly et al., 1996; Treviño, 1986; Vardi & Wiener, 1996) deal with the relationship between personality traits and OMB, suggesting that thorough selection procedures designed to address these characteristics prior to actual hiring (i.e., applying selection as a prevention strategy) may help reduce the likelihood of OMB. Denenberg and Braverman (1999) argue that trying to identify the cause of violence (and, for that matter, any form of OMB) makes less practical sense than examining the organization's capacity to respond to the signs of stress or potential danger, whatever their origin. Prevention, they argued, lies in recognizing the need for a prompt and effective response as soon as early signs (e.g., distress) appear. Hence, a crucial question, they claimed, is not what causes organizational misbehavior, but rather how well (i.e., quickly and efficiently) the system responds to misbehavior (irrespective of the cause).

A combined approach, suggesting that counterproductive behavior can be controlled through the prevention of dysfunctional activities, maintenance of functional work behavior, and termination of counterproductive employees, was proposed by Collins and Griffin (1998). Prevention, they claimed, begins with personnel selection using cognitive ability (e.g., critical reasoning, and problem-solving) and personality (e.g., reliability) tests designed to predict both productive and counterproductive performance. Maintenance involves the integration and socialization of newcomers through regulated practices, procedures, and culture. Following Sonnenstuhl and Trice (1991), they suggested that supervision, the degree of prominence and visibility of job performance, and work roles may serve to better integrate the new employee into the organization. In contrast, engaging in counterproductive behaviors becomes more difficult for work roles that are well supervised and interdependent of other tasks, where performance is visible, when there is limited geographical mobility, and changes among fellow workers and supervisors are infrequent.

Similarly, the organization might act to mitigate organizational-motivated violence (OMV; O'Leary-Kelly et al., 1996) in two ways. First, the firm may mitigate OMV by altering individual, group, or organizational characteristics that may prompt aggressive behavior before (i.e., prevention) or after (i.e., response) violence has occurred. Neuman and Baron (1997) suggested that some tactics such as the use of personnel selection procedures designed to screen for potentially aggressive employees, sanctions to discourage aggressive acts, strategies designed to reduce feelings or perceptions of injustice and inequity, and implementation of training programs (to provide individuals with improved social skills, coping strategies, and behavioral alternatives to aggression) may prove useful in preventing and controlling OMB. Second, the firm may intervene before aggressive action leads to violence by use of control mechanisms such as security and monitoring systems. For OMB management to be effective, it should be not only reactive but proactive as well.

The Rationale for OMB Management

OMB may have nefarious effects (Vardi & Weitz, 2002b), economically (e.g., productivity loss and liability compensation) and socially (e.g., mental and physical injuries, psychological withdraw, and decreased job satisfaction). A closer look at the costs of three of the more pernicious forms of OMB—theft, substance abuse, and violence—reveals a stark picture.

Costs of Employee Theft

In 2008, The Institute for Corporate Productivity surveyed managers and executives at 392 varied US companies. Of the sample, 18 percent reported that they had noticed a rise in monetary theft among employees, such as fraudulent transactions or missing cash. Twenty-four percent reported an increase in stolen non-monetary items, such as retail products and office supplies (Needleman, 2008). Estimates of the costs of employee theft run as high as $51 billion annually in the United States alone (Global Retail Theft Barometer, 2011). In 2014, The National Retail Security Survey inventory found that of $44 billion in losses due to retailers' inventory shrinkage employee/internal theft accounted for 34.5 percent (National Retail Security Survey, 2015).

Costs of Substance Abuse

In 2005, 15.3 percent of the US workforce reported drinking before work, drinking during work hours, or working under the influence of alcohol; 3.1 percent of the workforce reported illicit drug use before work or during work hours and 2.9 percent reported working under the influence of illicit drugs (Frone, 2006). According to the National Survey on Drug Use and Health, combined data from 2008 to 2012 indicate that approximately 9 percent of full-time workers aged 18 to 64 used alcohol heavily in the past month, approximately 9 percent used illicit drugs in the past month, and 9.5 percent were dependent on or abused alcohol or illicit drugs in the past year (Bush & Lipary, 2015). The costs of lost productivity due to excessive alcohol consumption were about $162 billion in 2006 (Frone, 2013). In 2007, a US Justice Department study found that the economic costs of drug abuse in the United States were $120 billion in lost productivity, mainly due to labor participation costs. A different study indicated that in 2007, workplace productivity costs due to use of prescription pain relievers for non-medical purposes were about $26 billion (almost half of total societal costs!). Of these costs, premature death accounted for $11.2 billion, lost wages/employment accounted for $7.9 billion, and *presenteeism* (i.e., "diminished on-the-job productivity"; Birnbaum et al., 2011, p. 661) accounted for $2 billion. Excess medically related absenteeism and incarceration costs accounted for comparable amounts of $1.8 billion (Birnbaum et al., 2011).

Costs of Violence

Workplace violence became a major organizational problem in the 1980s, making homicide the second leading cause of work-related deaths by 1990. The number of violent acts in the workplace increased by 300 percent during the 1990s alone. In 2001 it was reported that an average of 20 people per week were murdered while at work in the United States, 18,000 were assaulted each week, and that workplace homicides are the fastest-growing form of murder in the United States (Towler, 2001b). In 2010, the Bureau of Labor Statistics Census of Fatal Occupational Injuries (CFOI) reported that of 4,547 fatal workplace injuries that occurred in the US, approximately 11 percent were workplace homicides. However, while most of the attention tends to focus on workplace homicides, injury rates of non-fatal violence constitute the vast majority of workplace violence incidents. Between 2011 and 2013, workplace assaults ran as high as 25,630 annually. Most of the assaults occurred in health care and social service settings (US Department of Labor, 2015).

According to the 2011 Society for Human Resource Management (SHRM) survey, of 267 organizations, 27 percent reported incidents of violence. The most common costs associated with workplace violence are management time/expense of being distracted from focusing on managing business operations, productivity loss, staff replacement costs resulting from turnover caused by the incident, and increased training and security expenses. Apart from inflicting direct damage, workplace violence bears some dire indirect consequences as well: Employees who witness and have firsthand knowledge about violent acts tend to suffer from increased stress, lower morale, a growing sense of insecurity, decreased trust in management, HR and coworkers, decreased productivity, and increased absenteeism and turnover (SHRM, 2011).

When it comes to violence, human resource managers are commonly victims (Kurland, 1993), and women, for whom homicide is the leading cause of death in the workplace (Nomani, 1995), are particularly likely to be targeted (Women's Bureau, US Department of Labor, 1994). A 1993 survey conducted by Northwestern National Life Insurance Company found that one of four workers reported being harassed, threatened, or physically attacked on the job during the previous 12 months. A survey of 500 human resource managers by the American Management Association showed that more than half of the survey participants reported incidents of threats of violence in the previous four years. Thirty percent of the managers reported multiple occurrences (see Chappell & DiMartino, 1998). The International Labour Organization concluded that workplace violence was a worldwide phenomenon—one that transcends the boundaries of a particular country, work setting, or occupational group (Chappell & DiMartino, 1998).

In 1997 alone, this translated into $16 billion in lost wages (Towler, 2001b). In addition, survivors of workplace violence, families of the victims, and even the violent offenders can and do sue employers, adding substantial liability costs to those already mentioned. For example, Towler (2001b) reported a supermarket chain found liable for the actions of an employee who attacked a boy urinating on the building. The child was awarded $150,000. In another case, the family of a female employee who was stalked and killed by a fellow worker sued the company for negligent hiring and retention of the killer. Overall, the cost of lost productivity and lawsuits due to organizational violence was estimated to reach $4.2 billion in 1992, and the total cost of workplace violence in the United States was estimated to be $4–6 billion per year (Towler, 2001b).

The Need for a Model of OMB Management

The economics of OMB are indeed staggering, and the price tag increases when the costs of misbehaviors such as fraud, sabotage, industrial espionage, and so on are factored into the equation. In addition, from a wider perspective, it becomes clear that employees engaging in OMB may negatively influence investors' decisions, influence customers' intentions not to return, or avoid purchasing the company's products, manipulate suppliers to break contracts, and sway coworkers to be less satisfied and even leave their positions. Obviously such costs affect bottom-line performance and productivity and may even pose a threat to the organization's very survival (Analoui & Kakabadse, 1992). Despite the fact that such costs may be offset by the benefits that often follow organizational improvements due to misbehaviors, such as whistleblowing, bootlegging, or new quality and monitoring regulations and practices, it can be easily understood why OMB may have such insidious effects on the organization and its stakeholders.

That OMB may have negative effects is clear. The dollar costs of OMB may be high. That alone may give sufficient reason for management to attempt to control it. There is the legal aspect to consider as well: Many forms of OMB (e.g., theft, homicide, fraud, sexual harassment, and discrimination) are legally forbidden by state regulations that employers are obliged to enforce. Moreover, companies are typically considered liable for their employees' actions even when these actions are not in accordance with company policies, and firms can be held responsible for employees' OMB (Towler, 2001a, 2001b). For example, employers may be held liable for negligent hiring or negligent retention of employees with a known propensity for violence (Amernic, 2001; Towler, 2001a, 2001b).

The wide range of recorded manifestations (see Appendix 4) and the heavy socioeconomic price tag they bear clearly indicate that OMB cannot be perceived as a marginal aspect of the organizational life and it should not be overlooked. Managers need to be aware of the phenomenon, its negative consequences to the organization and its stakeholders, and their need to alleviate the problem. The next section presents an integrative model of OMB management designed to assist managers, human resources practitioners, consultants, organization development (OD) practitioners, and management researchers.

The OMB Management Model

Figure 11.1 presents the new integrative model of OMB management following and developing the model developed in Vardi and Weitz (2004). This model expands the framework depicted in Figure 2.1 (see Chapter 2). In addition to the assertion that the intention to misbehave is assumed to mediate the relationship between the antecedents and expressions of OMB, the model posits that misbehavior is a complex and temporal phenomenon and its management, therefore, is an ongoing dynamic process, in which the costs associated with it determine the type, timing, and scope of the intervention(s) necessary to cope with OMB. The model identifies four phases of intervention designed to decrease the likelihood of OMB and, as a result, minimize the financial, individual, and social costs associated with it. These interventions are assumed to influence the future recurrence of misbehavior by affecting actors' intention to misbehave directly or indirectly.

One major implication derived from this model suggests that the effects of OMB may have an influence on the antecedents of OMB and increase the recurrence of a specific manifestation of OMB. For example, an employee's chronic absenteeism or cyberloafing (expressions of production misbehavior) may increase the stress (individual-level antecedent) and pressure (task-level antecedent) of a coworker, which in turn may result in violence toward a third party (expression of interpersonal misbehavior). When more than one employee is engaged in social loafing, it might become a group norm, leading to even more employees' counterproductive conduct. As discussed at length in Chapter 3, acts of misbehavior have long-term ramifications on organizational careers.

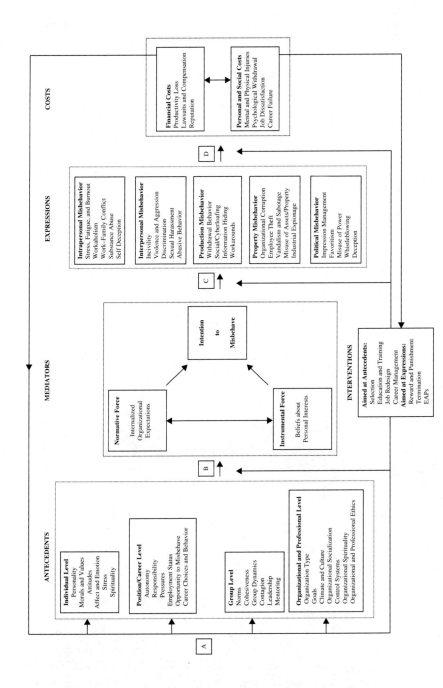

FIGURE 11.1 A revised integrative model of organizational misbehavior management

OMB Management: Interventions

Following Ivancevich et al. (2014) we refer to *OMB interventions* as the "Management of Employee Misbehavior (MEM)" (p. 205), which we define as any planned actions taken by management to cope (i.e., prevent, control) with organization members' (rank-and-file and managers alike) misbehavior, designed to reduce its frequency, scope, and costs. Figure 11.1 suggests four points (marked A, B, C, and D) of intervention in the MEM cycle, in which a firm seeks strategies to cope with misbehavior, to intervene and lower the probability of OMB taking place. These four action levers address the main stages in the temporal process:

- Phase A, pre-employment, is the costs ⇨ antecedents stage that deals with misbehavior prior to actual employment.
- Phase B is the antecedents ⇨ intention stage that deals with the attempt to reduce the motivation to engage in OMB.
- Phase C is the intention ⇨ manifestations stage, which focuses on the strategy to deter (not prevent) acts of misbehavior.
- Phase D is the manifestations ⇨ costs stage, which is designed to minimize the costs and to provide assistance following acts of OMB.

The MEM model assumes that all points of the intervention influence the future recurrence of misbehavior by affecting actors' and colleagues' intentions to misbehave, either directly (Phases B and C) or indirectly (Phases A and D). These four points of intervention are elaborated below.

MEM Phase A: Pre-Employment

The preliminary stage (Phase A) is the period in which the prospective employee has not yet entered the organization (pre-employment stage); it represents the timeframe in which one cycle of OMB has been completed and another one is about to begin (due to the adverse impact of the costs on the antecedents). At this stage, interventions can be designed to prevent misbehavior or alter the existing antecedents to prevent misbehavior. Use of selection techniques and careful job design and redesign methodologies are two examples of such interventions. For example, the goal at this stage is to keep OMB-prone individuals from entering the firm by use of integrity tests (e.g., Lee et al., 2005) to weed out applicants who are more likely to steal from the organization. To prevent substance abuse, firms may test prospective employees for drug use (e.g., Kitterlin & Moreo, 2012). However, such tactics may sometimes be problematic, as with the case of a job that requires assertiveness (e.g., salespeople)—a personality trait usually desirable, yet not too dissimilar and not easily differentiated in the selection stage from aggressiveness, which might lead to violent behavior on the job.

MEM Phase B: Socialization

The intention to misbehave is a function of two separate forces: The normative force, reflecting internalized organizational expectations, and instrumental forces, reflecting beliefs about personal interests. Vardi and Wiener (1992, 1996) argued that variables such as organizational socialization, culture, cohesiveness, and goals affect the normative force, whereas personal circumstances, dissatisfaction, built-in opportunity to misbehave, and control systems contribute to the formation of the instrumental force. Variables such as employees' primary socialization, personality, values, and cognitions may be related to both forces. The intention formation stage (Phase B) calls for two forms of intervention: One aimed at affecting the normative force and the other aimed at the instrumental force. In both cases, the goal is to lower the possibility of a given antecedent(s) to trigger the intention to misbehave. Interventions at this stage need to arouse a sense of wrongdoing within the individual—internalizing that, for example, stealing is, under all circumstances, wrong; bullying is abhorred, and that sexual harassment will not be tolerated—and reduce the instrumental motive to misbehave ("If I am caught stealing, I might get fired").

An intervention at Phase B may address a specific antecedent (e.g., personal attitudes and built-in opportunity) or, assuming that the antecedents have common denominators, be designed to address one or more of the four possible antecedent levels: Individual, task/position, group, and organization. For example, job redesign may reduce the built-in opportunity to misbehave (i.e., reduce the instrumental force), whereas a system-wide effort to disseminate, communicate, and implement a zero tolerance for misbehavior policy (i.e., cultural change) throughout the organization may reduce the normative force (Denenberg & Braverman, 1999). Some interventions may influence both normative and instrumental forces. For example, a formal mentorship program may help communicate values of proper conduct to newcomers (normative) as well as the possible sanctions facing misbehavior (instrumental).

MEM Phase C: Behavior Control

At this stage the intentions to misbehave already exist. Therefore, strategies shift from prevention to deterrence. Reward, control, and sanction systems, which may deter employees from carrying out their intentions because of fear of the associated punishment, play a major role. Consider the use of tracking devices (control) combined with use of bonuses and employee stock options (rewards). Embittered employees may choose not to misbehave if they know that they are being closely monitored and that if caught they may lose a bonus or, in more serious cases, their job.

One major influence on an employee's decision to misbehave is the perception of fairness and justice; it is a prominent antecedent of workplace misconduct

(Berry et al., 2007). As discussed earlier in the book, we distinguish between three types of fairness: (1) *procedural justice*—the perceived fairness of organizational procedures and decision-making processes; (2) *distributive justice*—the perceived fairness of decisions outcomes (e.g., pay), and the extent to which they are equitable; and (3) *interactional fairness*—the perceived fairness of the interpersonal treatment received by decision-makers (Colquitt et al., 2013; Ambrose et al., 2002). Interactional fairness is further divided into two facets: (1) *interpersonal fairness*—the extent to which interpersonal communication is respectful and appropriate, and (2) *informational fairness*—the extent to which explanations are truthful and adequate (Colquitt et al., 2013).

Recently, scholars have suggested that employees' fairness judgments are better illustrated through the construct of *overall justice* (general assessment of fairness) than specific facets of justice (e.g., Ambrose & Schminke, 2009). Priesemuth et al. (2014) examined the joint impact of overall justice and justice climate on bad behaviors in groups and found that group-level perceptions of overall justice are directly and positively related to both interpersonal deviance and political behavior in workgroups. These relationships were stronger under conditions of low interdependence between workgroup members.

Clearly, MEM calls for constant vigilance and continuous emphasis on organizational overall justice and fairness. Enhancing employees' perception of justice and fairness will lead not only to less misbehavior but also to improved organizational performance.

MEM Phase D: Corrective Measures

Phase D interventions have two goals: Minimizing the costs of misbehavior, and providing assistance to both perpetrators and targets of OMB. For example, periodical drug testing may help identify substance abuse and thus lower the rate of accidents on the job. The substance abusers can participate in rehabilitation programs. Similarly, employee assistance programs (EAPs) for victims of violence or sexual harassment may contribute to their early return to work and reduce the possibility of second-order misbehavior perpetrated against their aggressor or a third party. They may reduce the possibility of victims suing their employers. As in Phase A, interventions at this stage may address a specific manifestation (e.g., theft or sexual harassment) or, assuming a common denominator(s), one or more of the five categories of manifestations (i.e., production, property, interpersonal, intrapersonal, and political misbehavior). Hence, sanctions may reduce future absenteeism, whereas team-building interventions can be designed to cope with high levels of observed interpersonal misbehavior (e.g., aggression, bullying, withholding information, and lack of cooperation) associated with a specific group or team within the organization. Many factors may cause workers to withhold effort when they are working within the framework of a team, which may eventually lead to a decrease in the efficiency of the team and the organization as a whole.

To improve the work of the team, managers may have to take a number of commonsense steps. First, before handing over the project to the team, managers should ensure that the task is challenging, complex, and perceived as important. The greater the importance ascribed to it by the team members and the more they identify with it, the greater will be their commitment to perform well. Furthermore, the person in charge should acknowledge individual effort and output so that workers (rank-and-file as well as managers) feel appreciated, leading them to invest personal effort. Managers should be aware that the steps to be taken should not be merely instrumental; they should also take into account the norms developing in the team and possibly even assist in forging them. These norms may influence the willingness of each one of the team members to contribute to the collective effort. If a team has a tendency to behave fairly and altruistically, a sincere desire to collaborate, and the belief that all members are contributing according to their ability, then its commitment to the task will increase, which may lead to greater individual effort and reduce undesirable phenomena.

MEM Implications

The complex, dynamic, temporal, and highly contingent nature of the OMB phenomenon suggests that a generic, one-size-fits-all solution to OMB is unlikely. We have yet to find a panacea for OMB. As Analoui and Kakabadse (1992) argued, the multidimensional factors involved in the inception, emergence, and expression of each act of OMB make it difficult, if not impossible, to predict the exact time or place of its occurrence. Hence, every organization needs to constantly monitor itself, assess its needs (i.e., types of misbehavior and associated costs), and design means (i.e., interventions) for coping with OMB. We suggest that for MEM to be effective, the general phenomenon of OMB should be examined thoroughly and carefully analyzed (antecedents and/or manifestations), and that an effective coping strategy be devised. Management may design and implement a combination of several interventions aimed at different types and categories of OMB to be applied simultaneously. The application of such a strategy means, in fact, a culture change—delivering a clear and definitive organization-wide message of zero tolerance for OMB. For example, in a transportation company whose drivers were involved in accidents (costs) due to substance abuse (manifestation), it may be wise to establish periodical drug-testing programs and send substance abusers to rehabilitation programs (Phase D interventions). Also, new employees may be tested for substance abuse prior to hiring as part of the selection process (Phase A interventions).

Applying our OMB model as a practical tool enables management to forecast possible manifestations and costs given a specific antecedent and vice versa. One may zoom in on a certain antecedent (e.g., stress) and check for the possible outcomes (e.g., absenteeism, violence, and substance abuse) that need to be dealt with. Similarly, one can focus on a manifestation (e.g., violence) and trace its causes (e.g., stress and sense of injustice).

Imagine a situation in which the yearly job attitude survey and the performance appraisal system indicate that employees report high levels of job dissatisfaction and that they attribute this dissatisfaction to a sense of pay inequity. What are the forms of misbehavior that managers may expect? Research indicates that such frustration can lead to individual or group complaints (which are a legitimate action grounded in labor relations) and to production misbehavior (e.g., restriction of output), property misbehavior (e.g., sabotage), interpersonal misbehavior (e.g., violence toward supervisor), and intrapersonal misbehavior (e.g., substance abuse).

Or assume that a department reports high rates of absenteeism and rule-breaking. A thorough inquiry should be made to determine the causes of these phenomena, especially with regard to the different antecedents of OMB. Prevalent rule-breaking may indicate the presence of inadequate and non-comprehensive normative and substantive rules and/or a lack of concern or skills on the part of the management to enforce protective regulation (Analoui & Kakabadse, 1992). Absenteeism and rule-breaking may also be forms of resistance and protest against an authoritarian leadership (Ackroyd & Thompson, 1999). Hence, solutions may range from sending the manager to a management skills development program to transferring or terminating the manager and appointing a new one. However, if these behaviors reflect a built-in opportunity to be absent and taking advantage of a lax environment, a job redesign intervention may be called for.

A word of caution is in order: As can be easily understood from the discussion thus far, OMB interventions might have an adverse impact on misbehavior. That is, OMB interventions, if not designed and applied carefully and correctly, might foster OMB. For example, punishment needs to be perceived as justified and proportional relative to the severity of the act to be accepted as legitimate. If sanctions are perceived to be unjustified or non-proportional to the misbehavior, the levels of dissatisfaction and frustration may increase, resulting in a more severe form of misbehavior, as in the following case:

> Wastage and destruction were used as forms of unconventional behavior and were observed to be employed in both overt and covert forms, in order to show the discontent experienced. For example, security cameras were installed in bar (L) and as a consequence the staff could not "help themselves" to an occasional drink or two; even those which were genuine

mistakes or rejects brought back by customers. The staff then threw every-thing away instead of attempting to sell or save some of them as they were requested by the management. Phrases such as, "If I don't get, he (manager) doesn't either," were used. These phrases showed the intentions of the actors involved.

(Analoui & Kakabadse, 1992, p. 22)

Consider too the case of Arturo Reyes Torres, a highway worker for Caltrans, a Californian transportation organization, who was discharged for theft in 1997 after 15 years of service. Overtaken with anger and feelings of perceived unfairness, he returned to his former workplace and killed his former supervisor, along with three other employees, whom he held responsible for his termination (Denenberg & Braverman, 1999). We cannot overemphasize that OMB interventions need to be carefully designed and implemented so that the interventions do not induce further, secondary, and perhaps more costly and severe types of misbehavior.

The suggested guidelines for OMB management and interventions for its con-trol are the following:

- MEM is a temporal, dynamic, ongoing process similar to other conven-tional practices of administration and development and is, in fact, an integral part of it.
- There exists no panacea for OMB. Control mechanisms for its reduction need to be based on the specific needs of the organization, its members, and the organizational context.
- There are four main phases of intervention through which the organization may attempt to control OMB. The intervention phases differ in relation to their focus, yet the general purpose of all OMB interventions should be minimizing (i.e., weakening) the relationships among antecedents, mediators, expressions, and consequences of the OMB cycle with the intention to pre-vent undesirable behaviors (just as OD interventions are designed to enhance desirable ones).
- Some interventions or mechanisms may be used in more than one point throughout this process, and different interventions may be applied simul-taneously. A successful coping strategy calls for applying a combination of interventions at different stages simultaneously.
- OMB interventions should be designed so that they are perceived by employ-ees as legitimate and justified if they are to be effective. Perceived lack of fairness may lead to more severe forms of misbehavior in reaction to the sanctions imposed. This leads to the assertion that OMB interventions, like any other managerial practices, need to be constantly assessed for efficiency and effectiveness relative to their goals.

- While designing interventions, managers should consider the possibility that an intervention may have undesired effects (e.g., faulty design, improper application, or inappropriateness) and may even trigger misbehavior.

Summary

There is a tendency to focus on the positive aspects of work at the expense of exposing the dark side of organizations. Methodological and conceptual obstacles remain. We discussed these at length in the previous chapter and raised some useful suggestions for future endeavors. We still have a lot to learn, but we do have a good start. We believe the OMB framework presented in this book sheds light on the topic and contributes to our understanding. It also offers a broad canvas for future research, which may proceed in varied directions:

- The systematic study of the direct relationships between specific types of antecedents and manifestations—for example, the examination of the relationship between personality traits and the predisposition to bully.
- The exploration of the interaction between two or more variables within a level (e.g., the individual level) and their contribution to the intention to misbehave—for example, personality × stress ⇨ intention to misbehave. Similarly, the interaction between antecedents across levels—for example, values (individual level) × built-in opportunity (task level) ⇨ intention to misbehave.
- The exploration of the relationships between one or more antecedents and misbehaviors (with the intention to misbehave as mediator)—for example, personality × stress ⇨ theft, attitudes × job characteristics ⇨ sabotage.
- The examination of the interactions between manifestations within or across categories—for example, theft × sabotage, violence × sexual harassment, and drug use × aggression.
- The examination of the dynamic, temporal relationship between misbehavior and careers.

This model also draws a framework for the development and assessment of specific models of interventions aimed at the following:

- Specific antecedents or manifestations (e.g., selection tests designed to detect personality traits considered as predictors of violence).
- Aggregate level of antecedents or manifestations (e.g., team-building interventions at the group level and EAPs for rehabilitation to help victims of inter- or intrapersonal misbehavior).
- The system-wide level (e.g., designing a formal senior function to coordinate all efforts of OMB management).

A major implication of this model for both researchers and practitioners is that it combines prevention and deterrence strategies; it offers a means for determining the appropriate strategy for OMB assessment and control and the different intervention(s) by their efficacy. We are now in a better position to examine the results of a given intervention (or interventions) in lowering the rate and the costs of a given type of OMB. We can better examine the effect that drug testing has on lowering the rate and costs of accidents in a given organization or the effects of integrity testing on lowering the rate and costs of employee theft. Future research regarding the probability of a given intervention to meet its goals is needed.

We have reviewed the phenomenon of OMB and suggested an integrative model of OMB management with implications for management as well as directions for future research. The framework posits that OMB and the management of such behaviors are part of a dynamic, intentional, ongoing process in which the intention to misbehave is assumed to mediate the relationship between the antecedents and manifestations of OMB. The intention, in turn, is a function of two distinct, yet possibly related forces—an instrumental force reflecting beliefs about personal interests, and a normative force reflecting internalized organizational expectations. The varied antecedents in this model are grouped into categories reflecting four possible organizational levels of analysis: Individual, task/position, group, and organization. Manifestations are classified into five distinct categories of misbehavior: Intrapersonal, interpersonal, production, property, and political.

There are four main phases of intervention, or action levers, along the MEM cycle in which the organization may act to control the likelihood of OMB, thus reducing its associated costs. These four phases differ in their timing (regarding the OMB process), and in their focus, and call for an ongoing organizational effort to control OMB through the constant use of multiple interventions aimed at multiple forms of misbehaviors in varied steps of their formation and execution. If not applied sensitively and correctly, OMB interventions might in fact foster OMB and therefore require cautious consideration, preparation, implementation, and evaluation. The model also implies that the distinction between prevention and response strategies is of less importance than the question of the probability that a given intervention (or type of interventions) will lower the rate and costs of a given type of OMB.

The framework proposes that the costs of OMB—real or projected—determine to a large extent the type, timing, scope, and severity of the intervention(s) to be used. Other considerations are legal. Perhaps the most important lesson one may draw from this model is the assertion that, because of the highly contingent and dynamic nature of OMB, there is no one best solution. Every organization needs to assess its own situation and design its own means of coping with these phenomena. Before considering action, we offer the reader the following general propositions to consider:

- OMB bears significant financial and social costs, which in turn determine the need for interventions and their type, timing, scope, and severity.
- OMB costs may have an adverse impact on the antecedents of OMB, thus increasing the likelihood of the recurrence of the initial manifestation of OMB and inducing other forms of misbehavior. These secondary forms of misbehavior may be perpetrated by and targeted at the initial perpetrator(s) and target(s), as well as a third party.
- OMB management may reduce the frequency, scope, severity, and costs of OMB using varied action plans designed to minimize the relationship among the different variables associated with this process in four main phases of intervention along the OMB cycle.
- OMB interventions may have an adverse impact on the antecedents of OMB, thus increasing the likelihood of the recurrence of the initial manifestation as well as inducing other forms of misbehavior. These secondary forms of misbehavior may be perpetrated by and targeted at the initial perpetrator(s) and target(s), as well as a third party.
- The complex, dynamic, temporal, and highly contingent nature of OMB prohibits a generic, one-size-fits-all approach. It calls, instead, for a localized and specifically tailored MEM solution and an ongoing appraisal of its effectiveness.

The OMB management model, the MEM model, is a useful and practical tool for management to analyze the dynamics of the processes in varied levels and design appropriate intervention(s). It may also contribute to future research by drawing a general framework for the study of OMB in varied settings, such as the study of interactions among different variables in varied levels of analysis. Finally, this framework can be extended to encompass a wide range of organizational behaviors, and it can be developed into a general model of organizational behavior management and development.

Appendix 1

OVERALL OMB: QUESTIONNAIRE—OTHERS

(VARDI & WEITZ)

The following items (translated from Hebrew) pertain to different behaviors at work. Please indicate how often people in this organization behave this way:

Item	Very often	Often	Hardly ever	Never
1 Make private phone calls from the factory phone during work hours or breaks	3	2	1	0
2 Are late to work or leave it earlier without permission	3	2	1	0
3 Accept bribes or presents from suppliers, customers, or other sources	3	2	1	0
4 Use the copying machine for private purposes	3	2	1	0
5 Take a longer lunch break than permitted	3	2	1	0
6 Drink alcohol before or during work or during breaks	3	2	1	0
7 Take unnecessary risks by ignoring safety regulations	3	2	1	0
8 Use the expense account not according to formal procedure	3	2	1	0
9 Attend to personal or political matters during work hours	3	2	1	0
10 Sabotage factory machines or equipment	3	2	1	0
11 Work slowly on purpose	3	2	1	0
12 Waste factory money or materials	3	2	1	0
13 Take factory equipment or materials home without permission	3	2	1	0
14 Miss work without a reasonable justification	3	2	1	0
15 Favor a certain employee	3	2	1	0

Item	Very often	Often	Hardly ever	Never
16 Report on their colleagues	3	2	1	0
17 Blame colleagues for their own mistakes	3	2	1	0
18 Sexually harass colleagues	3	2	1	0
19 Verbally abuse colleagues	3	2	1	0
20 Steal from their colleagues	3	2	1	0
21 Endanger their colleagues	3	2	1	0
22 Fire an employee without justification	3	2	1	0
23 Go against management decisions	3	2	1	0

Appendix 2

MAIN TOPICS IN OB LITERATURE REVIEWS (2000–15)

Annual Review of Psychology

Year	Authors	Topic
2000	Macrae & Bodenhausen	Social cognition
	Lubinski	Individual differences
	Wood	Attitude change, social influence
2001	Maslach, Schaufeli, & Leiter	Job burnout
	Salas & Cannon-Bowers	Training
	Ajzen	Attitudes and behavior
	Miller	Injustice, disrespect, anger, retaliation, and withdrawal
	Pashler, Johnston, & Ruthruff	Attention and performance
	Hastie	Judgment and decision-making
2002	Eccles & Wigfield	Motivational beliefs, values, and goals
	Ellemers, Spears, & Doosje	Self and social identity, group commitment, social context, identity threat
	Brief & Weiss	Moods and emotions, job satisfaction, positive and negative affectivity, work environments, job performance
	Shafir & LeBoeuf	Judgment, choice, decision-making, normative theories, cognition
	Hewstone, Rubin, & Willis	Conflict, discrimination, prejudice, social categorization, stereotyping
2003	Olson & Olson	Human–computer interaction
	Rusbult & Van Lange	Attribution, communication, interpersonal processes, self-presentation, social motivation

Year	Authors	Topic
2004	Cialdini & Goldstein	Compliance and obedience
	Kerr & Tindale	Group motivation, process losses and gains, group information processing, shared cognitions
	Runco	Creativity
2005	Latham & Pinder	Work motivation: Needs, values, goals, affect, behavior
	Penner, Dovidio, Piliavin, & Schroeder	Prosocial behavior
	Major & O'Brien	Social identity, identity threat, stress and coping, stereotyping, prejudice, discrimination
	Ilgen, Hollenbeck, Johnson, & Jundt	Teamwork, workgroup, groups, coordination, cooperation
	Rynes, Gerhart, & Parks	Appraisal, pay, motivation, incentives, feedback
2006	Crano & Prislin	Attitudes and persuasion
	Ozer & Benet-Martínez	Individual differences, traits, consequential outcomes
	Crosby, Iyer, & Sincharoen	Affirmative action
2007	Leary	Motivational and emotional aspects of the self
		Ostracism
	Williams	Cross-cultural OB and work motivation,
	Gelfand, Erez, & Aycan	individual–organization relationship, psychological contracts, justice, citizenship behavior, person–environment fit
	Van Knippenberg & Schippers	Workgroup diversity, group performance, teams, team effectiveness
	Fouad	Career development, career decision-making, career self-efficacy, career adaptability, person–environment fit
2008	Higgins & Pittman	Motivation, attribution, self-presentation, impression management, communication
	Hodgkinson & Healey	Managerial and organizational cognition, OB, information processing, decision-making
	Sackett & Lievens	Personnel selection, job performance, ability, personality
2009	Weber & Johnson	Mindful judgment, decision-making
	Avolio, Walumbwa, & Weber	Leadership
	Aguinis & Kraiger	Training and development
	Barling, Dupré, & Kelloway	Workplace aggression and violence
	Aquino & Thau	Workplace victimization
2010	Lord, Diefendorff, Schmidt, & Hall	Motivation and self-regulation
	Hennessey & Amabile	Creativity
	Eby, Maher, & Butts	Emotion, moods, work attitudes, family attitudes, non-work experiences
2011	Bohner & Dickel	Attitudes
	Gigerenzer & Gaissmaier	Heuristic decision-making

Year	Authors	Topic
2012	Judge & Kammeyer-Mueller	Job attitudes, job satisfaction, mood, emotions, personality, performance
	Wanberg	Job loss, job search, job seeker, layoff, re-employment, mental health
2014	Jetten & Hornsey	Deviance and dissent in groups
	Treviño, Nieuwenboer, & Kish-Gephart	Organizational ethics, ethical decision-making, ethical leadership, moral identity, ethical infrastructures
	Parker	Job design, autonomy, job enrichment, job characteristics, self-managing teams
2015	Oppenheimer & Kelso	Information processing as a paradigm for decision-making
	Frese & Keith	Learning, action errors, error management, innovation

Annual Review of Organizational Psychology and Organizational Behavior

Year	Authors	Topic
2014	Edmondson & Lei	Psychological safety, organizational learning, teams, team learning
	Schmitt	Personality and cognitive ability as predictors of effective job performance
	Anderson & Brion	Power, hierarchy, politics, status, person-perception, groups
	Allen, Cho & Meier	Boundary management, work-family conflict
	Robinson, Wang, & Kiewitz	The impact of coworker deviant behavior upon individual employees
	Morrison	Employee voice and silence
	Lee, Burch, & Mitchell	Job embeddedness, voluntary turnover, organizational outcomes
	Noe, Clarke, & Klein	Training, development, informal learning, human capital resources, knowledge sharing, continuous learning
	Dutton, Workman, & Hardin	Compassion at work
	Zhou & Hoever	Innovation, team creativity, person-context interaction
	Greenhaus & Kossek	A work-home perspective on contemporary careers
	Bakker, Demerouti, & Sanz-Vergel	Employee engagement, burnout, job demands-resources model, job design
	Tjosvold, Wong, & Feng Chen	Constructively managing conflicts in organizations

Appendix 3
A SCENARIO-BASED MEASURE OF OMB TYPES

(a) *OMB Type S Scenario*: As part of your monthly salary, you receive reimbursement for using your own car for visiting your customers. Like many others in the company, you think the real costs you incur are not covered by this extra pay. Occasionally you join a fellow employee for the ride to visit customers. In such cases, would you report those trips for reimbursement to increase your income?

(b) *OMB Type D Scenario*: You work as an engineer in the research and development department of a high-tech company. Your team is highly cohesive, but you do not really feel part of it. Actually you are quite bitter because you think people are talking about you behind your back. Recently you had a brilliant idea that could improve the product your team is working on, but you have no desire to share it with them. Your good friend from college works for a competing firm. Would you tell your idea to him so his team could beat your company in the competition?

(c) *OMB Type O Scenario*: You are a veteran and loyal salesman in a company that markets technological products. You are proud of your company, although at this time it is not doing too well financially. In addition, it was recently discovered that one of the most popular products that you sell has a defect (albeit not a critical one). Headquarters issued a directive to the salesforce to stop marketing the product until further notice. You know that such a move will hurt the financial conditions of the company. Would you keep selling the product to your customers to minimize the economic damage to your company?

Appendix 4

AN ALPHABETIC LIST OF CONSTRUCTS, DEFINITIONS, AND MANIFESTATIONS OF OMB

Term	Authors	Definition
Abusive supervision	Tepper (2000)	"Subordinates' perceptions of the extent to which supervisors engage in the sustained display of hostile verbal and non verbal behaviors, excluding physical contact" (p. 178).
Antisocial behavior	Giacalone & Greenberg (1997)	"Any behavior that brings harm, or is intended to bring harm to the organization, its employees, or its stakeholders" (p. vii).
Bad behavior in organizations	Griffin & Lopez (2005)	"Any form of intentional (as opposed to accidental) behavior that is potentially injurious to the organization and/or to individuals within the organization" (p. 988).
Blue-collar crime	Horning (1970)	"Illegal acts which are committed by non salaried workers and which involve the operative's place of employment either as the victim (e.g., the theft of materials, the destruction of company property, the falsification of production records) or as a contributory factor by providing the locus for the commissions of an illegal act (e.g., fighting on company property, the theft of personal property, gambling on company premises, the selling of obscene literature on company premises)" (pp. 47–48).

Term	Authors	Definition
Citizenship fatigue	Bolino, Hsiung, Harvey, & LePine (2015)	"A state in which feeling worn out, tired, or on edge is attributed to engaging in OCB" (p. 57).
Corporate psychopath	Boddy (2010)	"A psychopath who works and operates in the organizational area" (p. 369).
Corruption	Ashforth, Gioia, Robinson, & Treviño (2008)	"The concept of corruption reflects not just the corrupt behavior of any single individual – defined as the illicit use of one's position or power for perceived personal or collective gain1– but also the dangerous, viruslike 'infection' of a group, organization, or industry" (p. 671).
Counterproductive work behavior	Fox & Spector (2005)	"Volitional acts that harm or are intended to harm organizations or people in organizations" (p. 151).
Counterproductive workplace behavior	Sackett & DeVore (2001)	"Any intentional behavior on the part of an organization member viewed by the organization as contrary to its legitimate interests" (p. 145).
Cyberbullying	Smith et al. (2008)	"An aggressive, intentional act carried out by a group or individual, using electronic form of contact, repeatedly and over time against a victim who cannot easily defend him or herself" (p. 376).
Cyberdeviancy	Weatherbee (2010)	"[V]oluntary behavior using information and communications systems which either threatens or results in harm to an organization, its members, or stakeholders" (p. 39).
Detrimental citizenship behavior (DCB)	Pierce & Aguinis (2015)	"[D]iscretionary employee behavior that goes beyond reason and necessity to promote specific organizational goals and, in so doing, harms legitimate stakeholder interests" (p. 71).
Dysfunctional behavior	Griffin, O'Leary-Kelly, & Collins (1998b)	"Motivated behavior by an employee or group of employees that has negative consequences for an individual within the organization, a group of individuals within the organization, and/or the organization itself" (p. 67).

Term	Authors	Definition
Dysfunctional behavior	Griffin & Lopez (2005)	"Motivated behavior by an employee or group of employees that is intended to have negative consequences for another individual and/or group and/ or the organization" (p. 1001).
Employee deviance	Hollinger & Clark (1982)	"Unauthorized acts by employees which are intended to be detrimental to the formal organization" (p. 97).
Employee deviance	Warren (2003)	"Behavioral departures from the norms of reference group" (p. 22).
Employee deviance	Robinson & Bennett (1995)	"Voluntary behavior that violates significant organizational norms and in so doing threatens the well-being of an organization, its members, or both" (p. 556).
Employee misconduct	Leatherwood & Spector (1991)	"Employee decisions to pursue self-interest at the expense of their principals or employer" (p. 553).
Employee sabotage	Crino (1994), cited in Skarlicki, Van Jaarsveld, & Walker (2008)	"[R]efers to behavior that can damage or disrupt the organization's operations by creating delays in production, damaging property, the destruction of relationships, or the harming of employees or customers" (p. 312).
Gender harassment	Fitzgerald, Gelfand, & Drasgow (1995)	"A broad range of verbal and nonverbal behaviors not aimed at sexual cooperation but that convey insulting, hostile, and degrading attitudes" (p. 430).
Generalized workplace harassment (GWH)	Rospenda & Richman (2004)	"Negative workplace interactions that affect the terms, conditions, or employment decisions related to an individual's job, or create a hostile, intimidating or offensive working environment, but which are not based on legally-protected social status characteristics" (p. 96).
Impression management	Bolino, Kacmar, Turnley, & Gilstrap (2008)	"Efforts by an actor to create, maintain, protect, or otherwise alter an image held by a target audience" (p. 1080).

Term	Authors	Definition
Insidious workplace behavior (IWB)	Greenberg (2010)	"[A] form of intentionally harmful workplace behavior that is legal, subtle, and low level (rather than severe), repeated over time, and directed at individuals or organizations" (p. 4).
Misconduct	Treviño (1992)	"Behavior that falls short of the [punishing] agent's moral or technical (work) standards" (p. 648).
Non-compliant behaviors	Puffer (1987)	"Non-task behaviors that have negative organizational implications" (p. 615).
Normal organizational wrongdoing	Palmer (2012)	"Any behavior that organizational participants perpetrate in the course of fulfilling their organizational roles (e.g., directors, managers, and/or employees) that the state judges to be wrongful" (p. 35).
Occupational crime	Colman (1985), cited in Greenberg & Scott (1996)	"White collar crime committed by an individual or a group of individuals exclusively for personal gain" (p. 117).
Organizational aggression	Spector (1978)	"Any behavior intended to hurt the organization" (p. 821).
Organizational aggression	O'Leary-Kelly, Griffin, & Glew (1996)	General definition: "Any injurious or destructive actions that affect organizational employees, property, or relationships" (p. 228). Restricted definition: "Injurious actions and events that are prompted by some factor in the organization itself" (p. 228).
Organizational miasma	Gabriel (2012)	"A highly toxic state of affairs capable of afflicting everybody and of corrupting the institutional and moral fabric of a social unit" (p. 1145).
Organizational misbehavior (OMB)	Vardi & Wiener (1996)	"Any intentional action by members of organizations that violates core organizational and/or societal norms" (p. 151).
Organizational misbehavior	Ackroyd & Thompson (1999)	"Anything you do at work you are not supposed to do" (p. 2).
Organizational retaliation behavior	Skarlicki & Folger (1997)	"Adverse reactions to perceived unfairness by disgruntled employees toward their employer" (p. 434).

Term	Authors	Definition
Organization-motivated aggression (OMA)	O'Leary-Kelly, Griffin, & Glew (1996)	"Attempted injuries or destructive behavior initiated by either an organizational insider or outsider that is instigated by some factor in the organizational context" (p. 229).
Organization-motivated violence (OMV)	O'Leary-Kelly, Griffin, & Glew (1996)	"Significant negative effects on person or property that occur as a result of organizational-motivated aggression" (p. 229).
Research misconduct	US Office of Science and Technology Policy (UTSP) Federal Policy on Research Misconduct, cited in Martinson, Anderson, & De Vries (2005)	"Fabrication, falsification, or plagiarism (FFP) in proposing, performing, or reviewing research, or in reporting research results" (p. 737).
Self-deception	Peck (1983), cited in Caldwell (2009)	"A denial of the duty owed to the self when it causes an individual to avoid confronting the need to modify one's behavior" (p. 397).
Sex-based harassment	Berdahl (2007)	"Behavior that derogates, demeans, or humiliates an individual based on that individual's sex" (p. 644).
Sexual orientation harassment	Ryan & Wessel (2012)	"Displaying unwanted behavior toward an individual in the workplace on the basis of the perceived or actual sexual orientation of that individual" (p. 489).
Social undermining	Duffy, Ganster, & Pagon (2002)	"[B]ehavior intended to hinder, over time, the ability to establish and maintain positive interpersonal relationships, work-related success, and favorable reputation" (p. 332).
Unconventional practices	Analoui & Kakabadse (1992)	"Incidents of indiscipline, pilferage, non-co-operation, and the misuse of facilities, as well as more taboo and sensitive practices such as disruption and destruction of the work environment" (p. 5).
Unethical behavior	Kish-Gephart, Harrison, & Treviño (2010)	"Any organizational member action that violates widely accepted (societal) moral norms" (p. 2).

Term	Authors	Definition
Whistleblowing	Mayer, Nurmohamed, Treviño, Shapiro, & Schminke (2013)	"Reporting work-related practices that are perceived to be illegal, immoral, or illegitimate to organizational authorities" (p. 89).
Workaholism	Schaufeli, Taris, & Van Rhenen (2008)	"Workaholics work harder than their job prescriptions require and put much more effort into their jobs than is expected by the people with whom or for whom they work, and in doing so they neglect their life outside the job" (p. 4).
Work–family conflict	Greenhaus & Beutell (1985)	"A form of interrole conflict in which the role pressures from the work and family domains are mutually incompatible in some respect. That is, participation in the work (family) role is made more difficult by virtue of participation in the family (work) role" (p. 77).
Workplace aggression	Greenberg & Alge (1998)	"Injurious actions and events that are prompted by some factor in the organization… excluding sources of aggression stemming from outside the organization, such as robbery" (p. 85).
Workplace aggression	Neuman & Baron (2005)	"Any form of behavior directed by one or more persons in a workplace toward the goal of harming one or more others in that workplace (or the entire organization) in ways the intended targets are motivated to avoid" (p. 18).
Workplace bullying	Matthiesen & Einarsen (2007)	"[S]ituation in which one or more persons systematically and over a long period of time perceive themselves to be on the receiving end of negative treatment on the part of one or more persons, in a situation in which the person(s) exposed to the treatment have difficulty in defending themselves against this treatment" (p. 735).

Term	Authors	Definition
Workplace incivility	Andersson & Pearson (1999)	"Low intensity deviant behavior with ambiguous intent to harm the target, in violation of workplace norms for mutual respect. Uncivil behaviors are characteristically rude and discourteous, displaying a lack of regard for others" (p. 457).
Workplace mistreatment	Cortina & Magley (2003)	"Specific, antisocial variety of organizational deviance, involving a situation in which at least one organizational member takes counternormative negative actions – or terminates normative positive actions – against another member… interpersonal mistreatment can thus range from subtle social slights to general incivility to blatant harassment and violence" (p. 247).
Workplace victimization	Aquino & Thau (2009)	"Individual's perception of having been exposed, either momentarily or repeatedly, to the aggressive acts of one or more other persons" (p. 721).

REFERENCES

Abdel Halim, A. A. (1978). Employee affective responses to organizational stress: Moderating effects of job characteristics. *Personnel Psychology*, 31, 561–578.

Abrahamson, E. (1996). Management fashion. *Academy of Management Review*, 21, 254–285.

Abrahamson, E. (1997). The emergence and prevalence of employee management rhetoric: The effects of long waves, labor union, and turnover, 1875 to 1992. *Academy of Management Journal*, 40, 491–533.

Abrams, D. & Hogg, M. A. (Eds.) (1990). *Social identity theory: Constructive and critical advances.* London: Harvester Wheatsheaf.

Academy of Management (2002). *Newsletter*, August. Radcliff Manor, NY: Author.

Ackroyd, S. & Thompson, P. (1999). *Organizational misbehaviour.* London: Sage.

Adams, A. & Crawford, N. (1992). *Bullying at work: How to confront and overcome it.* London: Virago Press.

Adams, J. S. (1963). Toward an understanding of inequity. *Journal of Abnormal and Social Psychology*, 67, 422–436.

Adams, J. S. (1965). Inequity in social exchange. In L. Berkowitz (Ed.), *Advances in experimental social psychology* (Vol. 2, pp. 267–299). New York: Academic Press.

Adams, S. (1996). *The Dilbert principle.* New York: Harper Business.

Adebayo, D., Akanmode, J., & Udegbe, I. (2007). The importance of spirituality in the relationship between psychological contract violation and cynicism in the Nigeria police. *The Police Journal*, 80(2), 141–166.

Adkins, C. L., Werbel, J. D., & Farh, J. (2001). A field study of job insecurity during a financial crisis. *Group & Organization Management*, 26(4), 463–483.

Agervold, M. (2007). Bullying at work: A discussion of definitions and prevalence, based on an empirical study. *Scandinavian Journal of Psychology*, 48(2), 161–172.

Aggarwal, A. P. & Gupta, M. M. (2000). *Sexual harassment in the workplace* (3rd edn). Vancouver, BC: Butterworths.

Aguilera, R. V. & Vadera, A. K. (2008). The dark side of authority: Antecedents, mechanisms, and outcomes of organizational corruption. *Journal of Business Ethics*, 77(4), 431–449.

Aguinis, H. & Kraiger, K. (2009). Benefits of training and development for individuals and teams, organizations, and society. *Annual Review of Psychology*, 60(1), 451–474.

Aguinis, H., Henle, C. A., & Ostroff, C. (2001). Measurement in work and organizational psychology. In N. Anderson, D. S. Ones, H. K. Sinangil, & C. Viswesvaran (Eds.), *Handbook of industrial, work and organizational psychology* (Vol. 1, pp. 27–50). London: Sage.

Ailon-Souday, G. (2001). *Merging ourselves apart: A study of identities in an Israeli high-tech corporation undergoing a merger with an American competitor* (Unpublished doctoral dissertation). Tel-Aviv University, Israel.

Ajzen, I. (1985). From intentions to actions: A theory of planned behavior. In J. Kurhl & J. Beckman (Eds.), *Consistency in social behavior: The Ontario symposium* (Vol. 2, pp. 3–15). Hillsdale, NJ: Lawrence Erlbaum Associates.

Ajzen, I. (2001). Nature and operation of attitudes. *Annual Review of Psychology*, 52(1), 27–58.

Ajzen, I. & Fishbein, M. (1980). *Understanding attitudes and predicting social behavior*. Englewood Cliffs, NJ: Prentice-Hall.

Aldrich, H. E. (1979). *Organizations and environments*. Englewood Cliffs, NJ: Prentice-Hall.

Allcorn, S. (1994). *Anger in the workplace: Understanding the causes of aggression and violence*. Westport, CT: Quorum Books.

Allen, T. D., Cho, E., & Meier, L. L. (2014). Work–family boundary dynamics. *Annual Review of Organizational Psychology and Organizational Behavior*, 1(1), 99–121.

Allen, V. L. & Greenberger, D. B. (1980). Destruction and perceived control. In A. Baum & J. E. Singer (Eds.), *Applications of personal control* (Vol. 2, pp. 85–109). Hillsdale, NJ: Lawrence Erlbaum Associates.

Allinson, R. E. (1998). Ethical values as part of the definition of business enterprise and part of the internal structure of the business organization. *Journal of Business Ethics*, 17, 1015–1028.

Allison, G. T. (1971). *Essence of decision: Explaining the Cuban missile crisis*. Boston, MA: Little, Brown.

Allport, F. H. (1924). *Social psychology*. Cambridge, MA: Riverside.

Allport, F. H. (1924). Response to social stimulation in the group. In F.H. Allport (Ed.), *Social psychology* (pp. 260–291). Hillsdale, NJ: Lawrence Erlbaum Associates.

Allport, G. W. (1961). *Pattern and growth in personality*. New York: Holt, Rinehart & Winston.

Alter, S. (2014). Theory of workarounds. *Communications of the Association for Information Systems*, 34(1), 1041–1066.

Altheide, D. L., Adler, P. A., Adler, P., & Altheide, D. A. (1978). The social meanings of employee theft. In J. M. Johnson & J. D. Douglas (Eds.), *Crime at the top* (pp. 90–124). Philadelphia, PA: Lippincott.

Ambrose, M. L. & Schminke, M. (2009). The role of overall justice judgments in organizational justice research: A test of mediation. *Journal of Applied Psychology*, 94(2), 491–500.

Ambrose, M. L., Seabright, M. A., & Schminke, M. (2002). Sabotage in the workplace: The role of organizational injustice. *Organizational Behavior and Human Decision Processes*, 89(1), 947–965.

Amernic, J. (2001). *Applicant background checks*. Retrieved from the human resources social network website: www.hr.com.

Analoui, F. & Kakabadse, A. (1991). *Sabotage: How to recognize and manage employee defiance*. London: Mercury.

Analoui, F. & Kakabadse, A. (1992). Unconventional practices at work: Insight and analysis through participant observation. *Journal of Managerial Psychology*, 7, 1–31.

Anand, V., Ashforth, B. C., & Joshi, M. (2004). Business as usual: The acceptance and perpetuation of corruption in organizations. *The Academy of Management Executive*, 18(2), 39–55.

Anandarajan, M. (2002). Internet abuse in the workplace. *Communications of the ACM*, 45(1), 53–54.

Anandarajan, M. & Simmers, C. A. (2005). Developing human capital through personal web use in the workplace: Mapping employee perceptions. *Communications of the Association for Information Systems*, 15(1), 776–791.

Andersen, H.C. (1837). *Fairy tales told for children: First collection*. Copenhagen: C. A. Reitzel.

Anderson, C. & Brion, S. (2014). Perspectives on power in organizations. *Annual Review of Organizational Psychology and Organizational Behavior*, 1(1), 67–97.

Andersson, L. M. (1996). Employee cynicism: An examination using a contract violation framework. *Human Relations*, 49, 1395–1418.

Andersson, L. M. & Bateman, T. S. (1997). Cynicism in the workplace: Some causes and effects. *Journal of Organizational Behavior*, 18, 449–469.

Andersson, L. M. & Pearson, C. M. (1999). Tit for tat? The spiraling effect of incivility in the workplace. *Academy of Management Review*, 24, 452–471.

Anthony, R. N. & Dearden, J. (1976). *Management control systems: Text and cases* (3rd edn). Homewood, IL: Irwin.

Aquino, K. & Thau, S. (2009). Workplace victimization: Aggression from the target's perspective. *Annual Review of Psychology*, 60, 717–741.

Archer, E. R. (1994). Words of caution on the temporary workforce. *HR magazine*, 39, 168–170.

Argyris, C. (1957). *Personality and organization: The conflict between system and the individual*. New York: Harper.

Argyris, C. (1960). *Understanding organizational behavior*. Homewood, IL: Dorsey.

Argyris, C. (1964). *Integrating the individual and the organization*. New York: Wiley.

Arthur, M. B., Claman, P. H., & DeFillippi, R. J. (1995). Intelligent enterprise, intelligent careers. *Academy of Management Executive*, 9, 7–22.

Arthur, M. B. & Rousseau, D. M. (Eds.) (1996). *The boundaryless career*. New York: Oxford University Press.

Arthur, M. B., Inkson, K., & Pringle, J. K. (1999). *The new careers: Individual action and economic change*. London: Sage.

Asch, S. E. (1956). Studies of independence and conformity: A minority of one against a unanimous majority. *Psychological Monographs: General and Applied*, 70(9), 1–70.

Ashforth, B. E. & Anand, V. (2003). The normalization of corruption in organizations. *Research in Organizational Behavior*, 25, 1–52.

Ashforth, B. E. & Humphrey, R. H. (1995). Emotions in the workplace: A reappraisal. *Human Relation*, 48, 97–125.

Ashforth, B. E. & Mael, F. (1989). Social identity theory and the organization. *Academy of Management Review*, 14, 20–39.

Ashforth, B. E., Gioia, D. A., Robinson, S. L., & Treviño, L. K. (2008). Re-viewing organizational corruption. *Academy of Management Review*, 33(3), 670–684.

Ashkanasy, N. M. & Jackson, C. R. A. (2001). Organizational culture and climate. In N. Anderson, D. S. Ones, H. K. Sinangil, & C. Viswesvaran (Eds.), *Handbook of industrial, work and organizational psychology* (Vol. 2, pp. 398–415). London: Sage.

Ashkenas, R., Ulrich, D., Jick, T., & Kerr, S. (1995). *The boundaryless organization: Breaking the chains of organizational structure*. San Francisco, CA: Jossey-Bass.

Ashmos, D. & Duchon, D. (2000). Spirituality at work: A conceptualization and measure. *Journal of Management Inquiry*, 9(2), 134–145.

Ashton, M. C. (1998). Personality and job performance: The importance of narrow traits. *Journal of Organizational Behavior*, 19, 289–303.

Ashton, M. C., Lee, K., & Son, C. (2000). Honesty as the sixth factor of personality: Correlations with Machiavellianism, primary psychopathy, and social adroitness. *European Journal of Personality*, 14, 359–368.

Askew, K., Buckner, J. E., Taing, M. U., Ilie, A., Bauer, J. A., & Coovert, M. D. (2014). Explaining cyberloafing: The role of the theory of planned behavior. *Computers in Human Behavior*, 36, 510–519.

Association for Certified Fraud Examiners (2014). *2014 global fraud survey*. Retrieved from: www.acfe.com/rttn-summary.aspx.

Astor, S. D. (1972). Twenty steps for preventing theft in business. *Management Review*, 61, 34–35.

Augsdorfer, P. (2005). Bootlegging and path dependency. *Research Policy*, 34(1), 1–11.

Avolio, B. J. (1999). *Full leadership development: Building the vital forces in organizations*. Thousand Oaks, CA: Sage.

Avolio, B. J., Walumbwa, F. O., & Weber, T. J. (2009). Leadership: Current theories, research, and future directions. *Annual Review of Psychology*, 60(1), 421–449.

Babiak, P. & Hare, R. D. (2006). *Snakes in suits: When psychopaths go to work*. New York: Regan Books.

Bacharach, S. B. (1989). Organizational theories: Some criteria for evaluation. *Academy of Management Review*, 14, 496–515.

Bacharach, S. B. & Lawler, E. J. (1980). *Power and politics in organizations*. San Francisco: Jossey-Bass.

Bacharach, S. B., Bamberger, P., & Sonnenstuhl, W. J. (2002). Driven to drink: Managerial control, work related risk factors and employee drinking behavior. *Academy of Management Journal*, 45, 637–658.

Bachman, R. (1994). *Violence and theft in the workplace*. Washington, DC: Bureau of Justice Statistics, US Department of Justice.

Baillien, E., Bollen, K., Euwema, M., & De Witte, H. (2014). Conflicts and conflict management styles as precursors of workplace bullying: A two-wave longitudinal study. *European Journal of Work and Organizational Psychology*, 23(4), 511–524.

Bakker, A. B., Demerouti, E., De Boer, E., & Schaufeli, W. B. (2003). Job demands and job resources as predictors of absence duration and frequency. *Journal of Vocational Behavior*, 62(2), 341–356.

Bakker, A. B., Demerouti, E., & Sanz-Vergel, A. (2008). How job demands affect partners' experience of exhaustion: Integrating work–family conflict and crossover theory. *Journal of Applied Psychology*, 93(4), 901–911.

Bakker, A. B., Demerouti, E., & Sanz-Vergel, A. (2014). Burnout and work engagement: The JD–R approach. *Annual Review of Organizational Psychology and Organizational Behavior*, 1(1), 389–411.

Bamberger, P. A. & Sonnenstuhl, W. J. (1998). Introduction: Research on organizations and deviance—some basic concerns. In S. Bacharach (Ed.), *Research in the sociology of organizations* (Vol. 15, pp. vii–xviii). Greenwich, CT: JAI Press.

Bandura, A. (1969). *Principles of behavior modification*. New York: Holt, Rinehart & Winston.

Bandura, A. (1973). *Aggression: A social learning analysis*. Englewood Cliffs, NJ: Prentice-Hall.

Bandura, A. (2001). Social cognitive theory: An agentic perspective. *Annual Review of Psychology*, 52(1), 1–26.

Baritz, L. (1960). *The servants of power: A history of the use of social science in American industry.* Middletown, CT: Wesleyan University Press.

Barling, J., Clegg, S. R., & Cooper, C. L. (Eds.) (2008). *The Sage handbook of organizational behavior: Macro approaches* (Vol. 2). London: Sage.

Barling, J., Dupré, K. E., & Kelloway, E. K. (2009). Predicting workplace aggression and violence. *Annual Review of Psychology*, 60, 671–692.

Baron, R. A. & Neuman, J. H. (1996). Workplace violence and workplace aggression: Evidence on their relative frequency and potential causes. *Aggressive Behavior*, 22, 161–173.

Baron, S. A. (1993). *Violence in the workplace: A prevention and management guide for businesses.* Oxnard, CA: Pathfinder.

Barrick, M. R. & Mount, M. K. (1991). The big five personality dimensions and job performance: A meta-analysis. *Personnel Psychology*, 44, 1–27.

Barrick, M. R. & Mount, M. K. (1993). Autonomy as a moderator of the relationships between the big five personality dimensions and job performance. *Journal of Applied Psychology*, 78, 111–118.

Barrick, M. R., Mount, M. K., & Strauss, J. P. (1993). Conscientiousness and performance of sales representatives: Test of the mediating effects of goal setting. *Journal of Applied Psychology*, 78, 715–722.

Barrick, M. R., Mount, M. K., & Strauss, J. P. (1994). Antecedents of involuntary turnover due to reduction in force. *Personnel Psychology*, 47, 515–536.

Barsade, S. G. & Gibson, D. E. (2007). Why does affect matter in organizations? *Academy of Management Perspectives*, 21(1), 36–59.

Baruch, Y. (2004). *Managing careers: Theory and practice.* Harlow: FT-Prentice Hall/Pearson.

Baruch, Y. (2005). Bullying on the net: Adverse behavior on e-mail and its impact. *Information & Management*, 42(2), 361–371.

Baruch, Y. & Jenkins, S. (2007). Swearing at work and permissive leadership culture: When anti-social becomes social and incivility is acceptable. *Leadership & Organization Development Journal*, 28(6), 492–507.

Baruch, Y. & Peiperl, M. A. (2000). Career management practices: An empirical survey and theoretic implications. *Human Resource Management*, 39, 347–366.

Baruch, Y. & Quick, J. C. (2007). Understanding second careers: Lessons from a study of US navy admirals. *Human Resource Management*, 46(4), 471–491.

Baruch, Y. & Vardi, Y. (2015). A fresh look at the dark side of contemporary careers: Toward a realistic discourse. *British Journal of Management.* Advance online publication. doi: 10.1111/1467–8551.12107.

Batson, D. C. (1975). Rational processing or rationalization? The effect of disconfirming information on a stated religious belief. *Journal of Personality and Social Psychology*, 32(1), 176–184.

Baucus, M. S. & Near, J. P. (1991). Can illegal corporate behavior be predicted? An event history analysis. *Academy of Management Journal*, 34, 9–36.

Baysinger, M. A., Scherer, K. T., & LeBreton, J. M. (2014). Exploring the disruptive effects of psychopathy and aggression on group processes and group effectiveness. *Journal of Applied Psychology*, 99(1), 48.

BBC News (2014). *The interview: A guide to the cyber attack on Hollywood.* BBC News, December 29. Retrieved from BBC news website: www.bbc.com/news/entertainment-arts-30512032.

Becker, T. E. & Martin, S. L. (1995). Trying to look bad at work: Methods and motives for managing poor impressions in organizations. *Academy of Management Journal*, 38, 174–199.

Beehr, T. A. (1995). *Psychological stress in the workplace*. London: Routledge.

Bell, M. P., Özbilgin, M. F., Beauregard, T. A., & Sürgevil, O. (2011). Voice, silence, and diversity in 21st century organizations: Strategies for inclusion of gay, lesbian, bisexual, and transgender employees. *Human Resource Management*, 50(1), 131–146.

Bendix, R. (1956). *Work and authority in industry: Ideologies of management in the course of industrialization*. New York: Harper & Row.

Bennett, R. J. & Robinson, S. L. (2000). Development of measure of workplace deviance. *Journal of Applied Psychology*, 85, 349–360.

Ben-Shahar, T. (2007). *Happier: Learn the secrets to daily joy and lasting fulfillment*. New York: McGraw-Hill.

Bensman, J. & Gerver, I. (1963). Crime and punishment in the factory: The function of deviancy in maintaining the social system. *American Sociological Review*, 28, 588–598.

Benson, P. G., Hanley, G. M., & Scroggins, W. A. (2013). Human resource management and deviant/criminal behavior in organizations. In S. M. Elias (Ed.), *Deviant and criminal behavior in the workplace* (pp. 128–151). New York: New York University Press.

Berdahl, J. L. (2007). Harassment based on sex: Protecting social status in the context of gender hierarchy. *Academy of Management Review*, 32, 641–658.

Berger, P. L. & Luckmann, T. (1966). *The social construction of reality: A treatise on the sociology of knowledge*. Garden City, NY: Anchor Books.

Bergeron, D. M., Shipp, A. J., Rosen, B., & Furst, S. A. (2013). Organizational citizenship behavior and career outcomes: The cost of being a good citizen. *Journal of Management*, 39(4), 958–984.

Berry, C. M., Ones, D. S., & Sackett, P. R. (2007). Interpersonal deviance, organizational deviance, and their common correlates: A review and meta-analysis. *Journal of Applied Psychology*, 92(2), 410.

Berta, D. (2003). Employee behavior study alarms operators. *Nation's Restaurant News*, 37(31), 1.

Beugré, C. D. (1998). Understanding organizational insider-perpetrated workplace aggression: An integrative model. *Research in Sociology of Organizations*, 15, 163–196.

Bies, R. J. & Tripp, T. M. (1995). The use and abuse of power: Justice as social control. In R. Cropanzano & K. M. Kacmar (Eds.), *Organizational politics, justice, and support: Managing the social climate at the workplace* (pp. 131–145). Westport, CT: Quorum.

Bies, R. J. & Tripp, T. M. (1996). Beyond distrust: "Getting even" and the need for revenge. In R. M. Kramer & T. R. Tyler (Eds.). *Trust in organizations: Frontiers of theory and research* (pp. 246–260). Thousand Oaks, CA: Sage.

Bies, R. J. & Tripp, T. M. (1998). Revenge in organizations: The good, the bad and the ugly. In R. W. Griffin, A. M. O'Leary-Kelly, & J. M. Collins (Eds.), *Dysfunctional behavior in organizations: Non-violent dysfunctional behavior* (Vol. 23, Part B, pp. 49–67). Stamford, CT: JAI Press.

Bies, R. J., Tripp, T. M., & Kramer, R. M. (1997). At the breaking point: Cognitive and social dynamics of revenge in organizations. In R. A. Giacalone & J. Greenberg (Eds.), *Antisocial behavior in organizations* (pp. 18–36). Thousand Oaks, CA: Sage.

Birnbaum, H. G., White, A. G., Schiller, M., Waldman, T., Cleveland, J. M., & Roland, C. L. (2011). Societal costs of prescription opioid abuse, dependence, and misuse in the United States. *Pain Medicine*, 12(4), 657–667.

Blake, R. & Mouton, J. (1964). *The managerial grid: The key to leadership excellence*. Houston, TX: Gulf.

Blau, P. M. (1964). *Exchange and power in social life*. New York: Wiley.

Blauner, R. (1964). *Alienation and freedom: The factory worker and his industry*. Chicago, IL: University of Chicago Press.

Bliss, E. C. & Aoki, I. S. (1993). *Are your employees stealing you blind?* San Diego, CA: Pfeiffer.

Boddy, C. R. (2006). The dark side of management decisions: Organizational psychopaths. *Management Decision*, 44(10), 1461–1475.

Boddy, C. R. (2011). Corporate psychopaths, bullying and unfair supervision in the workplace. *Journal of Business Ethics*, 100(3), 367–379.

Boddy, C. R. (2014). Corporate psychopaths, conflict, employee affective well-being and counterproductive work behavior. *Journal of Business Ethics*, 121(1), 107–121.

Bohner, G. & Dickel, N. (2011). Attitudes and attitude change. *Annual Review of Psychology*, 62(1), 391–417.

Bolino, M. C. (1999). Citizenship and impression management: Good soldiers or good actors? *Academy of Management Review*, 24, 82–98.

Bolino, M. C., Kacmar, K. M., Turnley, W. H., & Gilstrap, J. B. (2008). A multi-level review of impression management motives and behaviors. *Journal of Management*, 34(6), 1080–1109.

Bolino, M. C., Hsiung, H., Harvey, J., & LePine, J. A. (2015). "Well, I'm tired of tryin'!" Organizational citizenship behavior and citizenship fatigue. *Journal of Applied Psychology*, 100(1), 56–74.

Bolton, L. R., Becker, L. K., & Barber, L. K. (2010). Big five trait predictors of differential counterproductive work behavior dimensions. *Personality and Individual Differences*, 49(5), 537–541.

Bommer, M., Gratto, C., Gravander, J., & Tuttle, M. (1987). A behavioral model of ethical and unethical decision making. *Journal of Business Ethics*, 6, 265–280.

Bordia, P., Restubog, S. L. D., & Tang, R. L. (2008). When employees strike back: Investigating mediating mechanisms between psychological contract breach and workplace deviance. *Journal of Applied Psychology*, 93(5), 1104–1117.

Boudreau, J. W. & Ramstad, P. M. (2007). *Beyond HR: The new science of human capital*. Cambridge, MA: Harvard Business School Press.

Bowers, T. & Hook, B. (2002). *Hostile work environment: A manager's legal liability*, Tech Republic, October 22. Retrieved from Tech Republic website: www.Techrepublic. com/article/hostile-Work-Environment-a-Managers-Legal-Liability.

Bowie, N. E. & Dunka, R. F. (1990). *Business ethics*. Englewood Cliffs, NJ: Prentice-Hall.

Bowling, N. A. (2010). Effects of job satisfaction and conscientiousness on extra-role behaviors. *Journal of Business and Psychology*, 25(1), 119–130.

Bowling, N. A. & Beehr, T. A. (2006). Workplace harassment from the victim's perspective: A theoretical model and meta-analysis. *Journal of Applied Psychology*, 91(5), 998–1012.

Bowling, N. A. & Eschleman, K. J. (2010). Employee personality as a moderator of the relationships between work stressors and counterproductive work behavior. *Journal of Occupational Health Psychology*, 15(1), 91–103.

Bowling, N. A. & Gruys, M. L. (2010). Overlooked issues in the conceptualization and measurement of counterproductive work behavior. *Human Resource Management Review*, 20(1), 54–61.

Boyd, R. G. (1990). How employee thievery can plague an acquisition. *Mergers and Acquisitions*, 24, 58–61.

Boye, M. W. & Jones, J. W. (1997). Organizational culture and employee counterproductivity. In R. A. Giacalone & J. Greenberg (Eds.), *Antisocial behavior in organizations* (pp. 172–184). Thousand Oaks, CA: Sage.

Braithwaite, J. (1985). White collar crime. *Annual Review of Sociology*, 11, 1–25.

Braverman, H. (1974). *Labor and monopoly capital: The degradation of work in the twentieth century*. New York: Monthly Review Press.

Breaugh, J. A. (1985). The measurement of work autonomy. *Human Relations*, 38, 551–570.

Brief, A. P. & Motowidlo, S. J. (1986). Prosocial organizational behaviors. *Academy of Management Review*, 11, 710–725.

Brief, A. P. & Weiss, H. M. (2002). Organizational behavior: Affect in the workplace. *Annual Review of Psychology*, 53(1), 279–307.

Briner, B. & Hockey, R. G. (1988). Operator stress and computer-based work. In C. L. Cooper & R. Payne (Eds.), *Causes, coping, and consequences of stress at work* (pp. 115–140). New York: Wiley.

Brown, M. A. (1976). Values—a necessary but neglected ingredient of motivation on the job. *Academy of Management Review*, 1, 15–23.

Brown, M. E., Treviño, L. K., & Harrison, D. A. (2005). Ethical leadership: A social learning perspective for construct development and testing. *Organizational Behavior and Human Decision Processes*, 97(2), 117–134.

Bruer, W. (2015). FBI sees Chinese involvement amid sharp rise in economic espionage cases. *Washington CNN*, July 24. Retrieved from: http://edition.cnn.com/2015/07/24/politics/fbi economic-espionage.

Brummer, J. (1985). Business ethics: Micro and macro. *Journal of Business Ethics*, 4, 81–91.

Bryson, J. B. (1977). *Situational determinants of the expression of jealousy*. Paper presented at the annual meeting of the American Psychology Association, San Francisco, CA.

Bukowski, C. (2009). *Post office*. London: Virgin Books.

Burack, E. H. (1999). Spirituality in the workplace. *Journal of Organizational Change Management*, 12(4), 280–292.

Bureau of Labor Statistics (1999). *Fatal occupational injuries by event and exposure, 1993–1998*. Washington, DC: US Department of Labor.

Burke, R. J. (1999). Workaholism in organizations: The role of personal beliefs and fears. *Anxiety, Stress and Coping*, 13, 53–65.

Burton, J. P., Taylor, S. G., & Barber, L. K. (2014). Understanding internal, external, and relational attributions for abusive supervision. *Journal of Organizational Behavior*, 35(6), 871–891.

Bush, D. M. & Lipary, R. M. (2015). *The CBHSQ report: Substance use and substance use disorder, by industry*. Retrieved from the Substance Abuse and Mental Health Services administration website: www.samsa.gov/data/sites/defult/files/report_1959.

Buss, A. H. (1961). *The psychology of aggression*. New York: Wiley.

Buss, D. (1993). Ways to curtail employee theft. *Nation's Business*, 81, 36–37.

Byron, K. (2005). A meta-analytic review of work–family conflict and its antecedents. *Journal of Vocational Behavior*, 67(2), 169–198.

Calabrese, K. R. (2000). Interpersonal conflict and sarcasm in the workplace. *Genetic, Social, and General Psychology Monographs*, 126(4), 459–494.

Caldwell, C. (2009). Identity, self-awareness, and self-deception: Ethical implications for leaders and organizations. *Journal of Business Ethics*, 90, 393–406.

Caldwell, D. F. & O'Reilly, C. A., III (1982). Responses to failure: The effects of choice and responsibility on impression management. *Academy of Management Journal*, 25, 121–136.

Callahan, E. S. & Dworkin, T. M. (2000). The state of state whistleblower protection. *American Business Law Journal*, 38(1), 99–175.

Cappelli, P. & Chauvin, K. (1991). An interplant test of the efficiency wage hypothesis. *The Quarterly Journal of Economics*, 106, 769–787.

Cappelli, P. & Sherer, P. D. (1991). The missing role of context in OB: The need for a meso-level approach. In B. M. Staw & L. L. Cummings (Eds.), *Research in organizational behavior* (Vol. 13, pp. 55–110). Greenwich, CT: JAI Press.

Carlson, D., Ferguson, M., Hunter, E., & Whitten, D. (2012). Abusive supervision and work–family conflict: The path through emotional labor and burnout. *The Leadership Quarterly*, 23(5), 849–859.

Carr, A. Z. (1968). Is business bluffing ethical? *Harvard Business Review*, 46, 143–153.

Carroll, A. B. (1978). Linking business ethics to behavior in organizations. *SAM Advanced Management Journal*, 43, 4–11.

Cash, K. C. & Gray, G. R. (2000). A framework for accommodating religion and spirituality in the workplace. *Academy of Management Executive*, 14(3), 124–133.

Caudron, S. (1995). Fighting the enemy within. *Industry Week*, 44, 36–38.

Cerne, M., Nerstad, C. G. L., Dysvik, A., & Skerlavaj, M. (2014). What goes around comes around: Knowledge hiding, perceived motivational climate, and creativity. *Academy of Management Journal*, 37(1), 172–192.

Chan, M. E. & McAllister, D. J. (2014). Abusive supervision through the lens of employee state paranoia. *Academy of Management Review*, 39(1), 44–66.

Chappell, D. & DiMartino, V. (1998). *Violence at work*. Geneva: International Labour Organization.

Chatman, J. A. (1989). Improving interactional organizational research: A model of person–organization fit. *Academy of Management Review*, 14, 333–349.

Cherrington, D. J. (1980). *The work ethic: Working values and values that work*. New York: Amacom.

Cherrington, D. J. & Cherrington, J. O. (1985). The climate of honesty in retail stores. In W. Terris (Ed.), *Employee theft: Research, theory, and applications* (pp. 51–65). Park Ridge, IL: London House Press.

Chiu, S. & Peng, J. (2008). The relationship between psychological contract breach and employee deviance: The moderating role of hostile attributional style. *Journal of Vocational Behavior*, 73(3), 426–433.

Christian, M. S. & Ellis, A. P. J. (2011). Examining the effects of sleep deprivation on workplace deviance: A self-regulatory approach. *Academy of Management Journal*, 54(5), 913–934.

Cialdini, R. B. & Goldstein, N. J. (2004). Social influence: Compliance and conformity. *Annual Review of Psychology*, 55(1), 591–621.

Clark, M. A., Michel, J. S., Zhdanova, L., Pui, S. Y., & Baltes, B. B. (2014). All work and no play? A meta-analytic examination of the correlates and outcomes of workaholism. *Journal of Management*. Advance online publication. doi:10.1177/0149206314522301.

Cleveland, J. N. & Kerst, M. E. (1993). Sexual harassment and perceptions of power: An under-articulated relationship. *Journal of Vocational Behavior*, 42, 49–67.

Cleveland, J. N., Stockdale, M., & Murphy, K. R. (2000). *Women and men in organizations: Sex and gender issues at work*. Mahwah, NJ: Lawrence Erlbaum Associates.

Clinard, M. B. & Quinney, R. (1973). *Criminal behavior systems: A typology* (2nd edn). New York: Holt, Rinehart & Winston.

Cohen, G. (1999). *The relationship between different types of commitment in the workplace and organizational misbehavior* (Unpublished master's thesis). Tel Aviv University, Israel.

Cohen, J. (1992). Statistical power analysis. *Current Directions in Psychological Science*, 1(3), 98–101.

Cohen, M. D., March, J. G., & Olsen, J. P. (1972). A garbage can model of organizational choice. *Administrative Science Quarterly*, 17, 1–25.

Cohen, S. (1973). Property destruction: Motives and meanings. In C. Ward (Ed.), *Vandalism* (pp. 23–53). London: Architectural Press.

Cohen, S. & Edwards, J.R. (1989). Personality characteristics as moderators of the relationship between stress and disorder. In R. Neufeld (Ed.), *Advances in the investigation of psychological stress* (pp. 235–283). New York: Wiley.

Cohen-Charash, Y. & Spector, P. E. (2001). The role of justice in organizations: A meta-analysis. *Organizational Behavior and Human Decision Processes*, 86(2), 278–321.

Coker, B. L. (2013). Workplace internet leisure browsing. *Human Performance*, 26(2), 114–125.

Coleman, J. W. (1987). Toward an integrated theory of white-collar crime. *American Journal of Sociology*, 93, 406–439.

Coleman, J. W. (1994). *The criminal elite: The sociology of white-collar crime.* New York: St. Martin's Press.

Collins, J. M. & Griffin, R. W. (1998). The psychology of counterproductive job performance. In R. W. Griffin, A. M. O'Leary-Kelly, & J. M. Collins (Eds.), *Dysfunctional behavior in organizations* (Vol. 23, Part A, pp. 219–242). Stamford, CT: JAI Press.

Collins, J. M. & Schmidt, F. L. (1993). Personality, integrity, and white-collar crime: A construct validity study. *Personnel Psychology*, 46, 295–311.

Collins, O., Dalton, M., & Roy, D. (1946). Restriction of output and social cleavage in industry. *Applied Anthropology*, 5, 1–14.

Colquitt, J. A., Scott, B. A., Rodell, J. B., Long, D. M., Zapata, C. P., Conlon, D. E., & Wesson, M. J. (2013). Justice at the millennium, a decade later: A meta-analytic test of social exchange and affect-based perspectives. *Journal of Applied Psychology*, 98(2), 199–236.

Connelly, C. E., Zweig, D., Webster, J., & Trougakos, J. P. (2012). Knowledge hiding in organizations. *Journal of Organizational Behavior*, 33(1), 64–88.

Conner, S. (2012). Employees really do waste time at work. *Forbes*, July 17. Retrieved from: www.forbes.com/sites/cherylsnappconner/2012/07/17/employees-really-do-waste-time-at-work.

Cooper, C. L. & Rousseau, D. M. (Eds.) (1999). *The virtual organization: Trends in organizational behavior* (Vol. 6). New York: Wiley.

Copes, H. (2003). Societal attachments, offending frequency, and techniques of neutralization. *Deviant Behavior*, 24(2), 101–127.

Cornwall, H. (1987). *Datatheft: Computer fraud, industrial espionage, and information crime.* London: Heinemann.

Cortina, L. M. & Magley, V. J. (2003). Raising voice, risking retaliation: Events following interpersonal mistreatment in the workplace. *Journal of Occupational Health Psychology*, 8(4), 247–265.

Cortina, L. M. & Magley, V. J. (2009). Patterns and profiles of response to incivility in the workplace. *Journal of Occupational Health Psychology*, 14(3), 272–288.

Costa, P. T. & McCrae, R. R. (1988). Personality in adulthood: A six-year longitudinal study of self-reports and spouse ratings on the NEO personality inventory. *Journal of Personality and Social Psychology*, 54, 853–863.

Crane, A. (2005). In the company of spies: When competitive intelligence gathering becomes industrial espionage. *Business Horizons*, 48(3), 233–240.

Crano, W. D. & Prislin, R. (2006). Attitudes and persuasion. *Annual Review of Psychology*, 57(1), 345–374.

Cressey, D. R. (1953). *Other people's money: The social psychology of embezzlement.* New York: The Free Press.

Crino, M. D. & Leap, T. L. (1988). Sabotage: Protecting your company means dealing with the dark side of human nature. *Success*, 35(1), 52–55.

Crosby, F. J., Iyer, A., & Sincharoen, S. (2006). Understanding affirmative action. *Annual Review of Psychology*, 57(1), 585–611.

Crowne, D. P. & Marlowe, D. (1960). A new scale of social desirability independent of psychopathology. *Journal of Consulting Psychology*, 24, 349–354.

Crozier, M. (1964). *The bureaucratic phenomenon.* London: Tavistock Publications.

Cullen, J. B., Victor, B., & Stephens, C. (1989). An ethical weather report: Assessing the organization's ethical climate. *Organizational Dynamics*, 18, 50–63.

Dabney, D. A. & Hollinger, R. C. (1999). Illicit prescription drug use among pharmacists. *Work and Occupation*, 26, 77–106.

Daft, R. L. (1980). The evaluation of organization analysis in ASQ, 1959–1979. *Administrative Science Quarterly*, 25, 623–636.

Daft, R. L. (1995). *Organization theory and design.* St. Paul, MN: West.

Daft, R. L. (2000). *Management.* Fort Worth, TX: Dryden.

Daft, R. L. (2013). *Management.* Mason, OH: Cengage Learning.

Daft, R. L. & Lewin, A. Y. (1993). Where are the theories for the "new" organizational form? An editorial essay. *Organizational Science*, 4(4), i–iv.

Daft, R. L. & Noe, R. A. (2001). *Organizational behavior.* New York: Harcourt.

Dalal, R. S. (2005). A meta-analysis of the relationship between organizational citizenship behavior and counterproductive work behavior. *Journal of Applied Psychology*, 90(6), 1241–1255.

Dalton, D. R., Johnson, J. L., & Daily, C. M. (1999). On the use of "intent to…" variables in organizational research: An empirical and cautionary assessment. *Human Relations*, 52, 1337–1350.

Danet, B. (1981). Client-organization relationships. In P. C. Nystrom & W. H. Starbuck (Eds.), *Handbook of organizational design* (Vol. 2, pp. 382–428). New York: Oxford University Press.

Darley, J.M. (2005). The cognitive and social psychology of organizational corruption. *Brooklyn Law Review*, 70, 1177–1194.

De George, R. T. (1986). Theological ethics and business ethics/replies and reflections on theology and business ethics. *Journal of Business Ethics*, 5, 421–437.

DeGoey, P. (2000). Contagious justice: Exploring the social construction of justice in organizations. In B. M. Staw & R. I. Sutton (Eds.), *Research in organizational behavior* (Vol. 22, pp. 51–102). Stamford, CT: JAI Press.

Dehler, G. E. & Welsh, M. A. (1994). Spirituality and organizational transformation: Implications for the new management paradigm. *Journal of Managerial Psychology*, 9(6), 17–26.

Dehler, G. E. & Welsh, M. A. (1997). Discovering the keys: Spirit in teaching and the journey of learning. *Journal of Management Education*, 21(4), 496–508.

Delaney, J. (1993). Handcutting employee theft. *Small Business Report*, 18, 29–38.

Demerouti, E., Bakker, A. B., Nachreiner, F., & Schaufeli, W. B. (2001). The job demands-resources model of burnout. *Journal of Applied Psychology*, 86(3), 499.

DeMore, S. W., Fisher, J. D., & Baron, R. M. (1988). The equity-control model as a predictor of vandalism among college students. *Journal of Applied Social Psychology*, 18, 80–91.

Denenberg, R. V. & Braverman, M. (1999). *The violence-prone workplace: A new approach to dealing with hostile, threatening, and uncivil behavior.* Ithaca, NY: ILR Press.

Deutsch, M. (1985). *Distributive justice: A social-psychological perspective*. New Haven, CT: Yale University Press.

Diamond, M. A. (1997). Administrative assault: A contemporary psychoanalytic view of violence and aggression in the workplace. *American Review of Public Administration*, 27, 228–247.

Digman, J. M. (1990). Personality structure: Emergence of the five-factor model. *Annual Review of Psychology*, 41, 417–440.

Ditton, J. (1977). Perks, pilferage, and the fiddle: The historical structure of invisible wages. *Theory and Society*, 4, 39–71.

Drescher, K. D. & Foy, D. W. (1995). Spirituality and trauma treatment: Suggestions for including spirituality as a coping resource. *National Center for PTSD Clinical Quarterly*, 5(1), 4–5.

Drory, A. (1993). Perceived political climate and job attitudes. *Journal of Applied Psychology*, 83, 392–407.

Drory, A. & Romm, T. (1990). The definition of organizational politics: A review. *Human Relations*, 43, 1133–1154.

Dubinsky, A. & Loken, B. (1989). Analyzing ethical decision making in marketing. *Journal of Business Research*, 19, 83–107.

Dubois, P. (1976). *Sabotage in industry*. Middlesex: Pelican.

Duffy, M. K., Ganster, D. C., & Pagon, M. (2002). Social undermining in the workplace. *Academy of Management Journal*, 45, 331–351.

Duffy, M. K., Ganster, D. C., Shaw, J. D., Johnson, J. L., & Pagon, M. (2006). The social context of undermining behavior at work. *Organizational Behavior and Human Decision Processes*, 101(1), 105–126.

Duffy, M. K., Scott, K. L., Shaw, J. D., Tepper, B. J., & Aquino, K. (2012). A social context model of envy and social undermining. *Academy of Management Journal*, 55(3), 643–666.

Dutton, J. E., Workman, K. M., & Hardin, A. E. (2014). Compassion at work. *Annual Review of Organizational Psychology and Organizational Behavior*, 1(1), 277–304.

Duxbury, L., Higgins, C., Smart, R., & Stevenson, M. (2014). Mobile technology and boundary permeability. *British Journal of Management*, 25(3), 570–588.

Dworkin, T. M. & Near, J. P. (1997). A better statutory approach to whistleblowing. *Business Ethics Quarterly*, 7, 1–16

Eby, L. T., Maher, C. P., & Butts, M. M. (2010). The intersection of work and family life: The role of affect. *Annual Review of Psychology*, 61(1), 599–622.

Eccles, J. S. & Wigfield, A. (2002). Motivational beliefs, values, and goals. *Annual Review of Psychology*, 53(1), 109–132.

Eder, P. & Eisenberger, R. (2008). Perceived organizational support: Reducing the negative influence of coworker withdrawal behavior. *Journal of Management*, 34(1), 55–68.

Edmondson, A. C. & Lei, Z. (2014). Psychological safety: The history, renaissance, and future of an interpersonal construct. *Annual Review of Organizational Psychology and Organizational Behavior*, 1(1), 23–43.

Edwards, R. (1979). *Contested terrain: The transformation of the workplace in the twentieth century*. New York, NY: Basic Books.

Einarsen, S., Hoel, H., & Notelaers, G. (2009). Measuring exposure to bullying and harassment at work: Validity, factor structure and psychometric properties of the negative acts questionnaire-revised. *Work & Stress*, 23(1), 24–44.

Einarsen, S., Hoel, H., Zapf, D., & Cooper, C. L. (2011). The concept of bullying and harassment at work: The European tradition. In S. Einarsen, H. Hoel, D. Zapf, & C. L. Cooper (Eds.), *Bullying and harassment in the workplace: developments in theory, research, and practice* (2nd edn, pp. 3–40). Boca Raton, FL: CRC Press.

Eisenhardt, K. (1985). Control: Organizational and economic approaches. *Management Science*, 31, 134–149.

Eisenhardt, K. (1989). Agency theory: An assessment and review. *Academy of Management Review*, 14, 57–74.

Elangovan, A. R. & Shapiro, D. L. (1998). Betrayal of trust in organizations. *Academy of Management Review*, 23, 547–566.

Ellemers, N., Spears, R., & Doosje, B. (2002). Self and social identity. *Annual Review of Psychology*, 53(1), 161–186.

Ellis, S. & Arieli, S. (1999). Predicting intentions to report administrative and disciplinary infractions: Applying the reasoned action model. *Human Relations*, 52, 947–967.

Erez, M. & Early, P. C. (1993). *Culture, self, and identity*. New York: Oxford University Press.

Eschleman, K.J., Bowling, N.A., & LaHuis, N. (2014). The moderating effects of personality on the relationship between change in work stressors and change in counterproductive work behaviors. *Journal of Occupational and Organizational Psychology*. Advance online publication. doi: 10.1111/joop.12090.

Etzioni, A. (1961). *A comparative analysis of complex organizations*. Glencoe, IL: The Free Press.

Ewing, J. A. (1984). Detecting alcoholism: The CAGE questionnaire. *Journal of the American Medical Association*, 252, 1905–1907.

Fallan, J. D., Kudisch, J. D., & Fortunato, V. J. (2000, April). *Using conscientiousness to predict productive and counter productive work behavior*. Paper presented at the 15th annual conference of Society for Industrial and Organizational Psychology, New Orleans, LA.

Fallding, H. (1965). A proposal for the empirical study of values. *American Sociological Review*, 30, 223–233.

Fandt, P. M. & Ferris, G. R. (1990). The management of information and impressions: When employees behave opportunistically. *Organizational Behavior and Human Decision Processes*, 45, 140–158.

Fanelli, D. (2009). How many scientists fabricate and falsify research? A systematic review and meta-analysis of survey data. *PLoS One*, 4(5), e5738.

Fanelli, D. (2011). Negative results are disappearing from most disciplines and countries. *Scientometrics*, 90(3), 891–904.

Farley, L. (1978). *Sexual shakedown: The sexual harassment of women on the job*. New York: Warner Books.

Farrell, D. (1983). Exit, voice, loyalty, and neglect as responses to job dissatisfaction: A multidimensional scaling study. *Academy of Management Journal*, 26, 596–607.

Farrell, D. & Petersen, J. C. (1982). Patterns of political behavior in organizations. *Academy of Management Review*, 7, 403–412.

Feldman, D. C. (1981). The multiple socialization of organization members. *Academy of Management Review*, 6, 309–318.

Ferguson, M. J. (2007). *From bad to worse: A social contagion model of organizational misbehavior* (Unpublished doctoral dissertation). Vanderbilt University, Nashville, TN.

Ferrell, O. C. & Fraedrich, J. (1994). *Business ethics: Ethical decision making*. Boston, MA: Houghton Mifflin.

Ferrell, O. C. & Gresham, L. G. (1985). A contingency framework for understanding ethical decision making in marketing. *Journal of Marketing*, 49, 87–96.

Ferrell, O. C., Gresham, L. G., & Fraedrich, J. (1989). A synthesis of ethical decision modes in marketing. *Journal of Macro Marketing*, 9, 55–64.

Ferris, G. R. & Kacmar, K. M. (1988). *Organization politics and affective reactions*. Paper presented at the annual meeting of the Southwest Division of the Academy of Management, San Antonio, TX.

Ferris, G. R., Russ, G. S., & Fandt, P. M. (1989). Politics in organizations. In R. A. Giacalone & P. Rosenfeld (Eds.), *Impression management in the organization* (pp. 143–170). Hillsdale, NJ: Lawrence Erlbaum Associates.

Festinger, L. (1954). A theory of social comparison processes. *Human Relations*, 7, 117–140.

Festinger, L. (1957). *A theory of cognitive dissonance*. Stanford, CA: Stanford University Press.

Fiedler, F. E. (1967). *A theory of leadership effectiveness*. New York: McGraw-Hill.

Fimbel, N. & Burstein, J. S. (1990). Defining the ethical standards of the high-technology industry. *Journal of Business Ethics*, 9, 929–948.

Fishbein, M. & Ajzen, I. (1975). *Belief, attitude, intention and behavior: An introduction to theory research*. Reading, MA: Addison-Wesley.

Fisher, C. D. & Ashkanasy, N. M. (2000). The emerging role of emotions in work life: An introduction. *Journal of Organizational Behavior*, 21, 123–129.

Fisher, J. D. & Baron, R. M. (1982). An equity-based model of vandalism. *Population and Environment*, 5, 182–200.

Fitness, J. (2000). Anger in the workplace: An emotion script approach to anger episodes between workers and their supervisors. *Journal of Organizational Behavior*, 21, 147–162.

Fitzgerald, L. F. (1993). Sexual harassment: Violence against women in the workplace. *American Psychologist*, 48, 1070–1076.

Fitzgerald, L. F., Shullman, S. L., Bailey, N., Richards, M., Swecker, J., Gold, Y., Ormerol, A. J., & Weitzman, L. (1988). The incidence and dimensions of sexual harassment in academia and the workplace. *Journal of Vocational Behavior*, 32, 152–175.

Fitzgerald, L. F., Gelfand, M. J., & Drasgow, F. (1995). Measuring sexual harassment: Theoretical and psychometric advances. *Basic and Applied Social Psychology*, 17, 425–445.

Fitzgerald, L. F., Drasgow, F., Hulin, C. L., Gelfand, M. J., & Magley, V. J. (1997a). Antecedents and consequences of sexual harassment in organizations: A test of an integrated model. *Journal of Applied Psychology*, 82(4), 578–589.

Fitzgerald, L. F., Swan, S., & Magley, V. J. (1997b). But was it really sexual harassment? Legal, behavioral, and psychological definitions of the workplace victimization of women. In W. O'Donohue (Ed.), *Sexual harassment: Theory, research and treatment* (pp. 5–28). Boston, MA: Allyn & Bacon.

Fleishman, E. A. (1953). The measurement of leadership attitudes in industry. *Journal of Applied Psychology*, 37, 153–158.

Fleishman, E. A. & Harris, E. F. (1962). Patterns of leadership behavior related to employee grievance and turnover. *Personnel Psychology*, 15, 43–56.

Foa, E. B. & Foa, V. G. (1980). Resource theory: Interpersonal behavior as exchange. In M. K. Gergen, M. S. Greenberg, & R. H. Willis (Eds.), *Social exchange* (pp. 77–102). New York: Plenum.

Folger, R. & Skarlicki, D. P. (1998). A popcorn metaphor for employee aggression. In R. W. Griffin, A. M. O'Leary-Kelly, & J. M. Collins (Eds.), *Dysfunctional behavior in organizations* (pp. 43–81). Stamford, CT: JAI Press.

Fouad, N. A. (2007). Work and vocational psychology: Theory, research, and applications. *Annual Review of Psychology*, 58(1), 543–564.

Fox, S. & Spector, P. E. (1999). A model of work frustration-aggression. *Journal of Organizational Behavior*, 20, 915–931.

Fox, S. & Spector, P. E. (Eds.) (2005). *Counterproductive work behavior: Investigations of actors and targets*. Washington, DC: American Psychological Association.

Fox, S., Spector, P. E., & Miles, D. (2001). Counterproductive work behavior (CWB) in response to job stressors and organizational justice: Some mediator and moderator tests for autonomy and emotions. *Journal of Vocational Behavior*, 59(3), 291–309.

Francis, L., Holmvall, C. M., & O'Brien, L. E. (2015). The influence of workload and civility of treatment on the perpetration of email incivility. *Computers in Human Behavior*, 46, 191–201.

Freeman, R. E. & Gilbert, D. R. Jr. (1988). *Corporate strategy and the search for ethics*. Englewood Cliffs, NJ: Prentice-Hall.

Frese, M. & Keith, N. (2015). Action errors, error management, and learning in organizations. *Annual Review of Psychology*, 66(1), 661–687.

Friedman, M. (1970). The social responsibility of business. In T. L. Beauchamp & N. E. Bowie (Eds.), *Ethical theory and business* (pp. 173–178). Englewood Cliffs, NJ: Prentice-Hall.

Frijda, N. H. (1993). Moods, emotion episodes and emotions. In M. Lewis & J. M. Haviland (Eds.), *Handbook of emotions* (pp. 381–403). New York: Guilford.

Frone, M. R. (2006). Prevalence and distribution of illicit drug use in the workforce and in the workplace: Findings and implications from a US national survey. *Journal of Applied Psychology*, 91, 856–869.

Frone, M. R. (2008). Are work stressors related to employee substance use? The importance of temporal context assessments of alcohol and illicit drug use. *Journal of Applied Psychology*, 93(1), 199–206.

Frone, M. R. (2013). *Alcohol and illicit drug use in the workforce and workplace*. Washington, DC: American Psychological Association.

Frone, M. R. & Brown, A. L. (2010). Workplace substance-use norms as predictors of employee substance use and impairment: A survey of US workers. *Journal of Studies on Alcohol and Drugs*, 71(4), 526–534.

Fugate, M., Prussia, G. E., & Kinicki, A. J. (2012). Managing employee withdrawal during organizational change: The role of threat appraisal. *Journal of Management*, 38(3), 890–914.

Furnham, A. & Zacherl, M. (1986). Personality and job satisfaction. *Personality and Individual Differences*, 7, 453–459.

Furnham, A., Hyde, G., & Trickey, G. (2014). Do your dark side traits fit? Dysfunctional personalities in different work sectors. *Applied Psychology*, 63(4), 589–606.

Gabriel, Y. (1998). An introduction to the social psychology of insults in organizations. *Human Relations*, 51, 1329–1354.

Gabriel, Y. (2012). Organizations in a state of darkness: Towards a theory of organizational miasma. *Organization Studies*, 33(9), 1137–1152.

Gaertner, K. N. (1980). The structure of organization careers. *Sociology of Education*, 53, 7–20.

Galbraith, J. R. (1977). *Organization design*. Reading, MA: Addison-Wesley.

Gale, E. K. (1993). *Social influences on absenteeism* (Unpublished doctoral dissertation). Purdue University, Lafayette, IN.

Galmor, E. (1996). *The effect of employment status (temporary/permanent) on the organizational misbehavior* (Unpublished master's thesis). Tel Aviv University, Israel.

Galperin, B. L. & Aquino, K. (1999, August). *Individual aggressiveness and minority status as moderators of the relationship between perceived injustice and workplace deviance*. Paper presented at the Academy of Management meeting, Chicago, IL.

Ganot. S. (1999). *Subjective pressure, job satisfaction and workplace misbehavior among R&D employees in a high-tech organization* (Unpublished master's thesis). Tel Aviv University, Israel.

Ganster, D. C. (1989). *Stress, personal control and health*. London: Wiley.

Gardner, H. (1983). *Frames of mind*. New York: Basic Books.

Gardner, W. L. III & Martinko, M. J. (1998). An organizational perspective of the effects of dysfunctional impression management. In R. W. Griffin, A. M. O'Leary-Kelly, &

J. M. Collins (Eds.), *Dysfunctional behavior in organizations: Non-violent dysfunctional behavior* (Vol. 23, Part B, pp. 69–125). Stamford, CT: JAI Press.

Gayford, J. J. (1979). Battered wives. *British Journal of Hospital Medicine*, 22, 496–503.

Gelfand, M. J., Erez, M., & Aycan, Z. (2007). Cross-cultural organizational behavior. *Annual Review of Psychology*, 58(1), 479–514.

George, J. M. (1989). Mood and absence. *Journal of Business Psychology*, 74, 317–324.

George, J. M. & Brief, A. P. (1996). Motivational agendas in the workplace: The effects of feelings on focus of attention and work motivation. *Research in Organizational Behavior*, 18, 75–109.

Giacalone, R. A. & Greenberg, J. (1997). *Antisocial behaviors in organizations*. Thousand Oaks, CA: Sage.

Giacalone, R. A. & Jurkiewicz, C. K. (Eds.) (2003). *Handbook of workplace spirituality and organizational performance*. Armonk, NY: M.E. Sharpe.

Giacalone, R. A. & Rosenfeld, P. (1987). Reasons for employee sabotage in the workplace. *Journal of Business Psychology*, 1, 367–378.

Giacalone, R. A. & Rosenfeld, P. (Eds.) (1991). *Applied impression management: How image-making affects managerial decisions*. Thousand Oaks, CA: Sage.

Giacalone, R. A., Riordan, C. A., & Rosenfeld, P. (1997). Employee sabotage: Toward a practitioner–scholar understanding. In R. A. Giacalone & J. Greenberg (Eds.), *Antisocial behavior in organizations* (pp. 109–129). Thousand Oaks, CA: Sage.

Gigerenzer, G. & Gaissmaier, W. (2011). Heuristic decision making. *Annual Review of Psychology*, 62(1), 451–482.

Gladstein, D. (1984). Groups in context: A model of task group effectiveness. *Administrative Science Quarterly*, 29, 499–517.

Glambek, M., Matthiesen, S. B., Hetland, J., & Einarsen, S. (2014). Workplace bullying as an antecedent to job insecurity and intention to leave: A six-month prospective study. *Human Resource Management Journal*, 24(3), 255–268.

Global Retail Theft Barometer (2011). Thorofare, NJ: Checkpoint systems. Retrieved from the Center for Retail Research website: www.retailresearch.org.

Gobillot, E. (2007). *The connected leader: Creating agile organizations for people, performance and profit*. Philadelphia, PA: Kogan Page.

Goffman, A. (2014). *On the run: Fugitive life in an American city*. Chicago, IL: University of Chicago Press.

Goffman, E. (1959). *The presentation of self in everyday life*. Garden City, NY: Doubleday Anchor.

Goldberg, L. R. (1992). The development of marker variables for the big-five factor structure. *Psychological Assessment*, 4, 26–42.

Goldschmid-Aron, L. (1997). *Individual and organizational antecedents of workaholism* (Unpublished master's thesis). Tel Aviv University, Israel.

Goleman, D. (1995). *Emotional intelligence*. New York: Bantam Books.

Goleman, D. (1998). *Working with emotional intelligence*. New York: Bantam Books.

Goleman, D. & Cherniss, C. (Eds.) (2001). *The emotionally intelligent workplace: How to select for, measure, and improve emotional intelligence in individuals*. San Francisco, CA: Jossey-Bass.

Goleman, D., Boyatzis, R., & McKee, A. (2013). *Primal leadership: Realizing the power of emotional intelligence* (10th edn). Boston, MA: Harvard Business School Press.

Golembiewski, R. T. & Munzenrider, R. (1975). Social desirability as an intervening variable in interpreting OD effects. *Journal of Applied Behavioral Science*, 11, 317–332.

Gothelf, J. (2014). Bring agile to the whole organization. *Harvard Business Review*, November 14. Retrieved from: https://hbr.org/2014/11/bring-Agile-to-the-Whole-Organization.

Gotsis, G. & Kortezi, Z. (2008). Philosophical foundations of workplace spirituality: A critical approach. *Journal of Business Ethics*, 78(4), 575–600.

Gouldner, A. W. (1954). *Patterns of industrial bureaucracy: A case study of modern factory administration*. New York: The Free Press.

Gouldner, A. W. (1960). The norm of reciprocity. *American Sociological Review*, 25, 161–178.

Granovetter, M. S. (1985). Economic action and social structure: The problem of embeddedness. *American Journal of Sociology*, 91, 481–510.

Granovetter, M. S. (1992). Problems of explanation in economic sociology. In N. Nohria & R. G. Eccles (Eds.), *Networks and organizations: Structure, form and action* (pp. 25–56). Boston, MA: Harvard Business School Press.

Grant, S. L. (2013). The role of occupational stress in workplace deviance. In S. M. Elias (Ed.), *Deviant and criminal behavior in the workplace* (pp. 77–98). New York: New York University Press.

Gray-Toft, P. & Anderson, J. G. (1981). The nursing stress scale: Development of an instrument. *Journal of Behavioral Assessment*, 3, 11–23.

Graziano, W. G. & Eisenberg, N. (1997). Agreeableness: A dimension of personality. In R. Hogan, J. Johnson & S. R. Briggs (Eds.), *Handbook of personality psychology* (pp. 795–824). San Diego, CA: Academic Press.

Green, R. M. (1994). *The ethical manager: A new method for business ethics*. New York: Macmillan.

Greenberg, D. B. & Strasser, S. (1986). Development and application of a model of personal control in organizations. *Academy of Management Review*, 11, 164–177.

Greenberg, J. (1990a). Employee theft as a response to underemployment inequity: The hidden cost of pay cuts. *Journal of Applied Psychology*, 75, 561–568.

Greenberg, J. (1990b). Organizational justice: Yesterday, today and tomorrow. *Journal of Management*, 16, 399–432.

Greenberg, J. (1993). Stealing in the name of justice: Informational and interpersonal moderators of theft reactions to underpayment inequity. *Organizational Behavior and Human Decision Processes*, 54, 81–103.

Greenberg, J. (Ed.) (1994). *Organizational behavior: The state of the science*. Hillsdale, NJ: Lawrence Erlbaum Associates.

Greenberg, J. (1995). Employee theft. In N. Nicholson (Ed.), *The Blackwell encyclopedic dictionary of organizational behavior* (pp. 154–155). Oxford: Blackwell.

Greenberg, J. (1997). The STEAL motive: Managing the social determinants of employee theft. In R. A. Giacalone & J. Greenberg (Eds.), *Antisocial behavior in organizations* (pp. 85–107). Thousand Oaks, CA: Sage.

Greenberg, J. (1998). The cognitive geometry of employee theft: Negotiating "the line" between stealing and taking. In In R. W. Griffin, A. M. O'Leary-Kelly, & J. M. Collins (Eds.), *Dysfunctional behavior in organizations: Non-violent dysfunctional behavior* (Vol. 23, Part B, pp. 147–193). Stamford, CT: JAI Press.

Greenberg, J. (2010). *Insidious workplace behavior*. New York: Routledge.

Greenberg, J. & Alge, B. J. (1998). Aggressive reactions to workplace injustice. In R. W. Griffin, A. M. O'Leary-Kelly, & J. M. Collins (Eds.), *Dysfunctional behavior in organizations: Violent and deviant behavior* (Vol. 23, Part A, pp. 83–117). Stamford, CT: JAI Press.

Greenberg, J. & Barling, J. (1996). Employee theft. In C. L. Cooper & D. M. Rousseau (Eds.), *Trends in organizational behavior* (pp. 49–64). New York: Wiley.

Greenberg, J. & Baron, R. B. (1997). *Behavior in organizations* (6th edn). Englewood Cliffs, NJ: Prentice-Hall.

Greenberg, J. & Scott, K. S. (1996). Why do workers bite hands that feed them? Employee theft as a social exchange process. In B. M. Staw & L. L. Cummings (Eds.), *Research in organizational behavior* (Vol. 18, pp. 111–156). Greenwich, CT: JAI Press.

Greenberg, L. & Barling, J. (1999). Predicting employee aggression against coworkers, subordinates and supervisors: The roles of person behaviors and perceived workplace factors. *Journal of Organizational Behavior*, 20, 897–913.

Greenhaus, J. H. & Beutell, N. J. (1985). Sources of conflict between work and family roles. *Academy of Management Review*, 10(1), 76–88.

Greenhaus, J. H. & Foley, S. (2007). The intersection of work and family lives. In H. Gunz & M. Peiperl (Eds.), *Handbook of career studies* (pp. 131–152). Thousand Oaks, CA: Sage.

Greenhaus, J. H. & Kossek, E. E. (2014). The contemporary career: A work–home perspective. *Annual Review of Organizational Psychology and Organizational Behavior*, 1(1), 361–388.

Greenhaus, J. H. & Powell, G. N. (2003). When work and family collide: Deciding between competing role demands. *Organizational Behavior and Human Decision Processes*, 90(2), 291–303.

Greineisen, M. L. & Zhang, M. (2012). A comprehensive survey of retracted articles from the scholarly literature. *PLOS One*, 7(10), e44118.

Griffin, R. W. & Lopez, Y. P. (2005). "Bad behavior" in organizations: A review and typology for future research. *Journal of Management*, 31(6), 988–1005.

Griffin, R. W., O'Leary-Kelly, A. M., & Collins, J. M. (Eds.) (1998a). *Dysfunctional behavior in organizations: Non-violent dysfunctional behavior* (Vol. 23, Part B). Stamford, CT: JAI Press.

Griffin, R. W., O'Leary-Kelly, A. M., & Collins, J. M. (1998b). Dysfunctional work behaviors in organizations. In C. L. Cooper & D. M. Rousseau (Eds.), *Trends in organizational behavior* (pp. 65–82). New York: Wiley.

Grisham, L. (2015). Timeline: North Korea and the Sony pictures hack. *USA Today*, January 5. Retrieved from: www.usatoday.com/story/news/nation-now/2014/12/18/sony-hack-timeline-interview-north-korea/20601645.

Grover, S. L. (2010). Lying to bosses, subordinates, peers, and the outside world: Motivations and consequences. In J. Greenberg (Ed.), *Insidious Workplace Behavior* (pp. 237–235). New York: Routledge.

Gruys, M. L. (1999). *The dimensionality of deviant employee performance in the workplace* (Unpublished doctoral dissertation). University of Minnesota, Minneapolis, MN.

Guillory, W. (2000). *The living organizations: Spirituality in the workplace. A guide for adapting to chaotically changing workplace.* Salt Lake City, UT: Innovations International.

Guinsel, J. (1997). *Cyberwars: Espionage on the internet.* Cambridge, MA: Perseus Books.

Guion, R. M. & Gottier, R. F. (1965). Validity of personality measures in personnel selection. *Personnel Psychology*, 18, 135–164.

Gunz, H. P. & Peiperl, M. A. (Eds.) (2007). *Handbook of career studies.* Thousand Oaks, CA: Sage.

Gutek, B. A. (1985). *Sex in the workplace.* San Francisco, CA: Jossey-Bass.

Guzzo, R. A. & Dickson, M. W. (1996). Teams in organizations: Recent research on performance and effectiveness. *Annual Review of Psychology*, 47, 307–338.

Hackman, J. R. & Oldham, G. R. (1976). Motivation through the design of work: Test of a theory. *Organization Behavior and Human Performance*, 16, 250–279.

Hackman, J. R. & Oldham, G. R. (1980). *Work redesign.* Reading, MA: Addison-Wesley.

Hall, D. T. (1976). *Careers in organizations.* Pacific Palisades, LA: Goodyear.

Hall, D. T. (2004). The protean career: A quarter-century journey. *Journal of Vocational Behavior*, 65(1), 1–13.

Hall, D. T. & Schneider, B. (1972). Correlates of organizational identification as a function of career pattern and organizational type. *Administrative Science Quarterly*, 17, 340–350.

Hall, R. H. (1999). *Organizations: Structures, processes and outcomes*. Englewood Cliffs, NJ: Prentice-Hall.

Halverson, R. (1998). Employee theft drives shrink rate. *Discount Store News*, 9, 2–12.

Hammer, T. H., Saksvik, P. Ø., Nytrø, K., Torvatn, H., & Bayazit, M. (2004). Expanding the psychosocial work environment: Workplace norms and work-family conflict as correlates of stress and health. *Journal of Occupational Health Psychology*, 9(1), 83–97.

Hanisch, K. A. & Hulin, C. L. (1991). General attitudes and organizational withdrawal: An evaluation of a causal model. *Journal of Vocational Behavior*, 39, 110–128.

Hannah, S. T., Schaubroeck, J. M., Peng, A. C., Lord, R. G., Treviño, L. K., Kozlowski, S. W. J., Avolio, B. J., Dimotakis, N., & Doty, J. (2013). Joint influences of individual and work unit abusive supervision on ethical intentions and behaviors: A moderated mediation model. *Journal of Applied Psychology*, 98(4), 579–592.

Harper, D. & Emmert, F. (1963). Work behavior in a service industry. *Social Forces*, 42, 216–225.

Harrell, T. & Alpert, B. (1979). The need for autonomy among managers. *Academy of Management Review*, 4, 259–267.

Harris, M. M. & Greising, L. A. (1998). Alcohol and drug abuse as dysfunctional workplace behaviors. In R. W. Griffin, A. M. O'Leary-Kelly, & J. M. Collins (Eds.), *Dysfunctional behavior in organizations: Non-violent dysfunctional behavior* (Vol. 23, Part B, pp. 21–48). Stamford, CT: JAI Press.

Harvey, M., Treadway, D., Heames, J. T., & Duke, A. (2009). Bullying in the 21st century global organization: An ethical perspective. *Journal of Business Ethics*, 85(1), 27–40.

Hastie, R. (2001). Problems for judgment and decision making. *Annual Review of Psychology*, 52(1), 653–683.

Hauge, L. J., Skogstad, A., & Einarsen, S. (2009). Individual and situational predictors of workplace bullying: Why do perpetrators engage in the bullying of others? *Work & Stress*, 23(4), 349–358.

Hauge, L. J., Skogstad, A., & Einarsen, S. (2010). The relative impact of workplace bullying as a social stressor at work. *Scandinavian Journal of Psychology*, 51(5), 426–433.

Hauge, L. J., Einarsen, S., Knardahl, S., Lau, B., Notelaers, G., & Skogstad, A. (2011). Leadership and role stressors as departmental level predictors of workplace bullying. *International Journal of Stress Management*, 18(4), 305–323.

Healthy Workplace Bill (2015). *The Healthy Workplace Campaign*. Retrieved from Healthy Workplace Bill website: www.healthyworkplacebill.org.

Hegarty, W. H. & Sims, H. P. (1978). Some determinants of unethical decision behavior: An experiment. *Journal of Applied Psychology*, 63, 451–457.

Heinemann, P. P. (1972). *Mobbning—gruppvåld bland barn och vuxna* [Bullying: Group violence among children and adults]. Stockholm: Natur och Kultur.

Helldorfer, M. C. (1987). Church professionals and work addiction. *Studies in Formative Spirituality*, 8(2), 199–210.

Hellriegel, D., Slocum, J. W., & Woodman, R. W. (2001). *Organizational behavior* (9th edn). Cincinnati, OH: South-Western College Publishing.

Henle, C. A. & Blanchard, A. L. (2008). The interaction of work stressors and organizational sanctions on cyberloafing. *Journal of Managerial Issues*, 20(3), 383–400.

Hennessey, B. A. & Amabile, T. M. (2010). Creativity. *Annual Review of Psychology*, 61(1), 569–598.

Hersey, P. & Blanchard, K. (1982). *Management of organizational behavior* (4th edn). Englewood Cliffs, NJ: Prentice-Hall.

Hershcovis, M. S. (2011). "Incivility, social undermining, bullying... oh my!": A call to reconcile constructs within workplace aggression research. *Journal of Organizational Behavior*, 32(3), 499–519.

Hershcovis, M. S. & Barling, J. (2010). Towards a multi-foci approach to workplace aggression: A meta-analytic review of outcomes from different perpetrators. *Journal of Organizational Behavior*, 31(1), 24–44.

Hershcovis, M. S. & Reich, T. C. (2013). Integrating workplace aggression research: Relational, contextual, and method considerations. *Journal of Organizational Behavior*, 34, S26–S42.

Hershcovis, M. S., Turner, N., Barling, J., Arnold, K. A., Dupré, K. E., Inness, M., LeBlanc, M. M., & Sivanathan, N. (2007). Predicting workplace aggression: A meta-analysis. *Journal of Applied Psychology*, 92(1), 228.

Herzberg, F. (1968). One more time: How do you motivate employees? *Harvard Business Review*, 46, 53–62.

Hewstone, M., Rubin, M., & Willis, H. (2002). Intergroup bias. *Annual Review of Psychology*, 53(1), 575–604.

Hicks, D. A. (2003). *Religion and the workplace: Pluralism, spirituality, leadership*. Cambridge, MA: Cambridge University Press.

Higgins, E. T. & Pittman, T. S. (2008). Motives of the human animal: Comprehending, managing, and sharing inner states. *Annual Review of Psychology*, 59(1), 361–385.

Hirschi, T. (1969). *Causes of delinquency*. Berkeley, CA: University of California Press.

Hirschman, A. O. (1970). *Exit, voice, and loyalty: Responses to decline in firms, organizations and states*. Cambridge, MA: Harvard University Press.

Hobfoll, S. E. (2002). Social and psychological resources and adaptation. *Review of General Psychology*, 6(4), 307–324.

Hochschild, A. R. (1983). *The managed heart: Commercialization of human feeling*. Berkeley, CA: University of California Press.

Hodgkinson, G. P. & Healey, M. P. (2008). Cognition in organizations. *Annual Review of Psychology*, 59(1), 387–417.

Hofstede, G. (1993). Cultural constraints in management theories. *Academy of Management Executive*, 7, 81–94.

Hogan, J. & Hogan, R. (1989). How to measure employee reliability. *Journal of Applied Psychology*, 74, 273–279.

Hogan, R. & Ones, D. S. (1997). Conscientiousness and integrity at work. In R. Hogan, J. A. Johnson, & S. R. Briggs (Eds.), *Handbook of personality psychology* (pp. 849–870). San Diego, CA: Academic Press.

Holbeche, L. (1998). *Motivating people in lean organizations*. Oxford: Butterworth-Heinemann.

Holland, J. L. (1985). *Making vocational choices: A theory of vocational personalities and work environment* (2nd edn). Englewood Cliffs, NJ: Prentice-Hall.

Hollinger, R. C. (1986). Acts against the workplace: Social bonding and employee deviance. *Deviant Behavior*, 7, 53–75.

Hollinger, R. C. (1989). *Dishonesty in the workplace: A manager's guide to preventing employee theft*. Park Ridge, IL: London House Press.

Hollinger, R. C. & Clark, J. (1982). Employee deviance: A response to the perceived quality of the work experience. *Work and Occupations*, 9, 97–114.

Hollinger, R. C. & Clark, J. (1983). Deterrence in the workplace: Perceived certainty, perceived severity and employee theft. *Social Forces*, 62(2), 398–418.

Hollinger, R. C. & Davis, J. (2006). Employee theft and staff dishonesty. In M. Gill (Ed.), *The handbook of security* (pp. 203–228). New York: Palgrave Macmillan.

Holsti, O. R. (1968). Content analysis. In G. Lindzeye & E. Aronson (Eds.), *The handbook of social psychology* (Vol. 2, pp. 596–692). Reading, MA: Addison-Wesley.

Holt, T. J. & Schell, B. H. (2011). *Corporate hacking and technology-driven crime*. New York: Information Science Reference.

Holtsman-Chen, E. (1984). *The effects of entry jobs on the chances for promotion* (Unpublished master's thesis). Tel Aviv University, Israel.

Homans, G. C. (1950). *The human group*. New York: Harcourt, Brace.

Hoobler, J. M. & Brass, D. J. (2006). Abusive supervision and family undermining as displaced aggression. *Journal of Applied Psychology*, 91(5), 1125–1133.

Hoobler, J. M. & Hu, J. (2013). A model of injustice, abusive supervision, and negative affect. *The Leadership Quarterly*, 24(1), 256–269.

Horning, D. N. M. (1970). Blue collar theft: Conceptions of property, attitudes toward pilferage, and work group norms in a modern industrial plant. In E. O. Smigel & H. L. Ross (Eds.), *Crimes against bureaucracies* (pp. 46–64). New York: Van Nostrand Reinhold.

Hosmer, T. L. (1987). Ethical analysis and human resource management. *Human Resource Management*, 26, 313–330.

Hosmer, T. L. (1991). *The ethics of management*. Boston, MA: Irwin.

Hough, L. M. (1992). The "big-five" personality variables-construct confusion: Description versus prediction. *Human Performance*, 5, 139–155.

Hough, L. M. & Schneider, R. J. (1996). Personality traits, taxonomies, and applications in organizations. In K. R. Murphy (Ed.), *Individual differences and behavior in organizations* (pp. 31–88). San Francisco, CA: Jossey-Bass.

Hough, L. M., Eaton, M. K., Dunnette, M. D., Kamp, J. D., & McCloy, R. A. (1990). Criterion-related validities of personality constructs and the effect of response distortion on those validities. *Journal of Applied Psychology*, 75, 581–595.

House, R. J. & Podsakoff, P. M. (1994). Leadership effectiveness: Past perspectives and future directions for research. In J. Greenberg (Ed.), *Organizational behavior: The state of the science* (pp. 45–82). Hillsdale, NJ: Lawrence Erlbaum Associates.

House, R., Rousseau, D., & Themas-Hurt, M. (1995). The meso paradigm: A framework for the integration of micro and macro organizational behavior. *Research in Organizational Behavior*, 17, 71–114.

Howard, L. W. & Cordes, C. L. (2010). Flight from unfairness: Effects of perceived injustice on emotional exhaustion and employee withdrawal. *Journal of Business and Psychology*, 25(3), 409–428.

Howell, J. M. & Shamir, B. (2005). The role of followers in the charismatic leadership process: Relationships and their consequences. *Academy of Management Review*, 30(1), 96–112.

Hulin, C. L., Fitzgerald, L. F, & Dragsow, F. (1996). Organizational influences on sexual harassment. In M. S. Stockdale (Ed.), *Sexual harassment in the workplace* (pp. 127–150). Thousand Oaks, CA: Sage.

Humphreys, L. G. (1977). Predictability of employee theft: Importance of the base rate. *Journal of Applied Psychology*, 62, 514–516.

Hunt, S. T. (1996). Generic work behavior: An investigation into the dimensions of entry level, hourly job performance. *Personnel Psychology*, 49, 51–83.

Ilgen, D. R., O'Driscoll, M. P., & Hildreth, K. (1992). Time devoted to job and off job activities, interrole conflict and affective experiences. *Journal of Applied Psychology*, 77, 272–279.

Ilgen, D. R., Hollenbeck, J. R., Johnson, M., & Jundt, D. (2005). Teams in organizations: From input-process-output models to IMOI models. *Annual Review of Psychology*, 56(1), 517–543.

Inkson, K. (2007). *Understanding careers: The metaphors of working lives*. Thousand Oaks, CA: Sage.

Inkson, K., Gunz, H., Ganesh, S., & Roper, J. (2012). Boundaryless careers: Bringing back boundaries. *Organization Studies*, 33(3), 323–340.

Isaac, R. G. (1993). Organizational culture: Some new perspectives. In R. T. Golembiewski (Ed.), *Handbook of organizational behavior* (pp. 91–112). New York: Marcel Dekker.

Isen, A. M. & Baron, R. A. (1991). Positive affect as a factor on categorization. In L. L. Cummings & B. M. Staw (Eds.), *Research in organizational behavior* (Vol. 13, pp. 1–53). Greenwich, CT: JAI Press.

Issa, T. & Pick, D. (2010). Ethical mindsets: An Australian study. *Journal of Business Ethics*, 96(4), 613–629.

Itzkovich, Y. (2014). Incivility: The moderating effect of hierarchical status: Does a manager inflict more damage? *Journal of Management Research*, 6(3), 86–98.

Ivancevich, J. M., Konopaske, R., & Matteson, M. T. (2014). *Organizational behavior and management*. New York: McGraw-Hill.

Izraeli, D. (1994). *Marketing: Theory and practice*. Tel Aviv: Cherikover.

Jaccard, J. & Davidson, A. R. (1975). A comparison of two models of social behavior: Results of a survey sample. *Sociometry*, 38(4), 497–517.

James, G. G. (1984). In defense of whistle blowing. In W. H. Shaw & V. Barry (Eds.), *Moral issues in business* (6th edn, pp. 409–417). Belmont, CA: Wadsworth.

James, M. S. L. (2005). *Antecedents and consequences of cynicism in organizations: An examination of the potential positive and negative effects on school systems* (Unpublished doctoral dissertation). University of Florida, Gainesville, FL.

Janis, I. L. (1982). *Victims of groupthink: A psychological study of foreign-policy decisions and fiascoes* (rev. ed.). Boston, MA: Houghton-Mifflin.

Janoff-Bulman, R. (1992). *Shattered assumptions: Towards a new psychology to trauma*. New York: The Free Press.

Jensen, G. F. & Hodson, R. (1999). Synergies in the study of crime and the workplace. *Work and Occupations*, 26, 6–20.

Jensen, J. M. & Patel, P. C. (2011). Predicting counterproductive work behavior from the interaction of personality traits. *Personality and Individual Differences*, 51(4), 466–471.

Jensen, J. M., Opland, R. A., & Ryan, A. M. (2010). Psychological contracts and counterproductive work behaviors: Employee responses to transactional and relational breach. *Journal of Business and Psychology*, 25(4), 555–568.

Jetten, J. & Hornsey, M. J. (2014). Deviance and dissent in groups. *Annual Review of Psychology*, 65(1), 461–485.

Jick, T. D. (1979). Mixing qualitative and quantitative methods: Triangulation in action. *Administrative Science Quarterly*, 24, 602–611.

John, O. P. (1989). Towards a taxonomy of personality descriptions. In D. M. Buss & N. Cantor (Eds.), *Personality psychology: Recent trends and emerging directions* (pp. 261–271). New York: Springer-Verlag.

Johns, G. (1997). Contemporary research on absence from work: Correlations, causes and consequences. *International Review of Industrial and Organizational Psychology*, 12, 115–174.

Johns, G. (2001). The psychology of lateness, absenteeism, and turnover. In N. Anderson, D. S. Ones, H. K. Sinangil, & C. Viswesvaran (Eds.), *Handbook of industrial, work and organizational psychology* (Vol. 2, pp. 232–252). London: Sage.

Johnson, P. & Gill, J. (1993). *Management control and organizational behavior.* London: Paul Chapman.

Johnson, P. R. & Indvik, J. (1994). Workplace violence. *PUBLIC Personnel Management*, 23, 515–523.

Jonason, P. K., Slomski, S., & Partyka, J. (2012). The dark triad at work: How toxic employees get their way. *Personality and Individual Differences*, 52(3), 449–453.

Jones, E. E. & Gerard, H. B. (1967). *Foundations of social psychology.* New York: Wiley.

Jones, J. W. & Terris, W. (1983). Predicting employees theft in home improvement centers. *Psychological Reports*, 52, 187–201.

Jones, S. (2008). *Not "part of the job": Sexual harassment policy in the US, the Equal Employment Opportunity Commission, and women's economic citizenship, 1975–1991* (Unpublished doctoral dissertation). Bowling Green University, OH.

Jones, T. M. (1991). Ethical decision making by individuals in organizations: An issue-contingent model. *Academy of Management Review*, 16, 366–395.

Judge, T. A. & Kammeyer-Mueller, J. (2012). Job attitudes. *Annual Review of Psychology*, 63(1), 341–367.

Judge, T. A., Matocchio, J. J., & Thoresen, C. J. (1997). Five-factor model of personality and employee absence. *Journal of Applied Psychology*, 82, 745–755.

Jung, H. S. & Yoon, H. H. (2012). The effects of emotional intelligence on counterproductive work behaviors and organizational citizen behaviors among food and beverage employees in a deluxe hotel. *International Journal of Hospitality Management*, 31(2), 369–378.

Jurkiewicz, C. L. & Giacalone, R. A. (2004). A values framework for measuring the impact of workplace spirituality on organizational performance. *Journal of Business Ethics*, 49(2), 129–142.

Kabat-Farr, D. & Cortina, L. M. (2014). Sex-based harassment in employment: New insights into gender and context. *Law and Human Behavior*, 38(1), 58–72.

Kacmar, K. M. & Carlson, D. S. (1994). Using impression management in women's job search processes. *American Behavioral Scientist*, 37, 682–696.

Kacmar, K. M. & Carlson, D. S. (1998). A qualitative analysis of the dysfunctional aspects of political behavior in organizations. In R. W. Griffin, A. M. O'Leary-Kelly, & J. M. Collins (Eds.), *Dysfunctional behavior in organizations: Non-violent dysfunctional behavior* (Vol. 23, Part B, pp. 195–218). Stamford, CT: JAI Press.

Kahn, R. L., Wolfe, D. M., Quinn, R. P., Snoek, J. D., & Rosenthal, R. A. (1964). *Organizational stress: Studies in role conflict and ambiguity.* New York: Wiley.

Kanter, D. L. & Mirvis, P. H. (1989). *The cynical Americans: Living and working in an age of discontent and disillusion.* San Francisco, CA: Jossey-Bass.

Kanter, R. M. (1977). *Men and women of the corporation.* New York: Basic Books.

Kantor, H. (1999). *Misbehavior among social workers in welfare agencies: Its relationship with professional commitment, burnout at work, and the violence of patients* (Unpublished master's thesis). Tel Aviv University, Israel.

Karakas, F. (2009). Spirituality and performance in organizations: A literature review. *Journal of Business Ethics*, 94(1), 89–106.

Karasek, R. A. & Theorell, T. (1990). *Healthy work: Stress, productivity, and the reconstruction of working life.* New York: Basic Books.

Karau, S. J. & Williams, K. D. (1993). Social loafing: A meta-analytic review and theoretical integration. *Journal of Personality and Social Psychology*, 65, 681–706.

Katz, D. & Kahn, R. L. (1966). *The social psychology of organizations*. New York: Wiley.

Katz, D. & Kahn, R. L. (1978). *The social psychology of organizations* (2nd edn). New York: Wiley.

Katzell, R. A. & Austin, J. T. (1992). From then to now: The development of industrial-organizational psychology in the United States. *Journal of Applied Psychology*, 77, 803–835.

Keashly, L. & Harvey, S. (2005). Emotional abuse in the workplace. In S. Fox & P. E. Spector (Eds.), *Counterproductive work behavior: Investigations of actors and targets* (pp. 201–235). Washington, DC: American Psychological Association.

Keashly, L. & Jagatic, K. (2003). By any other name: American perspectives on workplace bullying. In S. Einarsen, H. Hoel, D. Zapf, & C. L. Cooper (Eds.), *Bullying and emotional abuse in the workplace: International perspectives in research and practice*. London: Taylor & Francis.

Kelloway, E. K., Barling, J., & Hurrell, J. J. (Eds.) (2006). *Handbook of workplace violence*. Thousand Oaks, CA: Sage.

Kemper, T. D. (1966). Representative roles and the legitimization of deviance. *Social Problems*, 13, 288–298.

Kerr, N. L. & Tindale, R. S. (2004). Group performance and decision making. *Annual Review of Psychology*, 55(1), 623–655.

Khan, A. K., Quratulain, S., & Bell, C. M. (2014). Episodic envy and counterproductive work behaviors: Is more justice always good? *Journal of Organizational Behavior*, 35(1), 128–144.

Kidwell, R. E. (2010). Loafing in the 21st century: Enhanced opportunities—and remedies—for withholding job effort in the new workplace. *Business Horizons*, 53(6), 543–552.

Kidwell, R. E. & Bennett, N. (1993). Employee propensity to withhold effort: A conceptual model to intersect three avenues of research. *Academy of Management Review*, 18, 429–456.

Killinger, B. (1991). *Workaholics: The respectable addicts*. New York: Simon & Schuster.

Kilman, R. H. (1985). Managing your organization's culture. *Nonprofit World Report*, 3, 12–15.

Kinjerski, V. & Skrypnek, B.J. (2006). *Measuring the intangible: Development of the spirit at work scale*. Paper presented at the annual meeting of the Academy of Management, Atlanta, GA.

Kipnis, D., Schmidt, S. M., & Wilkinson, I. (1980). Intraorganizational influence tactics: Exploration in getting one's way. *Journal of Applied Psychology*, 65, 440–452.

Kish-Gephart, J. J., Harrison, D. A., & Treviño, L. K. (2010). Bad apples, bad cases, and bad barrels: Meta-analytic evidence about sources of unethical decisions at work. *Journal of Applied Psychology*, 95(1), 1–31.

Kitterlin, M. & Moreo, P. J. (2012). Pre-employment drug-testing in the full-service restaurant industry and its relationship to employee work performance factors. *Journal of Human Resources in Hospitality & Tourism*, 11(1), 36–51.

Klockars, C. (1974). *The professional fence*. New York: The Free Press.

Knoke, D. (1990). *Organizing for collective action: The political economies of associations*. Hawthorne, NY: Aldine de Gruyter.

Kohlberg, L. (1969). Stage and sequence: The cognitive-developmental approach to socialization. In D. A. Goslin (Ed.), *Handbook of socialization theory and research* (pp. 347–480). Chicago, IL: Rand McNally.

Kohlberg, L. (1984). *The psychology of moral development*. New York: Harper & Row.

Kolodinsky, R. W., Giacalone, R. A., & Jurkiewicz, C. L. (2008). Workplace values and outcomes: Exploring personal, organizational, and interactive workplace spirituality. *Journal of Business Ethics*, 81(2), 465–480.

Konovsky, M. A. & Cropanzano, R. (1991). Perceived fairness of employee drug testing as a predictor of employee attitudes and job performance. *Journal of Applied Psychology*, 76(5), 698–707.

Korman, A. K. (1971). Organizational achievement, aggression and creativity: Some suggestions toward an integrated theory. *Organizational Behavior and Human Performance*, 6, 593–613.

Korman, A. K. (1976). Hypothesis of work behavior revisited and an extension. *Academy of Management Review*, 1, 50–63.

Kossek, E. E. & Ozeki, C. (1999). Bridging the work-family policy and productivity gap: A literature review. *Community, Work & Family*, 2(1), 7–32.

Kotter, J. P. (1973). The psychological contract: Managing the joining up process. *California Management Review*, 15, 91–99.

Kraut, A. I. (1975). Predicting turnover of employees from measured job attitudes. *Organizational Behavior and Human Performance*, 13, 233–243.

Kravitz, D. A. & Martin, B. (1986). Ringelmann rediscovered: The original article. *Journal of Personality and Social Psychology*, 50, 936–941.

Kreitner, R. & Kinicki, A. (1995). *Organizational behavior* (3rd edn). Chicago, IL: Irwin.

Krigel, K. (2001). *Relationship between personality traits (Big 5), organizational justice, and organizational misbehavior: A conceptual model* (Unpublished master's thesis). Tel Aviv University, Israel.

Kriger, M. P. & Hanson, B. J. (1999). A value-based paradigm for creating truly healthy organizations. *Journal of Organizational Change Management*, 12(4), 302–317.

Krishnakumar, S. & Neck, C. P. (2002). The "what," "why" and "how" of spirituality in the workplace. *Journal of Managerial Psychology*, 17(3), 153–164.

Kuchuk, I. (2015). *Who are you the knowledge hider? Knowledge hiding as a manifestation of organizational misbehavior* (Unpublished master's thesis). Tel Aviv University, Israel.

Kunda, G. (1992). *Engineering culture*. Philadelphia, PA: Temple University Press.

Kunda, G. (2006). *Engineering culture* (rev. edn). Philadelphia, PA: Temple University Press.

Kurland, N. B. (1995). Ethical intentions and the theories of reasoned action and planned behavior. *Journal of Applied Social Psychology*, 25, 297–313.

Kurland, O. M. (1993). Workplace violence. *Risk Management*, 40, 76–77.

Laabs, J., McClure, L., & Davidson, L. (1999). Employee sabotage: Don't be a target! *Workforce*, 78(7), 32–38.

Lam, H., Weiss, H. M., Welch, E. R., & Hulin, C. L. (2009). A within-person approach to work behavior and performance: Concurrent and lagged citizenship-counterproductivity associations, and dynamic relationships with affect and overall job performance. *Academy of Management Journal*, 52(5), 1051–1066.

Landy, F. J. (1985). *Psychology of work behavior* (3rd edn) Homewood, IL: Dorsey Press.

Langer, E. J. (1983). *The psychology of control*. Beverly Hills, CA: Sage.

Lasley, J. R. (1988). Toward a control theory of white collar offending. *Journal of Quantitative Criminology*, 4(4), 347–362.

Latané, B. (2000). Pressures to uniformity and the evolution of cultural norms: Modeling dynamic social impact. In D. R. Ilgen & C. L. Hulin (Eds.), *Computational modeling in organizations* (pp. 189–120). Washington, DC: American Psychological Association.

Latané, B., Williams, K., & Harkins, S. (1979). Many hands make light the work: The causes and consequences of social loafing. *Journal of Personality and Social Psychology*, 37, 822–832.

Latham, G. P. & Pinder, C. C. (2005). Work motivation theory and research at the dawn of the twenty-first century. *Annual Review of Psychology*, 56(1), 485–516.

Lau, V. C. S., Au, W. T., & Ho, J. M. C. (2003). A qualitative and quantitative review of antecedents of counterproductive behavior in organizations. *Journal of Business and Psychology*, 18(1), 73–99.

Lazarus, R. S. (1991). *Emotion and adaptation*. New York: Oxford University Press.

Lazarus, R. S. & Folkman, S. (1984). *Stress, appraisal, and coping*. New York: Springer-Verlag.

Le Bon, G. (1908). *The crowd: A study of the popular mind*. London: T. Fisher Unwin.

Le, K., Donnellan, M. B., Spilman, S. K., Garcia, O. P., & Conger, R. (2014). Workers behaving badly: Associations between adolescent reports of the big five and counterproductive work behaviors in adulthood. *Personality and Individual Differences*, 61–62, 7–12.

Leary, M. R. (2007). Motivational and emotional aspects of the self. *Annual Review of Psychology*, 58(1), 317–344.

Leatherwood, M. L. & Spector, L. C. (1991). Enforcements, inducements, expected utility and employee misconduct. *Journal of Management*, 17, 553–569.

Leavitt, H. J. (1972). *Managerial psychology* (3rd edn). Chicago, IL: University of Chicago Press.

Lee, C., Ashford, S. J., & Bobko, P. (1990). Interactive effects of "Type A" behavior and perceived control on worker performance, job satisfaction, and somatic complaints. *Academy of Management Journal*, 33, 870–881.

Lee, C. I. & Felps, W. (2013). *Towards a taxonomy of career studies*. Paper presented in the EGOS colloquium, Montreal, Canada.

Lee, K., Ashton, M. C., & de Vries, R. E. (2005). Predicting workplace delinquency and integrity with the HEXACO and five-factor models of personality structure. *Human Performance*, 18(2), 179–197.

Lee, R. M. (1993). *Doing research on sensitive topics*. London: Sage.

Lehman, W. E. K. & Simpson, D. D. (1992). Employee substance use and on the job behavior. *Journal of Applied Psychology*, 77, 309–321.

Lerner, H. (1980). Internal prohibitions against female anger. *American Journal for the Advancement of Psychoanalysis*, 40(2), 137–148.

Levin, D. (1989). *Investigating the concept of violence among social-workers in welfare agencies* (Unpublished master's thesis). Tel Aviv University, Israel.

Lewin, K. (1951). *Field theory in social science: Selected theoretical papers*. New York: Harper Bros.

Lewis, K. M. (2000). When leaders display emotions: How followers respond to negative emotional expression of male and female leaders. *Journal of Organizational Behavior*, 22, 221–234.

Leymann, H. (1996). The content and development of mobbing at work. *European Journal of Work and Organizational Psychology*, 5(2), 165–184.

Lian, H., Ferris, D. L., Morrison, R., & Brown, D. J. (2013). Blame it on the supervisor or the subordinate? Reciprocal relations between abusive supervision and organizational deviance. *Journal of Applied Psychology*, 99(4), 651–664.

Lian, H., Brown, D., Ferris, D. L., Liang, L., Keeping, L., & Morrison, R. (2014). Abusive supervision and retaliation: A self-control framework. *Academy of Management Journal*, 57(1), 116–139.

Library of Congress (2015). *Whistleblower Protection Act of 1989*. Retrieved from the Library of Congress website: http://thomas.loc.gov/cgi-bin/query/z?c101:S.20.ENR.

Liden, R. & Green, S. (1980). *On the measurement of career orientation*. Paper presented at the Midwest Academy of Management meeting, Cincinnati, OH.

Lim, S. & Cortina, L. M. (2005). Interpersonal mistreatment in the workplace: The interface and impact of general incivility and sexual harassment. *Journal of Applied Psychology*, 90(3), 483–496.

Lim, S., Cortina, L. M., & Magley, V. J. (2008). Personal and workgroup incivility: Impact on work and health outcomes. *Journal of Applied Psychology*, 93(1), 95–107.

Lim, V. K. (2002). The IT way of loafing on the job: Cyberloafing, neutralizing and organizational justice. *Journal of Organizational Behaviour*, 23(5), 675–694.

Lim, V. K. & Chen, D. J. (2012). Cyberloafing at the workplace: Gain or drain on work? *Behaviour & Information Technology*, 31(4), 343–353.

Lind, E. A. & Tyler, T. (1988). *The social psychology of procedural justice*. New York: Plenum.

Linstead, S. (1985). Breaking the purity rule: Industrial sabotage and the symbolic process. *Personnel Review*, 15, 12–19.

Lipman, M. & McGraw, W. R. (1988). Employee theft: A $40 billion industry. *Annals of the American Academy of Political and Social Science*, 498, 51–59.

Litwin, G. H. & Stringer, R. A. (1968). *Motivation and organizational climate*. Cambridge, MA: Harvard University Press.

Liu, S., Wang, M., Bamberger, P., Shi, J., & Bacharach, S. B. (2015). The dark side of socialization: A longitudinal investigation of newcomer alcohol use. *Academy of Management Journal*, 58(2), 334–355.

Locke, E. A. (1968). Toward a theory of task motivation and incentives. *Organizational Behavior and Human Performance*, 3(2), 157–189.

London House Press (1980). *Personnel selection inventory*. Park Ridge, IL: Author.

Lord, R. G., Diefendorff, J. M., Schmidt, A. M., & Hall, R. J. (2010). Self-regulation at work. *Annual Review of Psychology*, 61(1), 543–568.

Lovelock, C. H. (1983). Classifying services to gain strategic advantages: Marketing insights. *Journal of Marketing*, 47, 9–20.

Lu, G. J., Brockner, J., Vardi, Y., & Weitz, E. (2016). The dark side of job autonomy: Unethical behavior. Manuscript submitted for publication.

Lubet, S. (2015). Ethics on the run [Review of the book *On the run: Fugitive life in an American city*, by A. Goffman]. *The New Rambler*. Retrieved from: http://newramblerreview.com/book-reviews/law/ethics-on-the-run.

Lubinski, D. (2000). Scientific and social significance of assessing individual differences: "Sinking shafts at a few critical points." *Annual Review of Psychology*, 51(1), 405–444.

Luo, Y. (2005). An organizational perspective of corruption. *Management and Organization Review*, 1, 119–154.

Luthans, F. & Kreitner, R. (1985). *Organizational behavior modification and beyond: An operant and social learning approach*. Glenview, IL: Scott, Foresman.

Lynn, M., Naughton, M., & Vanderveen, S. (2009). Faith at work scale (FWS): Justification, development, and validation of a measure of Judeo-Christian religion in the workplace. *Journal of Business Ethics*, 85(2), 227–243.

Machlowitz, M. (1980). *Workaholics, living with them, working with them*. Reading, MA: Addison-Wesley.

Mackey, J. D., Ellen, B. P., Hochwarter, W. A., & Ferris, G. R. (2013). Subordinate social adaptability and the consequences of abusive supervision perceptions in two samples. *The Leadership Quarterly*, 24(5), 732–746.

Mackey, J. D., Frieder, R. E., Brees, J. R., & Martinko, M. J. (2015). Abusive supervision: A meta-analysis and empirical review. *Journal of Management*. Advance online publication. doi:10.1177/0149206315573997.

Macrae, C. N. & Bodenhausen, G. V. (2000). Social cognition: Thinking categorically about others. *Annual Review of Psychology*, 51(1), 93–120.

Mainiero, L. A. & Sullivan, S. E. (2006). *The opt-out revolt: Why people are leaving companies to create kaleidoscope careers*. Palo Alto, CA: Davies-Black.

Major, B. & O'Brien, L. T. (2005). The social psychology of stigma. *Annual Review of Psychology*, 56(1), 393–421.

Mangione, T. W. & Quinn, R. P. (1975). Job satisfaction, counterproductive behavior, and drug use at work. *Journal of Applied Psychology*, 60, 114–116.

Manning, F. V. (1981). *Managerial dilemmas and executive growth*. Reston, VA: Reston.

Mantell, M. (1994). *Ticking bombs: Defusing violence in the workplace*. Burr Ridge, IL: Irwin.

March, J. G. & Simon, H. A. (1958). *Organizations*. New York: Wiley.

Marcus, A. I. & Segal, H. P. (1989). *Technology in America: A brief history*. San Diego, CA: Harcourt, Brace, Jovanovich.

Mars, G. (1973). Chance, punters and the fiddle: Institutionalized pilferage in a hotel dining room. In M. Warner (Ed.), *The sociology of the workplace* (pp. 200–210). New York: Halsted.

Mars, G. (1974). Dock pilferage: A case study in occupational theft. In P. Rock & M. McIntosh (Eds.), *Deviance and social control* (pp. 209–228). London: Tavistock Publications.

Mars, G. (1982). *Cheats at work: An anthropology of workplace crime*. London: George Allen & Unwin.

Mars, G. (1987). Longshore drinking, economic security and union politics in Newfoundland. In M. T. Douglas (Ed.), *Constructive drinking* (pp. 91–101). Cambridge: Cambridge University Press.

Martin, T. C. (1996). The Comprehensive Terrorism Prevention Act of 1995. *Seton Hall Legislative Journal*, 20(1), 201–248.

Martinko, M. J. & Zellars, K. L (1998). Toward a theory of workplace violence and aggression: A cognitive appraisal perspective. In R. W. Griffin, A. M. O'Leary-Kelly, & J. M. Collins (Eds.), *Dysfunctional behavior in organizations: Violent and deviant behavior* (Vol. 23, Part A, pp. 1–42). Stamford, CT: JAI Press.

Martinko, M. J., Harvey, P., Brees, J. R., & Mackey, J. (2013). A review of abusive supervision research. *Journal of Organizational Behavior*, 34(S1), S120–S137.

Martinson, B. C., Anderson, M. S., & De Vries, R. (2005). Scientists behaving badly. *Nature*, 435(7043), 737–738.

Maslach, C., Schaufeli, W. B., & Leiter, M. P. (2001). Job burnout. *Annual Review of Psychology*, 52(1), 397–422.

Maslow, A. H. (1954). *Motivation and personality*. New York: Harper & Row.

Maslow, A. H. (1962). *Toward a psychology of being*. Princeton, NJ: D. Von Nostrand.

Masuch, M. (1985). Vicious circles in organizations. *Administrative Science Quarterly*, 30, 14–33.

Matthiesen, S. B. & Einarsen, S. (2007). Perpetrators and targets of bullying at work: Role stress and individual differences. *Violence and Victims*, 22(6), 735–753.

Mayer, D. M., Nurmohamed, S., Treviño, L. K., Shapiro, D. L., & Schminke, M. (2013). Encouraging employees to report unethical conduct internally: It takes a village. *Organizational Behavior and Human Decision Processes*, 121(1), 89–103.

Mayo, E. (1933). *The human problems of an industrial civilization*. New York: Macmillan.

Mazzetti, G., Schaufeli, W. B., & Guglielmi, D. (2014). Are workaholics born or made? Relations of workaholism with person characteristics and overwork climate. *International Journal of Stress Management*, 21(3), 227.

McCann, D. (2005). *Sexual harassment at work: National and international responses*. Geneva: International Labor Office.

McCormick, D. W. (1994). Spirituality and management. *Journal of Managerial Psychology*, 9(6), 5–8.

McCrae, R. R. & Costa, P. T. (1997). Conceptions and correlates to openness to experience. In R. Hogan, J. A. Johnson, & S. R. Briggs (Eds.), *Handbook of personality psychology* (pp. 825–846). San Diego, CA: Academic Press.

McCrae, R. R. & John, O. P. (1992). An introduction to the five-factor model and its applications. *Journal of Personality*, 60, 175–215.

McDonald, P. (2012). Workplace sexual harassment 30 years on: A review of the literature. *International Journal of Management Reviews*, 14(1), 1–17.

McFarlin, S. K. & Fals-Stewart, W. (2002). Workplace absenteeism and alcohol use: A sequential analysis. *Psychology of Addictive Behaviors*, 16(1), 17–21.

McGrath, J. E. (1976). Stress and behavior in organizations. In M. D. Dunnette (Ed.), *Handbook of industrial and organizational psychology* (pp. 1351–1395). Chicago, IL: Rand McNally.

McGregor, D. (1960). *The human side of enterprise*. New York: McGraw-Hill.

McGurn, R. (1988). Spotting the thieves who work among us. *Wall Street Journal*, March 7, pp. A16.

McKenna, R. J. (1996). Explaining amoral decision making: An external view of a human disaster. *Journal of Business Ethics*, 15(6), 681–694.

Mclean Parks, J. (1997). The fourth arm of justice: The art and science of revenge. In R. J. Lewicki, R. J. Bies, & B. H. Sheppard (Eds.), *Research on negotiation in organizations* (Vol. 6, pp. 113–144). Greenwich, CT: JAI Press.

McNutt, M. (2015). Editorial retraction. *Science*, 346(6215), 1366–1369.

Meglino, B. M. (1977). Stress and performance: Are they always incompatible? *Supervisory Management*, 22, 2–12.

Meglino, B. M., Ravlin, E. C., & Adkins, C. L. (1989). A work values approach to corporate culture: A field test of the value congruence process and its relationship to individual outcomes. *Journal of Applied Psychology*, 74, 424–432.

Mensch, B. S. & Kandel, D. B. (1988). Do job conditions influence the use of drugs? *Journal of Health and Social Behavior*, 29(2), 169–184.

Merriam, D. H. (1977). Employee theft. *Criminal Justice Abstracts*, 9, 375–410.

Merton, R. K. (1953). *Social theory and social structure*. Glencoe, IL: The Free Press.

Merton, R. T. (1938). Social structure and anomie. *American Sociological Review*, 3, 672–682.

Meyer, J. P. & Allen, N. J. (1997). *Commitment in the workplace: Theory, research, and application*. Thousand Oaks, CA: Sage.

Miceli, M. P. & Near, J. P. (1992). *Blowing the whistle: The organizational and legal implications for companies and employees*. New York, NY: Lexington.

Miceli, M. P. & Near, J. P. (1997). Whistle blowing as antisocial behavior. In R. A. Giacalone & J. Greenberg (Eds.), *Antisocial behavior in organizations* (pp. 130–149). Thousand Oaks, CA: Sage.

Miceli, M. P., Near, J. P., & Dworkin, T. M. (2008). *Whistle-blowing in organizations*. New York: Routledge.

Michaels, E., Handfield-Jones, H., & Axelrod, B. (2001). *The war for talent*. Boston, MA: Harvard Business School Press.

Miles, R. E. & Snow, C. C. (1978). *Organizational strategy, structure and process*. New York: McGraw-Hill.

Miller, D. T. (2001). Disrespect and the experience of injustice. *Annual Review of Psychology*, 52(1), 527–553.

Miner, J. B. (2002). *Organizational behavior: Foundations, theories, and analyses*. New York: Oxford University Press.

Minor, W. (1981). Techniques of neutralization: A reconceptualization and empirical examination. *Journal of Research in Crime and Delinquency*, 18(2), 295–318.

Mintzberg, H. (1983). *Power in and around organizations*. Englewood Cliffs, NJ: Prentice-Hall.

Mintzberg, H. (1989). *Mintzberg on Management: Inside our Strange World of Organizations*. New York, NY: Free Press.

Mitchell, M. S. & Ambrose, M. L. (2007). Abusive supervision and workplace deviance and the moderating effects of negative reciprocity beliefs. *Journal of Applied Psychology*, 92(4), 1159–1168.

Mitchell, T. R. (1979). Organizational behavior. *Annual Review of Psychology*, 30, 243–281.

Mitroff, I. I. & Denton, E. A. (1999). A study of spirituality in the workplace. *MIT Sloan Management Review*, 40(4), 83–92.

Mitroff, I. I. & Kilmann, R. H. (1984). *Corporate tragedies: Product tampering, sabotage, and other catastrophes*. New York: Praeger.

Moberg, D. J. (1997). On employee vice. *Business Ethics Quarterly*, 7, 41–60.

Molstad, C. (1988). Control strategies used by industrial brewery workers: Work avoidance, impression management and solidarity. *Human Organization*, 47, 354–360.

Moore, G. A. (1995). *Inside the tornado: Marketing strategies from Silicon Valley's cutting edge*. New York: Harper Business.

Moorman, R. H. & Podaskoff, P. M. (1992). A meta analytic review and empirical test of the potential confounding effects of social desirability response sets in organizational behavior research. *Journal of Occupational and Organizational Psychology*, 65, 131–149.

Morin, W. J. (1995). Silent sabotage: Mending the crisis in corporate values. *Management Review*, July 1, pp. 10–14.

Morrison, E. W. (2014). Employee voice and silence. *Annual Review of Organizational Psychology and Organizational Behavior*, 1(1), 173–197.

Mosier, S. K. (1983). *Workaholics: An analysis of their stress, success and priorities* (Unpublished master's thesis). University of Texas, Austin, TX.

Mount, M. & Barrick, M. R. (1995). The big five personality dimensions: Implications for research and practice in human resources management. *Research in Personality and Human Resource Management*, 13, 153–200.

Mount, M., Ilies, R., & Johnson, E. (2006). Relationship of personality traits and counterproductive work behaviors: The mediating effects of job satisfaction. *Personnel Psychology*, 59(3), 591–622.

Mowday, R. T. & Sutton, R. I. (1993). Organizational behavior: Linking individuals and groups to organizational contexts. *Annual Review of Psychology*, 44, 195–229.

Muchinsky, P. M. (2000). Emotions in the workplace: The neglect of organizational behavior. *Journal of Organizational Behavior*, 21, 801–805.

Murphy, K. R. (1996). Individual differences and behavior in organizations: Much more than g. In K. R. Murphy (Ed.), *Individual differences and behavior in organizations* (pp. 3–30). San Francisco, CA: Jossey-Bass.

Nadler, D. A. & Tushman, M. L. (1980). A model for diagnosing organizational behavior: Applying a congruence perspective. *Organizational Dynamics*, 9, 35–51.

Namie, G. (2007). The challenge of workplace bullying. *Employment Relations Today,* 34(2), 43–51.

Namie, G. & Namie, R., (2004). Workplace bullying: How to address America's silent epidemic. *Employee Rights and Employment Policy Journal,* 8(2), 315–334.

Namie, G. & Namie, R. (2009). US workplace bullying: Some basic considerations and consultation interventions. *Consulting Psychology Journal: Practice and Research,* 61(3), 202–219.

Nandkeolyar, A. K., Shaffer, J. A., Li, A., Ekkirala, S., & Bagger, J. (2014). Surviving an abusive supervisor: The joint roles of conscientiousness and coping strategies. *Journal of Applied Psychology,* 99(1), 138–150.

National Council on Crime and Delinquency (1975). *Workplace crime: Proceedings and resources of the internal business theft conference.* Chicago: Author.

National Retail Security Survey (2015). Gainesville, FL: University of Florida. Retrieved from the National Retail Federation website: https://nrf.com/resources/retail-library/national-retail-security-survey-2015#sthash.cEQ3KIb5.dpuf.

Naughton, T. J. (1987). A conceptual view of workaholism and implications for career counseling and research. *Career Development Quarterly,* 35(3), 180–187.

Neall, A. M. & Tuckey, M. R. (2014). A methodological review of research on the antecedents and consequences of workplace harassment. *Journal of Occupational and Organizational Psychology,* 87(2), 225–257.

Near, J. P. & Miceli, M. P. (1984). The relationship among beliefs, organizational position, and whistle-blowing status: A discriminant analysis. *Academy of Management Journal,* 27, 687–705.

Near, J. P. & Miceli, M. P. (1985). Organizational dissidence: The case of whistle-blowing. *Journal of Business Ethics,* 4, 1–16.

Near, J. P. & Miceli, M. P. (1986). Retaliation against whistle blowers: Predictors and effects. *Journal of Applied Psychology,* 71, 137–145.

Near, J. P. & Miceli, M. P. (1995). Effective whistle-blowing. *Academy of Management Review,* 20, 679–708.

Near, J. P., Baucus, M. S., & Miceli, M. P. (1993a). The relationship between values and practice: Organizational climates for wrongdoing. *Administration & Society,* 25, 204–226.

Near, J. P., Dworkin, T. M., & Miceli, M. P. (1993b). Explaining the whistle-blowing process: Suggestions from power theory and justice theory. *Organization Science,* 4, 392–411.

Needleman, S. E. (2008). Businesses say theft by their workers is up. *The Wall Street Journal,* December 11. Retrieved from: www.Wsj.com/articles/SB122896381748896999.

Neuman, J. H. & Baron, R. A. (1997). Aggression in the workplace. In R. A. Giacalone & J. Greenberg (Eds.), *Antisocial behavior in organizations* (pp. 37–67). Thousand Oaks, CA: Sage.

Neuman, J. H. & Baron, R. A. (2005). Aggression in the workplace: A social-psychological perspective. In S. Fox & P. E. Spector (Eds.), *Counterproductive work behavior: Investigations of actors and targets* (pp. 13–40). Washington, DC: American Psychological Association.

Neves, P. (2014). Taking it out on survivors: Submissive employees, downsizing, and abusive supervision. *Journal of Occupational and Organizational Psychology,* 87(3), 507–534.

Nicholson, N. (1998). How hardwired is human behavior? *Harvard Business Review,* 76, 134–147.

Nicholson, N. (2007). Destiny, drama and deliberation: Careers in the coevolution of lives and sciences. In H. Gunz & M. Peiperl (Eds.), *Handbook of career studies* (pp. 566–572). Thousand Oaks, CA: Sage.

Nielsen, M. B. & Einarsen, S. (2012). Outcomes of exposure to workplace bullying: A meta-analytic review. *Work & Stress*, 26(4), 309–332.

Nielsen, M. B., Skogstad, A., Matthiesen, S. B., Glasø, L., Aasland, M. S., Notelaers, G., & Einarsen, S. (2009). Prevalence of workplace bullying in Norway: Comparisons across time and estimation methods. *European Journal of Work and Organizational Psychology*, 18(1), 81–101.

Nielsen, M. B., Matthiesen, S. B., & Einarsen, S. (2010). The impact of methodological moderators on prevalence rates of workplace bullying: A meta-analysis. *Journal of Occupational and Organizational Psychology*, 83(4), 955–979.

Noe, R. A., Clarke, A. D. M., & Klein, H. J. (2014). Learning in the twenty-first-century workplace. *Annual Review of Organizational Psychology and Organizational Behavior*, 1(1), 245–275.

Nomani, A. Q. (1995). Women likelier to face violence in the workplace. *The Wall Street Journal*, October, p. A16.

Norman, W. T. (1963). Toward an adequate taxonomy of personality attributes: Replicated factor structure in peer nomination personality ratings. *Journal of Abnormal and Social Psychology*, 66, 483–574.

Oates, W. E. (1971). *Confessions of a workaholic: The facts about work addiction.* New York: World.

O'Farrell, C. & Nordstrom, C. R. (2013). Workplace bullying: Examining self-monitoring and organizational culture. *Journal of Psychological Issues in Organizational Culture*, 3(4), 6–17.

Ofer, R. (2003). *How do new employees learn to misbehave? The unexpected influence of organizational socialization* (Unpublished master's thesis). Tel Aviv University, Israel.

O'Leary-Kelly, A. M. & Bowes-Sperry, L. (2001). Sexual harassment as unethical behavior: The role of moral intensity. *Human Resource Management Review*, 11(1), 73–92.

O'Leary-Kelly, A. M., Griffin, R. W., & Glew, D. J. (1996). Organization-motivated aggression: A research framework. *Academy of Management Review*, 21, 225–253.

O'Leary-Kelly, A. M., Duffy, M. K., & Griffin, R. W. (2000a). Construct confusion in the study of antisocial behavior at work. *Research in Personnel and Human Resource Management*, 18, 275–303.

O'Leary-Kelly, A. M., Paetzold, R. L., & Griffin, R. W. (2000b). Sexual harassment as aggressive behavior: An actor-based perspective. *Academy of Management Review*, 25, 372–388.

O'Leary-Kelly, A. M., Bowes-Sperry, L., Bates, C. A., & Lean, E. R. (2009). Sexual harassment at work: A decade (plus) of progress. *Journal of Management*, 35, 503–536.

Olson, G. M. & Olson, J. S. (2003). Human-computer interaction: Psychological aspects of the human use of computing. *Annual Review of Psychology*, 54(1), 491–516.

Ones, D. S. & Viswesvaran, C. (1996). Integrity testing in organizations. In R. W. Griffin, A. M. O'Leary-Kelly, & J. M. Collins (Eds.), *Dysfunctional behavior in organizations: Non-violent dysfunctional behavior* (Vol. 23, Part B, pp. 243–276). Stamford, CT: JAI Press.

Ones, D. S., Viswesvaran, C., & Schmidt, F. L. (1993). Comprehensive meta-analysis of integrity test validities: Findings and implications for personnel selection and theories of job performance. *Journal of Applied Psychology*, 78, 679–703.

Ong, A. D., Bergeman, C. S., Bisconti, T. L., & Wallace, K. A. (2006). Psychological resilience, positive emotions, and successful adaptation to stress in later life. *Journal of Personality and Social Psychology*, 91(4), 730–749.

Oppenheimer, D. M. & Kelso, E. (2015). Information processing as a paradigm for decision making. *Annual Review of Psychology*, 66(1), 277–294.

Oravec, J. A. (2002). Constructive approaches to internet recreation in the workplace. *Communications of the ACM*, 45(1), 60–63.

Oravec, J.A. (2004). When work morphs into play: Using constructive recreation to support the flexible workplace. In M. Anandarajan (Ed.), *Personal web usage in the workplace: A guide to effective human resource management* (pp. 46–60). Hershey, PA: Idea Group.

O'Reilly, C.A. III. (1991). Organizational behavior: Where we've been, where we're going. *Annual Review of Psychology*, 42, 427–458.

Organ, D.W. (1988). *Organizational citizenship behavior: The good soldier syndrome*. Lexington, MA: Lexington Books.

Outmazgin, N. & Soffer, P. (2013). Business process workarounds: What can and cannot be detected by process mining. *Enterprise, Business Process and Information Systems Modeling*, 147, 48–62.

Ozer, D. J. & Benet-Martínez, V. (2006). Personality and the prediction of consequential outcomes. *Annual Review of Psychology*, 57(1), 401–421.

Ozer, D. J. & Reise, S. P. (1994). Personality assessment. *Annual Review of Psychology*, 45, 357–388.

Painter, K. (1991). Violence and vulnerability in the workplace: Psychological and legal implications. In M. J. Davidson & J. Earnshaw (Eds.), *Vulnerable workers: Psychosocial and legal issues* (pp. 159–178). New York: Wiley.

Palmer, D. (2012). *Normal organizational wrongdoing: A critical analysis of theories of misconduct in and by organizations*. New York: Oxford University Press.

Pandey, A. & Gupta, R. K. (2008). Spirituality in management: A review of contemporary and traditional thoughts and agenda for research. *Global Business Review*, 9(1), 65–83.

Parker, S. K. (2014). Beyond motivation: Job and work design for development, health, ambidexterity, and more. *Annual Review of Psychology*, 65(1), 661–691.

Pashler, H., Johnston, J. C., & Ruthruff, E. (2001). Attention and performance. *Annual Review of Psychology*, 52(1), 629–651.

Paulhus, D. L. & Williams, K. M. (2002). The dark triad of personality: Narcissism, Machiavellianism, and psychopathy. *Journal of Research in Personality*, 36(6), 556–563.

Paulsen, R. (2014). *Empty labor: Idleness and workplace resistance*. Cambridge, MA: Cambridge University Press.

Pawar, B. S. (2008). Individual spirituality, workplace spirituality and work attitudes: An empirical test of direct and interaction effects. *Leadership & Organization Development Journal*, 30(8), 759–777.

Pazy, A. & Zin, R. (1987). A contingency approach to consistency: A challenge to prevalent views. *Journal of Vocational Behavior*, 30, 84–101.

Pearson, C. M., Andersson, L. M., & Porath, C. L. (2000). Assessing and attacking workplace incivility. *Organizational Dynamics*, 29, 123–137.

Pearson, C. M., Andersson, L. M., & Porath, C. L. (2004). Workplace incivility. In S. Fox & P. Spector (Eds.), *Counterproductive work behavior: Investigations of actors and targets* (pp. 177–199). Washington, DC: American Psychology Association.

Peck, M. S. (1983). *People of the lie: The hope for healing human evil*. New York: Touchstone.

Peiperl, M. & Jones, B. (2001). Workaholics and overworkers: Productivity or pathology? *Group & Organization Management*, 26(3), 369–393.

Peled, Y. (2000). *Sexual harassment: Attitudes and behavior among doctors and nurses in a general hospital* (Unpublished master's thesis). Tel Aviv University, Israel.

Peng, A., Schaubroeck, J., & Li, Y. (2014). Social exchange implications of own and coworkers' experiences of supervisory abuse. *Academy of Management Journal*, 57(5), 1385–1405.

Penner, L. A., Dovidio, J. F., Piliavin, J. A., & Schroeder, D. A. (2005). Prosocial behavior: Multilevel perspectives. *Annual Review of Psychology*, 56(1), 365–392.

Perrow, C. (1984). *Normal accidents: Living with high risk technologies.* New York: Basic Books.

Perrow, C. (1986). *Complex organizations: A critical essay* (3rd edn). New York: McGraw-Hill.

Peters, T. J. & Waterman, R. H. (1982). *In search of excellence: Lessons from America's best-run companies.* Cambridge, MA: Harper & Row.

Petrick, J. A. & Manning, G. E. (1990). Developing an ethical climate for excellence. *Journal for Quality and Participation*, March, 84–90.

Petrick, J. A., Wagley, R. A., & Thomas, J. (1991). Structured ethical decision-making improving the prospects of managerial success in business. *SAM Advanced Management Journal*, 56, 28–34.

Pfeffer, J. (1981). *Power in organizations.* Marshfield, MA: Pitman.

Pierce, J. R. & Aguinis, H. (2015). Detrimental citizenship behaviour: A multilevel framework of antecedents and consequences. *Management and Organization Review*, 11(S01), 69–99.

Pilch, I. & Turska, E. (2015). Relationships between Machiavellianism, organizational culture, and workplace bullying: Emotional abuse from the target's and the perpetrator's perspective. *Journal of Business Ethics*, 128(1), 83–93.

Pillai, R., Schriesheim, C. A., & Williams, E. S. (1999). Fairness perceptions and trust as mediators for transformational and transactional leadership: A two-sample study. *Journal of Management*, 25, 897–933.

Pines, A. (1981). *Job stress and burnout: Research, theory and intervention perspectives.* Beverly Hills, CA: Sage.

Pines, A. & Kanner, A. D. (1982). Nurses' burnout: Lack of positive conditions and presence of negative conditions as two sources of stress. In E. A. McConnell (Ed.), *Burnout in the nursing profession* (pp. 139–145). St. Louis, MO: Mosby.

Pinsker, J. (2014). America's workers are out-stealing America's shoplifters. *The Atlantic*, November 13. Retrieved from: www.theatlantic.com/business/archive/2014/11/how-retail-workers-are-out-stealing-americas-shoplifters/382703.

Pinto, J., Leana, C. R., & Pil, F. K. (2008). Corrupt organizations or organizations of corrupt individuals? Two types of organization-level corruption. *Academy of Management Review*, 33(3), 685–709.

Piotrowski, C. (2012). From workplace bullying to cyberbullying: The enigma of e-harassment in modern organizations. *Organization Development Journal*, 30(4), 44–53.

Plutchik, R. (1993). Emotion and their vicissitudes: Emotions and psychopathology. In M. Lewis & J. M. Haviland (Eds.), *Handbook of emotion* (pp. 53–66). New York: Guilford.

Plutchik, R. (2001). The nature of emotions. *American Scientist*, 89, 344–350.

Poelmans, S. (1999). Workarounds and distributed viscosity in a workflow system: A case study. *ACM SIGGROUP Bulletin*, 20(3), 11–12.

Pomazal, R. J. & Jaccard, J. J. (1976). An informational approach to altruistic behavior. *Journal of Personality and Social Psychology*, 33, 317–326.

Popovich, P. M. & Warren, M. A. (2010). The role of power in sexual harassment as a counterproductive behavior in organizations. *Human Resource Management Review*, 20(1), 45–53.

Porath, C. L. & Pearson, C. M. (2010). The cost of bad behavior. *Organizational Dynamics*, 39(1), 64–71.

Porter, G. (1996). Organizational impact of workaholism: Suggestions for the researching the negative outcomes of excessive work. *Journal of Occupational Health Psychology*, 1(1), 70–84.

Porter, L. & Lawler, E. E. (1968). *Managerial attitudes and performance.* Homewood, IL: Irwin.

Porter, L. & Schneider, B. (2014). What was, what is, and what may be in OP/OB. *Annual Review of Organizational Psychology and Organizational Behavior*, 1, 1–21.

Porter, L. & Steers, R. M. (1973). Organizational work, and personal factors in employee turnover and absenteeism. *Psychological Bulletin*, 80, 151–176.

Porter, L., Lawler, E., & Hackman, J. (1975). *Behavior in organizations*. New York: McGraw-Hill.

Price, A. V. (1982). *Type A behavior pattern: A model for research and practice*. New York: Academic Press.

Priesemuth, M., Schminke, M., Ambrose, M. L., & Folger, R. (2014). Abusive supervision climate: A multiple-mediation model of its impact on group outcomes. *Academy of Management Journal*, 57(5), 1513–1534.

Privitera, C. & Campbell, M. A. (2009). Cyberbullying: The new face of workplace bullying? *CyberPsychology & Behavior*, 12(4), 395–400.

Puffer, S. M. (1987). Prosocial behavior, noncompliant behavior, and work performance among commission salespeople. *Journal of Applied Psychology*, 72, 615–621.

Punch, M. (1996). *Dirty business: Exploring corporate misconduct: Analysis and cases*. London: Sage.

Quinney, E. R. (1963). Occupational structure and criminal behavior: Prescription violation by retail pharmacists. *Social Problems*, 11, 179–185.

Raelin, J. A. (1984). An examination of deviant/adaptive behaviors in the organizational careers of professionals. *Academy of Management Review*, 9, 413–427.

Raelin, J. A. (1986). An analysis of professional deviance within organizations. *Human Relations*, 39, 1103–1130.

Raelin, J. A. (1994). Three scales of professional deviance within organizations. *Journal of Organizational Behavior*, 15, 483–501.

Rafaeli, A. & Sutton, R. I. (1987). Expression of emotion as part of the work role. *Academy of Management Review*, 12, 23–37.

Rafaeli, A. & Sutton, R. I. (1989). The expression of emotion in organization life. In L. L. Cummings & B. M. Staw (Eds.), *Research in Organizational Behavior* (Vol. 11, pp. 1–42). Greenwich, CT: JAI Press.

Randall, D. M. & Gibson, A. M. (1990). Methodology in business ethics research: A review and critical assessments. *Journal of Business Ethics*, 9, 457–471.

Raver, J. L. & Nishii, L. H. (2010). Once, twice, or three times as harmful? Ethnic harassment, gender harassment, and generalized workplace harassment. *Journal of Applied Psychology*, 95(2), 236.

Ravid-Robbins, T. (1999). *The relationship between attitudes, perceptions and personal characteristics & organizational misbehavior among hospital nurses* (Unpublished master's thesis). Tel Aviv University, Israel.

Reddin, W. J. (1967). The 3D management style theory: A typology based on task and relationships orientations. *Training and Development Journal*, 21, 8–17.

Reich, T. C. & Hershcovis, M. S. (2015). Observing workplace incivility. *Journal of Applied Psychology*, 100(1), 203.

Reichers, A. E., Wanous, J. P., & Austin, J. T. (1997). Understanding and managing cynicism about organizational change. *Academy of Management Executive*, 11(1), 48–59.

Reshef-Tamari, I. (1999). *Perceived organizational climate, job satisfaction and misbehavior among R&D employees in high-tech organization* (Unpublished master's thesis). Tel Aviv University, Israel.

Rest, J. R. (1986). *Moral development: Advances in research and theory*. New York: Praeger.

Rich, B. R. & Janos, L. (1994). *Skunk works: A personal memoir of my years at Lockheed*. New York: Little, Brown.

Richards, J. (2008). The many approaches to organisational misbehaviour: A review, map and research agenda. *Employee Relations*, 30(6), 653–678.

Riordan, C. M. & Vandenberg, R. J. (1994). A central question in cross-cultural research: Do employees of different cultures interpret work-related measures in an equivalent manner? *Journal of Management*, 20, 643–671.

Robinson, S. L. (1996). Trust and breach of the psychological contract. *Administrative Science Quarterly*, 41, 574–599.

Robinson, S. L. & Bennett, R. J. (1995). A typology of deviant workplace behaviors: A multidimensional scaling study. *Academy of Management Journal*, 38, 555–572.

Robinson, S. L. & Bennett, R. J. (1997). Workplace deviance: Its definition, its manifestations, and its causes. In R. J. Lewicki, R. J. Bies, & B. H. Sheppard (Eds.), *Research on negotiation in organizations* (Vol. 6, pp. 3–27). Greenwich, CT: JAI Press.

Robinson, S. L. & Greenberg, J. (1998). Employees behaving badly: Dimensions, determinants and dilemmas in the study of workplace deviance. In C. L. Cooper & D. M. Rousseau (Eds.), *Trends in organizational behavior* (Vol. 5, pp. 1–30). New York: Wiley.

Robinson, S. L. & O'Leary-Kelly, A. M. (1998). Monkey see, monkey do: The influence of work groups on the antisocial behavior of employees. *Academy of Management Journal*, 41, 658–672.

Robinson, S. L. & Rousseau, D. M. (1994). Violating the psychological contract: Not the exception but the norm. *Journal of Organizational Behavior*, 15, 245–259.

Robinson, S. L., Wang, W., & Kiewitz, C. (2014). Coworkers behaving badly: The impact of coworker deviant behavior upon individual employees. *Annual Review of Organizational Psychology and Organizational Behavior*, 1(1), 123–143.

Rodell, J. B. & Judge, T. A. (2009). Can "good" stressors spark "bad" behaviors? The mediating role of emotions in links of challenge and hindrance stressors with citizenship and counterproductive behaviors. *Journal of Applied Psychology*, 94(6), 1438–1451.

Roethlisberger, F. J. & Dickson, W. J. (1964). *Management and the worker*. Cambridge, MA: Harvard University Press.

Rokeach, M. (1973). *The nature of human values*. New York: The Free Press.

Rosenbaum, D. P. & Baumer, T. L. (1984). Measuring and controlling employee theft: A national assessment of the state of the art. *Journal of Security Administration*, 5, 67–80.

Rosenbaum, R. W. (1976). Predictability of employee theft using weighted application blanks. *Journal of Applied Psychology*, 61, 94–98.

Rospenda, K. M. & Richman, J. A. (2004). The factor structure of generalized workplace harassment. *Violence and Victims*, 19(2), 221–238.

Rospenda, K. M., Richman, J. A., Ehmke, J. L., & Zlatoper, K. W. (2005). Is workplace harassment hazardous to your health? *Journal of Business and Psychology*, 20(1), 95–110.

Rospenda, K. M., Richman, J. A., & Shannon, C. A. (2006). Patterns of workplace harassment, gender, and use of services: An update. *Journal of Occupational Health Psychology*, 11(4), 379.

Ross, L., Greene, D., & House, P. (1977). The "false consensus effect": An egocentric bias in social perception and attribution processes. *Journal of Experimental Social Psychology*, 13, 279–301.

Rothschild, J. & Miethe, T. D. (1999). Whistle-blowing disclosures and management retaliation. *Work and Occupations*, 26(1), 107–128.

Rousseau, D. M. (1989). Psychological and implied contracts in organizations. *Employee Responsibilities and Rights Journal*, 2, 121–139.

Rousseau, D. M. (1990). New hires' perceptions of their own and their employer's obligations: A study of psychological contracts. *Journal of Organizational Behavior*, 11, 389–400.

Rousseau, D. M. (1995). *Psychological contracts in organizations: Understanding written and unwritten agreements.* Thousand Oaks, CA: Sage.

Rousseau, D. M. (1997). Organizational behavior in the new organizational era. *Annual Review of Psychology*, 48, 515–546.

Rousseau, D. M. (1998). Why workers still identify with their organizations? *Journal of Organizational Behavior*, 19, 217–233.

Rousseau, D. M. & Parks, J. M. (1993). The contracts of individuals and organizations. *Research in Organizational Behavior*, 15, 1–43.

Rousseau, D. M. & Tijoriwala, S. A. (1998). Assessing psychological contracts: Issues, alternatives and measures. *Journal of Organizational Behavior*, 19, 679–696.

Rowe, M. (1974). *The progress of women in educational institutions: The Saturn's rings phenomenon.* Retrieved from MIT Sloan Management website: http://mrowe.scripts.mit.edu/Publications.html.

Roy, D. F. (1952). Quota restriction and goldbricking in a machine shop. *American Journal of Sociology*, 57, 427–442.

Roy, D. F. (1959). Banana time: Job satisfaction and informal interaction. *Human Organization*, 18, 158–168.

Roznowski, M. & Hulin, C. (1992). The scientific merit of valid measures of general constructs with special reference to job satisfaction and job withdrawal. In C. J. Cranny, P. C. Smith, & F. S. Stone (Eds.), *Job satisfaction: How people feel about their jobs and how it effects their performance* (pp. 123–163). New York: Lexington Books.

Rubin-Kedar, Y. (2000). *Organizational misbehavior in a fast-food restaurant chain: Task and organization influences* (Unpublished master's thesis). Tel Aviv University, Israel.

Runco, M. A. (2004). Creativity. *Annual Review of Psychology*, 55(1), 657–687.

Rusbult, C. E. & Van Lange, P. A. M. (2003). Interdependence, interaction, and relationships. *Annual Review of Psychology*, 54(1), 351–375.

Rusbult, C. E., Zembrodt, I. M., & Gunn, L. K. (1982). Exit, voice, loyalty and neglect: Responses to dissatisfaction in romantic involvements. *Journal of Personality and Social Psychology*, 43, 1230–1242.

Ryan, A. M. & Wessel, J. L. (2012). Sexual orientation harassment in the workplace: When do observers intervene? *Journal of Organizational Behavior*, 33(4), 488–509.

Rynes, S. L., Gerhart, B., & Parks, L. (2005). Personnel psychology: Performance evaluation and pay for performance. *Annual Review of Psychology*, 56(1), 571–600.

Sackett, P. R. & DeVore, C. J. (2001). Counterproductive behaviors at work. In N. Anderson, D. S. Ones, H. K. Sinangil, & C. Viswesvaran (Eds.), *Handbook of industrial, work and organizational psychology* (Vol. 1, pp. 145–164). London: Sage.

Sackett, P. R. & Lievens, F. (2008). Personnel selection. *Annual Review of Psychology*, 59(1), 419–450.

Sagie, A. (1998). Employee absenteeism, organizational commitment, and job satisfaction: Another look. *Journal of Vocational Behavior*, 52, 156–171.

Salancik, G. R. (1977). Commitment and the control of organization behavior and belief. In B. M. Staw & G. R. Salancik (Eds.), *New directions in organizational behavior* (pp. 1–54). Chicago: St. Clair Press.

Salancik, G. R. & Pfeffer, J. (1978). A social information processing approach to job attitudes and task design. *Administrative Science Quarterly*, 23, 224–253.

Salas, E. & Cannon-Bowers, J. (2001). The science of training: A decade of progress. *Annual Review of Psychology*, 52(1), 471–499.

Salin, D. (2008). The prevention of workplace bullying as a question of human resource management: Measures adopted and underlying organizational factors. *Scandinavian Journal of Management*, 24(3), 221–231.

Salovey, P. & Mayer, J. D. (1990). Emotional intelligence. *Imagination, Cognition and Personality*, 9, 185–211.

Samuels, H. (2003). Sexual harassment in the workplace: A feminist analysis of recent developments in the UK. *Women's Studies International Forum*, 26(5), 467–482.

Sarchione, C. D., Cuttler, M. J., Muchinsky, P. M., & Nelson-Gray, R. O. (1998). Prediction of dysfunctional job behavior among law enforcement officers. *Journal of Applied Psychology*, 83, 904–912.

Sauser, W. I. (2005). Ethics in business: Answering the call. *Journal of Business Ethics*, 58(4), 345–357.

Savery, L. K. (1988). Comparison of managerial and non-managerial employees' desire and perceived motivators and job satisfaction levels. *Leadership and Organization Development Journal*, 9, 17–22.

Schat, A. C. H., Frone, M. R., & Kelloway, E. K. (2006). Prevalence of workplace aggression in the US workforce: Findings from a national study. In E. K. Kelloway, J. Barling, & J. J. Hurrell (Eds.), *Handbook of workplace violence* (pp. 47–89). Thousand Oaks, CA: Sage.

Schaufeli, W. B., Taris, T. W., & Van Rhenen, W. (2008). Workaholism, burnout, and work engagement: Three of a kind or three different kinds of employee well-being? *Applied Psychology*, 57, 173–203.

Schaufeli, W. B., Bakker, A. B., & Van Rhenen, W. (2009). How changes in job demands and resources predict burnout, work engagement, and sickness absenteeism. *Journal of Organizational Behavior*, 30(7), 893–917.

Schein, E. H. (1969). *Process consultation: Its role in organization development*. Reading, MA: Addison-Wesley.

Schein, E. H. (1971). The individual, the organization and the career: A conceptual scheme. *Journal of Applied Behavioral Science*, 7, 401–426.

Schein, E. H. (1978). *Career dynamics: Matching individual and organizational needs*. Reading, MA: Addison-Wesley.

Schein, E. H. (1984). Coming to a new awareness of organizational culture. *Sloan Management Review*, 25, 3–16.

Schein, E. H. (1985). *Organizational culture and leadership: A dynamic view*. San Francisco, CA: Jossey-Bass.

Schein, E. H. (2004). *Organizational culture and leadership* (3rd edn). San Francisco, CA: Jossey-Bass.

Schein, V. E. (1979). Examining an illusion: The role of deceptive behaviors in organizations. *Human Relations*, 32, 287–295.

Schilpzand, P., De Pater, I. E., & Erez, A. (2014). Workplace incivility: A review of the literature and agenda for future research. *Journal of Organizational Behavior*. Advance online publication. doi: 10.1002/job.1976.

Schmidt, F. L. & Hunter, J. E. (1992). Development of a causal model of processes determining job performance. *Current Directions in Psychology Science*, 1, 89–92.

Schmidt-Wilk, J., Heaton, D. P., & Steingard, D. (2000). Higher education for higher consciousness: Maharishi University of Management as a model for spirituality in management education. *Journal of Management Education*, 24(5), 580–611.

Schmitt, N. (2014). Personality and cognitive ability as predictors of effective performance at work. *Annual Review of Organizational Psychology and Organizational Behavior*, 1(1), 45–65.

Schminke, M. (1998). *Managerial ethics: Moral management of people and processes*. Mahwah, NJ: Lawrence Erlbaum Associates.

Schneider, B. (1975). Organizational climate: An essay. *Personnel Psychology*, 28, 447–479.

Schneider, B. (1980). The service organization: Climate is crucial. *Organizational Dynamics*, 9, 52–65.

Schneider, B. (1987). The people make the place. *Personnel Psychology*, 40, 437–453.

Schneider, B. & Bowen, D. E. (1995). *Winning the service game*. Boston, MA: Harvard Business School Press.

Schneider, B. & Hall, D. T. (1972). Toward specifying the concept of work climate: A study of Roman Catholic diocesan priests. *Journal of Applied Psychology*, 56, 447–456.

Schneider, K. T., Swan, S., & Fitzgerald, L. F (1997). Job-related and psychological effects of sexual harassment in the workplace: Empirical evidence from two organizations. *Journal of Applied Psychology*, 82, 401–415.

Schwartz, S. H. & Tessler, R. C. (1972). A test of a model for reducing measured attitude-behavior discrepancies. *Journal of Personality and Social Psychology*, 24, 225–236.

Schyns, B. & Schilling, J. (2013). How bad are the effects of bad leaders? A meta-analysis of destructive leadership and its outcomes. *The Leadership Quarterly*, 24(1), 138–158.

Scott, B. A. & Judge, T. A. (2006). Insomnia, emotions, and job satisfaction: A multilevel study. *Journal of Management*, 32(5), 622–645.

Scott, K. S., Moore, K. S., & Miceli, M. P. (1997). An exploration of the meaning and consequences of workaholism. *Human Relations*, 50, 287–314.

Scott, W. R. (1998). *Organizations: Rational, natural and open systems*. Upper Saddle River, NJ: Prentice-Hall.

Seibert, S. E. & Kraimer, M. L. (1999). *The five factor model of personality and its relationship with career success*. Paper presented at the Academy of Management meeting, Chicago, IL.

Selznick, P. (1957). *The organizational weapon*. New York: McGraw-Hill.

Sennewald, C. A. (1986). Theft maxims. *Security Management*, September, p. 85.

Setter, O. (2001). *Entitlements and obligations: Psychological contracts of organizational members* (Unpublished doctoral dissertation). Tel Aviv University, Israel.

Sewell, G. (1998). The discipline of teams: The control of team-based industrial work through electronic and peer surveillance. *Administrative Science Quarterly*, 43, 397–428.

Shafir, E. & LeBoeuf, R. A. (2002). Rationality. *Annual Review of Psychology*, 53(1), 491–517.

Shain, M. (1982). Alcohol, drugs and safety: An updated perspective on problems and their management in the workplace. *Accident Analysis and Prevention*, 14, 239–246.

Shamir, B., House, R. J., & Arthur, M. B. (1993). The motivational effects of charismatic leadership: A self-concept based theory. *Organization Science*, 4, 577–594.

Shechter-Shmueli, L. (2005). *"Yakirevitch affair": A case study of the whistleblowing phenomenon* (Unpublished master's thesis). Tel Aviv University, Israel.

Sheppard, B. H., Hartwick, J., & Warshaw, P. R. (1988). The theory of reasoned action: A meta-analysis of past research with recommendations for modifications and future research. *Journal of Consumer Research*, 15, 325–343.

Shenhav, Y. (2002). *Manufacturing rationality: The engineering foundations of the managerial revolution*. New York: Oxford University Press.

Shirom, A. (1982). What is organizational stress? A facet analytic conceptualization. *Journal of Occupational Behavior*, 3, 21–37.

Shoss, M. K., Eisenberger, R., Restubog, S. L. D., & Zagenczyk, T. J. (2013). Blaming the organization for abusive supervision: The roles of perceived organizational support and supervisor's organizational embodiment. *Journal of Applied Psychology*, 98(1), 158–168.

SHRM (2011). *Workplace violence survey*. Retrieved from the SHRM website: www.shrm.org/research/surveyfindings/articles/pages/workplaceviolence.aspx.

Shulman, D. (2007). *From hire to liar: The role of deception in the workplace*. Ithaca, NY: Cornell University Press.

Sibbet, D. (1997). 75 years of management ideas and practice (1922–1997). *Harvard Business Review*, 75, 2–12.

Siegler, F.A. (1962). Demos on lying to oneself. *Journal of Philosophy*, 59, 469–475.

Skarlicki, D. P. & Folger, R. (1997). Retaliation in the workplace: The roles of distributive, procedural, and interactional justice. *Journal of Applied Psychology*, 82, 434–443.

Skarlicki, D. P., Folger, R., & Tesluk, P. (1999). Personality as a moderator in the relationship between fairness and retaliation. *Academy of Management Journal*, 42, 100–108.

Skarlicki, D. P., Van Jaarsveld, D. D., & Walker, D. D. (2008). Getting even for customer mistreatment: The role of moral identity in the relationship between customer interpersonal injustice and employee sabotage. *Journal of Applied Psychology*, 93(6), 1335–1347.

Sliter, M., Sliter, K., & Jex, S. (2012). The employee as a punching bag: The effect of multiple sources of incivility on employee withdrawal behavior and sales performance. *Journal of Organizational Behavior*, 33(1), 121–139.

Slora, K. B. (1989). An empirical approach to determining employee deviance base rates. *Journal of Business and Psychology*, 4, 199–219.

Smelser, N. J. (1999). Looking back at 25 years of sociology and the *Annual Review of Sociology*. *Annual Review of Sociology*, 25, 1–18.

Smith, S. F. & Lilienfeld, S. O. (2013). Psychopathy in the workplace: The knowns and unknowns. *Aggression and Violent Behavior*, 18(2), 204–218.

Smith, R. H. & Kim, S. H. (2007). Comprehending envy. *Psychological Bulletin*, 133(1), 46–64.

Smith, P. K., Mahdavi, J., Carvalho, M., Fisher, S., Russell, S., & Tippett, N. (2008). Cyberbullying: Its nature and impact in secondary school pupils. *Journal of Child Psychology and Psychiatry*, 49(4), 376–385.

Soffer, P., Outmazgin N., & Tzafrir S. (2015). *Why do employees work around business processes? Towards a motivational model.* (Unpublished manuscript.) Haifa University, Israel.

Somers, M. J. (2009). The combined influence of affective, continuance and normative commitment on employee withdrawal. *Journal of Vocational Behavior*, 74(1), 75–81.

Somers, J. J. & Casal, J. C. (1994). Organizational commitment and whistle blowing: A test of the reformer and the organization man hypothesis. *Group & Organization Management*, 19, 270–284.

Sonnenstuhl, W. J. (1996). *Working sober: The transformation of an occupational drinking culture.* Ithaca, NY: Cornell University Press.

Sonnenstuhl, W. J. & Trice, H. M. (1991). The workplace as locale for risks and interventions in alcohol abuse. In P. M. Roman (Ed.), *Alcohol: The development of sociological perspectives on use and abuse* (pp. 295–318). New Brunswick, NJ: Rutgers Center of Alcohol Studies.

Snir, R. & Harpaz, I. (2000). Workaholism and the meaning of work. In M. Koslowski & S. Stashevsky (Eds.), *Proceedings of the 7th International Conference on Work Values and Behavior* (pp. 593–598). Jerusalem, Israel.

Spector, P. E. (1975). Relationships of organizational frustration with reported behavioral reactions of employees. *Journal of Applied Psychology*, 60, 635–637.

Spector, P. E. (1978). Organizational frustration: A model and review of the literature. *Personnel Psychology*, 31, 815–829.

Spector, P. E. (1986). Perceived control by employees: A meta analysis of studies concerning autonomy and participation at work. *Human Relations*, 39, 1005–1016.

Spector, P. E. (1997a). *Job satisfaction: Application, assessment, causes, and consequences.* Thousand Oaks, CA: Sage.

Spector, P. E. (1997b). The role of frustration in antisocial behavior at work. In R. A. Giacalone & J. Greenberg (Eds.), *Antisocial behavior in organizations* (pp. 1–17). Thousand Oaks, CA: Sage.

Spector, P. E. (2001). Research methods in industrial and organizational psychology: Data collection and data analysis with special consideration to international issues. In N. Anderson, D. S. Ones, H. K. Sinangil, & C. Viswesvaran (Eds.), *Handbook of industrial, work and organizational psychology* (Vol. 1, pp. 10–26). London: Sage.

Spector, P. E. & Fox, S. (2002). An emotion-centered model of voluntary work behavior: Some parallels between counterproductive work behavior and organizational citizenship behavior. *Human Resource Management Review*, 12(2), 269–292.

Spence, J. T. & Robbins, A. S. (1992). Workaholism: Definition, measurement and preliminary results. *Journal of Personality Assessment*, 58, 160–178.

Sprouse, M. (1992). *Sabotage in the American workplace*. San Francisco, CA: Pressure Drop Press.

Sprouse, M. (1994). *Sabotage in the American workplace: Anecdotes of dissatisfaction, mischief, and revenge*. San Francisco, CA: Pressure Drop Press.

Stanton, J. M. (2002). Company profile of the frequent internet user. *Communications of the ACM*, 45(1), 55–59.

Staw, B. M. (1980). Rationality and justification in organizational life. In B. M. Staw & L. L. Cummings (Eds.), *Research in organizational behavior* (Vol. 2, pp. 45–80). Greenwich, CT: JAI Press.

Staw, B. M. (1984). Organizational behavior: A review and reformulation of the field's outcome variables. *Annual Review of Psychology*, 35, 627–666.

Staw, B. M., Bell, N. E., & Clausen, J. A. (1986). The dispositional approach to job attitudes: A lifetime longitudinal test. *Administrative Science Quarterly*, 31, 56–77.

Staw, B. M., Sutton, R. I., & Pelled, L. H. (1994). Employee positive emotion and favorable outcomes at the workplace. *Organization Science*, 5, 51–71.

Steers, R. M. (1991). *Introduction to organizational behavior*. New York: HarperCollins.

Steers, R. M. & Mowday, R. T. (1977). The motivational properties of tasks. *Academy of Management Review*, 2, 645–658.

Steers, R. M. & Porter, L. W. (1979). *Motivation and work behavior*. New York: McGraw-Hill.

Steers, R. M. & Spencer, D. G. (1977). The role of achievement motivation in job design. *Journal of Applied Psychology*, 62, 472–479.

Stevens, S. S. (1968). Measurement, statistics, and the schemapiric view. *Science*, 161, 849–856.

Stein, H. F. (2001). *Nothing personal, just business: A guided journey into organizational darkness*. Westport, CT: Quorum Books.

Strool, W. M. (1978). *Crime prevention through physical security*. New York: Marcel Dekker.

Sukenik, N. (2001). *Goal-oriented mechanisms designed by organizations to promote safety are often used instead to promote profits* (Unpublished doctoral dissertation) Tel Aviv University, Israel.

Sutherland, E. H. (1940). White-collar criminality. *American Sociological Review*, 5, 1–12.

Sutherland, E. H. (1949). *White collar crime*. New Haven, CT: Yale University Press.

Sykes, G. M. & Matza, D. (1957a). On neutralizing delinquent self-images. *American Sociological Review*, 22, 667–670.

Sykes, G. M. & Matza, D. (1957b). Techniques of neutralization: A theory of delinquency. *American Sociological Review*, 22, 664–670.

Takala, T. & Urpilainen, J. (1999). Managerial work and lying: A conceptual framework and an explorative case study. *Journal of Business Ethics*, 20, 181–195.

Taylor, F. W. (1895). A piece rate system: A step toward partial solution to the labor problem. *ASME Transactions*, 16, 856–893.

Taylor, F. W. (1903). *Shop management*. New York: Harper.

Taylor, F. W. (1911). *The principles of scientific management*. New York: Norton.

Taylor, L. & Walton, P. (1971). Industrial sabotage: Motives and meanings. In S. Cohen (Ed.), *Images of deviance* (pp. 219–245). Baltimore, MD: Penguin.

Tedeschi, J. T. & Reiss, M. (1981). Identities, the phenomenal self, and laboratory research. In J. T. Tedeschi (Ed.), *Impression management theory and social psychological research* (pp. 3–23). New York: Academic Press.

Tedeschi, R. G. & Calhoun, L. G. (1996). The posttraumatic growth inventory: Measuring the positive legacy of trauma. *Journal of Traumatic Stress*, 9(3), 455–471.

Tenbrunsel, A. E. & Messick, D. M. (2004). Ethical fading: The role of self-deception in unethical behavior. *Social Justice Research*, 17(2), 223–236.

Tepper, B. J. (2000). Consequences of abusive supervision. *Academy of Management Journal*, 43(2), 178–190.

Tepper, B. J. (2007). Abusive supervision in work organizations: Review, synthesis, and research agenda. *Journal of Management*, 33(3), 261–289.

Tepper, B. J. & Henle, C. A. (2011). A case for recognizing distinctions among constructs that capture interpersonal mistreatment in work organizations. *Journal of Organizational Behavior*, 32(3), 487–498.

Tepper, B. J., Carr, J. C., Breaux, D. M., Geider, S., Hu, C., & Hua, W. (2009). Abusive supervision, intentions to quit, and employees' workplace deviance: A power/dependence analysis. *Organizational Behavior and Human Decision Processes*, 109(2), 156–167.

Tepper, B. J., Moss, S. E., & Duffy, M. K. (2011). Predictors of abusive supervision: Supervisor perceptions of deep-level dissimilarity, relationship conflict, and subordinate performance. *Academy of Management Journal*, 54(2), 279–294.

Testimony given by Lin Farley (1975). Hearings on women in blue-collar, service, and clerical occupations, April 21. Commission on Human Rights of the City of New York.

Tett, R. P., Jackson, D. N., & Rothstein, M. (1991). Personality measures as predictors of job performance: A meta-analytic review. *Personnel Psychology*, 44, 703–742.

Thau, S., Crossley, C., Bennett, R. J., & Sczesny, S. (2007). The relationship between trust, attachment, and antisocial work behaviors. *Human Relations*, 60(8), 1155–1179.

Thompson, J. D. (1967). *Organizations in action*. New York: McGraw-Hill.

Thompson, S. C. (1981). Will it hurt less if I can control it? A complex answer to a simple question. *Psychological Bulletin*, 90, 89–101.

Tichy, N. M. (1982). Managing change strategically: The technical, political, and cultural keys. *Organizational Dynamics*, August, pp. 59–80.

Tischler, L. (1999). The growing interest in spirituality in business: A long-term socio-economic explanation. *Journal of Organizational Change Management*, 12(4), 273–280.

Tjosvold, D., Wong, A. S. H., & Feng Chen, N.Y. (2014). Constructively managing conflicts in organizations. *Annual Review of Organizational Psychology and Organizational Behavior*, 1(1), 545–568.

Toffler, B. L. (1986). *Tough choices: Managers talk ethics*. New York: Wiley.

Tomlinson, E. C. & Greenberg, J. (2007). Understanding and deterring employee theft with organizational justice. In J. Langan-Fox, C. L. Cooper, & R. J. Klimoski (Eds.), *Research companion to the dysfunctional workplace: Management challenges and symptoms* (pp. 285–301). Northampton, MA: Edward Elgar.

Towler, J. (2001a). *Finding employees with integrity*. Retrieved from: www.hr.com.

Towler, J. (2001b). *Don't hire a killer—how to avoid violence prone employees*. Retrieved from: www.hr.com.

Treviño, L. K. (1986). Ethical decision making in organizations: A person-situation interactionist model. *Academy of Management Review*, 11, 601–617.

Treviño, L. K. (1992). The social effects of punishment in organizations: A justice perspective. *Academy of Management Review*, 17, 647–676.

Treviño, L. K. & Nelson, K. A. (1994). *Managing business ethics: Straight talk about how to do it right.* New York: Wiley.

Treviño, L. K. & Nelson, K. A. (2011). *Managing business ethics.* New York: Wiley.

Treviño, L. K. & Youngblood, S. A. (1990). Bad apples in bad barrels: A causal analysis of ethical decision-making behavior. *Journal of Applied Psychology, 75,* 378–385.

Treviño, L. K., Weaver, G. R., & Reynolds, S. J. (2006). Behavioral ethics in organizations: A review. *Journal of Management, 32*(6), 951–990.

Treviño, L. K., den Nieuwenboer, N. A., & Kish-Gephart, J. (2014). (Un)ethical behavior in organizations. *Annual Review of Psychology, 65*(1), 635–660.

Trice, H. M. (1993). *Occupational subcultures in the workplace.* Ithaca, NY: ILR Press.

Trice, H. M. & Beyer, J. M. (1993). *The cultures of work organizations.* Englewood Cliffs, NJ: Prentice-Hall.

Turgeman-Goldschmidt, O. (2001). *To become a deviant: Reality construction among computer delinquents* (Unpublished doctoral dissertation). Hebrew University, Jerusalem, Israel.

Turner, A. N. & Lawrence, P. R. (1965). *Industrial jobs and the worker: An investigation of response to task attributes.* Boston, MA: Harvard University Press.

Turnley, W. H. & Feldman, D. C. (1999). The impact of psychological contract violations on exit, voice, loyalty, and neglect. *Human Relations, 52,* 895–922.

Turnley, W. H. & Feldman, D. C. (2000). Re-examining the effects of psychological contract violations: Unmet expectations and job dissatisfaction as mediators. *Journal of Organizational Behavior, 21,* 25–42.

Tziner, A. & Vardi, Y. (1982). Effects of command style and group cohesiveness on the performance effectiveness of self-selected tank crews. *Journal of Applied Psychology, 67,* 769–775.

Ugrin, J. C. & Michael Pearson, J. (2013). The effects of sanctions and stigmas on cyberloafing. *Computers in Human Behavior, 29*(3), 812–820.

Umphress, E. E. & Bingham, J. B. (2011). When employees do bad things for good reasons: Examining unethical pro-organizational behaviors. *Organization Science, 22*(3), 621–640.

US Department of Justice (2007). *The economic impact of illicit drug use on American society.* Retrieved from the national drug intelligence center website: www.justice.gov/archive/ndic.

US Department of Labor (2015). *Safety and health topics: Workplace violence.* Retrieved from the Occupational Safety & Health Administration (OSHA) website: www.osha.gov.

Usdiken, B. & Leblebici, H. (2001). Organization theory. In N. Anderson, D. S. Ones, H. K. Sinangil, & C. Viswesvaran (Eds.), *Handbook of industrial, work and organizational psychology* (Vol. 2, pp. 377–397). Thousand Oaks, CA: Sage.

Van Brakel, J. (1994). Emotions: A cross-cultural perspective on forms of life. In W. M. Wentworth & J. Ryan (Eds.), *Social perspectives on emotion* (Vol. 2., pp. 179–237). Greenwich, CT: JAI Press.

Van Dyne, L., Graham, J. W., & Dienesch, R. M. (1994). Organizational citizenship behavior: Construct redefinition, measurement, and validation. *Academy of Management Journal, 37,* 765–802.

Van Gils, S., Van Quaquebeke, N., Van Knippenberg, D., Van Dijke, M., & De Cremer, D. (2015). Ethical leadership and follower organizational deviance: The moderating role of follower moral attentiveness. *The Leadership Quarterly, 26*(2), 190–203.

Van Knippenberg, D. & Schippers, M. C. (2007). Work group diversity. *Annual Review of Psychology, 58*(1), 515–541.

Van Maanen, J. (1979). The fact of fiction in organization ethnography. *Administrative Science Quarterly, 24,* 539–550.

Van Maanen, J. & Barley, S. R. (1984). Occupational culture and control in organizations. *Research in Organizational Behavior*, 6, 287–365.

Van Wijhe, C. I., Peeters, M. C. W., & Schaufeli, W. B. (2014). Enough is enough: Cognitive antecedents of workaholism and its aftermath. *Human Resource Management*, 53(1), 157–177.

Vardi, Y. (1978). *Individual-level and organizational-level of career mobility patterns: An integrative model* (Unpublished doctoral dissertation). Cornell University, Ithaca, NY.

Vardi, Y. (1980). Organizational career mobility: An integrative model. *Academy of Management Review*, 5(3), 341–355.

Vardi, Y. (2001). The effects of organizational and ethical climates on misconduct at work. *Journal of Business Ethics*, 29, 325–337.

Vardi, Y. (2007). *Corals of time*. Jerusalem: Carmel Publishing.

Vardi, Y. (2011). *The pigheaded careerist: If you are climbing up a ladder, make sure your closets and conscience are spotless*. Paper presented at the 7th Critical Management Studies Conference, Naples, Italy.

Vardi, Y. & Kim, S. H. (2007). Considering the darker side of careers: Toward a more balanced perspective. In H. P. Gunz & M. A. Peiperl (Eds.), *Handbook of career studies* (pp. 502–510). Thousand Oaks, CA: Sage.

Vardi, Y. & Weitz, E. (2001). *Lead them not into temptation: Job autonomy as an antecedent of organizational misbehavior*. Paper presented at the annual meeting of the Academy of Management, Washington, DC.

Vardi, Y. & Weitz, E. (2002a). Antecedents of organizational misbehavior among caregivers. In M. A. Rahim, R. T. Golembiewski, & K. D. Mackenzie (Eds.), *Current topics in management* (Vol. 7, pp. 99–116). New Brunswick, NJ: Transaction Publishers.

Vardi, Y. & Weitz, E. (2002b). Organizational misbehavior: Hypotheses, research, and implications. In M. L. Pava & P. Primeaux (Eds.), *Re-imaging business ethics: Meaningful solutions for a global economy* (Vol. 4, pp. 51–84). New York: JAI Press.

Vardi, Y. & Weitz, E. (2002c). Using reasoned action theory to predict organizational misbehavior. *Psychological Reports*, 91, 1027–1040.

Vardi, Y. & Weitz, E. (2004). *Misbehavior in organizations*. Hillsdale, NJ: Lawrence Erlbaum Associates.

Vardi, Y. & Weitz, E. (2015). *Exploring the role of work groups in spreading job related misbehavior and the role of individual level mitigating factors*. Paper presented at the European Association of Work and Organizational Psychology Conference, Oslo, Norway.

Vardi, Y. & Wiener, Y. (1992). *Organizational misbehavior (OMB): Toward a motivational model*. Paper presented at the annual meeting of the Academy of Management, Miami, FL.

Vardi, Y. & Wiener, Y. (1996). Misbehavior in organizations: A motivational framework. *Organization Science*, 7(2), 151–165.

Vardi, Y., De Vries, D., & Gushpantz, T. (2000). Managerial deviant behavior: The stock regulation affair and illegalism in Israeli society. In H. Herzog (Ed.), *Reflection of a society* (pp. 37–68). Tel Aviv: Ramot (in Hebrew).

Vardi, Y., Weitz, E., & Gottfrid-Oz, T. (2014). *Is misbehavior contagious? An exploratory study of deviant workgroups and their members*. Paper presented at the 2nd Israel Organizational Behavior Conference (IOBC), Tel Aviv University, Israel.

Vaughan, D. (1999). The dark side of organizations: Mistake, misconduct, and disaster. *Annual Review of Sociology*, 25, 271–305.

Vecchio, R. P. (1995). It's not easy being green: Jealousy and envy in the workplace. In G. R. Ferris (Ed.), *Research in personnel and human resources management* (Vol. 13, pp. 201–244). Stamford CT: JAI Press.

Vecchio, R. P. (1997). Categorizing coping response for envy: A multidimensional analysis of workplace perceptions. *Psychological Reports*, 81, 137–138.

Vecchio, R. P. (2000). Negative emotion in the workplace: Employee jealousy and envy. *International Journal of Stress Management*, 7(3), 161–179.

Vega, G. & Comer, D. R. (2005). Sticks and stones may break your bones, but words can break your spirit: Bullying in the workplace. *Journal of Business Ethics*, 58, 101–109.

Victor, B. & Cullen, J. B. (1987). A theory and measure of ethical climate in organizations. *Research in Corporate Social Performance and Policy*, 9, 51–71.

Victor, B. & Cullen, J. B. (1988). The organizational bases of ethical work climates. *Administrative Science Quarterly*, 33, 101–125.

Vigoda, E. (1997). *Organizational politics: Characteristics, antecedents, and implications of interpersonal influence processes on employee performance in the Israeli public sector* (Unpublished doctoral dissertation). University of Haifa, Israel.

Vigoda, E. (2000). Organizational politics, job attitudes, and work outcomes: Exploration and implications for the public sector. *Journal of Vocational Behavior*, 57(3), 326–347.

Villanova, P. & Bernardin, H. J. (1989). Impression management in the context of performance appraisal. In R. A. Giacalone & P. Rosenfeld (Eds.), *Impression management in the organization* (pp. 299–314). Hillsdale, NJ: Lawrence Erlbaum Associates.

Vinchur, A. J., Schippmann, J. S., Switzer, F. S., & Roth, P. L. (1998). A meta-analytic review of predictors of job performance for salespeople. *Journal of Applied Psychology*, 83, 586–597.

Vinten, G. (Ed.) (1994). *Whistleblowing: Subversion or corporate citizenship?* London: Paul Chapman.

Vitak, J., Crouse, J., & LaRose, R. (2011). Personal internet use at work: Understanding cyberslacking. *Computers in Human Behavior*, 27(5), 1751–1759.

Volmer, J., Spurk, D., & Niessen, C. (2012). Leader–member exchange (LMX), job autonomy, and creative work involvement. *The Leadership Quarterly*, 23(3), 456–465.

Vroom, V. H. (1964). *Work and motivation*. New York: Wiley.

Wagner, D. T., Barnes, C. M., Lim, V. K., & Ferris, D. L. (2012). Lost sleep and cyberloafing: Evidence from the laboratory and a daylight saving time quasi-experiment. *Journal of Applied Psychology*, 97(5), 1068–1076.

Wagner-Marsh, F. & Conley, J. (1999). The fourth wave: The spiritually based firm. *Journal of Organizational Change Management*, 12(4), 292–302.

Wanberg, C. R. (2012). The individual experience of unemployment. *Annual Review of Psychology*, 63(1), 369–396.

Warren, D. E. (2003). Constructive and destructive deviance in organizations. *Academy of Management Review*, 28(4), 622–632.

Way, S. A., Lepak, D. P., Fay, C. H., & Thacker, J. W. (2010). Contingent workers' impact on standard employee withdrawal behaviors: Does what you use them for matter? *Human Resource Management*, 49(1), 109–138.

Wayne, S. J. Y. & Kacmar, K. M. (1991). The effects of impression management on the performance appraisal process. *Organizational Behavior and Human Decision Processes*, 48, 70–88.

WBI (2007, 2014). *The US workplace bullying survey*. Retrieved from the Workplace Bullying Institute website: www.workplacebullying.org/wbiresearch/wbi-2014-us-survey.

Weatherbee, T. G. (2010). Counterproductive use of technology at work: Information & communications technologies and cyberdeviancy. *Human Resource Management Review*, 20(1), 35–44.

Weber, E. U. & Johnson, E. J. (2009). Mindful judgment and decision making. *Annual Review of Psychology*, 60(1), 53–85.

Webroot (2015). *The societal costs of digital piracy.* Webroot, July 15. Retrieved from Webroot website: www.webroot.com/za/en/home/resources/tips/ethics-and-legal/the-societal-costs-of-digital-piracy.

Weick, K. E. (1979). *The social psychology of organizing.* Reading, MA: Addison-Wesley.

Weiner, B. (1974). *Achievement motivation and attribution theory.* Morristown, NJ: General Learning Press.

Weiss, H. M. & Adler, S. (1984). Personality and organizational behavior. *Research in Organizational Behavior,* 6, 1–50.

Weiss, H. M. & Cropanzano, R. (1996). Affective events theory: A theoretical discussion of the structure, causes and consequences of affective experiences at work. In B. M. Staw & L. L. Cummings (Eds.), *Research in organizational behavior* (Vol. 18, pp. 1–74). Stamford, CT: JAI Press.

Weitz, E. & Vardi, Y. (2008). Understanding and managing misbehavior in organizations. In C. Wankel (Ed.), *21st century management: A reference handbook* (Vol. 2, pp. 220–230). Thousand Oaks, CA: Sage.

Weitz, E., Vardi, Y., & Setter, O. (2012). Spirituality and organizational misbehavior. *Journal of Management, Spirituality & Religion,* 9(3), 255–281.

Welch, E. (1997). Business ethics in theory and practice: Diagnostic notes: A prescription for value. *Journal of Business Ethics,* 16, 309–313.

Welsh, S. (1999). Gender and sexual harassment. *Annual Review of Sociology,* 25, 169–190.

Westman, M. (1992). Moderating effect of decision latitude on stress-strain relationship: Does organizational level matter? *Journal of Organizational Behavior,* 13, 713–722.

Wheeler, A. R., Halbesleben, J. R., & Shanine, K. (2010). Eating their cake and everyone else's cake, too: Resources as the main ingredient to workplace bullying. *Business Horizons,* 53(6), 553–560.

Wheeler, H. N. (1976). Punishment theory and industrial discipline. *Industrial Relations,* 15, 235–243.

White, G. L. & Mullen, P. E. (1989). *Jealousy: Theory, research, and clinical strategies.* New York: Guilford.

Whitener, E. M. (1999). *The effects of cynicism on the development of interpersonal trust.* Paper presented at the annual meeting of the Academy of the Management, Chicago, IL.

Wiener, Y. (1982). Commitment in organizations: A normative view. *Academy of Management Review,* 7, 418–428.

Wiener, Y. (1988). Forms of value systems: A focus on organizational effectiveness and cultural change and maintenance. *Academy of Management Review,* 13, 534–545.

Wiener, Y. & Vardi, Y. (1990). Relationship between organizational culture and individual motivation: A conceptual integration. *Psychological Reports,* 67, 295–306.

Wiggins, J. S. & Pincus, A. L. (1992). Personality: Structure and assessment. *Annual Review of Psychology,* 43, 473–504.

Wille, B., De Fruyt, F., & De Clercq, B. (2013). Expanding and reconceptualizing aberrant personality at work: Validity of five-factor model aberrant personality tendencies to predict career outcomes. *Personnel Psychology,* 66(1), 173–223.

William Lee, T., Burch, T. C., & Mitchell, T. R. (2014). The story of why we stay: A review of job embeddedness. *Annual Review of Organizational Psychology and Organizational Behavior,* 1(1), 199–216.

Williams, C. L., Giuffre, P. A., & Dellinger, K. (1999). Sexuality in the workplace: Organizational control, sexual harassment, and the pursuit of pleasure. *Annual Review of Sociology,* 25, 73–93.

Williams, K. D. (2007). Ostracism. *Annual Review of Psychology,* 58(1), 425–452.

Williams, M. & Dutton, J. E. (1999). Corrosive political climates: The heavy toll of negative political behavior in organizations. In R.E. Quinn, R.M. O'Neill, & L. St. Clair (Eds.), *The pressing problems of modern organizations: Transforming the agenda for research and practice* (pp. 3–30). New York: American Management Association.

Willness, C. R., Steel, P., & Lee, K. (2007). A meta-analysis of the antecedents and consequences of workplace sexual harassment. *Personnel Psychology*, 60(1), 127–162.

Wimbush, J. C. & Dalton, D. R. (1997). Base rate for employee theft: Convergence of multiple methods. *Journal of Applied Psychology*, 82, 756–763.

Withey, M. J. & Cooper, W. H. (1989). Predicting exit, voice, loyalty, and neglect. *Administrative Science Quarterly*, 34, 521–539.

Wolfgang, A. P. (1988). Career satisfaction of physicians, nurses and pharmacists. *Psychological Reports*, 62, 938–941.

Women's Bureau, US Department of Labor. (1994). *Sources of information on the incidence of domestic violence at work and its effects* (Briefing memo). Washington, DC: US Government.

Wood, R. E. & Mitchell, T. R. (1981). Manager behavior in a social context: The impact of impression management on attributions and disciplinary actions. *Organizational Behavior and Human Performance*, 28, 356–378.

Wood, W. (2000). Attitude change: Persuasion and social influence. *Annual Review of Psychology*, 51(1), 539–570.

Wortman, C. B. & Breham, J. W. (1975). Responses to uncontrollable outcomes: An integration of reactance theory and the learned helplessness model. In L. Berkowitz (Ed.), *Advances in experimental social psychology* (pp. 278–336). New York: Academic Press.

Wu, L., Kwan, H.K., Liu, J., & Resick, C.J. (2012). Work-to-family spillover effects of abusive supervision. *Journal of Managerial Psychology*, 27(7), 714–731.

Xu, E., Huang, X., Lam, C. K., & Miao, Q. (2012). Abusive supervision and work behaviors: The mediating role of LMX. *Journal of Organizational Behavior*, 33(4), 531–543.

Yamada, D. C. (2004). Crafting a legislative response to workplace bullying. *Employee Rights and Employment Policy Journal*, 8, 475–519.

Yamada, D. C. (2008). Workplace bullying and ethical leadership. *Journal of Values-Based Leadership*, 1(2), 49–65.

Yanai, D. (1998). *Sexual harassment in the workplace: Women battery* (Unpublished master's thesis). Tel Aviv University, Israel.

Yang, J. & Diefendorff, J. M. (2009). The relations of daily counterproductive workplace behavior with emotions, situational antecedents, and personality moderators: A diary study in Hong Kong. *Personnel Psychology*, 62(2), 259–295.

Yang, L., Caughlin, D. E., Gazica, M. W., Truxillo, D. M., & Spector, P. E. (2014). Workplace mistreatment climate and potential employee and organizational outcomes: A meta-analytic review from the target's perspective. *Journal of Occupational Health Psychology*, 19(3), 315.

Yang, Y. & Konrad, A. M. (2011). Understanding diversity management practices: Implications of institutional theory and resource-based theory. *Group & Organization Management*, 36(1), 6–38.

York, K. M. (1989). Defining sexual harassment in workplaces: A policy-capturing approach. *Academy of Management Journal*, 32, 830–850.

Yosifon, H. (2001). *The relationship between job satisfaction and organizational misbehavior among employees* (Unpublished master's thesis). Tel Aviv University, Israel.

Zerbe, W. J. & Paulhus, D. L. (1987). Socially desirable responding in organizational behavior: A re-conception. *Academy of Management Review*, 12, 250–264.

Zey-Ferrell, M. & Ferrell, O. C. (1982). Role set configuration and opportunity as predictors of unethical behavior in organizations. *Human Relations*, 35, 587–604.

Zhou, J. & Hoever, I. J. (2014). Research on workplace creativity: A review and redirection. *Annual Review of Organizational Psychology and Organizational Behavior*, 1(1), 333–359.

Zilberman, S. (2002). *Emotional intelligence and workplace deviance among managers: A pioneering research study* (Unpublished master's thesis). Tel Aviv University, Israel.

Zohar, D. & Marshall, I. (2004). *Spiritual capital*. London: Bloomsbury.

AUTHOR INDEX

SUBJECT INDEX